TCP/IP
Network Administration

TCP/IP
Network Administration

by Craig Hunt

O'Reilly & Associates, Inc.
103 Morris Street, Suite A
Sebastopol, CA 95472

TCP/IP Network Administration

by Craig Hunt

Copyright © 1992 Craig Hunt. All rights reserved.
Printed in the United States of America.

Editor: Mike Loukides

Printing History:

August 1992:	First Edition.
March 1993:	Minor corrections.

ISBN: 0-937175-82-X

Table of Contents

7: *Configuring Routing* *133*

8: *Configuring DNS Name Service* *167*

9: Network Applications   191

10: sendmail   213

11: Troubleshooting TCP/IP   257

12: Network Security   301

13: Internet Information Resources 337

A: Network Contacts 359

B: Forms, Forms, Forms 363

Figures

Tables

Preface

The Internet, the world's largest network, grew from fewer than 6000 computers at the end of 1986 to more than 600,000 computers five years later.* This explosive growth demonstrates the incredible demand for network services. This growth has taken place despite a lack of practical information for network administrators. Most administrators have been forced to content themselves with **man** pages, or protocol documents and scholarly texts written from the point of view of the protocol designer. For practical information, most of us have relied on the advice of friends who had already networked their computers. This book addresses the lack of information by providing practical, detailed network information for the UNIX system administrator.

Networks have grown so extravagantly because they provide an important service. It is in the nature of computers to generate and process information, but this information is frequently useless unless it can be shared with the people who need it. The network is the vehicle that enables data to be easily shared. Once you have networked your computer, you will never want to be stuck on an isolated system again.

The common thread that ties the enormous Internet together is TCP/IP network software. TCP/IP is a set of communications protocols that define how different types of computers talk to each other. This is a book about

---

*These figures are taken from page 4 of RFC 1296, *Internet Growth (1981-1991)*, by M. Lottor, SRI International. Read this book and you'll learn what an RFC is, and how to get your own free copy!

building your own network based on TCP/IP. It is both a tutorial covering the "why" and "how" of TCP/IP networking, and a reference providing the details about specific network programs.

Audience

This book is intended for everyone who has a UNIX computer connected to a TCP/IP network. This obviously includes the network managers and the system administrators who are responsible for setting up and running computers and networks, but the audience also includes any user who wants to understand how his or her computer communicates with other systems. The distinction between a "system administrator" and an "end-user" is growing increasingly fuzzy. You may think of yourself as an end-user, but if you have a UNIX workstation on your desk, you're probably also involved in system administration tasks.

We assume that you have a good understanding of computers and their operation, and that you're generally familiar with UNIX system administration. If you're not, the Nutshell Handbook, *Essential System Administration*, by AEleen Frisch will fill you in on the basics.

Organization

Conceptually, this book is divided into four parts. The first three chapters are a basic discussion of the TCP/IP protocols. This discussion provides the background necessary to understand the rest of the book. Chapters 4–7 discuss how to configure the basic software necessary to get a network running. Chapters 8–10 discuss how to set up various important network services. Many services "work" automatically, but a few require special configuration attention. The final chapters, 11–13, cover ongoing tasks: troubleshooting, security, and keeping up with changing network information.

This book contains the following chapters:

Chapter 1, *Overview of TCP/IP*, gives the history of TCP/IP, a description of the structure of the protocol architecture, and a basic explanation of how the protocols in this architecture function.

Chapter 2, *Delivering the Data*, describes addressing, and how data passes through a network to reach the proper destination.

Chapter 3, *Name Service Concepts*, discusses the relationship between the addresses and the names that identify computer systems. It also discusses the various tables and programs that are used to translate the numbers to names.

Chapter 4, *Getting Started*, begins the discussion of network setup and configuration. This chapter discusses the preliminary configuration planning needed before you configure the systems on your network. It also explains the official paperwork that may be required for your network.

Chapter 5, *Basic Configuration*, describes how to configure TCP/IP in the UNIX kernel, and how to configure the internet daemon that starts most of the network services.

Chapter 6, *Configuring the Interface*, tells you how to identify a network interface to the network software. This chapter provides examples of Ethernet, SLIP, and PPP interface configurations.

Chapter 7, *Configuring Routing*, describes how to set up routing so that systems on your network can communicate properly with other networks. It covers the static routing table, the RIP and EGP routing protocols, and **gated**, a package that provides the latest implementations of several routing protocols.

Chapter 8, *Configuring DNS Name Service*, describes how to administer the name server program that converts system names to Internet addresses.

Chapter 9, *Network Applications*, describes how to configure those common network services that require some special configuration. The chapter discusses the UNIX **r** utilities (**rlogin**, etc.), the Network Filesystem (NFS), and the Network Information System (NIS).

Chapter 10, *sendmail*, discusses how to configure **sendmail**, which is the daemon responsible for delivering electronic mail.

Chapter 11, *Troubleshooting TCP/IP*, tells you what to do when something goes wrong. It describes the techniques and tools used to troubleshoot TCP/IP problems, and gives examples of actual problems and their solutions.

Chapter 12, *Network Security*, discusses how to live on the Internet without excessive risk. This chapter covers the security threats brought by the network, and the plans and preparations you can make to meet those threats.

Chapter 13, *Internet Information Resources*, describes the information resources available on the Internet and how you can make use of them. It also describes how to set up an anonymous **ftp** server of your own.

Appendix A, *Network Contacts*, lists various providers of network services in the United States and other countries.

Appendix B, *Forms, Forms, Forms*, contains the forms needed to register your network properly with the Network Information Center (NIC).

Appendix C, *A gated Reference*, is a complete reference guide to the configuration language of the **gated** routing package.

Appendix D, *named Reference*, is a reference guide to the Berkeley Internet Name Domain (BIND) name server software.

Appendix E, *Sample sendmail.cf*, contains the sample **sendmail** configuration file developed in the step-by-step examples in Chapter 10.

Appendix F, *Selected TCP/IP Headers*, contains detailed protocol references, taken directly from the RFCs, that support the protocol troubleshooting examples in Chapter 11.

Appendix G, *Reference for passwd+*, is a reference guide for the configuration of **passwd+**, a package that enhances password security.

Appendix H, *Software Sources*, contains a table that identifies all of the free software used in this book. It lists each software package, along with instructions on how to obtain your own copy.

UNIX Versions

Most of the examples in this book are taken from SunOS 4.1.1, which is a Berkeley based operating system. System V examples were taken from SCO UNIX, which is based on System V Release 3.2. Fortunately, TCP/IP software is remarkably standard from system to system. Because the TCP/IP software is so uniform, the examples should be applicable to any System V or BSD-based UNIX system. There may be small variations in command output or command-line options, but these variations should not present a problem.

Some of the ancillary networking software is identified separately from the UNIX operating system by its own release number. Many such packages are discussed, and when appropriate are identified by their release numbers. The most important of these packages are:

gated   Our discussion of **gated** is based on version 2.0.1.14. Note that there are significant differences between this version and previous versions.

BIND   Our discussion of the BIND software is based on version 4.8.1, which is the version used in SunOS 4.1.1. The current version is 4.8.3; however, there are relatively few differences between these two releases.

sendmail Our discussion of **sendmail** is based on release 5.65. This version of **sendmail** has been in use for years.

Conventions

This book uses the following typographical conventions:

Italic   is used for the names of files, directories, host names, domain names, and to emphasize new terms when they are first introduced.

bold   is used for command names.

`constant-width`
          is used to show the contents of files or the output from commands.

`constant-bold` is used in examples to show commands or text that would be typed literally by you.

`constant-italic`
          is used in examples to show variables for which a context-specific substitution should be made. (The variable `filename`, for example, would be replaced by some actual filename.)

`%, #`   When we demonstrate commands that you would give interactively, we normally use the default C shell prompt (%). If the command must be executed as root, we use the default superuser prompt (#). Because the examples may include multiple systems on a network, the prompt may be preceded by the name of the system on which the command was given.

[*option*]   When showing command syntax, we place optional parts of the command within brackets. For example, **ls [-1]** means that the **-1** option is not required.

Acknowledgments

I would like to thank the many people who helped in the preparation of this book. Thanks to Peter Mui (ORA) for getting the ball rolling. Peter originally suggested to Tim O'Reilly that I be contacted about writing this book.

I would like to thank the people who provided expert technical advice. John Wack (NIST), Matt Bishop (Dartmouth), and Wietse Venema (Eindhoven) for their advice on computer security. Eric Allman (Berkeley) for his comments on the **sendmail** chapter, and for setting up my talk at USENIX that got Peter Mui thinking about this book in the first place. And special thanks to Jeff Honig (Cornell) and Scott Brim (Cornell) for commenting on multiple iterations of the **gated** material.

My thanks to Chris Durham (SCO), Eric Pearce (ORA), and Jim Mohr (SCO) for all the last-minute comments that helped me clean up the final copy.

I also want to give a special thanks to John Dorgan (NIST). John is a system programmer on our Cray. He doesn't work with TCP/IP, but he contributed his time to read every chapter and tell me when I was being too obscure. He helped me fill in the blanks that I couldn't see.

Mike Loukides, my editor, also deserves a special thanks. Mike pointed out to me that **last | grep 'S[au]'** is not a complete sentence. (I thought it was a compound sentence!) He reacquainted me with a powerful and flexible language that can be used to insert helpful comments between the code. It's called English, and I've come to appreciate its usefulness.

My thanks also go out to Eileen Kramer, who turned my rough draft into a finished book, and to Chris Reilly, who turned my rough, hand-drawn figures into finished graphics. All the people at O'Reilly and Associates have been very helpful.

Finally I want to thank my family, Kathy, Sara, David, and Rebecca, for having the patience to let me put on my earphones and pick up my book, every evening for the last 18 months.

1

Overview of TCP/IP

Just as the advent of powerful, affordable UNIX desktop computing systems has given many of us—engineers, educators, scientists, and business people—second careers as UNIX system administrators, networking these computers has given us new tasks as network administrators.

Network administration and system administration are two different jobs. System administration tasks such as adding users and doing backups are isolated to one independent computer system. Not so with network administration. Once you place your computer on a network, it interacts with many other systems. The way you do network administration tasks has effects, good and bad, not only on your system but on other systems on the network. A sound understanding of basic network administration benefits everyone.

This book is a practical, step-by-step guide to configuring and managing TCP/IP networking software on UNIX computer systems. TCP/IP is one of the software packages that currently dominates UNIX data communications. It plays a particularly important role as the leading communications software for UNIX local area networks.

The name TCP/IP refers to an entire suite of data communications protocols. The suite gets its name from two of the protocols that belong to it: the

Transmission Control Protocol and the Internet Protocol. Although there are many other protocols in the suite, TCP and IP are certainly two of the most important.

The first part of this book discusses the basics of TCP/IP and how it moves data across a network. The second part explains how to configure and run TCP/IP on a UNIX system. Let's start with a little history.

TCP/IP and the Internet

In 1969 the Defense Advanced Research Projects Agency (DARPA) funded a research and development project to create an experimental packet switching network. This network, called the *ARPANET,* was built to study techniques for providing robust, reliable, vendor-independent data communications. Many techniques of modern data communications were developed in the ARPANET.

The experimental ARPANET was so successful that many of the organizations attached to it began to use it for daily data communications. In 1975 the ARPANET was converted from an experimental network to an operational network, and the responsibility for administering the network was given to the Defense Communications Agency (DCA).* However, development of the ARPANET did not stop just because it was being used as an operational network; the basic TCP/IP protocols were developed after the ARPANET was operational.

The TCP/IP protocols were adopted as Military Standards (MIL STD) in 1983, and all hosts connected to the network were required to convert to the new protocols. To ease this conversion, DARPA funded Bolt, Beranek, and Newman (BBN) to implement TCP/IP in Berkeley (BSD) UNIX. Thus began the marriage of UNIX and TCP/IP.

About the time that TCP/IP was adopted as a standard, the term *Internet* came into common usage. In 1983, the old ARPANET was divided into MILNET, the unclassified part of the Defense Data Network (DDN), and a new, smaller ARPANET. The term Internet was used to refer to the entire network: MILNET plus ARPANET. In 1990, the ARPANET formally passed out of existence, but today the Internet is larger than ever and encompasses many networks worldwide.

---

*DCA has since changed its name to Defense Information Systems Agency (DISA).

The Internet has grown far beyond its original scope. The DDN is an important part of the network and agencies such as DISA still play an important role for the entire Internet. But new networks, such as NSFNET and the various regional networks, play an increasingly vital role in shaping and directing the Internet. The growth of the Internet has brought many new organizations into the network.

A sign of the network's success is the confusion that surrounds the term *internet*. Originally it was used only as the name of the network built upon the Internet Protocol. Now internet is a generic term used to refer to an entire class of networks. An *internet* (lowercase *i*) is any collection of separate physical networks, interconnected by a common protocol, to form a single logical network. The *Internet* (uppercase *I*) is the worldwide collection of interconnected networks, which grew out of the original ARPANET, that uses *Internet Protocol (IP)* to link the various physical networks into a single logical network. In this book both "internet" and "Internet" refer to networks that are interconnected by TCP/IP.

Because TCP/IP is required for Internet connection, the large number of diverse new organizations recently added to the Internet has spurred interest in TCP/IP. As more organizations become familiar with TCP/IP, they see that its power can be applied in other network applications. In the UNIX community, the Internet protocols are often used for local area networking, even when the local network is not connected to the larger Internet. It is common for a site to use TCP/IP for communication over a local Ethernet, while using UUCP for communicating with remote computer sites.

TCP/IP Features

The popularity of the TCP/IP protocols on the Internet did not grow rapidly just because the protocols were there, or because military agencies mandated their use. They met an important need (world-wide data communication) at the right time, and they had several important features that allowed them to meet this need. These are:

- Open protocol standards, freely available and developed independently from any specific computer hardware or operating system. Because it is so widely supported, TCP/IP is ideal for uniting different hardware and software, even if you don't communicate over the Internet.

- Independence from specific physical network hardware. This allows TCP/IP to integrate many different kinds of networks. TCP/IP can be run over an Ethernet, a token ring, a dial-up line, an X.25 net, and virtually any other kind of physical transmission media.

- A common addressing scheme that allows any TCP/IP device to uniquely address any other device in the entire network, even if the network is as large as the world-wide Internet.
- Standardized high-level protocols for consistent, widely available user services.

Protocol Standards

Protocols are formal rules of behavior. In international relations, protocols minimize the problems caused by cultural differences when various nations work together. By agreeing to a common set of rules that are widely known and independent of any nation's customs, diplomatic protocols minimize misunderstandings; everyone knows how to act and how to interpret the actions of others. Similarly when computers communicate, it is necessary to define a set of rules to govern their communications.

In data communications these sets of rules are also called *protocols*. In homogeneous networks, a single computer vendor specifies a set of communications rules designed to use the strengths of the vendor's operating system and hardware architecture. But homogeneous networks are like the culture of a single country—only the natives are truly at home in it. TCP/IP attempts to create a heterogeneous network with open protocols that are independent of operating system and architectural differences. TCP/IP protocols are available to everyone, and are developed and changed by consensus—not by the fiat of one manufacturer. Everyone is free to develop products to meet these open protocol specifications.

The open nature of TCP/IP protocols requires publicly available standards documents. All protocols in the TCP/IP protocol suite are defined in one of three Internet standards publications. A number of the protocols have been adopted as *Military Standards (MIL STD)*. Others were published as *Internet Engineering Notes (IEN)*—though the IEN form of publication has now been abandoned. But most information about TCP/IP protocols is published as *Requests for Comments (RFC)*. RFCs contain the latest versions of the specifications of all standard TCP/IP protocols.* As the name "Request for Comments" implies, the style and content of these documents is much less rigid then most standards documents. RFCs contain a wide range of interesting and useful information, and are not limited to the formal specification of data communications protocols.

---

*Interested in finding out how Internet standards are created? Read *The Internet Standards Process*, RFC 1310.

As a network system administrator, you will no doubt read ma
RFCs yourself. Some contain practical advice and guidance that is
understand. Other RFCs contain protocol implementation spe
defined in terminology that is unique to data communications.

A Data Communications Model

To discuss computer networking, it is necessary to use terms that have special meaning in data communications. Even other computer professionals
may not be familiar with all the terms in the networking alphabet soup. As
is always the case, English and computer-speak are not equivalent (or even
necessarily compatible) languages. Although descriptions and examples
should make the meaning of the networking jargon more apparent, sometimes terms are ambiguous. A common frame of reference is necessary for
understanding data communications terminology.

An architectural model developed by the International Standards Organization (ISO) is frequently used to describe the structure and function of data
communications protocols. This architectural model, called the *Open Systems Interconnect (OSI) Reference Model*, provides a common reference for
discussing communications. The terms defined by this model are well
understood and widely used in the data communications community—so
widely used, in fact, that it is difficult to discuss data communications without using OSI's terminology.

The OSI Reference Model contains seven *layers* that define the functions of
data communications protocols. Each layer of the OSI model represents a
function performed when data is transferred between cooperating applications across an intervening network. Figure 1-1 identifies each layer by
name and provides a short functional description for it. Looking at this figure, the protocols are like a pile of building blocks stacked one upon
another. Because of this appearance, the structure is often called a *stack* or
protocol stack.

A layer does not define a single protocol—it defines a data communications
function that may be performed by any number of protocols. Therefore,
each layer may contain multiple protocols, each providing a service suitable
to the function of that layer. For example, a file transfer protocol and an
electronic mail protocol both provide user services, and both are part of the
Application Layer.

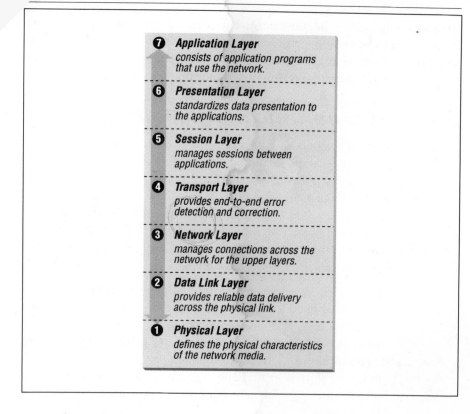

Figure 1.1: The OSI Reference Model

Every protocol communicates with its peer. A _peer_ is an implementation of the same protocol in the equivalent layer on a remote system; i.e., the local file transfer protocol is the peer of a remote file transfer protocol. Peer level communications must be standardized for successful communications to take place. In the abstract, each protocol is only concerned with communicating to its peer; it does not care about the layer above or below it.

However, there must also be agreement on how to pass data between the layers on a single computer, because every layer is involved in sending data from a local application to an equivalent remote application. The upper layers rely on the lower layers to transfer the data over the underlying network. Data is passed down the stack from one layer to the next, until it is transmitted over the network by the Physical Layer protocols. At the remote end, the data is passed up the stack to the receiving application. The individual layers do not need to know how the layers above and below them function; they only need to know how to pass data to them. Isolating network communications functions in different layers minimizes the impact of technological change on the entire protocol suite. New applications can be added without changing the physical network, and new network hardware can be installed without rewriting the application software.

Although the OSI model is useful, the TCP/IP protocols don't match its structure exactly. Therefore, in our discussions of TCP/IP we use the layers of the OSI model in the following way:

Application Layer   The Application Layer is the level of the protocol hierarchy where user-accessed network processes reside. In this text a TCP/IP application is any network process that occurs above the Transport Layer. This includes all of the processes that users directly interact with, as well as other processes at this level that users are not necessarily aware of.

Presentation Layer   For cooperating applications to exchange data, they must agree about how data is represented. In OSI, this layer provides standard data presentation routines. This function is handled within the applications in TCP/IP.

Session Layer   As with the Presentation Layer, the Session Layer is not identifiable as a separate layer in the TCP/IP protocol hierarchy. The OSI Session Layer manages the sessions (connection) between cooperating applications. In TCP/IP, this function largely occurs in the Transport Layer, and the term "session" is not used. For TCP/IP, the terms "socket" and "port" are used to describe the path over which cooperating applications communicate.

Transport Layer   Much of our discussion of TCP/IP is directed to the protocols that occur in the Transport Layer. The Transport Layer in the OSI reference model guarantees that the receiver gets the data exactly as it was sent. In TCP/IP this function is performed by the *Transmission Control Protocol (TCP)*. However, TCP/IP offers a second Transport Layer service, *User Datagram Protocol (UDP)* that does not perform the end-to-end reliability checks.

Network Layer	The Network Layer manages connections across the network and isolates the upper layer protocols from the details of the underlying network. The Internet Protocol (IP), which isolates the upper layers from the underlying network and handles the addressing and delivery of data, is usually described as TCP/IP's Network Layer.
Data Link Layer	The reliable delivery of data across the underlying physical network is handled by the Data Link Layer. TCP/IP rarely creates protocols in the Data Link Layer. Most RFCs that relate to the Data Link Layer talk about how IP can make use of existing data link protocols.
Physical Layer	The physical layer defines the characteristics of the hardware needed to carry the data transmission signal. Things such as voltage levels, and the number and location of interface pins, are defined in this layer. Examples of standards at the Physical Layer are interface connectors such as RS232C and V.35, and standards for local area network wiring such as IEEE 802.3. TCP/IP does not define physical standards—it makes use of existing standards.

The terminology of the OSI reference model helps us describe TCP/IP, but to fully understand it, we must use an architectural model that more closely matches the structure of TCP/IP. The next section introduces the protocol model we'll use to describe TCP/IP.

TCP/IP Protocol Architecture

While there is no universal agreement about how to describe TCP/IP with a layered model, it is generally viewed as being composed of fewer layers than the seven used in the OSI model. Most descriptions of TCP/IP define three to five functional levels in the protocol architecture. The four-level model illustrated in Figure 1-2 is based on the three layers (Application, Host-to-Host, and Network Access) shown in the DOD Protocol Model in the *DDN Protocol Handbook—Volume 1*, with the addition of a separate Internet layer. This model provides a reasonable pictorial representation of the layers in the TCP/IP protocol hierarchy.

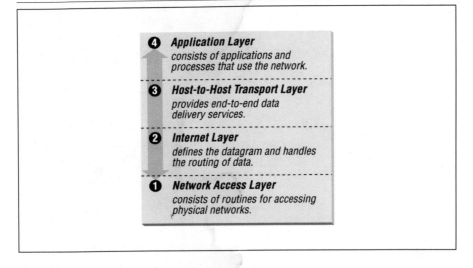

Figure 1.2: Layers in the TCP/IP Protocol Architecture

As in the OSI model, data is passed down the stack when it is being sent to the net, and up the stack when it is being received from the network. The four-layered structure of TCP/IP is seen in the way data is handled as it passes down the protocol stack from the Application Layer to the underlying physical network. Each layer in the stack adds control information to ensure proper delivery. This control information is called a *header* because it is placed in front of the data to be transmitted. Each layer treats all of the information it receives from the layer above as data and places its own header in front of that information. The addition of delivery information at every layer is called *encapsulation*. (Figure 1-3 illustrates this.) When data is received, the opposite happens. Each layer strips off its header before passing the data on to the layer above. As information flows back up the stack, information received from a lower layer is interpreted as both a header and data.

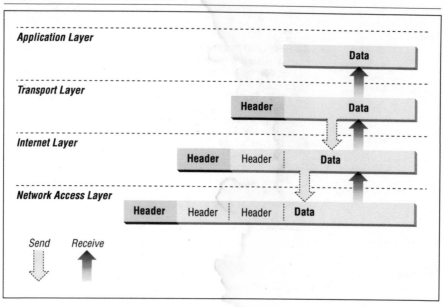

Figure 1.3: Data Encapsulation

Each layer has its own independent data structures. Conceptually a layer is unaware of the data structures used by the layers above and below it. In reality, the data structures of a layer are designed to be compatible with the structures used by the surrounding layers for the sake of more efficient data transmission. Still, each layer has its own data structure and its own terminology to describe that structure.

Figure 1-4 shows the terms used by different layers of TCP/IP to refer to the data being transmitted. Applications using TCP refer to data as a *stream*, while applications using the User Datagram Protocol (UDP) refer to data as a *message*. TCP calls data a *segment*, and UDP calls its data structure a *packet*. The Internet layer views all data as blocks called *datagrams*. TCP/IP uses many different types of underlying networks—each of which may have a different terminology for the data it transmits. Most networks refer to transmitted data as *packets* or *frames*. In our figure we assume a network that transmits pieces of data it calls *frames*. Each of these terms refers to the same thing—data to be transmitted. The terms vary as the view of the data varies from layer to layer.

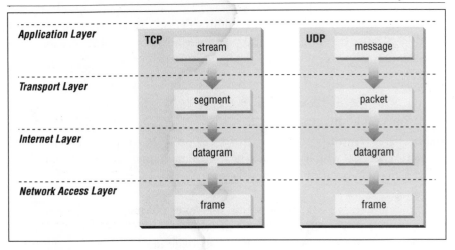

Figure 1.4: Data Structures

Let's look more closely at the function of each layer, working our way up from the Network Access Layer to the Application Layer.

Network Access Layer

The *Network Access Layer* is the lowest layer of the TCP/IP protocol hierarchy. The protocols in this layer provide the means for the system to deliver data to the other devices on a directly attached network. It defines how to use the network to transmit an IP datagram. Unlike higher-level protocols, Network Access Layer protocols must know the details of the underlying network (its packet structure, addressing, etc.) to correctly format the data being transmitted to comply with the network constraints. The TCP/IP Network Access Layer can encompass the functions of all three lower layers of the OSI reference Model (Network, Data Link, and Physical).

The Network Access Layer is often ignored by users. The design of TCP/IP hides the function of the lower layers, and the better known protocols (IP, TCP, UDP, etc.) are all higher-level protocols. As new hardware technologies appear, new Network Access protocols must be developed so that TCP/IP networks can use the new hardware. Consequently, there are many access protocols—one for each physical network standard.

Functions performed at this level include encapsulation of IP datagrams into the frames transmitted by the network, and mapping of IP addresses to the physical addresses used by the network. One of TCP/IP's strengths is its addressing scheme that uniquely identifies every host on the Internet. This IP address must be converted into whatever address is appropriate for the physical network over which the datagram is transmitted.

Two examples of RFCs that define network access layer protocols are:

- RFC 826, *Address Resolution Protocol (ARP)*, which maps IP addresses to Ethernet addresses
- RFC 894, *A Standard for the Transmission of IP Datagrams over Ethernet Networks*, which specifies how IP datagrams are encapsulated for transmission over Ethernet networks

As implemented in UNIX, protocols in this layer often appear as a combination of device drivers and related programs. The modules that are identified with network device names usually encapsulate and deliver the data to the network, while separate programs perform related functions such as address mapping.

Internet Layer

The layer above the Network Access Layer in the protocol hierarchy is the *Internet Layer*. The Internet Protocol, RFC 791, is the heart of TCP/IP and the most important protocol in the Internet Layer. IP provides the basic packet delivery service on which TCP/IP networks are built. All protocols, in the layers above and below IP, use the Internet Protocol to deliver data. All TCP/IP data flows through IP, incoming and outgoing, regardless of its final destination.

Internet Protocol

The Internet Protocol is the building block of the Internet. Its functions include:

- defining the datagram, which is the basic unit of transmission in the Internet;
- defining the Internet addressing scheme;
- moving data between the Network Access Layer and the Host-to-Host Transport Layer;
- routing datagrams to remote hosts;
- performing fragmentation and re-assembly of datagrams.

But before describing these functions in more detail, let's look at some of IP's characteristics. First, IP is a *connectionless protocol*. This means that IP does not exchange control information (called a "handshake") to establish an end-to-end connection before transmitting data. In contrast, a *connection-oriented protocol* exchanges control information with the remote system to verify that it is ready to receive data before sending it. When the handshaking is successful, the systems are said to have established a *connection*. Internet Protocol relies on protocols in other layers to establish the connection if they require connection-oriented service.

IP also relies on protocols in the other layers to provide error detection and error recovery. The Internet Protocol is sometimes called an *unreliable protocol* because it contains no error detection and recovery code. This is not to say that the IP protocol cannot be relied on—quite the contrary. IP can be relied upon to accurately deliver your data to the connected network, but it doesn't check whether the data was correctly received. Protocols in other layers of the TCP/IP architecture provide this checking when it is required.

The Datagram

The TCP/IP protocols were built to transmit data over the ARPANET, which was a *packet switching network*. A *packet* is a block of data that carries with it the information necessary to deliver it—in a manner similar to a postal letter, which has an address written on its envelope. A packet switching network uses the addressing information in the packets to switch packets from one physical network to another, moving them toward their final destination. Each packet travels the network independently of any other packet.

The *datagram* is the packet format defined by Internet Protocol. Figure 1-5 is a pictorial representation of an IP datagram. The first five or six 32-bit words of the datagram are control information called the *header*. By default, the header is five words long; the sixth word is optional. Because the header's length is variable, it includes a field called *Internet Header Length (IHL)* that indicates the header's length in words. The header contains all the information necessary to deliver the packet.

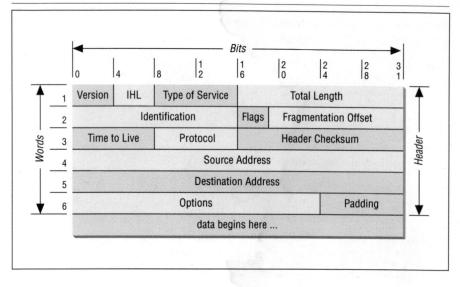

Figure 1.5: IP Datagram Format

The Internet Protocol delivers the datagram by checking the *Destination Address* in word 5 of the header. The Destination Address is a standard 32-bit IP address that identifies the destination network and the specific host on that network. (The format of IP addresses is explained in Chapter 2.) If the Destination Address is the address of a host on the local network, the packet is delivered directly to the destination. If the Destination Address is not on the local network, the packet is passed to a gateway for delivery. *Gateways* are devices that switch packets between the different physical networks. Deciding which gateway to use is called *routing*. IP makes the routing decision for each individual packet.

Routing Datagrams

Internet gateways are commonly (and perhaps more accurately) referred to as *IP routers* because they use Internet Protocol to route packets between networks. In traditional TCP/IP jargon, there are only two types of network devices—*gateways* and *hosts*. Gateways forward packets between networks and hosts don't. However, if a host is connected to more than one network (called a *multi-homed host*), it can forward packets between the networks. When a multi-homed host forwards packets, it acts just like any other gateway and is considered to be a gateway. Current data communications terminology sometimes makes a distinction between gateways and routers,* but we'll use the terms gateway and IP router interchangeably.

Figure 1-6 shows the use of gateways to forward packets. The hosts (or *end-systems*) process packets through all four protocol layers, while the gateways (or *intermediate-systems*) process the packets only up to the Internet Layer where the routing decisions are made.

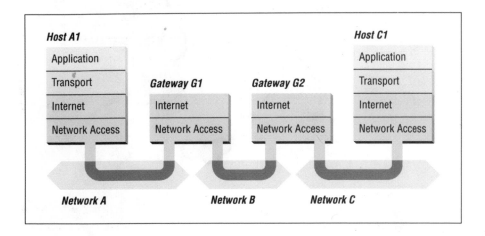

Figure 1.6: Routing Through Gateways

Systems can only deliver packets to other devices attached to the same physical network. Packets from *A1*, destined for host *C1*, are forwarded through gateways *G1* and *G2*. Host *A1* first delivers the packet to gateway *G1*, with which it shares network *A*. Gateway *G1* delivers the packet to *G2*, over network *B*. Gateway *G2* then delivers the packet directly to host *C1*, because they are both attached to network *C*. Host *A1* has no knowledge of any gateways beyond gateway *G1*. It sends packets destined for both networks *C* and *B* to that local gateway, and then relies on that gateway to properly forward the packets along the path to their destinations. Likewise, host *C1* would send its packets to *G2*, in order to reach a host on network *A*, as well as any host on network *B*.

---

*In current terminology, a gateway moves data between different protocols and a router moves data between different networks. So a system that moves mail between TCP/IP and OSI is a gateway, but a traditional IP gateway is a router.

Figure 1-7 shows another view of routing. This figure emphasizes that the underlying physical networks that a datagram travels through may be different and even incompatible. Host *A1* on the token ring network routes the datagram through gateway *G1*, to reach host *C1* on the Ethernet. Gateway *G1* forwards the data through the X.25 network to gateway *G2*, for delivery to *C1*. The datagram traverses three physically different networks, but eventually arrives intact at *C1*.

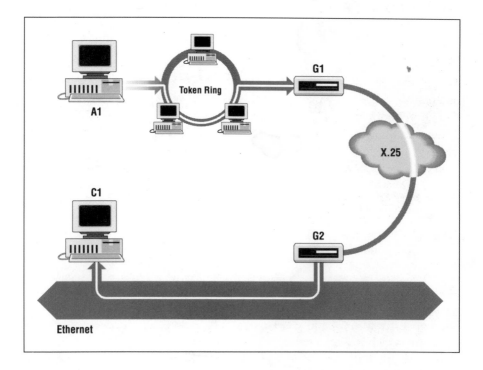

Figure 1.7: Networks, Gateways, and Hosts

Fragmenting Datagrams

As a datagram is routed through different networks, it may be necessary for the IP module in a gateway to divide the datagram into smaller pieces. A datagram received from one network may be too large to be transmitted in a single packet on a different network. This condition only occurs when a gateway interconnects dissimilar physical networks.

Each type of network has a *maximum transmission unit (MTU)*, which is the largest packet that it can transfer. If the datagram received from one network is longer than the other network's MTU, it is necessary to divide the datagram into smaller *fragments* for transmission. This process is called *fragmentation*. Think of a train delivering a load of steel. Each railway car can carry more steel than the trucks that will take it along the highway; so each railway car is unloaded onto many different trucks. In the same way that a railroad is physically different from a highway, an Ethernet is physically different from an X.25 network; IP must break an Ethernet's relatively large packets into smaller packets before it can transmit them over an X.25 network.

The format of each fragment is the same as the format of any normal datagram. Header word 2 contains information that identifies each datagram fragment and provides information about how to re-assemble the fragments back into the original datagram. The *Identification* field identifies what datagram the fragment belongs to, and the *Fragmentation Offset* field tells what piece of the datagram this fragment is. The *Flags* field has a *More Fragments bit* that tells IP if it has assembled all of the datagram fragments.

Passing Datagrams to the Transport Layer

When IP receives a datagram that is addressed to the local host, it must pass the data portion of the datagram to the correct Transport Layer protocol. This is done by using the *Protocol Number* from word 3 of the datagram header. Each Transport Layer protocol has a unique protocol number that identifies it to IP. Protocol numbers are discussed in Chapter 2.

You can see from this short overview that IP performs many important functions. Don't expect to fully understand datagrams, gateways, routing, IP addresses, and all the other things that IP does from this short description. Each chapter adds more details about these topics. So let's continue on with the other protocol in the TCP/IP Internet Layer.

Internet Control Message Protocol

An integral part of IP is the *Internet Control Message Protocol (ICMP)* defined in RFC 792. This protocol is part of the Internet Layer and uses the IP datagram delivery facility to send its messages. ICMP sends messages that perform the following control, error reporting, and informational functions for TCP/IP:

Flow control

When datagrams arrive too fast for processing, the destination host or an intermediate gateway sends an ICMP Source Quench Message back to the sender. This tells the source to temporarily stop sending datagrams.

Detecting unreachable destinations

When a destination is unreachable, the system detecting the problem sends a Destination Unreachable Message to the datagram's source. If the unreachable destination is a network or host, the message is sent by an intermediate gateway. But if the destination is an unreachable port, the destination host sends the message. (We discuss ports in Chapter 2.)

Redirecting routes

A gateway sends the ICMP Redirect Message to tell a host to use another gateway, presumably because the other gateway is a better choice. This message can only be used when the source host is on the same network as both gateways. To better understand this, refer to Figure 1-7. If a host on the X.25 network sent a datagram to *G1*, it would be possible for *G1* to redirect that host to *G2* because the host, *G1*, and *G2* are all attached to the same network. On the other hand, if a host on the token ring network sent a datagram to *G1*, the host could not be redirected to use *G2*. This is because *G2* is not attached to the token ring.

Checking remote hosts

A host can send the ICMP Echo Message to see if a remote system's Internet Protocol is up and operational. When a system receives an echo message, it sends the same packet back to the source host. The UNIX **ping** command uses this message.

Transport Layer

The protocol layer just above the Internet Layer is the *Host-to-Host Transport Layer*. This name is usually shortened to *Transport Layer*. The two most important protocols in the Transport Layer are *Transmission Control Protocol (TCP)* and *User Datagram Protocol (UDP)*. TCP provides reliable data delivery service with end-to-end error detection and correction. UDP provides low-overhead, connectionless datagram delivery service. Both protocols deliver data between the Application Layer and the Internet

Layer. Applications programmers can choose whichever service is more appropriate for their specific applications.

User Datagram Protocol

The User Datagram Protocol gives application programs direct access to a datagram delivery service, like the delivery service that IP provides. This allows applications to exchange messages over the network with a minimum of protocol overhead.

UDP is an unreliable, connectionless datagram protocol. (As noted before, "unreliable" merely means that there are no techniques in the protocol for verifying that the data reached the other end of the network correctly.) Within your computer, UDP will deliver data correctly. UDP uses 16-bit *Source Port* and *Destination Port* numbers in word 1 of the message header, to deliver data to the correct applications process. Figure 1-8 shows the UDP message format.

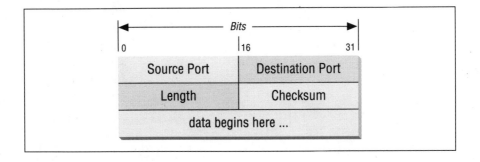

Figure 1.8: UDP Message Format

Why do applications programmers choose UDP as a data transport service? There are a number of good reasons. If the amount of data being transmitted is small, the overhead of creating connections and ensuring reliable delivery may be greater than the work of re-transmitting the entire data set. In this case, UDP is the most efficient choice for a Transport Layer protocol. Applications that fit a "query-response" model are also excellent candidates for using UDP. The response can be used as a positive acknowledgment to the query. If a response isn't received within a certain time period, the application just sends another query. Still other applications provide their own techniques for reliable data delivery, and don't require that service from the transport layer protocol. Imposing another layer of acknowledgment on any of these types of applications is inefficient.

Transmission Control Protocol

Applications that require the transport protocol to provide reliable data delivery use TCP because it verifies that data is delivered across the network accurately and in the proper sequence. TCP is a *reliable, connection-oriented, byte-stream* protocol. Let's look at each of the terms—reliable, connection-oriented, and byte-stream—in more detail.

TCP provides reliability with a mechanism called *Positive Acknowledgment with Re-transmission (PAR)*. Simply stated, a system using PAR sends the data again, unless it hears from the remote system that the data arrived okay. The unit of data exchanged between cooperating TCP modules is called a *segment* (see Figure 1-9). Each segment contains a checksum that the recipient uses to verify that the data is undamaged. If the data segment is received undamaged, the receiver sends a *positive acknowledgment* back to the sender. If the data segment is damaged, the receiver discards it. After an appropriate time-out period, the sending TCP module re-transmits any segment for which no positive acknowledgment has been received.

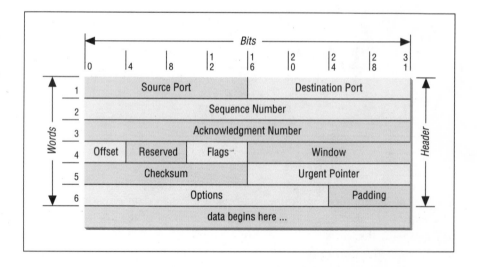

Figure 1.9: TCP Segment Format

TCP is connection-oriented. It establishes a logical end-to-end connection between the two communicating hosts. Control information, called a *handshake*, is exchanged between the two endpoints to establish a dialogue before data is transmitted. TCP indicates the control function of a segment by setting the appropriate bit in the *Flags* field in word 4 of the *segment header*.

The type of handshake used by TCP is called a *three-way handshake* because three segments are exchanged. Figure 1-10 show the simplest form of the three-way handshake. Host *A* begins the connection by sending host *B* a segment with the "Synchronize sequence numbers" (SYN) bit set. This segment tells host *B* that *A* wishes to set up a connection, and it tells *B* what sequence number host *A* will use as a starting number for its segments. (Sequence numbers are used to keep data in the proper order.) Host *B* responds to *A* with a segment that has the "Acknowledgment" (ACK) and SYN bits set. *B*'s segment acknowledges the receipt of *A*'s segment, and informs *A* which Sequence Number host *B* will start with. Finally, host *A* sends a segment that acknowledges receipt of *B*'s segment, and transfers the first actual data.

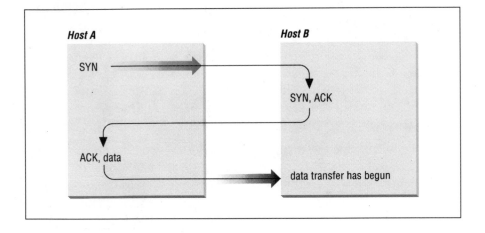

Figure 1.10: Three-way Handshake

After this exchange, host *A*'s TCP has positive evidence that the remote TCP is alive and ready to receive data. As soon as the connection is established, data can be transferred. When the cooperating modules have concluded the data transfers, they will exchange a three-way handshake with segments containing the "No more data from sender" bit (called the *FIN* bit) to close the connection. It is the end-to-end exchange of data that provides the logical connection between the two systems.

TCP views the data it sends as a continuous stream of bytes, not as independent packets. Therefore, TCP takes care to maintain the sequence in which bytes are sent and received. The "Sequence Number" and "Acknowledgment Number" fields in the TCP segment header keep track of the bytes.

The TCP standard does not require that each system start numbering bytes with any specific number; each system chooses the number it will use as a starting point. To keep track of the data stream correctly, each end of the connection must know the other end's initial number. The two ends of the connection synchronize byte-numbering systems by exchanging SYN segments during the handshake. The "Sequence Number" field in the SYN segment contains the *Initial Sequence Number* (ISN), which is the starting point for the byte-numbering system. Though not required by the protocol standard, the ISN is usually 0.

Each byte of data is numbered sequentially from the ISN, so the first real byte of data sent has a sequence number of ISN+1 (usually 1). The Sequence Number in the header of a data segment identifies the sequential position in the data stream of the first data byte in the segment. For example, if the first byte in the data stream was sequence number 1 (ISN=0) and 4000 bytes of data have already been transferred, then the first byte of data in the current segment is byte 4001, and the Sequence Number would be 4001.

The Acknowledgment Segment (ACK) performs two functions—*positive acknowledgment* and *flow control*. The acknowledgment tells the sender how much data has been received, and how much more the receiver can accept. The Acknowledgment Number is the sequence number of the last byte received at the remote end. The standard does not require an individual acknowledgment for every packet. The acknowledgment number is a positive acknowledgment of all bytes up through that number. For example, if the first byte sent was numbered 1 and 2000 bytes have been successfully received, the Acknowledgment Number would be 2000.

The Window field contains the number of bytes the remote end is able to accept. If the receiver is capable of accepting 6000 more bytes, the Window would be 6000. The window indicates to the sender that it can continue sending segments as long as the total number of bytes that it sends is smaller than the window of bytes that the receiver can accept. The receiver controls the flow of bytes from the sender by changing the size of the window. A zero window tells the sender to cease transmission until it receives a non-zero window value.

Figure 1-11 shows a TCP data stream that starts with an Initial Sequence Number of 0. The receiving system has received and acknowledged 2000 bytes, so the current Acknowledgment Number is 2000. The receiver also has enough buffer space for another 6000 bytes, so it has advertised a Window of 6000. The sender is currently sending a segment of 1000 bytes starting with Sequence Number 4001. The sender has received no acknowledgment for the bytes from 2001 on, but continues sending data as long as it is within the window. If the sender fills the window and receives no acknowledgment of the data previously sent, it will, after an appropriate time-out, send the data again starting from the first unacknowledged byte. In Figure 1-11, re-transmission would start from byte 2001 if no further acknowledgments are received. This procedure ensures that data is reliably received at the far end of the network.

TCP is also responsible for delivering data received from IP to the correct application. The application that the data is bound for is identified by a 16-bit number called the *port number.* The *Source Port* and *Destination Port* are contained in the first word of the segment header. Correctly passing data to and from the Application Layer is an important part of what the Transport Layer services do.

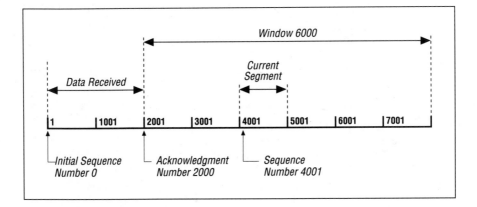

Figure 1.11: TCP Data Stream

Application Layer

At the top of the TCP/IP protocol architecture is the *Application Layer*. This layer includes all processes that use the Transport Layer protocols to deliver data. There are many applications protocols. Most provide user services, and new services are always being added to this layer. The most widely known and implemented applications protocols are:

- TELNET, the Network Terminal Protocol, provides remote login over the network.
- FTP, the File Transfer Protocol, is used for interactive file transfer.
- SMTP, the Simple Mail Transfer Protocol delivers electronic mail.

While FTP, SMTP, and TELNET are the most widely implemented TCP/IP applications, you will work with many others as both a user and a system administrator. Some other commonly used TCP/IP applications are:

- Domain Name Service (DNS)—Also called *name service*, this application maps IP addresses to the names assigned to network devices. DNS is discussed in detail in this book.
- Routing Information Protocol (RIP)—Routing is central to the way TCP/IP works. RIP is used by network devices to exchange routing information. Routing is also a major topic of this book.
- Network File System (NFS)—This protocol allows files to be shared by various hosts on the network.

Some protocols, such as TELNET and FTP, can only be used if the user has some knowledge of the network. Other protocols, like RIP, run without the user even knowing that they exist. As system administrator, you are aware of all these applications and all the protocols in the other TCP/IP layers.

Figure 1-12 shows the hierarchy of protocols in an imaginary computer. As you look at this figure, please remember that reducing the complexity of a protocol stack to a block diagram is, by its very nature, an oversimplification. This illustration is only to help you visualize the relationship of the many protocols in a single host. Not all of the protocols shown in Figure 1-12 have been discussed yet, but it should be helpful to get an idea of the overall structure. At the top of the figure are the applications protocols, like FTP and TELNET. Each protocol is shown with the number of the RFC that defines it. Lines run from each box to the lower layer service that the protocol uses. We see that FTP, TELNET, and SMTP rely primarily on TCP; while NFS, DNS, and RIP rely primarily on UDP. A few application-type

protocols, like the Exterior Gateway Protocol (EGP), another routing protocol, do not use Transport Layer services; they use IP services directly.

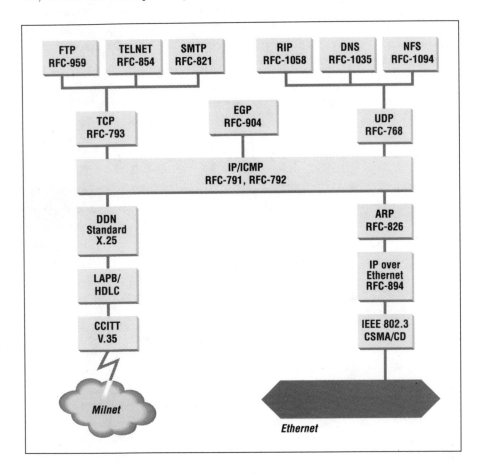

Figure 1.12: TCP/IP Protocols Inside a Sample Gateway

Below the applications are the Transport Layer protocols: TCP and UDP.
They interface directly with IP. All data, in and out of the system, flows
through IP. IP delivers data from the upper layers to the correct network,
and it delivers data from the network to the correct transport service. Likewise, the transport services deliver the data they receive from IP to the correct application.

We lump all of the protocols below IP together as Network Access protocols. The stacking of these protocols into three layers is not intended to imply some other hierarchy, though on the X.25 side these protocols correspond to the three lower layers of the OSI hierarchy (Network, Data Link, and Physical). For TCP/IP, all of these protocols are Network Access protocols.

In this chapter we discussed the structure of TCP/IP, the protocol suite upon which the Internet is built. In the next chapter we look at how the IP packet, the datagram, moves through a network when data is delivered between hosts.

2

Delivering the Data

In Chapter 1, we touched on the basic architecture and design of the TCP/IP protocols. From that discussion, we know that TCP/IP is a hierarchy of four layers. In this chapter, we explore in finer detail how data moves between the protocol layers and the systems on the network. We examine the structure of Internet addresses, including how addresses route data to its final destination, and how addressing rules are locally redefined to create subnets. We also look at the protocol and port numbers used to deliver data to the correct applications. These additional details move us from an overview of TCP/IP to the specific implementation details that affect your system's configuration.

Addressing, Routing, and Multiplexing

To deliver data between two Internet hosts, it is necessary to move the data across the network to the correct host, and within that host to the correct user or process. TCP/IP uses three schemes to accomplish these tasks:

Addressing	IP addresses, which uniquely identify every host on the Internet, deliver data to the correct host.
Routing	Gateways deliver data to the correct network.
Multiplexing	Protocol and port numbers deliver data to the correct software module within the host.

Each of these functions—addressing between hosts, routing between networks, and multiplexing between layers—is necessary to send data between two cooperating applications across the Internet. Let's examine each of these functions in detail.

To illustrate these concepts and provide consistent examples, we use an imaginary corporate network. Our imaginary company sells packaged nuts to the Army. Our company network is made up of several networks at our packing plant and sales office, as well as a connection to Milnet. We are responsible for managing the Ethernet in the computing center. This network's structure, or *topology*, is shown in Figure 2-1.

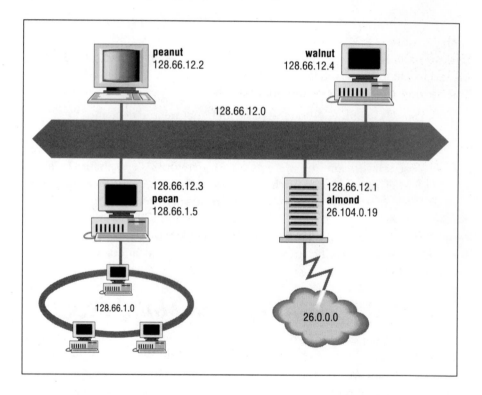

Figure 2.1: Sample Network

The icons in the figure represent computer systems. There are, of course, several other imaginary systems on our imaginary network. You'll just have to use your imagination! But we'll use the hosts *peanut* (a workstation) and *almond* (a system that serves as a gateway) for most of our examples. The thick line is our computer center Ethernet and the circle is the local network that connects our various corporate networks. The cloud is Milnet, one of the major segments of the Internet. What the numbers are, how they're used, and how datagrams are delivered are the topics of this chapter.

The IP Address

The Internet Protocol moves data between hosts in the form of datagrams. Each datagram is delivered to the address contained in the Destination Address (word 5) of the datagram's header. The Destination Address is a standard 32-bit IP address that contains sufficient information to uniquely identify a network and a specific host on that network.

An IP address contains a *network part* and a *host part*, but the format of these parts is not the same in every IP address. The number of address bits used to identify the network, and the number used to identify the host, vary according to the *class* of the address. The three main address classes are *class A, class B*, and *class C*. By examining the first few bits of an address, IP software can quickly determine the address' class, and therefore its structure. IP follows these rules to determine the address class:

- If the first bit of an IP address is 0, it is the address of a *class A network*. The first bit of a class A address identifies the address class. The next seven bits identify the network, and the last 24 bits identify the host. There are fewer than 128 class A network numbers, but each class A network can be composed of millions of hosts.

- If the first two bits of the address are 1 0, it is a *class B network* address. The first two bits identify class; the next fourteen bits identify the network, and the last sixteen bits identify the host. There are thousands of class B network numbers and each class B network can contain thousands of hosts.

- If the first three bits of the address are 1 1 0, it is a *class C network* address. In a class C address, the first three bits are class identifiers; the next 21 bits are the network address, and the last eight bits identify the host. There are millions of class C network numbers, but each class C network is composed of fewer than 254 hosts.

- If the first three bits of the address are 1 1 1, it is a special reserved address. These addresses are sometimes called *class D* addresses, but they don't really refer to specific networks. The numbers currently assigned in this range are multicast addresses. Multicast addresses are used to address groups of computers all at one time. Multicast addresses identify a group of computers that share a common protocol, as opposed to a group of computers that share a common network.

Luckily, this is not as complicated as it sounds. IP addresses are usually written as four decimal numbers separated by dots (periods).* Each of the four numbers is in the range 0-255 (the decimal values possible for a single byte). Because the bits that identify class are contiguous with the network bits of the address, we can lump them together and look at the address as composed of full bytes of network address and full bytes of host address. A first byte value:

- Less than 128 indicates a class A address; the first byte is the network number, and the next three bytes are the host address.

- From 128 to 191 is a class B address; the first two bytes identify the network, and the last two bytes identify the host.

- From 192 to 223 is a class C address; the first three bytes are the network address, and the last byte is the host number.

- Greater than 223, indicates the address is reserved. We can ignore reserved addresses.

Figure 2-2 illustrates how the address structure varies with address class. The class A address is 26.104.0.19. The first bit of this address is 0, so the address is interpreted as host 104.0.19 on network 26. One byte specifies the network and three bytes specify the host. In the address 128.66.12.1, the two high-order bits are 1 0 so the address refers to host 12.1 on network 128.66. Two bytes identify the network and two identify the host. Finally, in the class C example, 192.178.16.1, the three high-order bits are 1 1 0, so this is the address of host 1 on network 192.178.16—three network bytes and one host byte.

------

*Addresses are occasionally written in other formats, e.g., as hexadecimal numbers. However, the "dot" notation form is the most widely used. Whatever the notation, the structure of the address is the same.

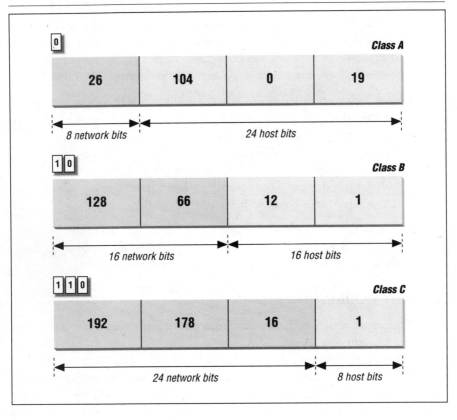

Figure 2.2: IP Address Structure

Not all network addresses or host addresses are available for use. We have already said that the addresses with a first byte greater than 223 are reserved. There are also two class A addresses, 0 and 127, that are reserved for special uses. Network 0 designates the *default route* and network 127 is the *loopback address*. The default route is used to simplify the routing information that IP must handle. The loopback address simplifies network applications by allowing the local host to be addressed in the same manner as a remote host. We use these special network addresses when configuring a host.

There are also some host addresses reserved for special uses. In all network classes, host numbers 0 and 255 are reserved. An IP address with all host bits set to zero identifies the network itself. For example, 26.0.0.0 refers to network 26, and 128.66.0.0 refers to network 128.66. Addresses in this form are used in routing table listings to refer to entire networks.

An IP address with all bits set to one is a *broadcast address.** A broadcast address is used to simultaneously address every host on a network. The broadcast address for network 128.66 is 128.66.255.255. A datagram sent to this address is delivered to every individual host on network 128.66.

IP addresses are often called host addresses. While this is common usage, it is slightly misleading. IP addresses are assigned to network interfaces, not to computer systems. A gateway, such as *almond* (see Figure 2-1), has a different address for each network it is connected to. The gateway is known to other devices by the address associated with the network that it shares with those devices. For example, *peanut* addresses *almond* as 128.66.12.1, while Milnet hosts address it as 26.104.0.19.

IP uses the network portion of the address to route the datagram between networks. The full address, including the host information, is used to make final delivery when the datagram reaches the destination network.

Address Depletion

The IP address, which provides universal addressing across all of the networks of the Internet, is one of the great strengths of the TCP/IP protocol suite. However, the structure of the IP address does have some problems. The TCP/IP designers did not envision the enormous scale of today's network. When TCP/IP was being designed, networking was limited to large organizations that could afford substantial computer systems. The idea of a powerful UNIX system on every desktop did not exist. At that time, a 32-bit address seemed so large that it was divided into classes to reduce the processing load on routers, even though dividing the address into classes sharply reduced the number of host addresses actually available for use. For example, assigning a large network a single class B address, instead of six class C addresses, reduces the load on the router because the router only needs to keep one route for that entire organization. However, the organization that was given the class B address probably does not have 64,000 computers, so most of the host addresses available to the organization will never be assigned.

The current address design, which favors routers over growth, is under critical strain from the rapid growth of the Internet. At the present rate of

---

*Unfortunately there are implementation-specific variations in broadcast addresses. Chapter 5 discusses these variations.

growth, all class B addresses could be exhausted within the next 15 months.* To prevent this, blocks of class C addresses are being assigned to organizations, but each class C address in the block requires its own entry within the routing table. This solution could cause the routing table to grow so rapidly that the routers will soon be overwhelmed.

These problems are being addressed by the ROAD (Routing and Addressing) working group of the Internet Engineering Task Force (IETF). The working group is looking for a scheme that:

- will alleviate the problem of address depletion, perhaps by moving to a larger address or to a "classless" address;
- will not accelerate the growth of the routing table, and will not increase the load on the routers;
- can be implemented in the routers, without requiring changes to the end-systems (the hosts).

The group is evaluating a few different proposals. One suggestion is to use Connectionless Network Protocol (CLNP) in the routers. CLNP is an OSI protocol similar to IP. It has a flexible 160 bit address that would be adequate for enormous growth in the Internet. However, unless the hosts also change to an OSI addressing scheme, some technique must be used in the routers to map from IP to OSI addresses.

Another suggestion is to assign large, contiguous blocks of class C addresses to "service providers."† The service providers then allocate chunks of these address blocks to the organizations to which they provide network services. This alleviates the short term shortage of class B addresses, but it aggravates the problems caused by a rapidly growing routing table.

To handle this other problem, each block of addresses is given only a single destination address in the routing table. This requires modifications to the routers and routing protocols. The protocols need to distribute, along with the destination addresses, address masks that define how the addresses are interpreted. The routers need to interpret these addresses as classless addresses, which are not evaluated according to the class rules discussed above, but according to the bit mask that accompanies the address. These

---

*The source for this prediction is the draft of *Supernetting: an Address Assignment and Aggregation Strategy*, by V. Fuller, T. Li, J. Yu, and K. Varadhan, March 1992.

†Service providers are entities that provide network services to other organizations, for example, a regional network. Some service providers are listed in Appendix A.

bit masks are just like the ones used for subnetting that we'll see in the next section. Using bit masks to create larger networks is called *supernetting*.

We don't know what techniques will be adopted by the IETF to overcome the problems of address depletion. If supernetting is adopted, it will probably be an interim step, because it does not address the basic limitation of the 32-bit address. But whatever happens, the changes should not have any near-term effect on your hosts. These changes are aimed at the routers that handle routing between the large national and regional networks. On your system, IP addresses will appear the same as they always have for some time to come.

Subnets

The standard structure of an IP address can be locally modified by using host address bits as additional network address bits. Essentially, the "dividing line" between network address bits and host address bits is moved, creating additional networks, but reducing the maximum number of hosts that can belong to each network. These newly designated network bits define a network within the larger network, called a *subnet*.

Organizations usually decide to subnet in order to overcome topological or organizational problems. Subnetting allows decentralized management of host addressing. With the standard addressing scheme, a single administrator is responsible for managing host addresses for the entire network. By subnetting, the administrator can delegate address assignment to smaller organizations within the overall organization—which may be a political expedient, if not a technical requirement. If you don't want to deal with the data processing department, assign them their own subnet and let them manage it themselves.

Subnetting can also be used to overcome hardware differences and distance limitations. IP routers can link dissimilar physical networks together, but only if each physical network has its own unique network address. Subnetting divides a single network address into many unique subnet addresses, so that each physical network can have its own unique address.

A subnet is defined by applying a bit mask, the *subnet mask*, to the IP address. If a bit is on in the mask, that equivalent bit in the address is interpreted as a network bit. If a bit in the mask is off, the bit belongs to the host part of the address. The subnet is only known locally. To the rest of the Internet, the address is still interpreted as a standard IP address.

For example, the subnet mask that would be associated with standard class B addresses is 255.255.0.0. The most commonly used subnet mask extends the network portion of a class B address by an additional byte. The subnet mask that does this is 255.255.255.0; all bits on in the first three bytes, and all bits off in the last byte. The first two bytes define the class B network; the third byte defines the the subnet address; the fourth byte defines the host on that subnet.

Many network administrators prefer to use byte-oriented masks because they are easier to read and understand. However, defining subnet masks on byte boundaries is not a requirement. The subnet mask is bit-oriented and can be applied to any address class. For example, a small organization could subdivide a class C address into four subnets with the mask 255.255.255.192. Applying this mask to a class C address defines the two high-order bits of the fourth byte as the subnet part of the address. This same mask, applied to a class B address, creates more than a thousand subnets because ten bits, the full third byte, and two bits of the fourth byte, are used to define the subnets. Table 2-1 shows the effect of various subnet masks on different network addresses.

Table 2.1: Effect of a Subnet Mask

IP Address	Subnet Mask	Interpretation
128.66.12.1	255.255.255.0	host 1 on subnet 128.66.12.0
130.97.16.132	255.255.255.192	host 4 on subnet 130.97.16.128
192.178.16.66	255.255.255.192	host 2 on subnet 192.178.16.64
132.90.132.5	255.255.240.0	host 4,5 on subnet 132.90.128.0
18.20.16.91	255.255.0.0	host 16.91 on subnet 18.20.0.0

or 1029

Confused? Don't be. If a subnet mask is used on your network, your network administrator will provide you with the correct value. If you're the network administrator, remember that you're not forced to use subnetting; you choose to use it to solve a specific organizational or topological problem. If you choose to use subnetting, select a mask that makes sense to you.

Internet Routing Architecture

In the traditional Internet structure, there was a hierarchy of gateways. This hierarchy reflected the history of the Internet, which was built upon the existing ARPANET. When the Internet was created, the ARPANET was the backbone of the network: a central delivery medium to carry long distance traffic. This central system was called the *core*, and the centrally managed gateways that interconnected it were called the *core gateways*.

When a hierarchical structure is used, routing information about all of the networks in the Internet is passed into the core gateways. The core gateways process this information, and then exchange it among themselves using the *Gateway to Gateway Protocol* (GGP). The processed routing information is then passed back out to the external gateways. You won't run GGP on your local gateway—it is only used by core gateways.

Outside of the Internet core are groups of independent networks called *autonomous systems* (AS). The term "autonomous system" has a formal meaning in TCP/IP routing. An autonomous system is not merely an independent network. It is a collection of networks and gateways with its own internal mechanism for collecting routing information and passing it to other independent network systems. The routing information passed to the other network systems is called *reachability information*. Reachability information simply says which networks can be reached through that autonomous system. The *Exterior Gateway Protocol* (EGP) is currently the protocol most frequently used to pass reachability between autonomous systems (see Figure 2-3).

The Defense Data Network (DDN) portion of the Internet still uses the core model to distribute routing information. But this hierarchical model has a major weakness—every route must be processed by the core. This places a tremendous processing burden on the core, and as the Internet grows larger the burden increases. In network-speak, we say that this routing model does not scale well and for this reason, a new model is emerging.

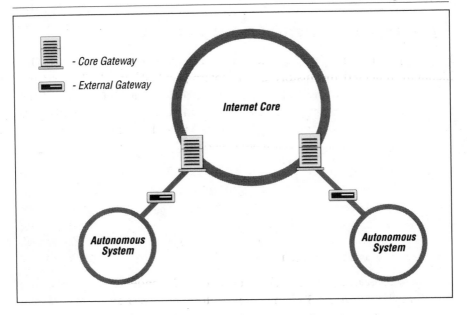

Figure 2.3: Gateway Hierarchy

The new routing model is based on co-equal collections of autonomous systems, called *routing domains*. Routing domains exchange routing information with other domains using *Border Gateway Protocol* (BGP) or EGP. Each routing domain processes the information it receives from other domains. Unlike the hierarchical model, this model does not depend on a single core system to choose the "best" routes. Each routing domain does this processing for itself; therefore, this model is more expandable. Figure 2-4 represents this model with three intersecting circles. Each circle is a routing domain. The overlapping areas are border areas, where routing information is shared. The domains share information, but do not rely on any one system to provide all routing information.

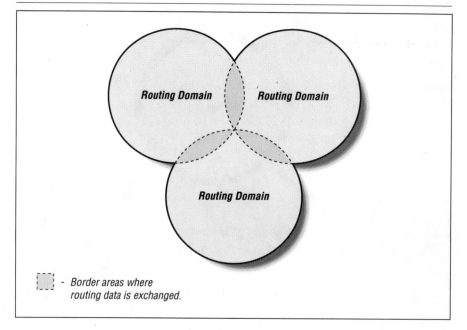

Figure 2.4: Routing Domains

No matter how it is derived, eventually the routing information winds up in your local gateway, where it is used by IP to make routing decisions.

The Routing Table

Gateways route data between networks; but all network devices, hosts as well as gateways, must make routing decisions. For most hosts, the routing decisions are simple:

- if the destination host is on the local network, the data is delivered to the destination host;
- if the destination host is on a remote network, the data is forwarded to a local gateway.

Because routing is network oriented, IP makes routing decisions based on the network portion of the address. The IP module determines the network part of the destination's IP address by checking the high-order bits of the address to determine the address class. The address class determines the portion of the address that IP uses to identify the network. If the destination network is the local network, the local subnet mask is applied to the destination address.

After determining the destination network, the IP module looks up the network in the local *routing table*.* Packets are routed toward their destination as directed by the routing table. The routing table may be built by the system administrator or by routing protocols, but the end result is the same; IP routing decisions are simple table look-ups.

You can display the routing table's contents with the **netstat —nr** command. The **—r** option tells **netstat** to display the routing table, and the **—n** option tells **netstat** to display the table in numeric form. It's useful to display the routing table in numeric form because the destination of most routes is a network, and networks are usually referred to by network numbers.

The **netstat** command displays a routing table containing the following fields:

Destination	The destination network (or host).
Gateway	The gateway to use to reach the specified destination.
Flags	The flags describe certain characteristics of this route. The possible flag values are:

    U   Indicates that the route is up and operational.

    H   Indicates this is a route to a specific host (most routes are to networks).

    G   Means the route uses a gateway. The system's network interfaces provide routes to directly connected networks. All other routes use remote gateways. Directly connected networks do not have the G flag set; all other routes do.

    D   Means that this route was added because of an ICMP redirect. When a system learns of a route via an ICMP redirect, it adds the route to its routing table, so that additional packets bound for that destination will not need to be redirected. The system, uses the D flag to mark these routes.

Refcnt	Shows the number of times the route has been referenced to establish a connection.

---

*This table is also called the *forwarding table*.

Use   Shows the number of packets transmitted via this route.

Interface   The name of the network interface* used by this route.

The only two fields important for our current discussion are the destination and gateway fields. The following is a sample routing table:

```
peanut% netstat -nr
Routing tables
Destination  Gateway      Flags  Refcnt   Use     Interface
127.0.0.1    127.0.0.1    UH     1        298     lo0
default      128.66.12.1  UG     2        50360   le0
128.66.12.0  128.66.12.2  U      40       111379  le0
128.66.2.0   128.66.12.3  UG     4        1179    le0
128.66.1.0   128.66.12.3  UG     10       1113    le0
128.66.3.0   128.66.12.3  UG     2        1379    le0
128.66.4.0   128.66.12.3  UG     4        1119    le0
```

The first table entry is the *loopback route* for the local host. This is the loopback address mentioned earlier as a reserved network number. Because every system uses the loopback route to send datagrams to itself, this entry is in every host's routing table. The H flag is set because it is a route to a specific host (127.0.0.1), not a route to an entire network (127.0.0.0). We'll see the loopback facility again when we discuss kernel configuration and the **ifconfig** command. For now, however, our real interest is in external routes.

Another unique entry in the routing table is the entry with the word "default" in the destination field. This entry is for the *default route*, and the gateway specified in this entry is the *default gateway*. The default gateway is used whenever there is no specific route in the table for a destination network address. For example, this routing table has no entry for network 192.178.16.0. If IP receives any datagrams addressed to this network, it will send the datagram via the default gateway 128.66.12.1.

You can tell from the sample routing table display that this host (*peanut*) is directly connected to network 128.66.12.0. The routing table entry for that network does not specify an external gateway; i.e., the routing table entry for 128.66.12.0 does not have the G flag set. Therefore, *peanut* must be directly connected to that network.

All of the gateways that appear in a routing table are on networks directly connected to the local system. In the sample shown above this means that, regardless of the destination address, the gateway addresses all begin with

---

*The network interface is the network access hardware and software that IP uses to communicate with the physical network. See Chapter 6 for details.

128.66.12. This is the only network to which *peanut* is directly attached, and therefore it is the only network to which *peanut* can directly deliver data. The gateways that *peanut* uses to reach the rest of the Internet must be on *peanut's* subnet.

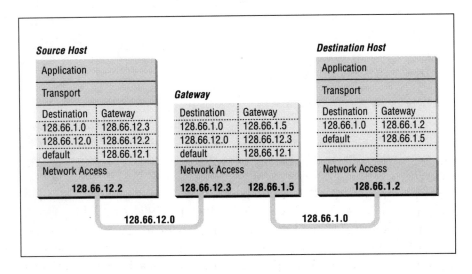

Figure 2.5: Table Based Routing

Figure 2-5 shows how routing works on our imaginary network. The IP layer of each host and gateway is replaced by a small piece of a routing table, showing destination networks and the gateways used to reach those destinations. When the source host (128.66.12.2) sends data to the destination host (128.66.1.2), it first determines that 128.66.1.2 is the local network's class B address and applies the subnet mask. (Network 128.66.0.0 is subnetted using the mask 255.255.255.0.) After applying the subnet mask, IP knows that the destination's network address is 128.66.1.0. The routing table in the source host shows that data bound for 128.66.1.0 should be sent to gateway 128.66.12.3. Gateway 128.66.12.3 makes direct delivery thorough its 128.66.1.5 interface. Examining the routing tables shows that all systems list only gateways on networks they are directly connected to. Note that 128.66.12.1 is the default gateway for both 128.66.12.2 and 128.66.12.3. But because 128.66.1.2 cannot reach network 128.66.12.0 directly, it has a different default route.

A routing table does not contain end-to-end routes. A route only points to the next gateway, called the *next hop*, along the path to the destination network. The host relies on the local gateway to deliver the data, and the gateway relies on other gateways. As a datagram moves from one gateway to another, it should eventually reach one that is directly connected to its destination network. It is this last gateway that finally delivers the data to the destination host.

Address Resolution

The IP address and the routing table direct a datagram to a specific physical network, but when data travels across a network, it must obey the physical layer protocols used by that network. The physical networks that underlay the TCP/IP network do not understand IP addressing. Physical networks have their own addressing schemes, and there are as many different addressing schemes as there are different types of physical networks. One task of the network access protocols is to map IP addresses to physical network addresses.

The most common example of this network access layer function is the translation of IP addresses to Ethernet addresses. The protocol that performs this function is *Address Resolution Protocol* (ARP), which is defined in RFC 826.

The ARP software maintains a table of translations between IP addresses and Ethernet addresses. This table is built dynamically. When ARP receives a request to translate an IP address, it checks for the address in its table. If the address is found, it returns the Ethernet address to the requesting software. If the address is not found in the table, ARP broadcasts a packet to every host on the Ethernet. The packet contains the IP address for which an Ethernet address is sought. If a receiving host identifies the IP address as its own, it responds by sending its Ethernet address back to the requesting host. The response is then cached in the ARP table.

The **arp** command displays the contents of the ARP table. To display the entire ARP table use the **arp −a** command. Individual entries can be displayed by specifying a host name on the **arp** command line. For example, to check the entry for *peanut* in the ARP table on *almond* enter:

```
almond% arp peanut
peanut (128.66.12.2) at 8:0:20:0:e:c8
```

Checking all entries in the table with the **–a** option produces the following output:

```
almond% arp -a
peanut.nuts.com (128.66.12.2) at 8:0:20:0:e:c8
pecan.nuts.com (128.66.12.3) at 8:0:20:1:77:fe
walnut.nuts.com (128.66.12.4) at 0:0:1d:0:bc:bb
```

This table tells you that when *almond* receives datagrams addressed to *peanut*, it puts those datagrams into Ethernet frames and sends them to Ethernet address 8:0:20:0:e:c8.

ARP tables shouldn't require any attention because they are built automatically by the ARP protocol, which is very stable.

RARP

The *Reverse Address Resolution Protocol* (RARP), defined in RFC 903, is a variant of the address resolution protocol. RARP also translates addresses, but in the opposite direction. It converts Ethernet addresses to IP addresses, instead of IP addresses to Ethernet addresses. The RARP protocol really has nothing to do with routing data from one system to another. We discuss it because of its close relationship to ARP, and because it is sometimes confused with ARP. ARP is the protocol that maps IP addresses to physical Ethernet addresses, so datagrams can be delivered from one host to another.

RARP helps configure diskless systems by allowing diskless workstations to learn their IP addresses. A diskless workstation has no disk to read its TCP/IP configuration from—not even its IP address. However, every system knows its Ethernet address because it is encoded in the Ethernet interface hardware. The diskless workstation uses the Ethernet broadcast facility to ask which IP address maps to its Ethernet address. When a server on the network sees the request, it looks up the Ethernet address in the table */etc/ethers*. If it finds a match, the server replies with the workstation's IP address.

The */etc/ethers* file is a simple text table that you create, using an editor. You need this file only if your system must provide support for diskless workstations; otherwise, you can do without it. */etc/ethers* is made up of single line entries that contain an Ethernet address, separated by blanks or tabs from a host name.

Host names are assigned by the network administrator, but the Ethernet address is assigned by the manufacturer, and therefore must be obtained from the network interface. Fortunately, it isn't too hard to figure out a system's Ethernet address. Most UNIX workstations display their Ethernet addresses while they are booting. The Ethernet address is usually displayed before the system tries to find any disks; so if you take a brand-new workstation out of the box, you should be able to find out its Ethernet address by turning it on and watching the display. To check the Ethernet address of a workstation that is already running, look at the output from the **dmesg** command or look in the file */usr/adm/messages*. For example:

```
peanut% grep ' addr' /usr/adm/messages
Jul 16 11:03:07 peanut vmunix: Ethernet address = 8:0:20:0:e:c8
```

Once the host names and Ethernet addresses are known, they are stored in the */etc/ethers* file. A small */etc/ethers* file is shown below:

```
almond% cat /etc/ethers
# ff:ff:ff:ff:ff:ff broadcast #
8:0:14:43:1:46     roasted
0:0:1d:0:bc:bb     walnut
8:0:20:1:1f:c3     brazil
8:0:20:1:77:fe     pecan
8:0:20:0:e:c8      peanut
```

If this host receives a RARP broadcast from Ethernet address 8:0:20:1:77:fe, it replies with the IP address of the host *pecan*.

Protocols, Ports, and Sockets

Once data is routed through the network and delivered to a specific host, it must be delivered to the correct user or process. As the data moves up or down the layers of TCP/IP, a mechanism is needed to deliver data to the correct protocols in each layer. The system must be able to combine data from many applications into a few transport protocols, and from the transport protocols into the Internet Protocol. Combining many sources of data into a single data stream is called *multiplexing*. Data arriving from the network must be *demultiplexed*: divided for delivery to multiple processes. To accomplish this, IP uses *protocol numbers* to identify transport protocols, and the transport protocols use *port numbers* to identify applications.

Some protocol and port numbers are reserved to identify *well-known services*. Well-known services are standard network protocols, such as FTP and TELNET that are commonly used throughout the network. The protocol numbers and port numbers allocated to well-known services are documented in the *Assigned Numbers* RFC. UNIX systems define protocol and port numbers in two simple text files.

Protocol Numbers

The protocol number is a single byte in the third word of the datagram header. The value identifies the protocol in the layer above IP to which the data should be passed.

On a UNIX system, the protocol numbers are defined in */etc/protocols*. This file is a simple table containing the protocol name and the protocol number associated with that name. The format of the table is a single entry per line, consisting of the official protocol name, separated by white space from the protocol number. The protocol number is separated by white space from the "alias" for the protocol name. Comments in the table begin with #. An */etc/protocol* file is shown below:

```
% cat /etc/protocols
#
# @(#)protocols 1.8 88/02/07 SMI
#
# Internet (IP) protocols #
ip      0       IP      # internet protocol, pseudo protocol number
icmp    1       ICMP    # internet control message protocol
igmp    2       IGMP    # internet group multicast protocol
ggp     3       GGP     # gateway-gateway protocol
tcp     6       TCP     # transmission control protocol
pup     12      PUP     # PARC universal packet protocol
udp     17      UDP     # user datagram protocol
```

The listing shown above is the contents of the */etc/protocols* file from an actual workstation. This list of numbers is by no means complete. If you refer to the Protocol Numbers section of the *Assigned Numbers* RFC, you'll see many more protocol numbers. However, a system only needs to include the numbers of the protocols that it actually uses. Even the list shown above is more than this specific workstation needed, but the additional entries do no harm.

What exactly does this table mean? When a datagram arrives and its destination address matches the local IP address, the IP layer knows that the datagram has to be delivered to one of the transport protocols above it. To decide which protocol should receive the datagram, IP looks at the datagram's protocol number. Using this table you can see that, if the datagram's protocol number is 6, IP delivers the datagram to TCP. If the protocol number is 17, IP delivers the datagram to UDP. TCP and UDP are the two transport layer services we are concerned with, but all of the protocols listed in the table use IP datagram delivery service directly. Some, such as ICMP and GGP, have already been mentioned. You don't need to be concerned with these minor protocols, but IGMP is an extension to IP for multicasting explained in RFC 988, and PUP is a packet protocol similar to UDP.

Port Numbers

After IP passes incoming data to the transport protocol, the transport protocol passes the data to the correct application process. Application processes (also called *network services*) are identified by port numbers, which are 16-bit values. The "source port number", which identifies the process that sent the data, and the "destination port number", which identifies the process that is to receive the data are contained in the first header word of each TCP segment and UDP packet.

On UNIX systems, port numbers are defined in the */etc/services* file. There are many more network applications than there are transport layer protocols, as the size of the table shows. Port numbers below 256 are reserved for "well-known services" (like FTP and TELNET) and are defined in the *Assigned Numbers* RFC. Ports numbered from 256 to 1024 are used for *UNIX-specific services*, which are services like **rlogin**, that were originally developed for UNIX systems. However, most of them are no longer UNIX-specific.

Port numbers are not unique between transport layer protocols; the numbers are only unique within a specific transport protocol. In other words, TCP and UDP can, and do, both assign the same port numbers. It is the combination of protocol and port numbers that uniquely identifies the specific process the data should be delivered to.

A partial */etc/services* file is shown below. The format of this file is very similar to the */etc/protocols* file. Each single-line entry starts with the official name of the service, separated by white space from the port number/protocol pairing associated with that service. The port numbers are paired with transport protocol names, because different transport protocols may use the same port number. An optional list of aliases for the official service name may be provided after the port number/protocol pair.

```
peanut% cat /etc/services
#
# @(#)services 1.12 88/02/07 SMI
#
# Network services, Internet style
#
```

```
echo            7/udp
echo            7/tcp
systat          11/tcp
netstat         15/tcp
ftp-data        20/tcp
ftp             21/tcp
telnet          23/tcp
smtp            25/tcp          mail
time            37/tcp          timserver
time            37/udp          timserver
name            42/udp          nameserver
whois           43/tcp          nicname
domain          53/udp          dns
domain          53/tcp
hostnames       101/tcp         hostname
#
# Host specific functions
#
tftp            69/udp
rje             77/tcp
finger          79/tcp
link            87/tcp          ttylink
supdup          95/tcp
pop-2           109/tcp                     # Post Office
uucp-path       117/tcp
nntp            119/tcp         usenet      # Network News Transfer
ntp             123/tcp                     # Network Time Protocol
#
# UNIX specific services
#
exec            512/tcp
login           513/tcp
shell           514/tcp         cmd         # no passwords used
biff            512/udp         comsat
who             513/udp         whod
syslog          514/udp
talk            517/udp
route           520/udp         router routed
```

This table, combined with the */etc/protocols* table, provides all of the information necessary to deliver data to the correct application. A datagram arrives at its destination based on the destination address in the fifth word of the datagram header. IP uses the protocol number in the third word of the datagram header, to deliver the data from the datagram, to the proper transport layer protocol. The first word of the data delivered to the transport protocol contains the destination port number that tells the transport protocol to pass the data up to a specific application. Figure 2-6 shows this delivery process.

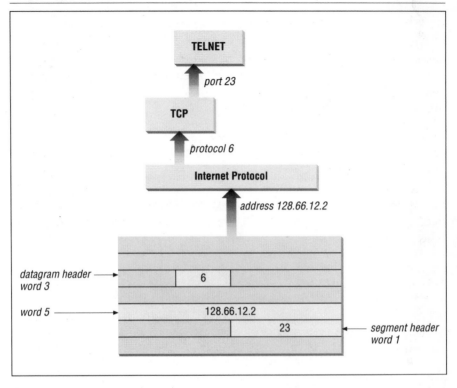

Figure 2.6: Protocol and Port Numbers

Sockets

Well-known ports are standardized port numbers that enable remote computers to know which port to connect to for a particular network service. This simplifies the connection process because both the sender and receiver know in advance that data bound for a specific process will use a specific port. For example, all systems that offer TELNET, offer it on port 23.

There is a second type of port number called a *dynamically allocated port*. As the name implies, dynamically allocated ports are not pre-assigned. They are assigned to processes when needed. The system ensures that it does not assign the same port number to two processes, and that the numbers assigned are above the range of standard port numbers.

Dynamically assigned ports provide the flexibility needed to support multiple users. If a TELNET user is assigned port number 23 for both the source and destination ports, what port numbers are assigned to the second concurrent TELNET user? To uniquely identify every connection, the source port is assigned a dynamically allocated port number, and the well-known port number is used for the destination port.

In the TELNET example, the first user is given a random source port number and a destination port number of 23 (TELNET). The second user is given a different random source port number and the same destination port. It is the pair of port numbers, source and destination, that uniquely identifies each network connection. The destination host knows the source port, because it is provided in both the TCP segment header and the UDP packet header. Both hosts know the destination port because it is a well-known port.

Figure 2-7 shows the exchange of port numbers during the TCP handshake. The source host randomly generates a source port, in this example 3044. It sends out a segment with a source port of 3044 and a destination port of 23. The destination host receives the segment, and responds back using 23 as its source port and 3044 as its destination port.

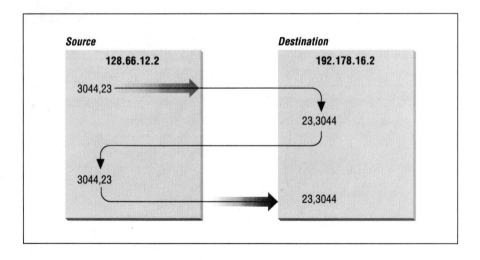

Figure 2.7: Passing Port Numbers

The combination of an IP address and a port number is called a *socket*. A socket uniquely identifies a single network process within the entire Internet. Sometimes the terms "socket" and "port number" are used interchangeably. In fact, well-known services are frequently referred to as "well-known sockets." In the context of this discussion, a "socket" is the combination of an IP address and a port number. A pair of sockets, one socket for the receiving host and one for the sending host, define the connection for connection-oriented protocols such as TCP.

Let's build on the example of dynamically assigned ports and well-known ports. Assume a user on host 128.66.12.2 uses TELNET to connect to host 192.178.16.2. Host 128.66.12.2 is the source host. The user is dynamically assigned a unique port number—3382. The connection is made to the TEL-NET service on the remote host which is, according to the standard, assigned well-known port 23. The socket for the source side of the connection is 128.66.12.2.3382 (IP address 128.66.12.2 plus port number 3382). For the destination side of the connection, the socket is 192.178.16.2.23 (address 192.178.16.2 plus port 23). The port of the destination socket is known by both systems because it is a well-known port. The port of the source socket is known, because the source host informed the destination host of the source socket when the connection request was made. The socket pair is therefore known by both the source and destination computers. The combination of the two sockets uniquely identifies this connection; no other connection in the Internet has this socket pair.

Networks, computers, and the applications within a computer can all be identified by special numeric values—IP addresses, protocol numbers, port numbers, and sockets. In the next chapter we discuss a network service that allows us to refer to computer systems by name instead of by number.

3

Name Service Concepts

The Internet Protocol document* defines names, addresses, and routes as follows:

> A name indicates what we seek. An address indicates where it is. A route indicates how to get there.

Names, addresses, and routes, all require the network administrator's attention. Routes and addresses are covered in the previous chapter. This chapter discusses names and how they are disseminated throughout the network.

Names and Addresses

Every network interface attached to a TCP/IP network is identified by a unique 32-bit IP address. A name (called a *host name*) can be assigned to any device that has an IP address. Names are assigned to devices because, compared to numeric Internet addresses, names are easier to remember and type correctly. The network software doesn't require names, but they do make it easier for humans to use the network.

---

*RFC 791, *Internet Protocol*, Jon Postel, ISI, 1981, page 7.

In most cases, host names and numeric addresses can be used interchangeably. A user wishing to **telnet** to the workstation at IP address 128.66.12.2 can enter:

```
% telnet 128.66.12.2
```

or use the host name associated with that address and enter the equivalent command:

```
% telnet peanut.nuts.com
```

Whether a command is entered with an address or a host name, the network connection always takes place based on the IP address. The system converts the host name to an address before the network connection is made. The network administrator is responsible for assigning names and addresses and storing them in the database used for the conversion.

Translating names into addresses isn't simply a "local" issue. The command **telnet peanut.nuts.com** is expected to work correctly on every host that's connected to the network. If *peanut.nuts.com* is connected to the Internet, hosts all over the world should be able to translate the name *peanut.nuts.com* into the proper address. Therefore, some facility must exist for disseminating the host name information to all hosts on the network

There are two common methods for translating names into addresses. The older method simply looks up the host name in a table called the *host table*.* The newer technique uses a distributed database system called *Domain Name Service* (DNS) to translate names to addresses. We'll examine the host table first.

The Host Table

The *host table* is a simple text file that associates IP addresses with host names. On most UNIX systems, the table is in the file */etc/hosts*. Each table entry in */etc/hosts* contains an IP address separated by white space from a list of host names associated with that address. Comments begin with #.

The host table on *peanut* might contain the following entries:

```
#
# Table of IP addresses and host names
#
128.66.12.2     peanut.nuts.com peanut
```

---

*Sun's Network Information Service (NIS) is an improved technique for accessing the host table. NIS is discussed in a later section.

```
127.0.0.1        localhost
128.66.12.1      almond.nuts.com almond loghost
128.66.12.4      walnut.nuts.com walnut
128.66.12.3      pecan.nuts.com pecan
128.66.1.2       filbert.nuts.com filbert
128.66.6.4       salt.plant.nuts.com salt.plant salt
```

The first entry in the sample table is for *peanut* itself. The IP address 128.66.12.2 is associated with the host name *peanut.nuts.com* and the alternate host name (or alias) *peanut*. The host name and all of its aliases resolve to the same IP address, in this case 128.66.12.2.

Aliases provide for name changes, alternate spellings, and shorter host names. They also allow for "generic host names." Look at the entry for 128.66.12.1. One of the aliases associated with that address is *loghost*. *loghost* is a special host name used by the syslog daemon, **syslogd**. Programs like **syslog** are written to direct their output to whichever host has been given a certain generic name. You can direct the output to any host you choose by assigning the appropriate generic host name as an alias. Other commonly used generic host names are *lprhost, mailhost,* and *dumphost*.

The second entry in the sample file assigns the address 127.0.0.1 to the host name *localhost*. As we have discussed, the class A network address 127 is reserved for the loopback network. The host address 127.0.0.1 is a special address used to designate the loopback address of the local host—hence the host name *localhost*. This special addressing convention allows the host to address itself the same way it addresses a remote host. The loopback address simplifies software by allowing common code to be used for communicating with local or remote processes. This addressing convention also reduces network traffic because the *localhost* address is associated with a loopback device that loops data back to the host before it is written out to the network.

Although the host table system has been superseded by DNS, it is still widely used for the following reasons:

- Most systems have a small host table containing name and address information about the important hosts on the local network. This small table is used when DNS is not running, such as during the initial system startup. Even if you use DNS, you should create a small */etc/hosts* file containing entries for your host, for *localhost*, and for the gateways and servers on your local net.

- Sites that use NIS use the host table as input to the NIS host database. You can use NIS in conjunction with DNS; but even when they are used together, most NIS sites create host tables that have an entry for every host on the local network. Chapter 9 explains how to use NIS with DNS.

- Very small sites, that are not connected to the Internet, sometimes use the host table. If there are few local hosts and the information about these hosts rarely changes, and there is no need to communicate via TCP/IP with remote sites, then there is little advantage to using DNS.

- Some sites run non-UNIX systems or older software that can't use DNS. If they can't be upgraded, these sites still have to use a large */etc/hosts* file.

Hosts connected to the Internet should use DNS. Despite this, large host tables are still used at some Internet sites. Because you will sometimes deal with sites that only use the host table, you should understand how it is built.

UNIX provides commands to automatically build */etc/hosts* and */etc/networks* with data available from the *Network Information Center* (NIC). I do not recommend that you use them to build */etc/hosts* because you should use DNS name service, not the NIC host table. However, these commands are still useful for building */etc/networks*, which is the file used to translate network addresses to network names. These commands are discussed in the following sections.

The NIC Host Table

The Network Information Center maintains a large table of Internet hosts called the *NIC host table*, which is stored on the host *nic.ddn.mil*, in the file *netinfo/hosts.txt*. Hosts included in the table are called *registered hosts*. Prior to adopting DNS, the NIC placed host names and addresses into this file for all sites on the Internet. Changes are still made to the host table, but new hosts are added only in special circumstances. Even when the host table was the primary means for translating host names to IP addresses, most sites registered only a limited number of key systems. But even with limited registration, the table grew so large that it became an inefficient way to convert host names to IP addresses. There is no way that a simple table could provide adequate service for the enormous number of hosts in today's Internet.

Another problem with the host table system is that it lacks a technique for automatically distributing information about newly registered hosts. Newly registered hosts can be referenced by name as soon as a site receives the new version of the host table. However, there is no way to guarantee that the host table is distributed to a site. (The NIC doesn't know who has a current version of the table, and who doesn't.) This lack of guaranteed uniform distribution is a major weakness of the host table system.

The NIC host table contains three types of entries: network records, gateway records, and host records. Figure 3-1 shows the format of the *hosts.txt* records. Each record begins with a keyword that identifies the record type, followed by an IP address, and one or more names associated with the address. The IP addresses and host names from the HOST records are extracted to construct the */etc/hosts* file. The network addresses and names from the NET records are used to create the */etc/networks* file.

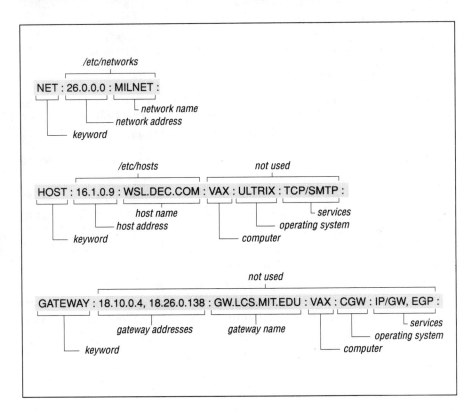

Figure 3.1: hosts.txt Records

The *hosts.txt* file contains a lot of information that UNIX does not use. The Gateway records aren't used at all. Neither are the fourth, fifth, and sixth fields of the HOST records. The fourth field describes the host computer hardware; the fifth field defines the operating system; and the sixth field defines the well-known services that the host is running. This information's accuracy is questionable; therefore it is not extracted from the *hosts.txt* file for any standard UNIX file.

The NIC host table must be converted to */etc/hosts* format before it can be used by UNIX. Let's look at how to build an */etc/hosts* and an */etc/networks* file from the NIC *hosts.txt* file.

Using gettable and htable

You can retrieve the *hosts.txt* file interactively from the NIC using FTP. However, on BSD systems the command **gettable** is specifically designed for this function. The command syntax is simply **gettable** *host*, where *host* is the host name of the remote site from which the *hosts.txt* file is retrieved. To get the *hosts.txt* file from *nic.ddn.mil*, enter:

```
% gettable nic.ddn.mil
```

Once the *hosts.txt* file is retrieved, it is converted to */etc/hosts* format using the **htable** command. The syntax of the command is **htable** *filename*, where *filename* is the name of the input file (normally *hosts.txt*).

In addition to the input file specified on the command line, **htable** looks for three other files:

localhosts   A locally-defined host table in the same format as an */etc/hosts* file. Use *localhosts* to list the hosts on your local network and any other hosts you want added to */etc/hosts* that aren't listed in *hosts.txt*.

localnetworks   A locally-defined listing of networks. This file is in the format of an */etc/networks* file, i.e., each entry starts with a network name, separated by white space from a network address. Use *localnetworks* to list your local networks, and any external networks you're interested in that aren't already listed in *hosts.txt*.

localgateways   This file is the same format as the */etc/gateways* file.*
localgateways can be ignored, because **htable** adds no
information to the file.

The **htable** command creates three output files: *hosts*, *networks*, and *gateways*. It does this by first copying the contents of the local files (*localhosts*, *localnetworks*, and *localgateways*) to the output files with no conversion. Then host and network information is extracted from *hosts.txt* and added to the appropriate output file. The **htable** command merely copies the *localgateways* file to the output *gateways* file without changing it.

Building /etc/hosts and /etc/networks

The following example shows the steps to add information from the NIC *hosts.txt* file to */etc/hosts* and */etc/networks*. In a temporary working directory, the administrator creates the *localhosts* and *localnetworks* files using a text editor. No *localgateways* file is created. Since **htable** contributes nothing to this file, it is simpler to just create */etc/gateways* directly.

First, change to the working directory and retrieve the latest version of the NIC *hosts.txt* file using the **gettable** command. In this case, the file is retrieved from *nic.ddn.mil*:

```
peanut% gettable nic.ddn.mil
Connection to nic.ddn.mil opened.
Host table received.
Connection to nic.ddn.mil closed
```

Now run **htable** to extract the host and network data from *hosts.txt*. A warning message is displayed because no *localgateways* file is found. You can ignore this.

```
peanut% htable hosts.txt
Warning, no localgateways file.
```

Check the output files to see that the NIC data has been appended. Listing the directory reveals that the newly created *networks* and *hosts* files are now thousands of lines long, while the *gateways* file is empty. Once processing is complete, remove the *gateways* file and the enormous *hosts.txt* file.

/etc/gateways contains information used by the Routing Information Protocol (RIP). It is discussed in Chapter 7.

```
peanut% ls -l
total 1266
-rw-r--r--  1 craig           0 May 10 17:02 gateways
-rw-r--r--  1 craig      232823 May 10 17:03 hosts
-rw-r--r--  1 craig      827858 May 10 16:32 hosts.txt
-rw-r--r--  1 craig         290 May 10 16:11 localhosts
-rw-r--r--  1 craig          16 May 10 16:11 localnetworks
-rw-r--r--  1 craig      194761 May 10 17:03 networks
peanut% rm hosts.txt
peanut% rm gateways
```

When you are confident that the hosts file and networks file produced by **htable** are correct, become superuser and move the files to the */etc* directory.

```
peanut# mv hosts /etc
peanut# mv networks /etc
```

The networks.txt File

Most of the information in the *hosts.txt* file is no longer used. The GATE-WAY records are ignored, and the HOST records are not needed because DNS now provides host name information. Only the NETWORK records provide useful information. The */etc/networks* file, which is created from the NETWORK records, is still used to map network addresses to network names because many network names are not included in the DNS database. The NIC produces a file, *networks.txt*, that contains only NETWORK records. If you only want to create the */etc/networks* file, use *networks.txt* instead of the larger *hosts.txt* file.

To create the */etc/networks* file, download the file *netinfo/networks.txt* via anonymous **ftp** from *nic.ddn.mil* into a local work directory. Run **htable networks.txt**. Discard the *hosts* file and the *gateways* file produced by **htable**, and move the *networks* file to the */etc* directory. That's all there is to it.

This is the last we'll speak of the NIC host table. The *hosts.txt* file has been superseded by DNS and only a small fraction of the hosts that are on the network are registered in the NIC host table.

Domain Name Service

The Domain Name System (DNS) overcomes both major weaknesses of the host table:

- DNS scales well. It doesn't rely on a single large table; it is a distributed database system that doesn't bog down as the database grows. DNS currently provides information on approximately 700,000 hosts, while less than 10,000 are listed in the host table.

- DNS guarantees that new host information will be disseminated to the rest of the network as it is needed.

Not only is information automatically disseminated, it is only disseminated to those who are interested. Here's how it works. If a DNS server receives a request for information about a host for which it has no information, it passes on the request to an *authoritative server*. An authoritative server is any server responsible for maintaining accurate information about the domain which is being queried. When the authoritative server answers, the local server saves (*caches*) the answer for future use. The next time the local server receives a request for this information, it answers the request itself. The ability to control host information from an authoritative source and to automatically disseminate accurate information makes DNS superior to the host table, even for small networks not connected to the Internet.

In addition to superseding the host table, DNS also replaces an earlier form of name service. Unfortunately, both the old and new services are commonly called *name service*. Both are listed in the */etc/services* file. In that file, the old software is assigned UDP port 42 and is called *nameservice*. DNS name service is assigned port 53 and is called *domain*. Naturally, there is some confusion between the two name servers. This text discusses DNS only; when we refer to "name service," we always mean DNS.

The Domain Hierarchy

DNS is a distributed hierarchical system for resolving host names into IP addresses. Under DNS, there is no central data base with all of the Internet host information. The information is distributed among thousands of name servers organized into a hierarchy similar to the hierarchy of the UNIX filesystem. DNS has a *root domain* at the top of the domain hierarchy that is served by a group of name servers called the *root servers*.

Just as directories in the UNIX filesystem are found by following a path from the root directory, through subordinate directories, to the target directory, information about a domain is found by tracing pointers from the root domain, through subordinate domains, to the target domain.

Directly under the root domain are the *top level domains*. There are two basic types of top-level domains—geographic and organizational. Geographic domains have been set aside for each country in the world, and are identified by a two-letter code. For example, the United Kingdom is domain UK, and Japan is domain JP. The country code for the United States (US) is not normally used. In fact, geographic domains are rarely used for hosts within the United States.*

Within the U.S. the top-level domains are organizational—that is, membership in a domain is based on the type of organization (commercial, military, etc.) to which the system belongs.† The top-level domains used in the United States are:

COM   commercial organizations

EDU   educational institutions

GOV   government agencies

MIL   military organizations

NET   network support organizations, such as network operation centers

ORG   organizations that don't fit in any of the above, such as non-profit organizations

Figure 3-2 illustrates the domain hierarchy. At the top is the root. Directly below the root domain are the top-level domains; in this figure only organizational top-level domains are shown. The root servers only have complete information about the top-level domains. No servers, not even the root servers, have complete information about all domains, but the root servers have pointers to the servers for the second level domains.‡ So while the root servers may not know the answer to a query, they know who to ask.

---

*When US is used as the top-level domain; the second-level domain is usually the state's two-letter postal abbreviation (e.g., WY for Wyoming). US geographic domains are usually used only by "personal systems" and other entities that don't fit any organizational category.

†There is no relationship between the organizational and geographic domains in the US. Each system belongs to either an organizational domain *or* a geographical domain, not both.

†‡*nib* under *gov* and *nuts* under *com* are the second-level domains shown in Figure 3-2.

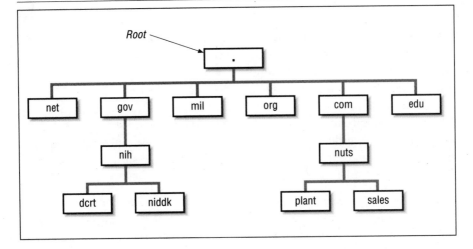

Figure 3.2: Domain Hierarchy

Creating Domains and Subdomains

The Network Information Center has the authority to allocate domains. To obtain a domain, you apply to the NIC for authority to create a domain under one of the top-level domains. Once the authority to create a domain is granted, you can create additional domains, called *subdomains*, under your domain. Let's look at how this works at our imaginary nut packing company.

Our company is a commercial profit-making (we hope) enterprise. It clearly falls into the *com* domain. We apply to the NIC for authority to create a domain named *nuts* within the *com* domain. The request for the new domain contains the host names and addresses of at least two servers that will provide name service for the new domain. (Chapter 4 discusses the domain name application.) When the NIC approves the request, it adds pointers in the *com* domain to the new domain's name servers. Now when queries are received by the root servers for the *nuts.com* domain, the queries are referred to the new name servers.

The NIC's approval grants us complete authority over our new domain. Any registered domain has authority to divide its domain into subdomains. Our imaginary company can create separate domains for the sales organization (*sales.nuts.com*) and for the packing plant (*plant.nuts.com*). This is done without consulting the NIC. The decision to add additional subdomains is completely up to the local domain administrator.

Name assignment is, in some ways, similar to address assignment. The NIC assigns a network address to an organization, and the organization assigns subnet addresses and host addresses within the range of that network address. Similarly, the NIC assigns a domain to an organization, and the organization assigns subdomains and host names within that domain. The NIC is the central authority that delegates authority and distributes control over names and addresses to individual organizations. Once that authority has been delegated, the individual organization is responsible for managing the names and addresses it has been assigned.

The parallel between subnet and subdomain assignment can cause confusion. Subnets and subdomains are not linked. A subdomain may contain information about hosts from several different networks. Creating a new subnet does not require creating a new subdomain, and creating a new subdomain does not require creating a new subnet.

A new subdomain becomes accessible when pointers to the servers for the new domain are placed in the domain above it (see Figure 3-2). Remote servers cannot locate the *nuts.com* domain until a pointer to its server is placed in the *com* domain. Likewise, the subdomains *sales* and *plant* cannot be accessed until pointers to them are placed in *nuts.com*. The DNS database record that points to the name servers for a domain is the NS (*name server*) record. This record contains the name of the domain and the name of the host that is a server for that domain. Chapter 8 discusses the actual DNS database. For now, let's just think of these records as pointers.

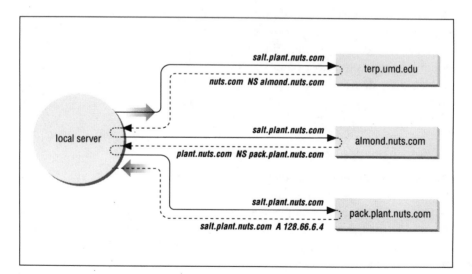

Figure 3.3: Non-recursive Query

Figure 3-3 illustrates how the NS records are used as pointers. A local server has a request to resolve *salt.plant.nuts.com* into an IP address. The server has no information on *nuts.com* in its cache, so it queries a root server (*terp.umd.edu* in our example) for the address. The root server replies with an NS record that points to *almond.nuts.com* as the source of information on *nuts.com*. The local server queries *almond*, which in turn points it to *pack.plant.nuts.com* as the server for *plant.nuts.com*. The local server then queries *pack.plant.nuts.com*, and finally receives the desired IP address. The local server caches the A (address) record and each of the NS records. The next time it has a query for *salt.plant.nuts.com*, it will answer the query itself. And the next time the server has a query for other information in the *nuts.com* domain, it will go directly to *almond* without involving a root server.

Figure 3-3 is an example of a non-recursive query. In a *non-recursive* query the remote server tells the local server who to ask next. The local server must follow the pointers itself. In a *recursive* search, the remote server follows the pointers and returns the final answer to the local server. The root servers generally perform only non-recursive searches.

Domain Names

Domain names reflect the domain hierarchy. Domain names are written from most specific (a host name) to least specific (a top-level domain), with each part of the domain name separated by a dot.* A fully qualified domain name (FQDN) starts with a specific host and ends with a top-level domain. *peanut.nuts.com.* is the FQDN of workstation *peanut*, in the *nuts* domain, of the *com* domain.

Domain names are rarely written as fully qualified domain names. Usually domain names are written relative to a *default domain* in the same way that UNIX pathnames are written relative to the current (default) working directory. DNS adds the default domain to the user input when constructing the query for the name server. For example, if the default domain is *nuts.com*, a user can omit the *nuts.com* extension for any host names in that domain. *almond.nuts.com* could be addressed simply as *almond*. DNS adds the default domain *nuts.com*.

---

* The root domain is identified by a single dot, i.e., the root name is a null name written simply as ".".

This feature is implemented in different ways on different systems, but there are two predominate techniques. On some systems the extension is added to every host name request unless it *ends* with a dot, i.e., is qualified out to the root. For example, assume that there is a host named *salt* in the subdomain *plant* of the *nuts.com* domain. *salt.plant* does not end with a dot, so *nuts.com* is added to it giving the domain name *salt.plant.nuts.com*. On some other systems, the extension is added only if there is *no dot* embedded in the requested host name. On this type of system *salt.plant* would not be extended and would therefore not be resolved by the name server because *plant* is not a valid top-level domain. But *almond*, which contains no embedded dot, would be extended with *nuts.com*, giving the valid domain name *almond.nuts.com*.

How the default domain is used and how queries are constructed varies depending on software implementation. It can even vary by release level. For this reason, you should exercise caution when embedding a host name in a program. Only an IP address is immune from changes in the name server software.

BIND, resolver, and named

The implementation of DNS used on most UNIX systems is the *Berkeley Internet Name Domain* (BIND) software. Descriptions in this text are based on the BIND name server implementation.

DNS name service software is conceptually divided into two components—a resolver and a name server. The *resolver* is the software that forms the query; it asks the questions. The *name server* is the process that responds to the query; it answers the questions.

The resolver does not exist as a distinct process running on the computer. Rather, the resolver is a library of software routines (called the "resolver code") that is linked into any program that needs to look up addresses. This library knows how to ask the name server for host information.

Under BIND, all computers use resolver code but not all computers run the name server process. A computer that does not run a local name server process and relies on other systems for all name service answers is called a *resolver-only* system. Resolver-only configurations are only common on single user systems. Most UNIX systems run a local name server process.

The BIND name server runs as a distinct process called *named* (pronounced "name" "d"). Name servers are classified differently depending on how they are configured. The three main categories of name servers are:

primary   The *primary server* is the server from which all data about a domain is derived. The primary server loads the domain's information directly from a disk file created by the domain administrator. Primary servers are *authoritative*, meaning they have complete information about their domain and their responses are always accurate. There should be only one primary server for a domain.

secondary   Secondary servers transfer the entire domain database from the primary server. A particular domain's database file is called a *zone file*; copying this file to a secondary server is called a *zone file transfer*. A secondary server assures that it has current information about a domain by periodically transferring the domain's zone file. Secondary servers are also authoritative for their domain.

caching-only Caching-only servers get the answers to all name service queries from other name servers. Once a caching server has received an answer to a query, it caches the information and will use it in the future to answer queries itself. Most name servers cache answers and use them in this way. What makes the caching-only server unique is that this is the only technique it uses to build its domain database. Caching servers are *non-authoritative*, meaning that their information is second-hand and incomplete, though usually accurate.

The relationship between the different types of servers is an advantage that DNS has over the host table for most networks, even very small networks. Under DNS, there should be only one primary name server for each domain. DNS data is entered into the primary server's database by the domain administrator. Therefore, the administrator has central control of the host name information. An automatically distributed, centrally controlled database is an advantage for any size network. When you add a new system to the network, you don't need to modify the */etc/hosts* files on every node in the network; you only modify the DNS database on the primary server. The information is automatically disseminated to the other servers by full zone transfers or by caching single answers.

Network Information Service

The *Network Information Service* (NIS)* is an administrative database system that was developed by Sun Microsystems. It provides central control and automatic dissemination of important administrative files. NIS can be used in conjunction with DNS, or as an alternative to it.

NIS and DNS have some similarities and some differences. Like DNS, the Network Information Service overcomes the problem of accurately distributing the host table, but unlike DNS, it only provides service for local area networks. NIS is not intended as a service for the Internet as a whole. Another difference is that NIS provides access to a wider range of information than DNS. As its name implies, Network Information Service provides much more than name-to-address conversions. It converts several standard UNIX files into databases that can be queried over the network. These databases are called *NIS maps*.

/etc/hosts and */etc/networks* are two of the files that NIS converts into maps. The maps can be stored on a central server where they can be centrally maintained while still being fully accessible to the NIS clients. Because the maps can be both centrally maintained and automatically disseminated to users, NIS overcomes a major weakness of the host table. But NIS is not an alternative to DNS for Internet hosts because the host table, and therefore NIS, contains only a fraction of the information available to DNS. For this reason DNS and NIS are usually used together.

This chapter has introduced the concept of host names and provided an overview of the various techniques used to translate host names into IP addresses. This is by no means the complete story. Assigning host names and managing name service are important tasks for the network administrator. These topics are revisited several times in this book and discussed in extensive detail in Chapter 8.

---

*Formerly called the "Yellow Pages," or *yp*. Although the name has changed, the abbreviation *yp* is still used.

4

Getting Started

This chapter departs from previous ones. Chapters 1–3 describe the TCP/IP protocols and how they work. We discussed why routing is required, what name service is, and other basic concepts. In this chapter, the emphasis shifts from how TCP/IP functions, to how it is configured. This chapter begins the network configuration process, and the first step in this process is planning.

Before configuring a host to run TCP/IP, you must have certain information. At the very least, every host must have a unique IP address and host name. You should also decide on the items below before configuring a system:

default gateway address If the system communicates with TCP/IP hosts that are not on its local network, a default gateway address may be needed.

routing protocol If a routing protocol is used on the network, each device needs to know what protocol it is.

name server addresses To resolve host names into IP addresses, each host needs to know the addresses of the domain name servers.

domain name	Hosts using the domain name service must know their correct domain name.
subnet mask	To communicate properly, each system on a network must use the same subnet mask.
broadcast address	To avoid broadcast problems, the broadcast address of every computer on a network must be the same.

If you're configuring a network from scratch, make these decisions before configuring any system. If you're adding a new system to an existing network, make sure that you find out the answers from your network administrator before putting the system online. The network administrator is responsible for making and communicating decisions about overall network configuration.

If you are creating a new TCP/IP network, you will have to make some basic decisions. Will the new network connect to the Internet? If it will, how is the connection to be made? How should the network number be chosen? How do I register a domain name? How do I choose host names? To formally obtain a network address or to register a domain name you must apply to the Network Information Center (NIC). In the rest of this chapter, we cover how these decisions are made and when they should be communicated to the NIC.

Connected and Non-connected Networks

First, you must decide whether or not your new network will be directly connected to the Internet. The Internet's administration makes a distinction between networks connected to the Internet and those that are not connected. A *connected network* is directly attached to the Internet and has full access to other networks on the Internet. A *non-connected network* is not directly attached to the Internet, and its access to Internet networks is limited. An example of a non-connected network is a TCP/IP network that attaches to the outside world via **uucp**. Users on the network can send mail to Internet hosts but they cannot **rlogin** to one of them.

Many TCP/IP networks (perhaps most) are not connected to the Internet. Many of you will probably have non-connected networks. On these networks, TCP/IP is only used for internal communication between the organization's various networks. Some other networking solution, like **uucp** or a public data network, is used for external communications.

There are two basic reasons why many sites do not connect to the Internet. One reason is the long-standing requirement for a government sponsor for direct Internet connection. Many organizations are not inclined to seek government sponsorship; the very fact that it is required makes them feel unwelcome. Many of them feel that they will not qualify for this sponsorship, or that their network traffic will be restricted in some way.

Don't let the "sponsorship" requirement deter you from joining the Internet. New policies are promoting connection to the Internet. Commercial TCP/IP networks, like PSInet and Alternet, are designed to support commercial customers, and the regional networks often have liberal acceptable-use policies that permit a wide variety of organizations to connect to the network. Appendix A contains a list of contacts for the regional networks and for the commercial TCP/IP networks. Contact them for information about how to get connected.

Cost is the second reason why many sites do not connect to the Internet. Low use or limited requirements, such as only needing e-mail access, may make the cost of an Internet connection exceed the benefit. But unless you have carefully determined what your needs are and what an Internet connection will cost, you cannot make that determination. The contacts in Appendix A can give you the various cost and performance alternatives.

Obtaining an IP Address

Every interface on a TCP/IP network must have a unique IP address. If a host is part of the Internet, its IP address must be unique within the entire Internet.* If a host's TCP/IP communications are limited to a local network, its IP address only needs to be unique locally. Because of this, administrators whose networks will not be connected to the Internet sometimes pick a network address without consulting the NIC. We recommend that you get an official network number from the NIC.

All networks, including those not planning to connect to the Internet, should obtain their network addresses from the NIC. Unless you have a crystal ball, the future is unknowable. Future events, changes in technology and network policy, or changes in your communications requirements may make the connection of your network to the Internet inevitable. As the

---

*The address 128.66.0.0 used in this book is a real IP address. *Do not* use this address on your network. It may already be assigned to another organization.

Internet grows and becomes more ubiquitous, the likelihood of your local network connecting to some regional or national network also grows.

Obtaining a network address from the NIC is simple and costs nothing. There are no advantages to choosing your own unofficial network address—except that you do not have to fill out an application. The advantage to filling out the application and obtaining your address from the NIC is that you will not have to change your address in the future if you do connect to the Internet. By getting an address from the NIC, you ensure that you won't have to reconfigure every system on your network when you decide to connect.

The Network Address Application

Before you submit any of the applications discussed in this chapter, check with your network service provider. The organization that provides your connection to the Internet may submit these forms for you. If they've already submitted the forms, you obviously won't need to. Even if they haven't submitted these forms, they may provide help in doing it. If you have access to such a service, take advantage of it. If you don't, read on.

To apply for a network address, submit a network address application form to the NIC. This can be done via postal mail or electronic mail. This application form, and all the other forms mentioned in this chapter, are reproduced in Appendix B, but getting your own copy from the NIC will ensure that you have the most recent version. To obtain the form through postal mail, send a request to the NIC at the address shown in Appendix B; return the completed form to the same address. If you have e-mail access to the Internet, mail the completed form to *hostmaster@nic.ddn.mil*.

The application form is largely self-explanatory, but a few items require some thought. The first question on the application asks for the name of the governmental organization sponsoring your connection to the Internet. Don't be discouraged by this question. It is directed only to applicants whose networks will be directly connected to the Internet. If you are not connecting to the Internet, just skip this question.

A connected network requires a sponsor, because it is allowed to pass data across the government subsidized segments of the Internet. A non-connected network does not pass data over these networks, and therefore does not require a government sponsor. Despite this distinction, the NIC grants network addresses and domain names to both connected and non-connected networks. You can, and should, get an "official" network address even if you aren't connected to the Internet.

The growing diversity of the global network makes the requirement for government sponsors less applicable. New segments of the network are emerging that are sponsored by commercial organizations, educational institutions, and foreign governments. Each of these networks has its own policies and guidelines for membership and usage. These new networks make the idea of government sponsorship obsolete. Unfortunately, the requirement is still with us, at least for the short term.

The administration of the Internet is planning to eliminate the requirement for sponsors. RFC 1174 explains the plan to replace sponsors with a more flexible concept based on *acceptable-use policies.* These policies define what uses are legitimate for a network, and they vary from network to network. For example, one network's policy might ban commercial traffic; another network's policy might allow it. Other networks look at a network's policy and decide, based on it, if they'll carry traffic from that network. The current requirement of government sponsorship for full network access will be completely replaced when RFC 1174 is fully implemented. By the time your network is connected to the Internet, RFC 1174 may have been implemented, and the question of sponsorship will be moot.

If you will be connected to the Internet, put the requested information about your Internet sponsor in Item 1. If you're not sure how to answer this question, talk to the people in charge of the network through which you connect to the Internet. Your network will connect to the Internet through some area, regional, or national network (probably one of the networks listed in Appendix A). These networks have network management organizations that can provide help and information about dealing with the network bureaucracy. Take advantage of the experts.

Item 2 requests information about the technical point-of-contact (POC) for the new network. The POC is the person responsible for the network. Two things may be confusing here. One is the request for a *NIC handle.* You have a NIC handle only if you are registered in the *NIC white pages.* The white pages (discussed in Chapter 12) is a directory of information about users, networks, hosts, and domains. A NIC handle is a record identifier for this directory. A personal NIC handle for a user entry is composed of the user's initials and perhaps a number. For example, my initials are *cwh* and my NIC handle is *cwh3.* It is unlikely that you will have a handle before you have a network number. If you don't have a handle, just leave 2a blank. The NIC will assign you one.

The other confusing thing in Item 2 is the request for a network mailbox. This appears to be a Catch-22. They want your e-mail address and they haven't given you a network number yet! In fact, it is not unusual to have access to e-mail on another network before your local network is set up. If you have an electronic mailbox that can be addressed from the Internet, provide it in answer to this question. If you don't have a mailbox, Item 2f can simply be left blank. If later you have a mailbox, let the NIC know what it is. The administrator of a network that is not connected to the Internet may never have a mailbox that can be reached by the NIC.

The network name requested in Item 3 is equivalent to the network name in the */etc/networks* file. Each network has a name associated with the assigned network number. This is where you inform the NIC of the name you have chosen for your network. The application submitted by our imaginary nut company contained the name *nuts-net* in answer to Question 3.

Item 4 asks for the postal address of your network site. Since you have already provided the mailing address of the network technical contact, this address may seem unnecessary. Usually this is the same address as the one provided for the technical contact, but this question is designed to find out where your network is located geographically—which *may* be different from the location of the technical staff. The old Internet number application asked for the longitude and latitude of your network site (jokingly called your ICBM address), so the forms are improving!

Item 5 is required only for Milnet connections. If you're connecting to Milnet, answer Question 5; otherwise skip it. Question 5 is used to inform the NIC that you want your network to be *announced* to NSFNET. Announcing your network includes it in the routing information exchanged between Milnet and NFSNET—allowing you to communicate with many more networks. If your network is not announced to NSFNET, it will only be reachable by other networks connected to the Milnet. It is possible that you don't want Milnet to announce your network to NFSNET because you have another, better path to NFSNET. Question 5b informs the NIC that you already have your own NSFNET connection.

Item 6 is self-explanatory. How many computers are connected to your network now, and how many do you expect to have connected in five years?

Item 7 needs to be filled in only if you will *not* accept a class C network number. If your requirements will not allow you to use a class C network number, you must state them here. Unless you require several subnets or hundreds of hosts, a class C address is probably sufficient. Class A and class B addresses are in short supply. Don't waste this valuable resource. Only use what you need.

Question 8 is self-explanatory. Classify your organization as either research, defense, government (non-defense), or commercial.

Question 9 requires a little thought. It asks the purpose of your network. How will your network be used to forward the goals of your organization? This can be answered in a short, simple, straightforward manner. A single sentence is often enough. Our imaginary company might answer Item 9 with the following statement:

> 9) To provide efficient, economical communications to support our customers in the Department of Defense.

The application for an IP network address has been covered in detail because everyone should fill out this form, whether or not they are connecting to the Internet. Obtaining a network address is the first step in creating a TCP/IP network. Once you obtain a network number, you're able to assign host addresses from that network number to the individual systems on your network.

Assigning Host Addresses

The NIC assigns *network numbers*. After submitting its application to the NIC, our imaginary company's network (*nuts-net*) was assigned network number 128.66. The network administrator is permitted to assign host addresses within the range of IP addresses* available to this class B address; i.e., the network administrator can assign the last two bytes of the four-byte address. A host address with all bits zero or with all bits one cannot be used, but beyond these two restrictions, you're free to assign host addresses in any way that seems reasonable to you.

Network administrators usually assign host addresses in one of two ways:

one address at a time	Each individual host is assigned an address, perhaps in sequential order, through the address range.
groups of addresses	Blocks of addresses are delegated to smaller organizations within the overall organization, which then assign the individual host addresses.

---

*The range of addresses is called the *address space*.

The assignment of groups of addresses is most common when the network is subnetted, and the address groups are divided along subnet boundaries. But assigning blocks of addresses does not require subnetting. It can just be an organizational device for delegating authority. Delegating authority for groups of addresses is often very convenient for large networks, while small networks tend to assign host addresses one at a time. No matter how addresses are assigned, someone must retain sufficient central control to prevent duplication, and to ensure that the addresses are recorded correctly on the domain name servers.

Obtaining a Domain Name

A domain name is also obtained by submitting an application to the NIC. You can obtain the latest version of the application form from the postal address given in Appendix B. If you want to submit the form via postal mail, send it to the same address. If you have access to e-mail, you can send the completed form to *hostmaster@nic.ddn.mil.*

This application is similar to the application for an IP address. You'll be asked to provide names, addresses, mailboxes, and NIC handles. The most difficult question is the request for the names and addresses of your primary and secondary name servers. The servers listed must be connected to the Internet. If you are going to provide the primary server yourself, you must obtain a connected network number before submitting the domain name application.* The difficulty arises when specifying the secondary name server.

The secondary server should be on a separate physical network from the primary server. Putting the secondary server on a different network guarantees that other sites can look up information about your network, even if access to your network is unavailable for some reason. A large organization may have multiple independent networks, but for most sites this requirement means asking another organization to provide a secondary name server. Who do you ask?

Again, you should turn to the people who are providing your Internet access. The network that connects you to the Internet may provide secondary name servers as a service to its users. If they do not, they may be able to point you to other organizations that do provide the service. It is even

---

*It isn't necessary to provide your own primary server; and if you aren't connected to the Internet, you can't provide your own primary. That situation is discussed below.

possible for two organizations who are both applying for new domains to provide secondary service for each other. In other words, you provide someone with a secondary server; in return, they provide a secondary server for you.

Question 9 may also cause some confusion. It asks if you have any registered hosts. As discussed in Chapter 3, registered hosts are hosts listed in the NIC host table. If you have never registered a host in the NIC host table, skip this question. It is unlikely that you'll need to answer this question unless you have been connected to the Internet for several years. The question gives you the opportunity to change the old registered host names to new names appropriate to your new domain. If you have a registered host name to change, enter the old host name, the IP address, and the new fully-qualified domain name. This information is used to update the NIC host table.

Even if you are not connected to the Internet, you may still want to register your domain name with the NIC. There are two reasons for doing this. The first is the same reason mentioned for registering your network address; the future is unknowable. In the future you may be connected to the Internet. The second is a more immediate reason. Many non-Internet networks have e-mail gateways to the Internet, and some of these networks allow Internet hosts to address mail to you based on an "Internet-style" domain name. Both UUNET and Bitnet offer this service. However, you cannot register a domain name unless someone on the Internet will provide primary and secondary name service for your domain. Luckily, in addition to forwarding the mail, UUNET and Bitnet provide both primary and secondary name service for their customers. Appendix B provides information on how to obtain applications for registering an Internet domain through UUNET and Bitnet. The applications are similar to the standard domain name application, except that the primary and secondary name server information is already filled in with the names of servers provided by UUNET and Bitnet. The forms contain special instructions for submitting these applications.

Obtaining an IN-ADDR.ARPA Domain

When you obtain your Internet domain name, you should also apply for an *in-addr.arpa* domain. This special domain is sometimes called a *reverse domain*. Chapter 8 contains more information about how the *in-addr.arpa* domain is set up and used, but basically the reverse domain maps numeric IP addresses into domain names. This is the reverse of the normal process, which converts domain names to addresses.

The application for a reverse domain is available in Appendix B and from the NIC. Again, submit the completed form to *hostmaster@nic.ddn.mil* (if you have e-mail) or to the NIC's postal address.

The form asks one three-part question. The three items requested are:

IN-ADDR.ARPA Domain Name

> Your *in-addr.arpa* domain name is constructed by reversing the individual numbers in your network number and tacking *in-addr.arpa* to the end. The network number of *nuts-net* is 128.66. So its reverse domain name is *66.128.in-addr.arpa.* The number 128.66 is reversed to 66 and 128, and *in-addr.arpa* is added to the end of this reversed numeric string.
>
> Reversing the network number to construct the domain name makes more sense when you remember that domain names are written from the most specific (host name) to the most general (top-level domain). IP addresses are written from the most general (network) to the most specific (host). Reversing the order of the numbers in an IP address makes the structure of the address agree with the structure of the domain name.

Network Name

> This is the same network name as Item 3 on your Internet number application. For example, the name of 128.66 is *nuts-net.*

IN-ADDR Servers

> These servers will probably be the same servers used in Items 7 and 8 of your domain name application. Two servers are required. Each should be identified by fully-qualified domain name, IP address, hardware type, and operating system.

The instructions written on the *in-addr.arpa* domain application contain a clear example of how to complete this form. If you are connecting to the Internet, do not overlook submitting this application.

Choosing a Host Name

Once you obtain a domain name, you are responsible for assigning host names within that domain. You must ensure that host names are unique within your domain or subdomain, in the same way that host addresses must be unique with a network or subnet. But there is more to choosing a host name than just making sure the name is unique. Choosing a host name can be a surprisingly emotional issue. Many people feel very strongly about the name of their computer because they identify their computer with themselves or their work.

RFC 1178 provides excellent guidelines on how to choose a host name. Some key suggestions from these guidelines are:

- Use real words that are short, easy to spell, and easy to remember. The point of using host names instead of IP addresses is that they are easier to use. If host names are difficult to spell and remember, they defeat their own purpose.

- Use theme names. For example, all hosts in a group could be named after human movements: fall, jump, hop, skip, walk, run, stagger, wiggle, stumble, trip, limp, lurch, hobble, etc. Theme names are often easier to choose then unrestricted names, and increase the sense of community among network users.

- Avoid using project names, personal names, acronyms, numeric names, and technical jargon. Projects and users change over time. Naming a computer after the person who is currently using it or the project it is currently assigned to, may just lead to renaming the computer in the future.

The only requirement for a host name is that it be unique within its domain. But a well-chosen host name can save future work and make the user happier.

Planning Routing

In Chapter 2, we learned that hosts only communicate directly with other computers connected to the same network. Gateways are needed to communicate with systems on other networks. If the hosts on your network need to communicate with computers on other networks, a route through a gateway must be defined. There are two ways to do this:

- Routing can be handled by a *static routing table* built by the system administrator. Static routing tables are most useful when the number of gateways is limited. Static tables do not dynamically adjust to changing network conditions, so each change in the table is made manually by the network administrator. Complex environments require a more flexible approach to routing then a static routing table provides.

- Routing can be handled by a *dynamic routing table* that responds to changing network conditions. Dynamic routing tables are built by routing protocols. Routing protocols exchange routing information which they use to update the routing table. Dynamic routing is used when there are multiple gateways on a network, and are essential when more then one gateway can reach the same destination.

Many networks use a combination of both static and dynamic routing. Some systems on the network use static routing tables, while others run routing protocols and have dynamic tables. While it is often appropriate for hosts to use static routing tables, gateways usually run routing protocols.

The network administrator is responsible for deciding what type of routing to use and for choosing the default gateway for each host. Make these decisions before you start to configure your system. Here are a few guidelines to help you plan routing. If you have:

- *A network with no gateways to other TCP/IP networks.* No special routing configuration is required in this case. The gateways referred to in this discussion are IP routers that interconnect TCP/IP networks. If you are not interconnecting TCP/IP networks, you do not need an IP router. Neither a default gateway nor a routing protocol needs to be specified.
- *A network with a single gateway.* If you only have one gateway, don't run any routing protocols. Specify the single gateway as the default gateway in a static routing table.
- *A network with internal gateways to other subnets and a single gateway to the world.* Here there is a real choice. You can statically specify each subnet route and make the gateway to the world your default route, or you can run a routing protocol. Decide which you want to do based on the effort involved in maintaining a static table versus the slight overhead of running a routing protocol on your hosts and networks. If you have more than a few hosts, running a routing protocol is probably easiest.
- *A network with multiple gateways to the world.* If you have multiple gateways that can reach the same destination, use a routing protocol. This allows the gateways to adapt to network changes, giving you redundant access to the remote networks.

Figure 4-1 shows a subnetted class B network with five gateways identified as *A* through *E*. A central subnet (128.66.1.0) interconnects five other subnets. One of the subnets has a gateway to an external class A network. The network administrator would probably choose to run a routing protocol on the central subnet (128.66.1.0) and perhaps on subnet 128.66.12.0, which is attached to the class A network (26.0.0.0). Dynamic routing is appropriate on these subnets because they have multiple gateways. Without dynamic routing, the administrator would need to update every one of these gateways manually whenever any change occurred in the network—for example, whenever a new subnet was added. A mistake during the manual update could disrupt network service. Running a routing protocol on these two subnets is simpler and more reliable.

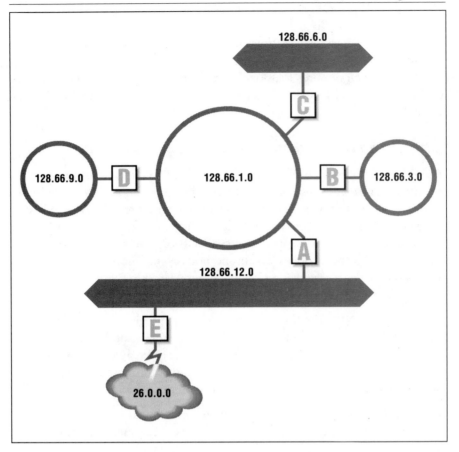

Figure 4.1: Routing and Subnets

On the other hand, the administrator would probably choose static routing for the other subnets (128.66.3.0, 128.66.6.0, and 128.66.9.0). These subnets each use only one gateway to reach all destinations. Changes external to the subnets, such as the addition of a new subnet, do not change the fact that these subnets still have only one routing choice. Newly added networks are still reached through the same gateway. The hosts on these subnets specify the subnet's gateway as their default route. In other words, the hosts on subnet 128.66.3.0 specify *B* as the default gateway, while the hosts on subnet 128.66.9.0 specify *D* as the default, no matter what happens on the external networks.

Some routing decisions are thrust upon you by the external networks that you connect to. In Figure 4-1, the local network connects to Milnet (26.0.0.0), which requires that Exterior Gateway Protocol (EGP) be used for routing. Therefore, gateway *E* has to run EGP to exchange routes with network 26.0.0.0.

Obtaining an Autonomous System Number

The Exterior Gateway Protocol (EGP) and Border Gateway Protocol (BGP) require that gateways have a special identifier called an *autonomous system number*. (Refer to the section on Internet Gateway Architecture in Chapter 2 for a discussion of autonomous systems.) If you plan to connect your network to an external network that uses BGP or EGP to exchange routing information, you must obtain an autonomous system number from the NIC. Unless you have this special requirement, you can skip this section.

The application for an autonomous system number is available in Appendix B and from the NIC. The form is very similar to the application for obtaining a network number; again it asks for an administrative and a technical contact. But this time, instead of asking for a name to be associated with a network number, it asks for a name to assign to the autonomous system number. For example, *nuts-net* chose the autonomous system name *nuts-as*.

You're also asked to identify the hardware and software used by your gateway. This is not complicated, but some details are requested. For example, *almond* is the *nuts-net* gateway. It is a Sun 4/360 with a Sun MCP hardware interface running the EGP software found in Cornell's *gated* software. (We configure *gated* in Chapter 7.) Therefore, Items 4, 5, and 6 of the *nuts-as* application are answered as follows:

4) The gateway is implemented with Cornell's *gated* software.

5) The gateway runs on a Sun 4/360 with a Sun MCP interface.

6) The gateway runs under the Sun OS 4.1.1 operating system and is implemented in C.

Question 7 is similar to Question 6 in the Internet number application. Here the question is, how many gateways interconnecting different networks are part of your autonomous system, and how large will the number of gateways be in five years? The answer is often one, and remains one for the entire five years. For example, *nuts-as* has one external gateway, which connects 128.66.0.0 to 26.0.0.0, and no plans to add additional external gateways. On the *nuts-as* application the answer to Question 7 is simply one. The internal gateways between subnets are not counted.

The form also asks for the IP addresses of all gateways. Remember that gateways always have more than one address. Again, don't worry about subnets. Therefore, the answer to Question 8 for *nuts-as* is as follows:

8) One gateway connecting MILNET and NUTS-NET with address 26.104.0.19 on MILNET and 128.66.12.1 on NUTS-NET.

Only a small percentage of Internet sites need to use EGP or BGP. A far more common concern is subnetting.

Defining the Subnet Mask

Chapter 2 describes the default structure of each class of network number and touches upon the reasons for subnetting. Unless you wish to change the default structure of your network number, you do not have to define a subnet mask. The decision to subnet is commonly driven by topological or organizational considerations.

The topological reasons for subnetting include:

- *Overcoming distance limitations.* Some network hardware has very strict distance limitations. Ethernet is the most common example. The maximum length of a "thick" Ethernet cable is 500 meters; the maximum length of a "thin" cable is 300 meters. If you need to cover a greater distance, you can use IP routers to link a series of Ethernet cables. Each cable still must not exceed the maximum allowable length, but the length of the network becomes the sum of the length of all the cables. Using this approach, every cable is a separate subnet.

- *Interconnecting dissimilar physical networks.* IP routers can be used to link together networks which have different and incompatible underlying network technologies. Figure 4-1 shows a central token ring subnet, 128.66.1.0, connecting to Ethernet subnets 128.66.6.0 and 128.66.12.0.

- *Filtering traffic between networks.* Local traffic stays on the local subnet. Only traffic intended for other networks is forwarded through the gateway.

Subnetting is not the only way to solve topology problems. Networks are implemented in hardware and can be altered by changing or adding hardware, but subnetting is an effective way to overcome these problems at the TCP/IP software level.

Of course, there are non-technical reasons for creating subnets. Subnets often serve organizational purposes such as:

- *Simplifying network administration.* Subnets can be used to delegate address management, troubleshooting, and other network administration responsibilities to smaller organizations within the overall organization. This is an effective tool for managing a large network with a limited staff. It places the responsibility for managing the subnet on the people who benefit from its use.

- *Recognizing organizational structure.* The structure of an organization (or simply office politics) may require independent network management for some divisions. Creating independently managed subnets for these divisions is preferable to having them go directly to the NIC to get their own independent network numbers.

- *Isolating traffic by organization.* Certain organizations may prefer to have their local traffic isolated to a network that is primarily accessible only to members of that organization. This is particularly appropriate when security is involved. For example, the payroll department might not want their network packets on the engineering network, where some clever person could figure out how to intercept them.

- *Isolating potential problems.* If a certain segment will be less reliable than the remainder of the net, you may want to make that segment a subnet. For example, if the research group puts experimental systems on the network from time to time, or experiments with the network itself, you expect this part of the network to be unstable. Make it a subnet to prevent experimental hardware or software from interfering with everyone else.

In a subnetted network, every interface must use the same subnet mask. The subnet mask has the same form as an IP address. It shows which bits form the "network part" of the address, and which bits form the "host part." Bits in the "network part" are turned *on* (i.e., one), while bits in the "host part" are turned *off* (i.e., zero). The network administrator decides if subnetting is required and defines the subnet mask for the network. Once a mask is defined, it must be disseminated to all hosts on the network.

The subnet mask used on *nuts-net* is 255.255.255.0. This mask subnets a class B address on a full byte boundary. The structure is clean, simple, and very easy to understand—this form of subnetting has been tested and debugged on the widest range of hardware and software. The *nuts-net* administrator has decided that this mask provides enough subnets, and that the individual subnets have enough hosts, to effectively use the address space of 253 hosts per subnet. Figure 4-1 shows an example of this type of subnetting. Applying this subnet mask to the addresses 128.66.1.0 and 128.66.12.0 causes them to be interpreted as the addresses of two different networks, not as two different hosts on the same network.

Specifying the Broadcast Address

The need to specify a broadcast address may not be as clear as, for example, the need to specify a subnet mask. The standard broadcast address is an address where all host bits are set to ones. This means the standard broadcast address on subnet 128.66.12.0 is 128.66.12.255. We want to use the standard broadcast address, so why worry about it?

The problem arises because some devices use the wrong broadcast address and do not allow the broadcast address to be corrected by the system administrator. The BSD 4.2 UNIX release used a broadcast address where the host bits were all set to zero, and there was no facility for changing the broadcast address. Most systems derived from BSD 4.2 have subsequently been patched or upgraded to resolve this problem. The problem does not exist in BSD 4.3. If you have systems on your network that use the wrong broadcast address, upgrade them to fix this problem. If they cannot be upgraded, they should be replaced.

If it is not possible to fix or replace the errant systems, it is possible to configure all other systems to use the incorrect broadcast address. This is not desirable, but it is possible. In Chapter 6 we discuss how the broadcast address is set using the **ifconfig** command.

Sample Planning Sheets

After gathering the basic information, the network administrator must disseminate it. The person responsible for configuring each end-system, normally the administrator of that system, must be given the necessary information. A simple way to do this is for the network administrator to create a short list of information for the system administrator.

A sample list for the workstation *peanut*, based on the topics we have discussed, provides basic configuration information. The information sheet lists the name, address, subnet mask, the fact that DNS is used, and the fact that RIP is used on subnet 128.66.12.0. The installation planning sheet for *peanut* contains the following:

Hostname:	peanut
IP address:	128.66.12.2
Subnet mask:	255.255.255.0
Default gateway:	128.66.12.1 (almond.nuts.com)
Broadcast address:	128.66.12.255
Domain name:	nuts.com
Name servers:	128.66.12.1 (almond.nuts.com)
	128.66.6.8 (pack.plant.nuts.com)
Routing protocol:	Routing Information Protocol (RIP)

A similar sheet prepared for *almond* varies slightly from the planning sheet for *peanut*. The names and address are different of course, but the real differences are caused by the fact that *almond* is a gateway. As a gateway, *almond* has more than one network interface, and each interface requires its own configuration. Each interface has its own address and can have its own name, subnet mask, and routing protocol. The planning sheet for *almond* is:

Hostname:	almond (128.66.12.1)
	mil-gw (26.104.0.19)
IP address:	128.66.12.1
	26.104.0.19
Subnet mask:	255.255.255.0 (128.66.12.1)
	default (26.104.0.19)
Default gateway:	none
Broadcast address:	128.66.12.255 (128.66.12.1)
	default (26.104.0.19)
Domain name:	nuts.com
Name servers:	128.66.12.1 (almond.nuts.com)
	128.66.6.8 (pack.plant.nuts.com)
Routing protocol:	Routing Information Protocol (RIP) (128.66.12.1)
	Exterior Gateway Protocol (EGP) (26.104.0.19)

We use the information from the planning sheet to configure these systems in subsequent chapters. Planning is the first step in configuring TCP/IP. In the following chapters we put these plans into action.

5

Basic Configuration

Every UNIX computer that runs TCP/IP has a technique for incorporating the basic transport and IP datagram services into the operating system. This chapter discusses two files fundamental to the basic configuration of TCP/IP on UNIX systems: the *kernel configuration* file and the */etc/inetd.conf* file. These files are so basic to network configuration that they often come from the manufacturer preconfigured to run TCP/IP.

We'll examine the contents of these configuration files and the role they play in linking TCP/IP and UNIX. With this information you should be able to modify these files for your own custom configurations.

Kernel Configuration

Kernel configuration is not really a network administration task. Configuring the kernel is a basic part of UNIX system administration, whether or not the computer is connected to a network. But TCP/IP networking, like other system functions, is integrated into the kernel. This chapter covers:

- the kernel configuration statements that are essential for TCP/IP
- an example of adding a new device to the kernel
- the system parameters that relate to TCP/IP

The two predominant UNIX families, AT&T System V and Berkeley BSD 4.3, have very different kernel configuration files. Even within a specific type of UNIX, there are variations from vendor to vendor. The kernel configuration statements in the following examples are drawn from both BSD and System

V, and are limited to those things which directly affect TCP/IP configuration. The sample kernel statements are from SCO UNIX, which is a variant of System V.3, and from SunOS 4.1.1, a variant of BSD 4.3.

For systems derived from BSD (Berkeley) UNIX, the kernel configuration file is preconfigured for TCP/IP. Rarely is there any need to modify the configuration for networking. The BSD kernel configuration file is normally only changed:

- to produce a smaller, more efficient kernel by removing unneeded items
- to add a new device
- to modify a system parameter

While there is rarely any need to modify the kernel network statements, it is useful to understand what these statements do. Looking into the kernel configuration file shows how UNIX is tied to the hardware and software of the network.

Some systems derived from System V are shipped with a minimal kernel, so changes may be needed to add TCP/IP to the kernel. However, when you install the network software, the kernel changes will probably be made automatically by the installation procedure, so you probably won't need to make the changes yourself. But it still helps to understand the configuration process.

CAUTION

The procedures and files used for kernel configuration vary dramatically depending on UNIX implementation. These variations make it essential that you refer to your system documentation before trying to configure the kernel on your system. Only your system documentation can provide you with the accurate, detailed instructions required to successfully complete this task.

The BSD Kernel Configuration File

The UNIX kernel is a C program compiled and installed by **make**. The **config** command reads the kernel configuration file and generates the files (including the Makefile) needed to compile and link the kernel. On BSD systems, the kernel configuration file is located in the directory */usr/sys/conf.**

/usr/sys is sometimes symbolically linked to */sys*. We use */usr/sys/conf* only as an example. Your system may use another directory.

There is no standard name for the BSD kernel configuration file. When you create a configuration file, you can choose any name you wish. But by convention, BSD kernel configuration filenames use uppercase letters.

A large kernel configuration file named *GENERIC* is delivered with the BSD system. The *GENERIC* kernel file configures all of the standard devices for your system—including everything necessary for TCP/IP. No modifications are necessary for the *GENERIC* kernel to run basic TCP/IP services.

If the kernel has been modified on your system, the system administrator will have chosen a new name for the configuration file. To find the name of the file, check for the identifying string stored in the kernel (*/vmunix*). For example, on *almond*, our imaginary Sun system **grep**'ing the output of **string /vmunix** for the string *SunOS* displays the following:

```
% strings /vmunix | grep SunOS
SunOS Release 4.1.1 (SMOKED) #1: Tue Apr 23 13:59:37 EDT 1991
```

The string enclosed in parentheses is the value from the *ident* statement* in the kernel, which should be the name of the configuration file. This message tells you that the kernel has been customized (a kernel that was not modified would be named GENERIC), and that the configuration file is named SMOKED. So on *almond* you should find the kernel configuration in the file */usr/sys/conf/SMOKED*. In addition to this configuration file, there may be a directory named */usr/sys/SMOKED*. A directory with the same name as the configuration file is created in */usr/sys* by **config** to hold the Makefile and other files used to generate the kernel. System administrators usually delete this directory because it is not needed after the kernel is built.

TCP/IP in the BSD Kernel

For a network administrator, it is more important to understand which kernel statements are necessary to configure TCP/IP than to understand the detailed structure of each statement. Three types of statements are used to configure TCP/IP in the BSD kernel: options, pseudo-device, and device statements.

---

*The *ident* statement simply identifies the kernel. It isn't related to TCP/IP, so it won't be discussed further.

The *options* statement tells the kernel to compile a software option into the system. The options statement that is important to TCP/IP is:

```
options INET          # basic networking support--mandatory
```

Every-BSD based system running TCP/IP has an **options INET** statement in its kernel configuration file. The statement produces a **–DINET** argument for the C complier, which in turn causes the IP, ICMP, TCP, UDP, and ARP modules to be compiled into the kernel. This single statement incorporates the basic transport and IP datagram services into the system. Never remove this statement from the configuration file.

The second statement required by TCP/IP in all BSD configurations is a pseudo-device statement. A *pseudo-device* is a device driver not directly associated with an actual piece of hardware. The pseudo-device required by TCP/IP is:

```
pseudo-device   loop          # loopback network--mandatory
```

The pseudo-device statement creates a header (*.h*) file that is identified by the pseudo-device name. For example, the statement shown above creates the file *loop.h* in the kernel directory. On *almond* a directory listing of */usr/sys/SMOKED* (the directory created by **config**) shows the header file *loop.h*. The loop pseudo-device is necessary to create the loopback device (lo0). This device is associated with the loopback address 127.0.0.1; it is defined as a pseudo-device because it is not really a piece of hardware.

Another pseudo-device that is used on every BSD TCP/IP system is:

```
pseudo-device   ether         # basic Ethernet support
```

This statement is necessary to support Ethernet. The pseudo-device *ether* is required for full support of ARP and other Ethernet specific functions. While it is possible that a system that does not have Ethernet may not require this statement, it is universally configured, and should remain in your kernel configuration.

The pseudo-terminals, or *ptys*, are another pseudo-device that is universally configured:

```
pseudo-device   pty           # pseudo-tty's
```

This statement defines the virtual terminal devices used by remote login services such as **rlogin** and **telnet**. Pseudo-terminals are also used by many other applications, such as Emacs, that have no direct connection to TCP/IP networking.

Real hardware devices are defined using the device statement. Every host attached to a TCP/IP network requires some physical hardware for that attachment. The hardware is declared with a device statement in the kernel configuration file. There are many possible network interfaces for TCP/IP, but the most common are Ethernet interfaces.

The *device* statement varies according to the interface being configured. But how do you know which hardware interfaces are installed in your system? A simple way to tell is to look at the messages displayed on the console at boot time. These messages show all of the devices, including network devices, that the system found during initialization.

The network devices available on a BSD UNIX system are listed in Intro(4) of the UNIX reference manual. The specific **man** pages in Section 4 provide detailed descriptions of the devices, including the text of the kernel statements necessary to configure them.

The example below shows a **grep** of the Intro(4) documentation. This manual entry shows that only two of the documented devices are Ethernet interfaces: le0 (Lance Ethernet Interface) and ie0 (Intel Ethernet interface). The output has been edited slightly to produce a cleaner display.

```
% man - 4 intro | grep Ether
      ie          ie(4S)       Intel 10 Mb/s Ethernet interface
      le          le(4S)       LANCE 10Mb/s Ethernet interface
```

To find which of these devices are configured, we can **grep** for the interface names in the output of the **dmesg** command or in the */usr/adm/messages* files. First we check for the Intel interface (ie0), but **grep** doesn't find any matching lines. Next we check for the Lance interface (le0) and get a match. This match shows that the Lance device was configured the last time the system booted.

```
% dmesg | grep ie0
% dmesg | grep le0
le0 at obio 0xf9000000 pri 3
```

The kernel configuration file contains the following device statement that was used to configure the le0 device:

```
device          le0 at obio ? csr 0xf9000000 priority 3
```

Some device statement, though not necessarily this one, is present in the kernel configuration file on your BSD system.

The options, pseudo-device, and device statements found in this kernel configuration file tell the system to include the TCP/IP, Ethernet, and loopback software in the kernel, and to configure a Lance Ethernet interface.

These sample TCP/IP kernel configuration statements are:

```
options INET           # basic networking support--mandatory
pseudo-device   loop   # loopback network--mandatory
pseudo-device   ether  # basic Ethernet support
pseudo-device   pty    # pseudo-tty's
device le0 at obio ? csr 0xf9000000 priority 3
```

The statements in your configuration may vary somewhat from those shown above. But you have the same basic statements in your kernel configuration file. With these basic statements, BSD UNIX is ready to run TCP/IP.

BSD TCP/IP System Parameters

BSD allows you to set some optional TCP/IP software variables from within the kernel configuration file by using the options statement:

IPFORWARDING

This parameter determines whether the system forwards IP datagrams destined for another computer. By default,* the system forwards datagrams only if it has more than one network interface; i.e., the system is assumed to be a gateway. The default value for the IPFORWARDING variable is 0. The value 1 means *always* forward datagrams; the value -1 means *never* forward datagrams.

Don't force a system with a single network interface to forward datagrams. Doing this can hide configuration problems on other systems on the network. If the other systems are incorrectly delivering datagrams to your host, forwarding the datagrams will make it appear as if they were correctly addressed and make it difficult to detect the real problem. On occasion, you might want to force a system not to forward datagrams by setting this variable to –1. This is useful if you want to prevent a multi-homed host (a host with two network interfaces) from acting as a gateway.

IPSENDREDIRECTS

This parameter determines if the system issues ICMP redirects. ICMP redirects are discussed more thoroughly in Chapter 1, but in short, a gateway sends a "redirect" message to tell a system that a better gateway is available for reaching a certain destination. This parameter is enabled by setting its value to 1, which is the default. To disable redirects, set the variable to 0.

---

*Refer to your system's documentation for details. The defaults and even the available parameters may be different for your system.

When systems have their routing set wrong, only gateways are expected to send redirects. If IPFORWARDING is disabled, no redirects are sent, regardless of the value set for IPSENDREDIRECTS, because the system is not acting as a gateway.

SUBNETSARELOCAL

This parameter determines the size of packets sent to other subnets of your network. The default value of SUBNETSARELOCAL is 1. When this default is set, the system assumes that subnets are local and that the MTU of the local network can be used when sending them packets. To override this default, set SUBNETSARELOCAL to 0. This causes the system to use a default packet length designed to avoid fragmentation; this default packet length is normally smaller then the MTU of your local network. (Chapter 1 discusses MTU and fragmentation in more detail.) Avoiding fragmentation can provide faster and more efficient data delivery. However, do not change SUBNETSARELOCAL to 0 unless your subnets are remotely connected to your local network, and the smallest MTU on the path to the subnets is smaller then the MTU of your local network. Otherwise you'll reduce your system's performance by forcing it to use a smaller packet size than is necessary.

DIRECTED_BROADCAST

This parameter determines whether the system routes packets that can cause a broadcast on the destination network. By default, DIRECTED_BROADCAST is set to 1; this means that broadcast packets are forwarded. To disable DIRECTED_BROADCAST, set it to 0. When disabled, packets that cause a broadcast on another network are not forwarded. This parameter is only significant if IPFORWARDING is enabled.

Use the options statement to set all of these parameters. This statement has the form **options** *parameter=value*, where *parameter* is the parameter name and *value* is a numeric value. For example, here's the statement that prevents a multi-homed host from forwarding packets by setting the IPFOR-WARDING parameter to −1:

```
options IPFORWARDING=-1
```

There are two other options that make BSD 4.3 TCP/IP more compatible with TCP/IP from BSD 4.2. However, don't use these options unless you have to, because they make 4.3 TCP/IP ignore errors. The compatibility options are:

COMPAT_42   This parameter disables UDP checksum calculations. The UDP checksum calculation in BSD 4.2 was incorrect, so when a host running 4.3 receives a UDP packet from a system running 4.2, it causes a checksum error. This parameter tells the system to ignore these errors.

TCP_COMPAT_42   This parameter prevents connections between 4.2 and 4.3 systems from hanging by adjusting 4.3 to ignore mistakes made by 4.2. In addition, setting this parameter prevents the system from sending TCP Sequence Numbers that are interpreted as negative numbers by 4.2 systems. With this option, the initial sequence number will be set to zero for each connection.

Since both of these options have names that contain numbers, we recommend that you double-quote them on the command line. For example:

```
options "TCP_COMPAT_42"
```

You will probably never change any of the variables discussed in this section. Like everything else in the kernel configuration file, they usually come correctly configured to run TCP/IP.

Adding Network Devices

In the BSD environment, the kernel comes ready to run TCP/IP. But on occasion, the kernel must be modified to add additional network devices. This normally occurs when new devices are developed, or when optional networking software and hardware are purchased.

The exact instructions for adding new network devices to the kernel are different for each device added. You *must* read the specific installation instructions provided with the new software and hardware. Generally this is a very simple procedure because the new driver is normally delivered with an installation script. All you need to do is invoke the script, answer some simple questions, and mount the necessary tapes, floppies, or CDs.

As an example, look at how *SunLink MCP 6.0* and *SunLink DDN 6.0* are installed on *almond*. First, the software is extracted from the tape using a program like **tar** or the Sun program **extract_unbundled**.* Then, an

---

*Unbundled software is optional, extra-cost software.

installation script is run from the directory where the extracted software was stored. Installation scripts are commonly used by both System V and BSD systems. SCO's instructions, *Installing Preconfigured Drivers*, say to run the installation script specific to the new driver. They give the sample syntax as *./scriptname*. Our sample installation of MCP on a Sun BSD system, uses a very similar command:

```
# ./install.mcp
```

The Sun installation script asks a few simple questions, including the name of the input kernel configuration file and the new name for the output file. Recall that the BSD kernel file can be renamed when modified. To make the following examples more understandable, we'll change the kernel configuration filename each time it is updated. For our sample MCP installation, the input name is GENERIC; we've chosen the ouput name MCP. After the script runs, the information added to the new configuration file can be checked with a **diff** of GENERIC and MCP.

```
# diff GENERIC MCP
57a58,71
> #
> # The following is for MCP and ALM-2
> #
> device mcp0 at vme32d16 ? csr 0x01000000 flags 0x1ffff priority 4
>        vector mcpintr 0x8b
> device mcp1 at vme32d16 ? csr 0x01010000 flags 0x1ffff priority 4
>        vector mcpintr 0x8a
> device mcp2 at vme32d16 ? csr 0x01020000 flags 0x1ffff priority 4
>        vector mcpintr 0x89
> device mcp3 at vme32d16 ? csr 0x01030000 flags 0x1ffff priority 4
>        vector mcpintr 0x88
> pseudo-device mcpa64
> pseudo-device mcph16
> pseudo-device ifd16
```

The **diff** shows that the MCP installation script added device statements for the MCP hardware and pseudo-device statements for the driver software.

Installing the DDN software is a similar operation. The DDN software is extracted from tape, and the device-specific installation script is run. The installation script (**./install.ddn**) also asks for the old kernel name, MCP, and a new kernel name for which we'll use DDN. After the script is completed, a **diff** of MCP and DDN shows the following:

```
# diff MCP DDN
71a72,77
> options         XPKT
> pseudo-device   hdlcline4 init      hdlc_init
> pseudo-device   zss2
```

```
> pseudo-device    xpkt4      init     "x25_init"
> pseudo-device    xvc4
> pseudo-device    imp1       init     "imp_init all"
```

The DDN software did not add any new physical devices; i.e., there are no new device statements. Only software options statements and pseudo-device statements have been added. But now the system can support X.25 and HDLC, which are required for our Milnet connection.

The point we want to make is that it isn't very hard—regardless of the system—to install optional software like MCP or DDN. Automated scripts or step-by step cookbooks are usually provided with all optional software. It is instructive, though not really necessary, to look at the kernel configuration file afterwards and see what has been changed.

System V Kernel Configuration

While the kernel configuration files and procedures used by AT&T System V and BSD are very different, the net result is the same: each system uses a **config** program to build an operational UNIX kernel. And there are other similarities. BSD has a single configuration file, but it contains separate sections for identifying the system and configuring the devices. System V does these same tasks using a Makefile for the system identification information and a separate file, the *kernel description file*, to configure the devices. All of the TCP/IP network configuration information is in the description file, so we'll concentrate our discussion on that.

There are very few general descriptions of how to configure an AT&T kernel.* Each implementation of System V has its own unique kernel configuration procedure. There were major differences between System V Releases 2, 3, and 4. The following examples are based on SCO UNIX, which is a version of System V, Release 3. The kernel configuration procedure for other variants of SVR3 (for example, Interactive's 386/ix) should be fundamentally similar, although (as with BSD UNIX) you must always check your documentation before making any changes.

Aside from the differences in specific configuration files, BSD and System V differ in that System V vendors have done more to automate the process. When you buy a new software package (like a TCP/IP networking pack-

---

*The most detailed description I found is in the Nutshell Handbook, *System Performance Tuning*, by Mike Loukides.

age), you will run a system configuration program to install the package and automatically make necessary kernel changes.

One other difference deserves mentioning. BSD systems usually come with a GENERIC kernel that has every possible device configured. System V takes the opposite approach. The kernel that's shipped with the system is minimal, and customizing it usually means adding extra facilities as needed. So, while you probably wouldn't need to create a custom kernel to run TCP/IP under BSD UNIX, you may need to under System V. As we said, most System V implementations have configuration programs that do this automatically. However, in this section we're going to look at the "low level" configuration, i.e., what the installation script does for you.

The SCO kernel description file is */etc/conf/cf.d/mdevice*. Unlike the BSD example, the filename *mdevice* is never changed, and every entry in the mdevice file has the same format. There are no keywords, like **device** or **pseudo-device**. Instead, each entry begins with a device name, followed by several fields that describe the device. There is an entry for every device driver installed in the kernel. For TCP/IP to function, you need an individual entry for each of the following devices: *arp, arpproc, cp, icmp, ip, llcloop, socket, tcp, ttyp, udp,* and *vty*.

Except for arpproc, each entry in mdevice has a corresponding file in the */dev* directory. A few of these devices are grouped together in the */dev/inet* subdirectory. The devices represented by files in */dev/inet* provide the same function as the **options INET** statement did in the BSD configuration. Each of these, IP (*/dev/inet/ip*), ICMP (*/dev/inet/icmp*), TCP (*/dev/inet/tcp*), UDP (*/dev/inet/udp*), and ARP (*/dev/inet/arp*) is configured by a statement in the mdevice file. But the net result is the same, the key protocols are included in the kernel. For example, the TCP and the IP entries in the SCO mdevice file look like this:

```
ip    ocis  iSc  ip   0  23  0  256  -1
tcp   ocis  iSc  tcp  0  33  0  256  -1
```

We won't explain the values in each field; the installation scripts will set up the entries correctly.

arpproc is required for ARP to run over Ethernet. The arpproc statement is similar in function to the **pseudo-device ether** statement in the BSD configuration file. The BSD pseudo-device *loop* is parallel to the llcloop entry SCO's *mdevice* file. llcloop defines the local loopback device in the SCO kernel. Additionally, the function of the BSD **pseudo-device pty** statement is provided by two devices in *mdevice*. These two devices, *ttyp* and *vty*, define the virtual terminal services.

The arpproc, llcloop, ttyp, and vty entries in the SCO mdevice file are:

```
ttyp      ocrwi  ict  ttyp 0  26 0   16  -1
vty       ocrwi  ic   vty  0  27 0   16  -1
arpproc   oci    iS   app  0   0 0  256  -1
llcloop   ocis   iSc  lo_  0  30 0  256  -1
```

Some other devices required in the mdevice file do not have direct parallels in the BSD configuration. These are the *socket compatibility* devices, *socket* and *cp*. They are required because TCP/IP was developed using Berkeley's socket I/O facility, while systems based on the AT&T kernel use the STREAMS facility. SCO UNIX requires the socket compatibility package to run TCP/IP on the streams-based system.*

A physical network interface is required on the SCO system, just as it was under BSD. There are many Ethernet interfaces available for SCO systems. Table 5-1 lists some of them.

Table 5.1: Ethernet Cards Supported by SCO

Interface Name	Description
e3A	3Com 501 EtherLink I
e3B	3Com 503 EtherLink II
e3C	3Com 523 EtherLink/MC
e3D	3Com 507 EtherLink 16
hpi	HP ISA card (various models)
hpe	HP 27248A EISA
i6E	Racal InterLan NI6510 ISA
i3B	Racal InterLan ES3210 EISA
tok	IBM Token Ring Adapter (various models)
exos	Excelan 205 Ethernet
wdn	Western Digital EtherCard PLUS (various models)

A possible entry in the mdevice file for a 3C501 Ethernet board is:

```
e3A0  I  iScH  e3c  0  28  1  1  -1
```

The H in the third field of this entry indicates a hardware device. All the entries previously shown had no H in the third field because they were

---

*Here "sockets" and "streams" refer to the different styles of I/O used by BSD and System V, not to the TCP/IP terms socket and stream discussed in Chapter 1.

pseudo-devices. So, even though the SCO configuration does not use key-words like device and pseudo-device, it does have a way to differentiate a hardware device from a software driver.

SCO, like most System V systems, does not require the administrator to make changes directly to the kernel configuration. The entries shown above are made for you by a configuration program. The SCO TCP/IP configuration program is called **netconfig**.

SCO's netconfig

netconfig is the program used to configure network devices. It installs the device drivers, configures the kernel, and modifies the startup files to support the newly installed device. The configuration tasks we cover in this chapter and in Chapter 6 are all handled by this single program.

The layers of the TCP/IP architecture are viewed by **netconfig** as links in a chain. The chain flows from the applications level, through the basic TCP/IP services to the physical network. **netconfig** represents these chains as a list of software and hardware linked together by -> symbols. For example, the chain of SCO NFS, SCO TCP/IP, and a Western Digital Ethernet card is written as:

```
sco_nfs->sco_tcp->wdn0
```

When a new service or device is being installed, you are creating a new chain. Likewise when a device is de-installed, **netconfig** says that you are removing a chain.

When it is run, **netconfig** displays the currently configured chains, and asks if you wish to add, remove, or reconfigure a chain. To install a new device select "Add a chain." The program then walks you through a series of menus that completely configure the new device. You will even be prompted for the IP address, the subnet mask, and the broadcast address. **netconfig** will use these to build an **ifconfig** statement for the new device. (We'll cover **ifconfig** in the next chapter.) Finally, **netconfig** will ask if you want to relink the kernel. If you tell it to, it will update the kernel files and rebuild the kernel for you. All of this from one simple menu system!

The Internet Daemon

The kernel configuration brings the basic transport and IP datagram services of TCP/IP into UNIX. But there is much more to the TCP/IP suite than just the basic services. How are these other protocols included in the UNIX configuration?

Some protocols are explicitly started by including them in the boot files. This technique is used, for example, to start the Routing Information Protocol (RIP) and the Domain Name Service (DNS). The daemons that service these protocols, **routed** and **named** respectively, are run from a startup file such as */etc/rc.local* on a Sun system or */etc/tcp* on an SCO UNIX system.*

Many other network daemons are not started individually. These daemons are started by a super-server that listens for network service requests and starts the appropriate daemon to process the request. This super server is called the *internet daemon*.

The internet daemon—**inetd** (pronounced "i net d")—is started at boot time from an initialization file such as */etc/rc*. When it is started, **inetd** reads its configuration from the */etc/inetd.conf* file. This file contains the names of the services that **inetd** listens for and starts. You can add or delete services by making changes to the *inetd.conf* file.

An example of a file entry is:

```
ftp   stream  tcp  nowait  root  /usr/etc/in.ftpd  in.ftpd
```

The fields in the *inetd.conf* entry are, from left to right:

name	The name of a service, as listed in the */etc/services* file. In the sample entry the value in this field is `ftp`.
type	The type of data delivery service used, also called *socket type*. The commonly used socket types are:

	stream	The stream† delivery service provided by TCP, i.e., TCP byte stream.
	dgram	The packet (datagram) delivery service, provided by UDP.

---

*Your system may not use either of these startup files, but startup files are usually in the */etc* directory and often have names that begin with *rc*.

†Here the reference is to TCP/IP sockets and TCP streams—not to AT&T streams I/O or BSD socket I/O.

| | raw | Direct IP datagram service. |

The sample shows that FTP uses a stream socket.

protocol   This is the name of a protocol, as given in the */etc/protocols* file. Its value is usually either "tcp" or "udp." The FTP protocol uses TCP as its transport layer protocol, so the sample entry contains `tcp` in this field.

wait-status   The value for this field is either "wait" or "nowait." Generally, but not always, datagram type servers require "wait," and stream type servers allow "nowait." If the status is "wait," **inetd** must wait for the server to release the socket before it begins to listen for more requests on that socket. If the status is "nowait," **inetd** can immediately begin to listen for more connection requests on the socket. Servers with a status of "nowait" use sockets other than the connection request socket for processing; i.e., they use dynamically allocated sockets.

uid   The user name under which the server runs. This is any valid user name, but it is normally *root*. There are two common exceptions. The **finger** service often runs as the user *nobody* or *daemon* for security reasons, and the **uucp** service is sometimes run as the user *uucp* to save space in the system's accounting files.

server   This is the full pathname of the server program started by **inetd**. Because our example is from a Sun system, the path is */usr/etc/in.ftpd*. On your system the path may be different, perhaps */etc/ftpd*.

It is more efficient for **inetd** to provide some small services directly than it is for **inetd** to start separate servers for these functions. For these small services, the value of the server field is the keyword "internal," which means that this service is an internal **inetd** service.

arguments   These are any command-line arguments that should be passed to the server program when it is invoked. This list always starts with `argv[0]` (the server's name). The valid command-line arguments for each program are documented on the program's **man** page. In the example only `in.ftpd`, the server's name, is provided.

There aren't many situations in which you need to modify the *inetd.conf* file, but there are some. For example, you may wish to disable a service. The default configuration provides a full array of servers. Not all of them are required on every system, and for security reasons you may want to disable non-essential services on some computers. To disable a service, place a # at the beginning of its entry (which turns the line into a comment) and pass a hang-up signal to the **inetd** server. When **inetd** receives a hang-up signal, it re-reads the configuration file and the new configuration takes effect immediately.

You may also need to add a service that has been previously disabled. Let's look in detail at an example of that. We'll begin by looking at the contents of the */etc/inetd.conf* file on *peanut*:

```
peanut% head -16 /etc/inetd.conf
# @(#)inetd.conf 1.17 88/02/07 SMI
ftp      stream tcp  nowait  root  /usr/etc/in.ftpd     in.ftpd
telnet   stream tcp  nowait  root  /usr/etc/in.telnetd in.telnetd
shell    stream tcp  nowait  root  /usr/etc/in.rshd     in.rshd
login    stream tcp  nowait  root  /usr/etc/in.rlogind in.rlogind
exec     stream tcp  nowait  root  /usr/etc/in.rexecd  in.rexecd
finger   stream tcp  nowait  root  /usr/etc/in.fingerd in.fingerd
#tftp dgram udp wait root /usr/etc/in.tftpd in.tftpd -s /tftpboot
comsat   dgram  udp  wait    root  /usr/etc/in.comsat   in.comsat
talk     dgram  udp  wait    root  /usr/etc/in.talkd    in.talkd
name     dgram  udp  wait    root  /usr/etc/in.tnamed  in.tnamed
daytime stream tcp  nowait  root     internal
time     stream tcp  nowait  root     internal
echo     dgram  udp  wait    root     internal
discard dgram  udp  wait    root     internal
time     dgram  udp  wait    root     internal
```

The first part of this file shows several standard TCP/IP services. One of these, **tftp**, is commented out. The TFTP protocol is a special version of FTP that allows file transfers without username/password verification. Because of this, it is a possible security hole and is often disabled in the *inetd.conf* file.

As an example of modifying the *inetd.conf* file, we'll reconfigure the system to provide **tftp** service, which is sometimes necessary for supporting diskless devices. First, use your favorite editor to remove the comment (#) from the **tftp** entry in *inetd.conf.* (The example uses **sed**, everyone's favorite editor!) Then find out the process ID for **inetd** and pass it the SIGHUP signal. The following steps show how this is done on *peanut.*

```
# cd /etc
# mv inetd.conf inetd.conf.org
# cat inetd.conf.org | sed s/#tftp/tftp/ > inetd.conf
# ps -acx | grep inetd
  144 ?  I     0:12 inetd
# kill -HUP 144
```

In some situations, you may also need to modify the pathname of a server or the arguments passed to a particular server when it is invoked. For example, look again at the **tftp** entry. This line contains command-line arguments that are passed to the **tftp** server when it is started. The **–s /tftpboot** option addresses the most obvious **tftp** security hole. It prevents **tftp** users from retrieving files that are not located in the directory specified after the **–s** option. If you want to use another directory for **tftp**, you must change the *inetd.conf* file. The only command-line arguments passed to servers started by **inetd** are those defined in the *inetd.conf* file.

These basic configuration files, the kernel configuration file and the */etc/inetd.conf* file, are necessary for installing the TCP/IP software on a UNIX system, but they require little attention from the system administrator. In Chapter 6 we configure the network interface, calling upon the planning we did in Chapter 4.

6

Configuring the Interface

When networking protocols only work with a single kind of physical network, there is no need to identify the network interface to the software. The software knows what the interface *must* be; no configuration issues are left for the administrator. However, one important strength of TCP/IP is its flexible use of different physical networks. This flexibility adds complexity to the system administrator's task, because you must tell TCP/IP which interface (or interfaces) to use, and you must define each interface's characteristics.

Because TCP/IP is independent of the underlying physical network, IP addresses are implemented in the network software—not in the network hardware. Unlike Ethernet addresses, which are determined by the Ethernet hardware, the system administrator assigns TCP/IP addresses to each network interface.

In this chapter, we use the **ifconfig** (interface configure) command to identify the network interface to TCP/IP and to assign the IP address, subnet mask, and broadcast address to the interface. We also configure a network interface to run Serial Line IP (SLIP), which is a commonly used (but nonstandard) Network Access Layer protocol. The SLIP configuration will allow us to configure an interface from "the ground up," and to see an example of an interface that is not configured with **ifconfig**.

The ifconfig Command

The **ifconfig** command sets, or checks, configuration values for network interfaces. Regardless of the vendor or version of UNIX, the **ifconfig** command is used to set the IP address, the subnet mask, and the broadcast address for each interface. Its most basic function is assigning the IP address. Here is the **ifconfig** command we use to configure the Ethernet interface on *peanut*:

```
# ifconfig le0 128.66.12.2 netmask 255.255.255.0 \
broadcast 128.66.12.255
```

Many other arguments can be used with the **ifconfig** command; we discuss several of these later. But a few important arguments provide the basic information required by TCP/IP for every network interface. These are:

interface   The name of the network interface that you want to configure with **ifconfig**. In the example above, this is the Ethernet interface le0.

address   The IP address assigned to this interface. Enter the address as either an IP address (in dotted decimal form) or as a host name. An IP address is preferable, because if a host name is used, **ifconfig** must resolve the host name to an address before the address can be assigned to the interface. If you decide to use a host name, place the host name and its address in the */etc/hosts* file. Your system must be able to find the host name in */etc/hosts* because **ifconfig** usually executes before DNS is running. The example uses the numeric IP address 128.66.12.2 as the *address* value.

netmask *mask*   The subnet mask for this interface. Ignore this argument if you're not dividing your network into subnets. If you are subnetting, remember that every system on the network must have the same subnet mask. The subnet mask chosen for our imaginary network is 255.255.255.0, so that is the value assigned to *peanut's* le0 interface.

broadcast *address*   The broadcast address for the network. Most, but not all, systems default to the standard broadcast address, which is an IP address with all host bits set to one. In the **ifconfig** sample we explicitly set the broadcast address to 128.66.12.255 to avoid any confusion. To avoid problems, every system on the subnet must agree on the broadcast address.

The network administrator provides the values for the address, subnet mask, and broadcast address. The values in our example are taken directly from the planning sheet we developed in Chapter 4. But the name of the interface, the first argument on every **ifconfig** command line, must be determined from the system's documentation.

In Chapter 5, we saw that the standard network interfaces are documented in Section 4 of the *Unix Reference Manual*, and that the specific interface used on a system can often be determined from the contents of */usr/adm/messages*. From this, we determined that the Ethernet interface used on *peanut* and *almond* is interface le0.

Optional interfaces are often not documented in the *Unix Reference Manual*. For example, *almond's* Milnet interface is only discussed in the documentation that comes with the optional DDN software. That documentation says to configure DDN Standard X.25 (*std0*) for Milnet. Only a system's documentation can provide accurate information about its interfaces and how they should be configured. But there is a software tool, **netstat**, that tells you what interfaces are available on your system.

Determining the Interface with netstat

You cannot always determine all available interfaces on your system by looking at the output of **dmesg**, nor by looking at device statements in the kernel configuration file. These only show you the physical hardware interfaces. In the TCP/IP protocol architecture, the Network Access Layer encompasses all functions that fall below the Internet Layer. This can include all three lower layers of the OSI Reference Model: the Physical Layer, the Data Link Layer, and the Network Layer. IP needs to know the specific interface in the Network Access Layer where packets should be passed for delivery to a particular network. This interface is not limited to a physical hardware driver. It could just as easily be a software interface into the network layer of another protocol suite. So how do you determine all the available network interfaces on your system? Use the **netstat** command. For example, to check the status of all available network interfaces, enter:

```
% netstat -ain
```

The **–i** option tells **netstat** to display the status of the configured network interfaces. The **–a** option modifies the command to include all network interfaces, not just those already configured, and the **–n** tells **netstat** to display its output in numeric form. The **netstat –ain** command displays the following fields:

Name   The Interface Name field shows the actual name assigned to the interface. This is the name that you give to **ifconfig** to identify the interface. An asterisk (*) in this field indicates that the interface is not enabled; i.e., the interface is not "up."

Mtu   The Maximum Transmission Unit shows the longest frame (packet) that can be transmitted by this interface without fragmentation. The MTU is displayed in bytes. MTU is discussed in the "Datagram" section of Chapter 1.

Net/Dest   The Network/Destination field shows the network or the destination host to which the interface provides access. In all of our examples, this field contains a network address. The network address is derived from the IP address of the interface and the subnet mask.

              This field only contains a host address if the interface was configured for a point-to-point (host-specific) link. A point-to-point link is a direct connection between two computers. You can create a point-to-point with the **ifconfig** command. To do this, place a destination address directly after the local interface's address on the **ifconfig** command line. The destination address is the address of the remote host at the other end of the point-to-point link.*

Address   The IP Address field shows the Internet address assigned to this interface.

Ipkts   The Input Packets field shows how many packets this interface has received.

Ierrs   The Input Errors field shows how many damaged packets the interface has received.

Opkts   The Output Packets field shows how many packets were sent out by this interface.

Oerrs   The Output Errors field shows how many of the packets caused an error condition.

---

*See the description of the H flag in the "Routing Table" section of Chapter 2.

Collis   The Collisions field shows how many Ethernet collisions
              were detected by this interface. Ethernet collisions are a nor-
              mal condition caused by Ethernet traffic contention. This
              field is not applicable to non-Ethernet interfaces.

Queue   The Packets Queued field shows how many packets are in
              the queue, awaiting transmission via this interface. Normally
              this is zero.

The output of a **netstat** command on *peanut* shows:

```
peanut% netstat -ain
Name  Mtu   Net/Dest    Address      Ipkts Ierrs Opkts Oerrs Collis Queue
le0   1500  128.66.0.0  128.66.12.2  1547  1     1127  0     135    0
lo0   1536  127.0.0.0   127.0.0.1    133   0     133   0     0      0
```

This display shows that *peanut*, like most workstations, has only two net-
work interfaces. In this case it is easy to identify each network interface.
The lo0 interface is the loopback interface, which every TCP/IP system has.
This is the same loopback device discussed in Chapter 5. le0 is a Lance
Ethernet interface, also discussed in Chapter 5.

On most systems, the loopback interface is part of the default configuration, so you usually don't need to configure it. If you need to configure lo0
on your system, use the following command:

```
# ifconfig lo0 127.0.0.1
```

The configuration of the Ethernet interface requires more attention. The
surprising thing about the sample **netstat** display is that we haven't yet
entered an **ifconfig** command for le0, and it already has an IP address!
peanut, like many systems, used an installation script to install UNIX. This
script requested the host address, which it then used to configure the interface. Later on we'll look at how good a job the installation script did setting
up this interface, but first let's look at what **netstat** shows about the interfaces on a more complex system.

While most hosts have only one real network interface, some hosts and all
gateways have multiple interfaces. Sometimes all interfaces are the same
type. For example, a gateway between two Ethernets has two Ethernet
interfaces. **netstat** on a gateway like this might display lo0, le0, and le1.
Deciphering a **netstat** display with multiple interfaces of the same type is
still very simple. But deciphering a system with many different types of network interfaces, such as *almond*, is more difficult. When we use **netstat** to
check the interfaces on *almond*, we see a long, confusing list of network
interfaces. Most of these will never be configured, making our job (figuring
out which interfaces we need to configure) rather difficult. Here is the

output from the **netstat –ain** command on *almond*; it has been edited for the sake of brevity:

```
almond% netstat -ain
Name Mtu  Net/Dest    Address     Ipkts Ierrs Opkts Oerrs Collis Queue
zss0* 1152 none        none        0     0     0     0     0      0
zss1* 1152 none        none        0     0     0     0     0      0
le0   1500 128.66.0.0  128.66.12.1 1547  1     1127  0     135    0
mcph0 1152 none        none        0     0     0     0     0      0
mcph1* 1152 none       none        0     0     0     0     0      0
hdlc0 1031 none        none        0     0     0     0     0      0
hdlc1* 1024 none       none        0     0     0     0     0      0
xpkt0  256 none        none        0     0     0     0     0      0
xpkt1* 256 none        none        0     0     0     0     0      0
xvc0*  256 none        none        0     0     0     0     0      0
xvc1*  256 none        none        0     0     0     0     0      0
ip0*     0 none        none        0     0     0     0     0      0
std0  1004 none        none        0     0     0     0     0      0
osixpkt0* 128 none     none        0     0     0     0     0      0
imp0* 1004 none        none        0     0     0     0     0      0
lo0   1536 loopback    localhost   133   0     133   0     0      0
```

Your system will probably show a completely different set of interfaces. These interfaces are specific to a Sun system with MCP hardware and Sun-Link DDN software.

We can ignore most of the devices shown in this **netstat** output. Only those related to *almond's* Ethernet and Milnet connections need to be configured. The interface le0 is configured for Ethernet, and the std0 (DDN Standard X.25) interface is configured for Milnet.* But several other interfaces shown in the **netstat** display are also used by the DDN Standard X.25 software.

X.25 protocols encompass all three lower layers of the OSI model, and each of these layers is represented by a network interface in the **netstat** display. The OSI Physical Layer is the MCP hardware interface (mcph0). The Data Link Layer is High Level Data Link Control (hdlc0) software, and the Network Layer is X.25 packet software (xpkt0). The Network Access protocol, DDN Standard X.25 (std0), links these lower layers to IP; i.e., std0 is IP's interface to X.25. Therefore, std0 is the interface configured for IP with the **ifconfig** command. The other X.25 layers have interface-specific configuration utilities of their own, but these are not standard parts of UNIX or TCP/IP. We'll look at examples of interface-specific configuration utilities later in this chapter when we configure SLIP.

---

*DDN Standard X.25 maps Internet addresses to X.25 addresses, and encapsulates IP datagrams in X.25 packets.

Despite the comprehensive display provided by **netstat**, in the final analysis, you must rely on the documentation that comes with optional software to choose the correct interface. It is possible to look at **netstat**'s output and guess that std0 stands for *Standard X.25*. But guessing is a highly unreliable way to do business. Optional software requires special documentation. When installing new network software always read the documentation carefully.

This long discussion about determining the network interface may have overshadowed the important **ifconfig** functions of assigning the IP address, subnet mask, and broadcast address. So let's return to these important topics.

Checking the Interface with ifconfig

As noted above, the UNIX installation script may configure the network interface. However, this configuration may not be exactly what you want. You can check the configuration of an interface with **ifconfig**. To display the current values assigned to the interface, enter **ifconfig** with an interface name and no other arguments. For example, to check interface le0:

```
% ifconfig le0
le0: flags=63<UP,BROADCAST,NOTRAILERS,RUNNING>
     inet 128.66.12.2 netmask ffff0000 broadcast 128.66.0.0
```

When used to check the status of an interface, the **ifconfig** command displays two lines of output. The first line shows the interface name and the flags that define the interface's characteristics. The flags are displayed as both a numeric value and a set of keywords. In our example the interface name is le0, and the interface's flags have the value 63, which corresponds to:

UP   The interface is enabled for use.

BROADCAST   The interface supports broadcasts, which means it is connected to a network that supports broadcasts, such as an Ethernet.

NOTRAILERS   This interface does not support trailer encapsulation. This is an Ethernet-specific characteristic which we discuss in more detail later.

RUNNING   This interface is operational.

The second line of **ifconfig** output displays information that directly relates to TCP/IP. The keyword "inet" is followed by the Internet address assigned to this interface. Next comes the keyword "netmask," followed by the subnet mask written in hexadecimal. Finally, the keyword "broadcast" and the broadcast address are displayed.

If we check the information displayed here against the configuration plan developed in Chapter 4, we see that the interface needs to be reconfigured. The default configuration provided by the UNIX installation script did not provide all of the values we planned. The address (128.66.12.2) is correct, but the subnet mask (ffff0000 or 255.255.0.0) and the broadcast address (128.66.0.0) are incorrect. Let's look at how these values are assigned, and how to correct them.

Assigning a Subnet Mask

In order to function properly, every interface on a specific physical network must have the same subnet mask. For le0 on *almond* and *peanut* the netmask value is 255.255.255.0, because both systems are attached to the same network. However, *almond's* le0 and std0 interfaces use different netmasks, even though they are parts of the same computer, because they are on different networks.

To assign a subnet mask, write the subnet mask value after the keyword "netmask" on the **ifconfig** command line. The subnet mask is usually written in the "dotted decimal" form used for IP addresses.* For example, the following command assigns the correct subnet mask to the le0 interface on *peanut*:

```
# ifconfig le0 128.66.12.2 netmask 255.255.255.0 \
broadcast 128.66.12.255
```

Putting the netmask value directly on the **ifconfig** command line is the most common, and usually the simplest, way to assign the subnet mask to an interface. But it is also possible to tell **ifconfig** to take the netmask value from a file instead of from the command line. Conceptually, this is similar to using a host name in place of an IP address. For example, the *nuts-net* administrator might add the following entry to */etc/networks*:

```
nuts-mask        255.255.255.0
```

---

*Hexadecimal notation can also be used for the subnet mask. To enter a netmask in hexadecimal, write the value as a single hex number starting with a leading 0x. For example, the hexadecimal form of 255.255.255.0 is 0xffffff00. Choose the form that is easier for you to understand.

Once this entry has been added, you can use the name *nuts-mask* on the **ifconfig** command line, instead of the actual mask. For example:

```
# ifconfig le0 128.66.5.2 netmask nuts-mask
```

The name *nuts-mask* resolves to 255.255.255.0, which is the correct netmask value for our sample systems.

On SunOS systems, you can also use */etc/netmasks* to set the subnet mask. The */etc/netmasks* file is a table of one-line entries, each containing a network address* separated from a subnet mask by white space. If a Sun system on *nuts-net* (128.66.0.0) has a */etc/netmasks* file that contains the entry:

```
128.66.0.0      255.255.255.0
```

then the following **ifconfig** command can be used to set the subnet mask:

```
# ifconfig le0 128.66.5.1 netmask +
```

The plus sign after the keyword "netmask" causes **ifconfig** to take the mask value from */etc/netmasks*. **ifconfig** searches the file for a network address that matches the network address of the interface being configured. It then extracts the subnet mask associated with that address and applies it to the interface.

Some systems take advantage of the fact that the IP address, subnet mask, and broadcast address can be set indirectly to reduce the extent that startup files need to be customized. Reducing customization lessens the chance that a system might hang while booting because a startup file was improperly edited, and it makes it possible to preconfigure these files for all of the systems on the network. The */etc/hosts, /etc/networks,* and */etc/netmasks* files that provide input to the **ifconfig** command, all produce NIS maps that can be centrally managed at sites that use NIS.

A disadvantage of setting the **ifconfig** values indirectly is that it can make troubleshooting more cumbersome. If all values are set in the boot file, you only need to check the values there. When network configuration information is supplied indirectly, you may need to check the boot file, the *hosts* file, the *networks* file, and the *netmasks* file to find problems. An error in any of these files could cause an incorrect configuration. To make debugging easier, many system administrators prefer to set the configuration values directly on the **ifconfig** command line.

---

*Use the official network address, not a subnet address.

Setting the Broadcast Address

RFC 919, *Broadcasting Internet Datagrams*, clearly defines the format of a broadcast address as an address with all host bits set to one. Since the broadcast address is so precisely defined, **ifconfig** should be able to compute it automatically, and you should be able to use the default in almost every situation. Unfortunately, this is not the case. TCP/IP was included in BSD 4.2 before RFC 919 was an adopted standard. BSD 4.2 used a broadcast address with all host bits set to zero, and didn't allow the broadcast address to be modified during configuration. Because of this history, some current releases of UNIX default to a "zero-style" broadcast address for compatibility with older systems, while other releases default to the standard "one-style" broadcast address.

You can avoid this confusion by defining a broadcast address for the entire network and ensuring that every device on the network explicitly sets it during configuration. Set the broadcast address in the **ifconfig** command using the keyword **broadcast** followed by the correct broadcast address. For example, the **ifconfig** command to set the broadcast address for *almond's* le0 interface is:

```
# ifconfig le0 128.66.12.1 netmask 255.255.255.0  \
broadcast 128.66.12.255
```

Note that the broadcast address is relative to the local subnet. *almond* views this interface as connected to network 128.66.12.0; therefore, its broadcast address is 128.66.12.255. *almond* would interpret the address 128.66.255.255 as host address 255 on subnet 255 of network 128.66.0.0, not as a broadcast address for *nuts-net* as a whole.

Assigning the Network Interface Address

If you only want to assign an IP address to a network interface, enter **ifconfig** with only the interface name and the IP address. Use the IP address that the network administrator has assigned for the given interface. Look at the configuration plan for *almond*; we see that the Milnet interface has been assigned the address 26.104.0.19. Therefore, we configure std0 by entering the following command:

```
almond# ifconfig std0 26.104.0.19
```

We can use a host name in place of an address in the **ifconfig** command. Assuming that */etc/hosts* contains the following entry:

```
26.104.0.19    mil-gw.nuts.com mil-gw
```

we can configure std0 with:

```
almond# ifconfig std0 mil-gw.nuts.com
```

The std0 interface does not require a subnet mask because Milnet is not subnetted, and it does not require a broadcast address because our std0 interface does not support broadcasts. Therefore, the simple **ifconfig** command shown above is all we need.

Putting ifconfig in the Startup Files

The **ifconfig** command is normally executed at boot time by a startup file. On BSD UNIX systems, the **ifconfig** commands are usually located in */etc/rc.boot* or */etc/rc.local.* System V UNIX presents a much more complex set of startup files, but the **ifconfig** statements are usually located in a file with a name like */etc/tcp* or */etc/init.d/tcp.** Because network access is important for some of the processes run by the startup files, the **ifconfig** statements execute near the beginning of the startup procedure. The simplest way to configure a network interface to suit your requirements is to edit the startup files and insert the correct **ifconfig** statements.

On *almond*, we edit */etc/rc.boot* and insert the two lines necessary to configure the Ethernet and Milnet connections. We use the *rc.boot* file because it runs early in *almond's* startup procedure. The two lines placed in the file are:

```
ifconfig std0 26.104.0.19
ifconfig le0 128.66.12.1 netmask 255.255.255.0 broadcast 128.66.12.255
```

Insert the new lines in place of any **ifconfig** lines that are already in */etc/rc.boot*, and comment out any **ifconfig** lines in */etc/rc.local.*† Don't remove an **ifconfig** line, such as the line for lo0, unless you replace it with one of your own. ·

This simple procedure ensures that the interfaces on the host are properly configured at every boot.

---

*A good description of the maze of System V initialization files is provided in the Nutshell Handbook, *Essential System Administration*, by AEleen Frisch.

†The *rc.local* script runs at the end of the BSD startup procedure, and we don't want it modifying the configuration changes we made in *rc.boot*.

The Other Command Options

We've used **ifconfig** to set the interface address, the subnet mask, and the broadcast address. These are certainly the most important functions of **ifconfig**, but it has other functions as well. It is also used to enable or disable "trailer encapsulation," the address resolution protocol, and the interface itself. **ifconfig** also provides a "routing metric" used by the Routing Information Protocol. We'll look at each of these functions.

Enabling and Disabling the Interface

The **ifconfig** command has two arguments, **up** and **down**, for enabling or disabling the network interface. The **up** argument enables the network interface and marks it ready for use. The **down** argument disables the interface so that it cannot be used for network traffic.

The **down** argument is used when reconfiguring an interface. Some configuration parameters, for example the IP address, cannot be changed unless the interface is down. First, the interface is brought down. Then the reconfiguration is done, and the interface is brought back up. For example, the following steps change the address for an interface:

```
# ifconfig le0 down
# ifconfig le0 129.66.1.2 up
```

After these commands execute, the interface operates with the new configuration values. The **up** argument in the second **ifconfig** command is not actually required because it is the default. However, an explicit **up** is commonly used after the interface has been disabled, or when an **ifconfig** command is used in a script file to avoid problems if the default is changed in a future release.

ARP and Trailers

Two options on the **ifconfig** command line, **arp** and **trailers**, are used only for Ethernet interfaces. The **trailers** option enables or disables negotiations for trailer encapsulation of IP packets. In Chapter 1 we discussed how IP packets are sent over different physical networks by being encapsulated in the frames that those networks transmit. Trailer encapsulation is an optional technique that reduces the number of memory-to-memory copies the receiving system needs to perform.

To enable trailer encapsulation, put the keyword **trailers** on the **ifconfig** command line. When trailer encapsulation is enabled, the system requests (via the ARP protocol) that other systems also use trailer encapsulation when sending it data.

The option **–trailers** disables trailer encapsulation. Trailer encapsulation is disabled for two basic reasons. First, the I/O architecture of some systems does not derive any benefit from trailer encapsulation. If a system doesn't do memory-to-memory copies when receiving data from the network, it doesn't benefit from trailer encapsulation. Second, there are some systems that have difficulties with the negotiations for trailer encapsulation. For these reasons some systems, the most notable example is Sun OS, ignore the **trailers** argument and never use trailer encapsulation, while other systems allow trailer encapsulation but default to **–trailers**. However, most systems enable trailer encapsulation by default. Check your system documentation for the default on your system.

Chapter 2 discusses the Address Resolution Protocol (ARP), an important protocol that maps IP addresses to physical Ethernet addresses. You can enable ARP with the **ifconfig** keyword **arp** and disable it with the keyword **–arp**. It is possible (though very rare) that a host attached to your network cannot handle ARP. This would only happen on a network using specialized equipment or developmental hardware. In these very rare circumstances, it may be necessary to disable ARP in order to interoperate with the non-standard systems, but it is hard to envision why this would be necessary. By default **ifconfig** enables ARP. As a general rule, you should leave ARP enabled on all your systems.

Metric

The **ifconfig** command creates an entry in the routing table for every interface that is assigned an IP address. Each interface is the route to a network. Even if a host isn't a gateway, its interface is still its "route" to the local network. **ifconfig** determines the route's destination network by applying the interface's subnet mask to the interface's IP address. For example, the le0 interface on *almond* has an address of 128.66.12.1 and a mask of 255.255.255.0. Applying this mask to the address provides the destination network, which is 128.66.12.0. The **netstat –in** display shows the destination address:

```
% netstat -in
Name Mtu  Net/Dest    Address     Ipkts   Ierrs Opkts   Oerrs Collis Queue
le0  1500 128.66.12.0 128.66.12.1 1125826 16    569786  0     8914   0
lo0  1536 127.0.0.0   127.0.0.1   94280   0     94280   0     0      0
```

The Routing Information Protocol (RIP) is the routing protocol most commonly used by UNIX. RIP does two things: it distributes routing information to other hosts, and it uses incoming routing information to build routing tables dynamically. The routes created by **ifconfig** are the ultimate source of the routing information distributed by RIP, and the **ifconfig metric** argument can be used to control how RIP uses this routing information.

RIP makes routing decisions based on the cost of a route. The route's cost is determined by a routing metric associated with the route. A routing metric is just a number. The lower the number, the lower the cost of the route. The higher the number, the higher the cost. When building a routing table, RIP favors low-cost routes over high-cost routes. Directly connected networks are given a very low cost. Therefore, the default metric is 0 for a route through an interface to a directly attached network. However, you can use the metric argument to supply a different routing metric for an interface.

To increase the cost of an interface to three, so that RIP prefers routes with values of 0, 1, or 2, use **metric 3** on the **ifconfig** command line:

```
# ifconfig std0 26.104.0.19 metric 3
```

Use the metric option only if there is another route to the same destination and you want to use it as the primary route. We did not use this command on *almond*, because it has only one interface connected to the outside world. But if it had a second connection, say through a higher speed link, then the command shown above could be used to direct traffic through the higher performance interface.

Newer routing software sets the RIP routing metric in a routing configuration file instead of on the **ifconfig** command line. This new approach to providing routing information is the preferred method. We discuss the format of the routing configuration file in the next chapter.

TCP/IP Over a Serial Line

TCP/IP will run over a wide variety of physical media. The media can be Ethernet cables, as in your local Ethernet, or telephone circuits, as in a wide area network. In the first half of this chapter, we used **ifconfig** to configure a local Ethernet interface. In this section, we use other commands to configure a network interface to use a telephone circuit.

Almost all data communications takes place via serial interfaces. A serial interface is just an interface that sends the data as a series of bits over a "single wire," as opposed to a parallel interface that sends the data bits in parallel over "several wires" simultaneously. This description of a serial interface would fit almost any communications interface (including Ethernet itself), but the term is usually applied to an interface that connects to a telephone circuit via a modem or similar device. Likewise, a telephone circuit is often called a serial line.

In the TCP/IP world, serial lines are used to create wide area networks (WAN). Unfortunately, TCP/IP has not always had a standard physical layer protocol for serial lines. Because of the lack of a standard, many designers choose to use a single brand of routers within their WAN to ensure successful physical layer communication. The growth of TCP/IP WANs has led to a strong interest in standardizing serial line communications to provide vendor independence.

Other forces that have increased interest in serial line communications are the advent of small affordable systems that run TCP/IP, and the advent of high-speed, dial-up modems that can provide "reasonable" TCP/IP performance. When the ARPANET was formed, computers were very expensive and dial-up modems were very slow. At that time, if you could afford a computer, you could afford a leased telephone line. In recent years, however, it has become possible for a user to own a UNIX system at home. In this new environment, there is an increasing demand for services that allow TCP/IP access over dial-up serial lines.

These two forces, the need for standardized wide area communications and the need for dial-up TCP/IP access, have led to the creation of two serial line protocols: Serial Line IP (SLIP) and Point-to-Point Protocol (PPP).*

The Serial Protocols

Serial Line IP was created first. It is a minimal protocol that allows isolated hosts to link via TCP/IP over the telephone network. The SLIP protocol defines a simple mechanism for "framing" datagrams for transmission across serial lines. SLIP sends the datagram across the serial line as a series of bytes, and it uses special characters to mark when a series of bytes should

---

*Dial-up modems are usually asynchronous. Both SLIP and PPP support asynchronous, dial-up service as well as synchronous leased-line service.

be grouped together as a datagram. SLIP defines two special characters for this purpose:

- The SLIP END character, a single byte with the decimal value 192, is the character that marks the end of a datagram. When the receiving SLIP encounters the END character, it knows that it has a complete datagram that can be sent up to IP.

- The SLIP ESC character, a single byte with the decimal value of 219, is used to "escape" the SLIP control characters. If the sending SLIP encounters a byte value equivalent to either a SLIP END character or a SLIP ESC character in the datagram it is sending, it converts that character to a sequence of two characters. The two-character sequences are ESC 220 for the END character, and ESC 221 for the ESC character itself.* When the receiving SLIP encounters these two byte sequences, it converts them back to single-byte values. This procedure prevents the receiving SLIP from incorrectly interpreting a data byte as the end of the datagram.

SLIP is described in RFC 1055, *A Nonstandard for Transmission of IP Datagrams Over Serial Lines: SLIP.* As the name of the RFC makes clear, SLIP is not an Internet standard. The RFC does not propose a standard; it documents an existing protocol. The RFC identifies the deficiencies in SLIP, which fall into two categories:

- The SLIP protocol does not define any link control information that could be used to dynamically control the characteristics of a connection. Therefore, SLIP systems must assume certain link characteristics. Because of this limitation, SLIP can only be used when both hosts know each other's address, and only when IP datagrams are being transmitted.

- SLIP does not compensate for noisy, low-speed telephone lines. The protocol does not provide error correction or data compression.

For many applications these problems are unimportant. You may only be interested in sending IP datagrams. You probably know the addresses of both hosts involved in the link, and can, at worst, provide these addresses manually. Additionally, today's modems provide their own compression and error correction. Given these conditions, SLIP is usually considered adequate for linking isolated hosts. However, in a dynamic environment such as a large WAN, SLIP's problems are generally viewed as major

---

*In this sentence ESC means the SLIP escape character, not the ASCII escape character.

weaknesses, and it is usually considered an inadequate protocol for linking routers.

To address SLIP's weaknesses, Point-to-Point Protocol (PPP) was developed as an Internet standard. Two RFCs that document Point-to-Point Protocol are: RFC 1171, *The Point-to-Point Protocol for the Transmission of Multi-Protocol Datagrams Over Point-to-Point Links*, and RFC 1172, *The Point-to-Point Protocol (PPP) Initial Configuration Options*. At this writing, there are several proposed RFCs that add to the PPP standard.*

PPP addresses the weaknesses of SLIP with a three-layered protocol:

Data Link Layer Protocol	The Data Link Layer Protocol used by PPP is a slightly modified version of High-level Data Link Control (HDLC). PPP modifies HDLC by adding a Protocol field that allows PPP to pass traffic for multiple Network Layer protocols. HDLC is an international standard protocol for reliably sending data over synchronous, serial communications lines. PPP also uses a proposed international standard for transmitting HDLC over asynchronous lines. So PPP can guarantee reliable delivery over any type of serial line.
Link Control Protocol	The Link Control Protocol (LCP) provides control information for the serial link. It is used to establish the connection, negotiate configuration parameters, check link quality, and close the connection. During the parameter negotiations, LCP can negotiate compression. LCP was developed specifically for PPP.
Network Control Protocols	The Network Control Protocols are individual protocols that provide configuration and control information for the Network Layer protocols. Remember, PPP is designed to pass data for a wide variety of network protocols. NCP allows PPP to be customized to do just that. Each network protocol (DECNET, IP, OSI, etc.) has its own NCP protocol. The NCP protocol

---

*If you want to make sure you have the very latest version of a standard, obtain the latest list of RFCs as described in Chapter 13.

> defined in RFCs 1171 and 1172 is the Internet Control Protocol (IPCP), which supports Internet Protocol.

PPP is a more robust protocol than SLIP, but it is also more difficult to implement and not as widely available. However, PPP's advantages make it the serial line protocol of the future, and the likely choice for router vendors seeking a standard mechanism for communicating over serial lines.

Choosing a Serial Protocol

Many network administrators debate over which serial protocol is best. In reality, the correct choice is not always the "best protocol" in abstract terms; rather it is the "right protocol" for a specific situation. If you have a large network, you will probably use both PPP and SLIP.

PPP is preferred because it is a proposed Internet standard. Therefore, it will ensure interoperability between systems from a wide variety of vendors. Additionally, PPP has more features, and is more robust, than SLIP. These features make PPP a good choice as a non-proprietary protocol for connecting routers over serial lines. However, because SLIP was the first widely available serial protocol for IP, and because it is simple to implement, SLIP is available for more kinds of hardware than PPP.

One of the largest applications for IP over serial lines is dial-up access. SLIP is more widely used for this than PPP is, because many of the systems that offer dial-up access only support SLIP. SLIP is available for most terminal servers, and in most PC implementations of TCP/IP. SLIP and PPP do not interoperate; they are completely different protocols. So if your terminal servers only have SLIP, the remote hosts that connect through these servers must also have SLIP. Because of its installed base, SLIP will continue to be widely used for the foreseeable future.

So which protocol should you use? The answer is both. PPP is the serial protocol of the future; use it where you can. For example, when you are designing a new serial line service, try to use PPP. However, you should continue to support SLIP. SLIP is adequate for most applications, and is often the only serial protocol available for a specific piece of hardware. Simply put, use PPP where you can and use SLIP where you must.

Installing SLIP

SLIP is available for most UNIX systems. On SCO systems it is included as part of the TCP/IP package; on IBM AIX systems SLIP is part of the operating system. The SLIP configuration of both of these systems is simple; but on some other UNIX systems, SLIP configuration requires more effort. As an example of a more complex configuration, we'll install SLIP on a Sun system. Let's start with the complicated installation first.

SLIP for Sun

SLIP software is available via anonymous **ftp** from several different sources. If your system doesn't have SLIP, use **archie** as described in Chapter 13 to locate a SLIP source for your system. In this example, we use the BSD version of SLIP modified to run on Sun OS 4.x systems. This software is available from *ai.toronto.edu* in *pub/slipware.tar.Z*. The compressed **tar** file contains the SLIP software and some helpful support packages. The *slipware* file contains:

SLIP   In our example, this is *slip-4.0*, which is the version of SLIP for Sun systems running Sun OS 4.x.

YAPT 5.5c   This is Yet Another Patch Tape (YAPT) 5.5c from Sun. It provides fixes for serial port problems. In addition to these patches, you should apply patch 100149-03. You can obtain this patch via anonymous **ftp** from *ftp.cs.toronto.edu* in the file *sun-patches/100149-03.tar.Z*.

tip   This is a version of the BSD **tip** program modified to support dial-up SLIP.

gated   **gated**, described in the next chapter, is required to support SLIP in a dynamic routing environment. **routed** does not properly support SLIP connections. Don't use the **gated** that comes in the *slipware* file; get the latest version of **gated** from Cornell.

Each of these packages is a **tar** file within the *slipware* **tar** file. Once the files are uncompressed and restored, they create a directory called *slipware* with subdirectories for *slip-4.0*, *tip*, and *yapt5.5c*.

The installation of SLIP on a Sun system is a good example of how the kernel is modified to support a "non-standard" network interface. Additionally, the configuration of the SLIP interface uses its own special configuration command, instead of **ifconfig**. In many ways installing SLIP is a more interesting, though less common, example of installing an optional network interface than the examples in Chapter 5. Let's look at the details of this installation.

Modifying System Files for SLIP

Assuming that the *slipware* directory has been created under */usr/local*, the directory containing the SLIP files is */usr/local/slipware/slip-4.0*. Our first step in installing SLIP is to copy the required SLIP files from this directory to the appropriate */sys* directory, as follows:

```
# cd /usr/local/slipware/slip-4.0
# cp tty_slip.c /sys/os/tty_slip.c
# cp slip.h /usr/include/sys/slip.h
# cp slip.h /sys/sys/slip.h
```

Next, modify the common files and structures used by the kernel so that they reference our newly installed SLIP files. First, edit */sys/conf.common/files.cmn* and insert:

```
os/tty_slip.c            optional slip
```

Then, edit */sys/sun/str_conf.c* and insert these three pieces of code:

```
...
#include "slip.h"
...
#if     NSLIP > 0
extern struct streamtab slipinfo;
#endif
...
#if     NSLIP > 0
        { "slip",        &slipinfo },
#endif
...
```

You must rebuild the kernel to make use of the newly installed files, but before doing that apply the *yapt5.5c* patches and the patch 100149-03. These patches also make kernel modifications; therefore, install the patches now so that you only rebuild the kernel once.

Patching the Kernel

Installing the patches from *yapt5.5c* is easy. *yapt5.5c* uses an installation script like those described in Chapter 5. To install the patches, simply change to the *yapt5.5c* directory and run **install**:

```
# cd /usr/local/slipware/yapt5.5c
# ./install
```

Installing the patch 100149-03 is slightly more difficult. The *100149.tar.Z* file contains the object module **ip_input.o**. This object file fixes a problem that can cause SLIP to crash your system with an "mclput () panic" error.

Assume that the patch file has been restored in the */tmp* directory. To install the new **ip_input.o** module:*

```
# cd /tmp
# mv /sys/sun4c/OBJ/ip_input.o /sys/sun4c/OBJ/ip_input.o.FCS
# cp ip_input.o /sys/sun4c/OBJ/ip_input.o
# chmod 444 /sys/sun4c/OBJ/ip_input.o
```

Patches change frequently; new patches are released, and individual patches are revised. Don't assume the patches in these examples are the latest versions, or the only ones you need. Check with your vendor for the latest information about patches for your system.

Rebuilding the Kernel

Now that the SLIP system files and kernel patches are installed, we need to rebuild the kernel in order to run SLIP. The first step in this process is to modify the kernel configuration file to add the SLIP pseudo-device.† In the example, we copy a small generic configuration file, *GENERIC_SMALL*, to the file we are going to modify. We're calling the new configuration file *SLIPPERY*.

```
# cd /sys/sun4c/conf
# cp GENERIC_SMALL SLIPPERY
```

We edit the new configuration file modifying the IDENT statement to identify the new configuration and adding a pseudo-device for SLIP:

```
IDENT    "SLIPPERY"
...
pseudo-device        slip5
```

Next, we rebuild the kernel using this new configuration:

```
# /etc/config SLIPPERY
Doing a "make depend"
# cd ../SLIPPERY
# make
cc -sparc -c -O -Dsun4c -DSLIP ...
        .
        .
        .
building vmunix_small.o
cc -sparc -I. -c -O -Dsun4c -DSLIP -DSUN4C_60 ...
loading vmunix_small
```

---

*The directory *sun4c* is architecture specific. Because we are installing SLIP for Sun 4.x, this directory could be either *sun4c* or *sun4*. To successfully modify the kernel on a Sun system, you must know which Sun architecture you are using.

†BSD kernels and pseudo-devices are discussed in Chapter 5.

```
rearranging symbols
text    data    bss     dec      hex
983040  154024  43784   1180848  1204b0
```

Examine the output from **config** and **make** carefully. There should be no errors. If there are any, don't use the new kernel. Instead, go back over every step of the SLIP installation and make sure you didn't make any mistakes or leave out any steps. If necessary, repeat the entire installation. When the **config** and **make** output is error free, move the new kernel* to the root directory, and **sync** and **reboot** your system:

```
# mv /vmunix /vmunix.org
# mv vmunix_small /vmunix
# sync
# reboot
```

If the system fails to reboot properly with the new kernel, reboot with the original kernel (*/vmunix.org* in our example). Check every step of the installation to see where things went wrong. Then repeat the entire installation correcting your mistake.

Configuring the SLIP Interface

SLIP is now installed in the kernel, but the SLIP network interface is not yet configured. In the same way we had to configure the Ethernet interface for TCP/IP, we must configure the SLIP interface. We used the **ifconfig** command for the Ethernet interface; to configure a SLIP interface, we'll use a SLIP-specific command. Unfortunately SLIP is not standardized; different systems use different commands. Two common SLIP configuration commands are **slattach**, used on various UNIX systems, and **sliplogin**, used with the *slipware* software. In this section we discuss both.

slattach

The syntax and function of **slattach** are similar to **ifconfig**. Like **ifconfig**, the **slattach** command assigns an IP address to a physical network interface. For example:

```
# slattach /dev/tty001 128.66.15.3 128.66.15.26
```

Here the superuser uses **slattach** to assign the address 128.66.15.3 to the device */dev/tty001*. Only two systems are directly connected to a serial line; one at each end. The second address on the command line is the

---

*This new kernel is called *vmunix_small* because that is the name on the **config** statement in the kernel configuration file.

destination address (the address of the host at the other end of the point-to-point link). The link created by this **slattach** command is a dedicated link between 128.66.15.3 and 128.66.15.26, and it is not available to any other system.

Notice that the **slattach** command identifies the serial device (*/dev/tty001*) instead of the IP network interface (*sl01*). The **slattach** and **sliplogin** commands both use the name of the serial device to configure a SLIP interface. However, when you use **netstat** to check the status of the SLIP interface, it displays the interface name.

Like **ifconfig**, the **slattach** command is stored in a startup file. It configures the serial interface when the system boots, and the interface remains dedicated to SLIP use unless some action is taken to detach it. With SCO's TCP/IP, the **sldetach** command is used to detach the serial device from the network interface as follows:

```
# sldetach sl01
```

Once the superuser runs **sldetach**, the serial device that was configured for SLIP is again available to be used as a "normal" terminal interface. **sldetach** undoes the work of **slattach**. But unlike **slattach**, **sldetach** uses the interface name instead of the device name.

None of the special kernel configuration tasks covered in the previous sections are required to install SLIP on systems that provide their own versions of SLIP. In fact, there is usually no need to explicitly enter the **slattach** command. For example, on an SCO system, the correct **slattach** command is placed in the */etc/tcp* script when **netconfig** is run to install SLIP. So, very little effort is necessary to configure a SLIP interface on an SCO system.

IBM AIX systems provide SLIP as part of the operating system. AIX also uses the **slattach** command, but its syntax varies from that used by SCO. AIX uses **ifconfig** to configure the interface, and **slattach** to attach the serial device to the configured interface. Instead of IP addresses on the **slattach** command line, AIX provides an option for a dial-string to create a dial-out SLIP connection. This dial-out feature allows an AIX user to set up a dial connection and attach SLIP to the interface, all in one command. For example:

```
# slattach /dev/tty1 ´""ATZ OK \pATDT5551212 CONNECT""´
```

The dial-string uses the BNU/UUCP chat syntax to define the commands used by the modem to set up a dial connection. In the example above, the dial-string does the following:

- Sends ATZ to rest the modem.
- Waits for the response OK from the modem.
- Pauses (\ p) 1 second.
- Sends the dial command (ATDT) to the modem requesting that it call 555-1212.
- Waits for a response that contains the word CONNECT.

slattach expects the physical connection to the remote system to exist when **slattach** is invoked. The physical connection can be a direct connection, a leased line or a dial line. But if a dial connection is used, some process, such as **cu** or **tip**, must establish the physical connection before **slattach** is invoked. The AIX dial-out feature eliminates the need for an external process to establish the link, however it only dials the phone, it does not configure the remote system for SLIP. The remote system must already be configured for SLIP for the link to work. In the next section, we'll see that the **sliplogin** command provides a login facility for configuring the remote system that allows the SLIP connection to be dynamically created.

The differences in the SCO and AIX **slattach** commands show that SLIP commands are not standardized. If your system comes with SLIP, carefully read your system's documentation so you'll know the exact syntax used on your system.

sliplogin

The *slipware* software uses **sliplogin** to configure the SLIP interface. However before using it, we must compile and install it with set-uid permission. Here's a sample installation:

```
# cd /usr/local/slipware/slip-4.0
# make
cc -DLCKDIR=\"/var/spool/uucp/LCK\" -target sun4 -o sliplogin sliplogin.c
# cp sliplogin /etc
# cd /etc
# chmod 4755 sliplogin
```

sliplogin can be used in two different ways. You can use it like **slattach** to configure a dedicated SLIP interface, identifying the IP addresses of both ends of the link, or you can use it to support dynamic dial-in SLIP access.

To configure a dedicated interface using **sliplogin**, the superuser enters a command like this:

```
# sliplogin 128.66.15.3 128.66.15.26 < /dev/ttyb &
```

This command assigns the address 128.66.15.3 to the local interface. The second address is the destination address—the address of the host at the remote end of this point-to-point link. The function of this command is similar to the SCO **slattach** command shown in the previous section.

Like **slattach**, this command does not specify the IP interface name. Instead, the serial device (*/dev/ttyb*) is defined on the command line. The SLIP interface names used by *slipware* are slip0 through slip4. Each interface is configured in order, as each **sliplogin** command is executed. In other words, the first **sliplogin** command configures slip0, the second configures slip1, and so on, for each command entered. The **netstat −ni** command shows which interfaces have been configured:

```
# netstat -ni
```

Name	Mtu	Net/Dest	Address	Ipkts	Ierrs	Opkts	Oerrs	Collis	Queue
le0	1500	128.66.15.0	128.66.15.1	1	0	4	0	0	0
lo0	1536	127.0.0.0	127.0.0.1	1712	0	1712	0	0	0
slip0	1006	128.66.15.26	128.66.15.3	0	0	0	0	0	0

The **sliplogin** command creates a host-specific route using the first address from the command line as the gateway for the route, and the second address as the destination.* **sliplogin** installs this host-specific route in the routing table. You can use **netstat** to see this effect on the routing table:

```
# netstat -nr
Routing tables
```

Destination	Gateway	Flags	Refcnt	Use	Interface
128.66.15.26	128.66.15.3	UH	0	0	slip0
127.0.0.1	127.0.0.1	UH	1	28	lo0
default	128.66.15.2	UG	0	0	le0
128.66.15.0	128.66.15.1	U	21	1687	le0

The contents of routing tables are explained in detail in the next chapter. For now, just notice that the first line in this table is a route to the remote host (128.66.15.26), and that the interface used for the route is slip0.

So far, we have used **sliplogin** in the same way that we used **slattach** on the SCO system, and the effects have been the same. However, **sliplogin** can also be used as a login shell to dynamically establish a dial-in SLIP link. **slattach** is run by the root user, and is normally run at startup to configure a dedicated serial link. **sliplogin** can be run by a non-root user, and can

---

*Routes and routing are discussed in Chapters 2 and 7.

be invoked at login, instead of at boot time. When **sliplogin** is used by a non-root user without any command-line arguments, it looks up the link configuration information in the */etc/hosts.slip* file. It uses the user's login name as the key for searching the file. When it finds the key, it uses the information stored under that key to configure the SLIP link. In this way, **sliplogin** can dynamically configure a SLIP link when the user logs in.

For example, assume that the gateway *pistachio* allows dial-up SLIP access from several remote hosts. The administrator of *pistachio* creates "pseudo" user accounts for each remote host. Each account has **sliplogin** as its login shell. This allows the SLIP link to be specifically configured for whichever host logs into the SLIP interface. One user account created by the administrator is *chestnut-slip*. When a user named *chestnut-slip* logs into the system, the system searches for the user name in */etc/hosts.slip*. If the system finds a record that begins with the string *chestnut-slip*, it applies the data stored in that record to the link configuration. Here are *pistachio's* */etc/hosts.slip* entries:

```
macadamia-slip normal 128.66.15.3 128.66.15.10
chopped-slip normal 128.66.15.3 128.66.15.11
chestnut-slip normal 128.66.15.3 128.66.15.12
roasted-slip normal 128.66.15.3 128.66.15.13
sales-slip normal 128.66.15.3 128.66.15.26
```

In our example, *pistachio* matches the login name *chestnut-slip* and uses the first address (128.66.15.3) as the local address, and the second address (128.66.15.12) as the remote address. The remote address is the address of the host (*chestnut*) that the user logs in from. The addresses are used exactly as if they were entered directly on the **sliplogin** command line. This dynamic link configuration allows the system administrator to define SLIP connections that are only created when the dial-in users actually log in.

For SLIP to function properly, both ends of the SLIP connection must know the address of the other end. The SLIP protocol does not have any facility for exchanging addresses. The SLIP connection must be configured manually at both ends. **sliplogin** makes this simple. To do this for a dial-up connection using **sliplogin**, these general step are performed:

- The user on the local system connects to the remote system using **tip**, **cu**, or some other standard UNIX facility for creating a remote terminal connection.*

---

*The dial-out facility shown for the AIX **slattach** command is unique. **sliplogin** does not provide this facility.

- The user logs into the remote system which causes **sliplogin** to run and to configure the remote system's interface using the information from the */etc/hosts.slip* file. The user is returned to his local system as soon as the **sliplogin** configuration command runs.
- The user then configures the SLIP interface on the local system with **sliplogin**. The SLIP interface will remain "attached" until the **sliplogin** process is killed.
- Working from the local system, the user can now use the SLIP interface as if it were any other TCP/IP interface. For example, if a user on *chestnut* enters an **ftp** command, the FTP packets flow out from *chestnut*, across the SLIP line to *pistachio*, and on to their destination. The isolated system becomes part of the network.

The root user can use */etc/hosts.slip* in a different way. The root user can invoke **sliplogin** with a search key on the command line, and **sliplogin** will set up a link using the addresses defined in */etc/hosts.slip*. For example, assuming the *hosts.slip* file shown above, **sliplogin** would set up a serial link between 128.66.15.3 and 128.66.15.26 if the following command was entered by the superuser:

```
# sliplogin sales-slip < /dev/ttyb &
```

These features, and the wide availability of SLIP, make it a frequent choice for supporting dial-in IP access. However, in situations that require more than a few SLIP ports, a dedicated terminal server is usually more cost effective than using a full UNIX system as a SLIP server.

Installing PPP

Point-to-Point Protocol (PPP) is available from many different sources on the Internet. The software used for the examples in this section was downloaded via anonymous **ftp** from *archive.cis.ohio-state.edu* in the file *ppp-sunos4.1.p16.tar.Z*. This installation is almost identical to the SLIP installation.

First, copy the PPP system files to */sys*:

```
# cp ppp_async.c /sys/os/ppp_async.c
# cp ppp_if.c /sys/os/ppp_if.c
# cp ppp_str.h /sys/sys/ppp_str.h
# cp slcompress.c /sys/os/slcompress.c
# cp slcompress.h /sys/os/slcompress.h
# cp slip_var.h /sys/sys/slip_var.h
# cp slip_var.h /usr/include/sys/slip_var.h
```

Next, edit */sys/conf.common/files.cmn*, inserting these lines:

```
os/slcompress.c          optional ppp
os/ppp_if.c              optional ppp
os/ppp_async.c           optional ppp
```

Then edit */sys/sun/str_conf.c*, adding these three pieces of code:

```
#include "ppp.h"
...
#if      NPPP > 0
extern struct streamtab ppp_asyncinfo;
extern struct streamtab ppp_ifinfo;
#endif
...
#if      NPPP > 0
         { "pppif",      &ppp_ifinfo },
         { "pppasync",   &ppp_asyncinfo },
#endif
```

At this point, I recommend that you apply the same patches we applied for SLIP. These patches are not specific to SLIP; they're patches for the serial interfaces. Because PPP uses the same serial interfaces, it will benefit from the same patches. Look in the SLIP section, "Patching the Kernel," for details about applying the patches.

Finally, edit the kernel configuration file and rebuild the kernel. The pseudo-device statement added to the kernel for PPP is:

```
pseudo-device    ppp5
```

These steps are identical to the configuration steps we followed for SLIP. Only the specifics of the individual steps are different. Installing most network services does not require modifying the kernel, but when it is required, these are the basic steps.

Configuring the PPP Interface

The PPP network interface is configured using the **ppp** command. The format of **ppp** is very similar to the **slattach** command we used for SLIP. For example, this **ppp** command would configure the serial device */dev/ttya* with a local address of 128.66.15.3 and a remote address of 128.66.15.26:

```
# ppp 128.66.15.3:128.66.15.26 /dev/ttya &
```

PPP's ability to learn the IP address of the remote system gives it the flexibility to handle dial-up links without using a static configuration file like */etc/hosts.slip*. It's a very simple feature to use. If you don't specify the remote host's IP address on the **ppp** command line, it will learn the correct address from the remote host. For example:

```
# ppp 128.66.15.3: /dev/ttya &
```

In this example, **ppp** assigns the local address (128.66.15.3) to the interface, but has no address for the remote host. The remote address is learned when a remote host connects to this system through this link. When a PPP connection is being established, link control information is exchanged. This information tells the system the IP address of the host at the other end of the link. As with **sliplogin**, the dial-up connection still needs to be established using a program such as **tip** or **cu**, but this **ppp** command is general enough to be used with any remote host. With **sliplogin**, the command, or the */etc/hosts.slip* entry, has to be written specifically for each remote host.

In this chapter we looked at various commands to configure the network interface. Each of these commands defines the IP address of the interface, and modifies the routing table to route data through the newly configured network interface. In the next chapter, we look at more complex routing configurations.

7

Configuring Routing

Routing is the glue that binds the Internet together. Without it, TCP/IP traffic would be limited to a single physical network. Routing allows traffic from your local network to reach its destination somewhere else in the world—perhaps after passing through many intermediate networks.

The important role of routing and the complex interconnection of Internet networks make the design of routing protocols a major challenge to network software developers. Consequently, most discussions of routing concern protocol design. Very little is written about the important task of properly configuring routing protocols. However, more day to day problems are caused by improperly configured routers than are caused by improperly designed routing algorithms. As system administrators, we need to ensure that the routing on our systems is properly configured. This is the task we tackle in this chapter.

Common Routing Configurations

A distinction should be made between routing and routing protocols. All systems route data, but not all systems run routing protocols. *Routing* is the act of forwarding datagrams based on the information contained in the routing table. *Routing protocols* are programs that exchange the information used to build routing tables.

The routing configuration of a specific network does not always require a routing protocol. In situations where the routing information does not change, for example, when there is only one possible route, the system administrator usually builds the routing table manually. Some networks have no access to any other TCP/IP networks, and therefore require no special action by the system administrator to build the routing table—either manually or with routing protocols. The three most common routing configurations are:*

minimal routing   A network completely isolated from all other TCP/IP networks requires only minimal routing. A minimal routing table is built by **ifconfig** when the network interface is configured. If your network doesn't have direct access to other TCP/IP networks, and if you are not using subnetting, this may be the only routing table you'll require. Isolated networks are not as rare as you might think. In the UNIX environment, it's common for a TCP/IP local area network to have access to the outside world only through UUCP.

static routing   A network with a limited number of gateways to other TCP/IP networks can be configured with static routing. A static routing table is constructed manually by the system administrator using the **route** command. Static routing tables do not adjust to network changes, so they should be used only where routes do not change. But when remote destinations can only be reached through one route, a static route is the best choice.

dynamic routing   A network with more than one possible route to the same destination should use dynamic routing. A dynamic routing table is built from the information exchanged by routing protocols. The protocols are

---

*Guidelines for choosing the correct routing configuration for your network are presented in Chapter 4.

designed to distribute information that dynamically adjusts routes to reflect changing network conditions. Routing protocols handle complex routing situations more quickly and accurately than the system administrator can. Routing protocols are designed not only to switch to a backup route when the primary route becomes inoperable; they are also designed to decide which is the "best" route to a destination. On any network where there are multiple paths to the same destination, a routing protocol should be used.

Routes are built by **ifconfig**, manually by the system administrator or dynamically by routing protocols. But no matter how routes are entered, they all end up in the routing table.

The Minimal Routing Table

Let's look at the contents of the routing table constructed by **ifconfig** when *peanut's* network interfaces were configured.

```
% netstat -rn
Routing tables
Destination        Gateway         Flags   Refcnt Use     Interface
127.0.0.1          127.0.0.1       UH      1      132      lo0
128.66.12.0        128.66.12.2     U       26     49041    le0
```

The first entry is the loopback route to *localhost* created when lo0 was configured. The other entry is the route to network 128.66.12.0 through interface le0. Address 128.66.12.2 is not a remote gateway address. It is the address assigned to the le0 interface on *peanut*.

Look at the Flags field for each entry. Both entries have the U (up) flag set, indicating that they are ready to be used, but neither entry has the G (gateway) flag set. The G flag indicates that a remote gateway is used. The G flag is not set because both of these routes are direct routes through local interfaces, not through external gateways.

The loopback route also has the H (host) flag set. This indicates that only one host can be reached through this route. The meaning of this flag becomes clear when you look at the destination field for the loopback entry. It shows that the destination is a host address, not a network address. The loopback network address is 127.0.0.0. The destination address shown (127.0.0.1) is the address of *localhost*, an individual host. This particular host route is in every routing table.

Although every host table has this host-specific route, most routes are routes to networks. One reason network routes are used is to reduce the size of the routing table. An organization may have only one network but hundreds of hosts. The Internet has a few thousand networks but hundreds of thousands of hosts. A routing table with a route for every host would be unmanageable.

Our sample table contains only one network route, 128.66.12.0. Therefore, *peanut* can only communicate with hosts located on that network. The limited capability of this routing table is easily verified with the **ping** command. **ping** uses the ICMP Echo Message to force a remote host to echo a packet back to the local host. If packets can travel to and from a remote host, it indicates that the two hosts can successfully communicate.

To check the routing table on *peanut*, first **ping** another host on the local network.

```
% ping -s almond
PING almond.nuts.com: 56 data bytes
64 bytes from almond.nuts.com (128.66.12.1): icmp_seq=0. time=11. ms
64 bytes from almond.nuts.com (128.66.12.1): icmp_seq=1. time=10. ms
^C
----almond.nuts.com PING Statistics----
2 packets transmitted, 2 packets received, 0% packet loss
round-trip (ms)  min/avg/max = 10/10/11
```

ping displays a line of output for each ICMP ECHO_RESPONSE received.* When **ping** is interrupted, it displays some summary statistics. All of this indicates successful communication with *almond*. But if we check a host that is not on *nuts-net*, say a host on Milnet, the results are different.

```
% ping 26.40.0.17
sendto: Network is unreachable
```

Here the message, "sendto: Network is unreachable," indicates that *peanut* does not know how to send data to the network that host 26.40.0.17 is on. There are only two routes in the *peanut* routing table and neither is a route to 26.0.0.0.

---

*Sun's **ping** would only display the message "almond is alive" if the –s option was not used. Some other **ping** implementations do not require the –s option.

Even other subnets on *nuts-net* cannot be reached using this routing table. To demonstrate this, **ping** a host on another subnet. For example:

```
% ping 128.66.1.2
sendto: Network is unreachable
```

These **ping** tests show that the routing table created by **ifconfig** only allows communication with other hosts on the local network. If your network does not require access to any other TCP/IP networks, this may be all you need. However, if it does require access to other networks, more routes must be added to the routing table.

Building a Static Routing Table

As we have seen, the minimal routing table only works to reach hosts on the directly connected physical networks. Routes through external gateways must be added to the routing table to reach remote hosts. One way to do this is by constructing a static routing table with **route** commands.

Use the UNIX **route** command to manually add or delete entries in the routing table. For example, to add a route to 26.0.0.0 to *peanut's* routing table, we enter:

```
# route add 26.0.0.0 128.66.12.1 1
add net 26.0.0.0: gateway almond
```

The first argument after the **route** command in this sample is the keyword **add**. The first keyword on every **route** command line is either **add** or **delete**, telling **route** either to add a new route or delete an existing one. There is no default; one of these keywords must be used.

The next value is the destination address, which is the address reached via this route. The destination address can be specified as an IP address, a network name from the */etc/networks* file, a host name from the */etc/hosts* file, or the keyword **default**. Because most routes are added early in the startup process, numeric IP addresses are used more than names. This is done so that the routing configuration is not dependent on the state of the name server software. Always use the complete numeric address (all four bytes). If you enter less than four bytes, **route** will expand the address, and the expanded address may not be what you intended.*

---

*Some implementations of **route** expand "26" to 0.0.0.26, even though "26" could mean Milnet (26.0.0.0).

If the keyword **default** is used for the destination address, **route** creates a *default route.** The default route is used whenever there is no specific route to a destination, and it is often the only route you need. If your network has only one gateway, use a default route to direct all traffic bound for remote networks through that gateway.

Next on the **route** command line is the gateway address. This is the IP address of the external gateway through which data is sent to the destination address. The address must be the address of a gateway on a directly connected network. TCP/IP routes specify the *next-hop* in the path to a remote destination. That next-hop must be directly accessible to the local host; therefore, it must be on a directly connected network.

The last argument on the command line is the routing metric. The metric argument is not used when routes are deleted, but it is required whenever a route is added. Despite being required, **route** only uses the metric to decide if this is a route through a directly attached interface or a route through an external gateway. If the metric is 0, the route is installed as a route through a local interface, and the G flag, which we saw in the **netstat -i** display, is not set. If the metric value is greater than 0, the route is installed with the G flag set, and the gateway address is assumed to be the address of an external gateway. Static routing makes no other use of the metric. Dynamic routing is required to make real use of varying metric values.

Adding Static Routes

As an example, let's configure static routing on the imaginary workstation *peanut*. Figure 7-1 shows the subnet 128.66.12.0. There are two gateways on this subnet, *almond* and *pecan*. *almond* is the gateway to thousands of networks on the Internet; *pecan* provides access to the other subnets on *nuts-net*. We'll use *almond* as our default gateway because it is used by thousands of routes. The smaller number of routes through *pecan* can easily be entered individually. The number of routes through a gateway, not the amount of traffic it handles, decides which gateway to select as the default. Even if most of *peanut's* network traffic goes through *pecan* to other hosts on *nuts-net*, the default gateway should be *almond*.

---

*The network address associated with the default route is 0.0.0.0.

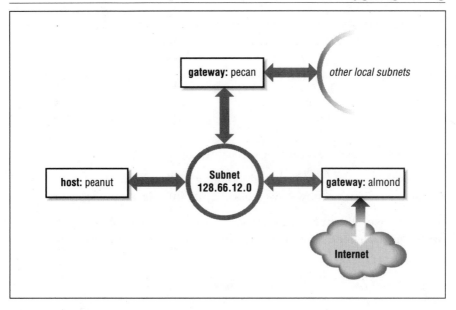

Figure 7.1: Routing on a Subnet

To install the default route on *peanut*, we enter:

```
# route -n add default 128.66.12.1 1
add net default: gateway 128.66.12.1
```

The destination is **default**, and the gateway address (128.66.12.1) is *almond's* address. Now *almond* is *peanut's* default gateway. The **–n** option is not required. It just tells **route** to display numeric addresses in its informational messages. When you add **route** commands to a startup file, use the **–n** option to prevent **route** from wasting time querying name server software that may not be running.

After installing the default route, you can examine the routing table to make sure the route has been added:

```
% netstat -rn
Routing tables
Destination     Gateway        Flags   Refcnt Use
Interface
127.0.0.1       127.0.0.1      UH      1      132       lo0
default         128.66.12.1    UG      0      0         le0
128.66.12.0     128.66.12.2    U       26     49041     le0
```

Try **ping** again to see whether *peanut* can now communicate with remote hosts. If we're lucky,* the remote host responds and we see:

```
% ping 26.40.0.17
PING 26.40.0.17: 56 data bytes
64 bytes from foo.army.mil (26.40.0.17): icmp_seq=0. time=110. ms
64 bytes from foo.army.mil (26.40.0.17): icmp_seq=1. time=100. ms
^C
----26.40.0.17 PING Statistics----
2 packets transmitted, 2 packets received, 0% packet loss
round-trip (ms)  min/avg/max = 100/105/110
```

This display indicates successful communication with the remote host, which means that we now have a good route to hosts on the Internet.

However, we still haven't installed routes to the rest of *nuts-net*. If we **ping** a host on another subnet, something interesting happens:

```
% ping 128.66.1.2
PING 128.66.1.2: 56 data bytes
ICMP Host redirect from gateway almond.nuts.com (128.66.12.1)
 to pecan.nuts.com (128.66.12.3) for filbert.nuts.com (128.66.1.2)
64 bytes from filbert.nuts.com (128.66.1.2): icmp_seq=1. time=30. ms
^C
----128.66.1.2 PING Statistics----
1 packets transmitted, 1 packets received, 0% packet loss
round-trip (ms)  min/avg/max = 30/30/30
```

peanut believes that all destinations are reachable through its default route. Therefore, even data destined for the other subnets is sent to *almond*. If *peanut* sends data to *almond* that should go through *pecan*, *almond* sends an ICMP Redirect to *peanut* telling it to use *pecan*. (See Chapter 1 for a description of the ICMP Redirect Message.) **ping** shows the ICMP Redirect in action.

Using **netstat** we can see the effect this redirect has on the routing table:

```
% netstat -nr
Routing tables
Destination      Gateway        Flags    Refcnt  Use      Interface
127.0.0.1        127.0.0.1      UH       1       1604     lo0
128.66.1.3       128.66.12.3    UGHD     0       514      le0
default          128.66.12.1    UG       3       373964   le0
128.66.12.0      128.66.12.1    U        31      686547   le0
```

The route with the D flag set was installed by the ICMP Redirect.

---

*It is possible that the remote host is down. If it is, **ping** receives no answer. Don't give up; try another host.

To avoid repeated ICMP Redirects, specific routes through *pecan* should be installed for each subnet, using these **route** statements:

```
# route -n add 128.66.1.0 128.66.12.3 1
add net 128.66.1.0: gateway 128.66.12.3
# route -n add 128.66.6.0 128.66.12.3 1
add net 128.66.6.0: gateway 128.66.12.3
# route -n add 128.66.3.0 128.66.12.3 1
add net 128.66.3.0: gateway 128.66.12.3
# route -n add 128.66.9.0 128.66.12.3 1
add net 128.66.9.0: gateway 128.66.12.3
```

netstat shows what the completed routing table looks like. *peanut* is directly connected to only 128.66.12.0, so all gateways in its routing table have addresses that begin with 128.66.12. The finished routing table is show below.

```
% netstat -rn
Routing tables
Destination      Gateway         Flags    Refcnt Use  Interface
127.0.0.1        127.0.0.1       UH       1      132       lo0
128.66.12.0      128.66.12.2     U        26     49041     le0
128.66.1.3       128.66.12.3     UGHD     1      514       le0
default          128.66.12.1     UG       0      0         le0
128.66.1.0       128.66.12.3     UG       1      4904      le0
128.66.6.0       128.66.12.3     UG       0      0         le0
128.66.3.0       128.66.12.3     UG       0      0         le0
128.66.9.0       128.66.12.3     UG       0      0         le0
```

The routing table we have constructed uses the default route (through *almond*) to reach external networks, and specific routes (through *pecan*) to reach other subnets within *nuts-net*. Rerunning the **ping** tests produces consistently successful results. However, if any subnets are added to the network, the routes to these new subnets must be manually added to the routing table. Additionally, if the system is rebooted, all static routing table entries are lost. Therefore, to use static routing you must ensure that the routes are re-installed each time your system boots.

Installing Static Routes at Startup

If you decide to use static routing, you need to make two modifications to your startup files:

1. Add the desired **route** statements to a startup file.
2. Remove any statements from the startup file that run a routing protocol.

As an example, let's see how we would add static routing to the startup procedure on *peanut*. Remember that *peanut* is an imaginary BSD UNIX system. Before making changes to your real system, check your system documentation. You may need to modify a different boot script and your system may start the routing protocol with */etc/routed* instead of */usr/etc/in.routed.* Only your system's documentation can provide the exact details for your system.

First, edit *rc.local* to add the **route** statements:

```
route -n add default 128.66.12.1 1 > /dev/console
route -n add 128.66.1.0 128.66.12.3 1 > /dev/console
route -n add 128.66.6.0 128.66.12.3 1 > /dev/console
route -n add 128.66.3.0 128.66.12.3 1 > /dev/console
route -n add 128.66.9.0 128.66.12.3 1 > /dev/console
```

Next, comment out the lines that start the routing protocol:

```
#       if [ -f /usr/etc/in.routed ]; then
#               in.routed;      echo -n ' routed' > /dev/console
#       fi
```

Although the startup filename may be different on your system, the procedure should be basically the same. These simple steps are all that is needed to set up static routing. The problem with static routing is not setting it up, but maintaining it if you have a changeable networking environment. Routing protocols are flexible enough to handle simple and complex routing environments. That is why startup procedures often run routing protocols by default.

The Variety of Routing Protocols

All routing protocols perform the same basic functions. They determine the "best" route to each destination, and they distribute routing information among the systems on a network. How they perform these functions, in particular how they decide which routes are best, is what makes routing protocols different from each other. The next two sections provide a quick overview of the routing protocols currently in use.

Interior Routing Protocols

Routing protocols are divided into two general groups: *interior* and *exterior* protocols. An interior protocol is a routing protocol used inside—interior to—an independent network system. In TCP/IP terminology, these independent network systems are called autonomous systems.* Within an autonomous system (AS), routing information is exchanged using an

---

*Autonomous systems are described in Chapter 2.

interior protocol chosen by the autonomous system's administration. There are several interior protocols to choose from.

The Routing Information Protocol (RIP) is the most commonly used interior protocol. RIP is widely available because it is included as part of the UNIX software delivered with most systems. It is very well suited for local area networks. If you run a routing protocol on your local network, it is probably RIP.

RIP selects the route with the lowest "hop count" (*metric*) as the best route. The RIP hop count represents the number of gateways through which data must pass to reach its destination. RIP assumes that the best route is the one that uses the fewest gateways; i.e., fewer gateways mean a shorter path, and the shortest path is the best path. This approach to choosing the best route is sometimes called a *distance-vector algorithm*.

The longest path that RIP accepts is 15 hops. If the metric of a route is greater than 15, RIP considers the destination unreachable and discards the route. For this reason RIP is *not* suitable for very large autonomous systems where routes may well pass through more than 15 gateways. Also, RIP's assumption that the shortest path is the best path does not take into account such things as congestion or delay on a route. Other interior protocols have been developed to overcome these limitations.

Hello is an interior protocol that was developed to use delay as the deciding factor when choosing the best route. *Delay* is the length of time it takes a datagram to make the round-trip between its source and destination. A Hello packet contains a timestamp indicating when it was sent. When the packet arrives at it destination, the receiving system subtracts the timestamp from the current time, to estimate how long it took the packet to arrive.

Hello is not widely used. It was the interior protocol of the original 56 kbps NSFNET backbone. Back then, it was used between NSFNET's LSI-11 routers, commonly called the *fuzzball routers*. Hello has had very little usage outside of NSFNET. NSFNET replaced Hello with another protocol when it removed the "fuzzballs" and upgraded to a T1 (1.554 mbps) backbone.

The routing protocol used on the T1 NSFNET backbone is a special version of the "Intermediate System to Intermediate System" (IS-IS) protocol, which is an OSI routing protocol. This special protocol is a "Shortest Path First" (SPF) or *link-state* protocol. Like RIP, it chooses the shortest path as the best path. But unlike RIP, it is well suited for very large networks with large numbers of routers.

Another link-state protocol, called "Open Shortest Path First" (OSPF), is being developed for more general use. OSPF is not yet available for most UNIX systems, but should be shortly. OSPF is suitable for very large networks and provides *equal cost multipath routing*. This mouthful means that OSPF can maintain several routes to the same destination. The multipath route feature may be very useful for specialized router systems, but the current versions of IP available in UNIX are not equipped to use multiple routes to the same destination. UNIX's implementation of IP assumes that the routing table only contains the best route to each location. Therefore, IP uses the first route that it finds in the table, and ignores duplicates. Changes to the UNIX implementation of IP are required before it can take full advantage of multipath routing.

Exterior Protocols

Exterior routing protocols are used to exchange routing information between autonomous systems. The routing information passed between autonomous systems is called *reachability information*. Reachability information is simply information about which networks can be reached through a specific autonomous system.

RFC 1163 defines Border Gateway Protocol, one of the exterior routing protocols, and it provides the following description of the routing function of an autonomous system:

> The classic definition of an Autonomous System is a set of routers under a single technical administration, using an interior gateway protocol and common metrics to route packets within the AS, and using an exterior gateway protocol to route packets to other ASs. ...
> ...the administration of an AS appears to other ASs to have a single coherent interior routing plan and presents a consistent picture of what networks are reachable through it. From the standpoint of exterior routing, an AS can be viewed as monolithic...

Moving routing information into and out of these monoliths is the function of exterior routing protocols. Don't confuse an *exterior routing protocol* with the Exterior Gateway Protocol (EGP). EGP is not a generic term; it is one of the exterior routing protocols. In fact, it is the most commonly used exterior protocol and the one we use in our examples.

A gateway running EGP announces that it can reach networks that are part of its autonomous system, and, except for a small subset of gateways that run as core gateways, an EGP gateway does not announce that it can reach networks outside its autonomous system. For example, *almond* is the gateway for our imaginary autonomous system *nuts-as. almond* can reach the entire Internet through its connection to Milnet, but only one network is contained in its autonomous system. Therefore, *almond* only announces one network (128.66.0.0) via EGP.

Unlike the interior protocols discussed above, EGP implementations do not attempt to choose the best route to a destination. EGP updates contain distance-vector information, but EGP does not evaluate this information. The distance-vector values from different autonomous systems are not directly comparable, because each AS may use different criteria for developing these values. Therefore, EGP leaves the choice of a "best" route to someone else.

When EGP was designed, the network relied upon a group of trusted core gateways to process and distribute the routes received from all of the autonomous systems. These core gateways were expected to have the information necessary to choose the best external routes. EGP reachability information was passed into the core gateways, where the information was combined and passed back out to the autonomous systems. Milnet still uses this system. In our sample network, *almond* sends an update packet into the Milnet core containing reachability information for one network (128.66.0.0), and *almond* receives back reachability information for thousands of other networks.

A routing structure that depends on a centrally controlled group of gateways does not scale well and is therefore inadequate for the rapidly growing Internet. As the number of autonomous systems and networks connected to the Internet grows, it becomes increasingly difficult for the core gateways to keep up with the expanding workload. This is one reason why the Internet is moving to a more distributed architecture that places a share of the burden of processing routes on each autonomous system. In a distributed architecture, the autonomous systems require routing protocols, interior and exterior, that can make intelligent routing choices.

A new exterior routing protocol, Border Gateway Protocol (BGP), is starting to replace EGP. BGP is currently used as an interior protocol in the T3 (45 mbps) NSFNET backbone and as the exterior protocol between the NSFNET backbone and some of the regional networks.

Like EGP, BGP exchanges reachability information between autonomous systems, but BGP provides more capabilities. BGP can provide more information about each route, and can use this information to select the "best" route. BGP calls this information *path attributes*. The attributes can include information used to select routes based on administrative preference. This type of routing—sometimes called *policy based routing*—uses non-technical reasons (for example, political, organizational, or security considerations) to make routing decisions. Thus BGP enhances the system's ability to choose between routes and to implement routing policies. These features are important for networks that do not rely on the core gateways to perform these tasks. BGP's capabilities are needed to implement a new network structure composed of equivalent autonomous systems that will be more expandable than the old hierarchical structure.

By far the most important thing to remember about exterior protocols is that most systems never run them. Exterior protocols are only required when an AS must exchange routing information with another AS. Most computers within an AS run an interior protocol such as RIP. Only those gateways that connect the AS to another AS need to run an exterior routing protocol. Unless you had to obtain an AS number (as described in Chapter 4) to connect your network to the outside world, you are not running your own AS. Your network is probably an independent part of an AS run by someone else. Regional networks, such as SURAnet, are good examples of autonomous systems made up of many independent networks.

Choosing a Routing Protocol

Although there are many routing protocols, choosing the one you'll use is usually easy. Most of the interior routing protocols mentioned above were developed to handle the special routing problems of very large networks. Some of the protocols have only been used by large national and regional networks. For local area networks, RIP is the most common choice. OSPF is not yet widely available; Hello was never widely used; and the weaknesses of RIP are only critical problems for very large networks.

If you must run an exterior routing protocol, the protocol that you use is often not a matter of choice. For two autonomous systems to exchange routing information, they must use the same exterior protocol. If the other AS is already in operation, its administrators have probably decided which protocol to use, and you will be expected to conform to their choice. Most often this choice is EGP, although the use of BGP is growing.

In the following sections we discuss two different ways that RIP and EGP are implemented on UNIX systems. First, we discuss software that implements each protocol individually, and then we examine the Gateway Routing Daemon (**gated**) software that combines the protocols into one software package.

There are reasons for covering both implementations. The software that implements the protocols individually is still widely used. Discussing the individual protocol implementations provides an opportunity to discuss each protocol in more detail. But the emphasis of this text is on **gated**. It provides the most recent implementation of each protocol, and it provides superior configuration control for the system administrator. I recommend using **gated** to run whichever routing protocol you choose.

Routing Information Protocol

As delivered with most UNIX systems, Routing Information Protocol (RIP), is run by the routing daemon, **routed** (pronounced "route" "*d*"). The routing daemon dynamically builds the routing table based on information received through RIP updates.

When **routed** is started, it issues a request for routing updates and then listens for responses to its request. When a system configured to supply RIP information hears the request, it responds with an update packet based on the information in its routing table. The update packet contains the destination addresses from the routing table, and the routing metric associated with each destination. Update packets are not just issued in response to requests, they are also issued periodically to keep routing information accurate.

When a RIP update is received, **routed** takes the information in the response and updates the routing table. If the routing update contains a route to a destination that does not exist in the local routing table, the new route is added. If the update describes a route whose destination is already in the local table, the new route is only used if it has a lower cost. The cost of a route is determined by adding the cost of reaching the gateway that sent the update to the metric contained in the RIP update packet. If the total metric is less than the metric of the current route, the new route is used.

RIP also deletes routes from the routing table. There are two ways that this is done. First, if the gateway to a destination says the cost of the route is greater than 15, the route is deleted. Second, RIP assumes that a gateway that doesn't send updates is dead. All routes through a gateway are deleted if no updates are received from that gateway for a specified time period. In general, routing updates are issued every 30 seconds. In many implementations, if a gateway does not issue routing updates for 180 seconds, all routes through that gateway are deleted from the routing table.

Running RIP with routed

To run RIP using the routing daemon (**routed**)* enter the following command:

```
# routed
```

The **routed** statement is generally used without any command-line arguments, but you may want to use the **–q** option. The **–q** option prevents **routed** from advertising routes. It just listens to the routes advertised by other systems. If your computer is not a gateway, you should probably use the **–q** option.

As we saw in the section on static routing, the **routed** statement is generally included in a startup file.† If the statement that starts **routed** is in your startup file, no other action is required to run RIP. Boot your system and RIP is running. Otherwise, add the following code to your startup:

```
#  Use /etc/routed on most systems, /usr/etc/in.routed on Sun systems
#
        if [ -f /etc/routed ]; then
                routed;        echo -n ' routed' > /dev/console
        fi
```

Creating Routes with /etc/gateways

routed can build a functioning routing table just using the RIP updates received from the RIP suppliers. However, it is sometimes necessary to supplement this information with, for example, an initial default route or information about a gateway that does not announce its routes. The */etc/gateways* file stores this additional routing information. **routed** reads */etc/gateways* at startup and adds its information to the routing table.

The most common use of the */etc/gateways* file is to define an active default route, so we'll use that as an example. This one example is sufficient because all entries in the */etc/gateways* file have the same basic format. On *peanut*, the following entry specifies *almond* as the default gateway:

```
net 0.0.0.0 gateway 128.66.12.1 metric 1 active
```

The entry starts with the keyword **net**. Every */etc/gateways* entry starts with the keyword **net** or the keyword **host** to indicate whether the address that follows is a network address or a host address. The destination address

---

*On Sun systems the routing daemon is */usr/etc/in.routed*; on most other systems it is */etc/routed*.
†This is the same code we commented out when we put static routing in the startup file.

0.0.0.0 is the address used for the default route. In the **route** command we used the keyword **default** to indicate this route, but in */etc/gateways* the default route is indicated by network address 0.0.0.0.

Next is the keyword **gateway** followed by the gateway's IP address. In this case it is the address of *almond* (128.66.12.1).

Then comes the keyword **metric** followed by a numeric metric value. The metric was almost meaningless when used with static routing. Now that we are running RIP, the metric is actually used to make routing decisions. The RIP metric represents the number of gateways through which data must pass to reach the final destination. But as we saw with **ifconfig**, the metric is really an arbitrary value used by the administrator to prefer one route over another. (The system administrator is free to assign any metric value.) However, it is only useful to vary the metric if you have more than one route to the same destination. With only one gateway to the Internet, the correct metric to use for *almond* is 1.

All */etc/gateways* entries end with either the keyword **passive** or the keyword **active**. Passive means the gateway listed in the entry is not required to provide RIP updates. Use passive to prevent RIP from deleting the route if no updates are received from the gateway. A passive route is placed in the routing table and kept there as long as the system is up. In effect, it becomes a permanent static route.

The keyword **active**, on the other hand, creates a route that can be updated by RIP. An active gateway is expected to supply routing information and will be removed from the routing table if, over a period of time, it does not provide routing updates. Active routes are used to "prime the pump" during the RIP startup phase, with the expectation that the routes will be updated by RIP when the protocol is up and running.

Our sample entry ends with the keyword **active**, which means that this default route will be deleted if no routing updates are received from *almond*. Default routes are convenient; this is especially true when you use static routing. But when you use dynamic routing, default routes should be used with caution, especially if you have multiple gateways that can reach the same destination. A passive default route prevents the routing protocol from dynamically updating the route to reflect changing network conditions. Use an active default route that can be updated by the routing protocol.

Exterior Gateway Protocol

To understand the commands used to configure Exterior Gateway Protocol (EGP), it is helpful to understand EGP terminology and a little bit about how it works. We know that EGP is a protocol for exchanging routing information with gateways in other autonomous systems. But before it sends routing information to a remote gateway, the system must first exchange EGP *Hello* and *I-Heard-You* (I-H-U) messages with that gateway. Hello and I-H-U messages are special EGP packets used to establish a dialog between two gateways that speak EGP. Computers communicating via EGP are called *EGP neighbors*, and the exchange of Hello and I-H-U messages is called *acquiring a neighbor.*

Once a neighbor is acquired, the system requests routing information from the neighbor. This request for information is called a *poll.* The neighbor responds by sending a packet of reachability information called an *update.* If the system receives a poll from its EGP neighbor, it responds with its own update packet.

When the system receives an update from its neighbor, it includes the routes from the update into its local routing table. But if the neighbor fails to respond to three consecutive polls, the system assumes that the neighbor is down and removes the neighbor's routes from its table.

Configuring the EGP User Process

EGP is run either as a separate process using the EGP User Process (**egpup**) or as part of the Gateway Routing Daemon (**gated**). Use **gated** to run EGP; don't use **egpup**. We'll look at how EGP is run using **egpup** only because it is still used at some sites, and someday you may be called upon to advise someone who is using it.

When **egpup** is started, it reads a configuration file, usually called */etc/egp.init.*[*] The following configuration commands can appear in the */etc/egp.init* file:

autonomoussystem *asn*

> This statement specifies the autonomous system number; *asn* should be the official number assigned to the system. Refer to Chapter 4 for information on obtaining an official AS number.

---

*Some systems use the filename */etc/egp.conf.*

egpneighbor *neighbor*

> This statement specifies a remote gateway used as an EGP neighbor. Most configuration files contain multiple **egpneighbor** statements to define a few possible neighbors. The value *neighbor* is the host name or IP address of the remote gateway with which you'll exchange routing information. Since EGP passes routing information between autonomous systems, the addresses of possible EGP neighbors must be obtained from the administration of the other AS. For example, in Milnet the possible EGP neighbors are defined by the Defense Information Systems Agency (DISA).

egpmaxacquire *number*

> This statement specifies the maximum number of EGP neighbors to acquire. EGP is capable of acquiring more than one neighbor at a time. Acquiring more than one neighbor increases the overhead of the protocol, but it also makes the protocol more robust if one neighbor does not reliably respond to polls.

egpnetsreachable *net1 net2 net3 ...*

> This statement specifies the networks you advertise as reachable to your EGP neighbors. If this statement is used, only the networks included on this statement are advertised. If the statement is not used, all networks directly connected to the system are advertised as reachable.

net *destination* **gateway** *address* **metric** *number*

> This statement directs EGP to install a static route. This statement is similar to the **net** statement in the */etc/gateways* file. However, EGP's **net** statement cannot specify an active or passive route. A route installed in this way by EGP is always passive and will not be updated. As we have discussed, it is not good to have a passive default route.

defaultgateway *address*

> This statement directs EGP to install an active default route. This default route is installed at startup but is removed when an EGP neighbor is acquired. This default route is re-installed when EGP makes an orderly shutdown.

A sample *egp.init* file is shown below:

```
#       configure EGP
#
autonomoussystem 249
egpmaxacquire   1
egpneighbor            26.1.0.49
```

```
egpneighbor          26.21.0.104
egpnetsreachable     128.66.0.0
#
```

In this sample configuration the autonomous system number is 249. The system only acquires one EGP neighbor and only attempts to acquire gateway 26.1.0.49 or 26.21.0.104. The only network announced as reachable is 128.66.0.0. This configuration defines no static or default routes.

The above configuration would work for *almond*, the *nuts-net* gateway, but we're not going to use *egpup* on *almond*. We'll use **gated** to configure our imaginary gateway.

Gateway Routing Daemon

gated is a single package that combines RIP, Hello, BGP, and EGP. The routing protocols in **gated** are compatible with the same protocols provided in other implementations. RIP in **gated** is the same as RIP in **routed**, and **gated**'s EGP is functionally equivalent to EGP in **egpup**. Despite these similarities, there are several reasons why you should use **gated**:

- On systems that run more than one routing protocol, **gated** combines the routing information learned from the protocols, and selects the "best" routes.

- Routes learned through an interior routing protocol can be announced via an exterior routing protocol. This allows the reachability information announced externally to adjust dynamically to changing interior routes.

- **gated** simplifies the routing configuration. All protocols are configured from a single file (*/etc/gated.conf*) using a single consistent syntax for the configuration commands.

- **gated** is constantly being upgraded. So even if you aren't running multiple protocols, using **gated** is a good way to ensure that you're running the most up-to-date software.

gated's Preference Value

There are two sides to every routing protocol implementation. One side, the external side, exchanges routing information with remote systems. The other side, the internal side, uses the information received from the remote systems to update the routing table. For example, when EGP exchanges Hello and I-H-U message to acquire a neighbor, it is an external protocol function. When EGP adds a route to the routing table, it is an internal function.

The external protocol functions implemented in **gated** are the same as those in other implementations of the protocols. However, the internal side of **gated** is unique. Internally, **gated** processes routing information from different routing protocols, each of which has its own metric for determining the best route, and combines that information to update the routing table. Before **gated** was written, **routed** and **egpup** would each write routes into the routing table without knowledge of each other's action. The route found in the table was the last one written, not necessarily the best route.

Table 7-1 shows the routing metrics used by the four protocols currently implemented in **gated**. Each metric represents something that is used to help the system choose the best route. This is either a hop count, the delay on the route, or an arbitrary value set by the administrator. For all of these metrics a low value is better than a high value. The table shows the range of possible values for each metric, as well as the value used by each protocol to indicate an unreachable destination.

Table 7.1: Routing Protocol Metrics

Protocol	Metric Represents	Range	Unreachable
RIP	distance (hop-count)	0-15	16
Hello	delay in milliseconds	0-29999	30000
BGP	unspecified	0-65534	65535
EGP	distance (unused)	0-254	255

gated uses these metrics when it advertises routes via these protocols. For example, when **gated** announces a route via RIP, it uses a valid RIP metric; when announcing a route via Hello, it uses a valid Hello metric. But when **gated** receives a route from one of these protocols, it needs more than that protocol's metric to select the best route.

With multiple routing protocols and multiple network interfaces, it is possible for a system to receive routes to the same destination from different protocols. **gated** compares these routes and attempts to select the best one. However, because the metrics used by different protocols are not directly comparable, **gated** uses its own value to prefer routes from one protocol or interface over another. This value is called *preference*.

Preference is used only by **gated** to help it combine routing information from several different sources into a single routing table. Table 7-2 lists the sources from which **gated** receives routes, and the default preference given to each source. Preference values range from 0 to 255 with the lowest number indicating the most preferred route. From this table you can see that **gated** prefers a route learned from RIP over the same route learned from EGP.

Table 7.2: Default Preference Values

Route Type	Default Preference
direct route	0
ICMP redirect	20
static route	50
Hello protocol	90
RIP	100
BGP	150
EGP	200

Preference can be set in the **gated** configuration file in several different configuration statements. It can be set to prefer routes from one network interface over another, from one protocol over another, or from one remote gateway over another. Preference values are not transmitted or modified by the protocols. Preference is only used in the configuration file. In the next section we'll look at the gated configuration file (*/etc/gated.conf*) and the configuration commands it contains.

Configuring gated

gated has recently undergone major changes. The last major release adopted a new configuration syntax that is consistent for every protocol. The previous syntax, used by **gated** 1.9.1.7, was adapted from the configuration commands of the individual protocols; the lines in a **gated** 1.9.1.7 configuration file that control RIP look like entries in an */etc/gateways* file, and the lines that control EGP look like lines from an */etc/egp.init* file. The new **gated** configuration language is quite different.

The new language is more structured. It resembles C code more than it does the configuration commands in */etc/egp.init* or */etc/gateways.* All statements end with a semicolon, and associated statements are grouped together by curly braces. This structure makes it simple to see what parts of the configuration are associated with each other, which is important when multiple protocols are configured in the same file. In addition to structure in the language, the */etc/gated.conf* file also has a structure.

The different configuration statements, and the order in which these statements must appear, divide *gated.conf* into four sections: *definition statements, protocol statements, static statements*, and *control statements.* Entering a statement out of order causes an error when parsing the file.

Two other types of statements do not fall into any of these categories. They are *directive statements* and *trace statements.* These can occur anywhere in the *gated.conf* file and do not directly relate to the configuration of any protocol. These statements provide instructions to the parser, and instructions to control tracing from within the configuration file.

All of the new **gated** configuration commands are summarized in Table 7-3. The table lists each command by name, identifies the statement type, and provides a very short synopsis of each command's function. The entire command language is covered in detail in Appendix C.

Table 7.3: gated Configuration Statements

Statement	Type	Function
%directory	directive	sets the directory for include files
%include	directive	includes a file into *gated.conf*
tracefile	trace	names the file for trace output
traceoptions	trace	specifies which events are traced
options	definition	defines gated options
autonomoussystem	definition	defines the AS number
interface	definition	defines interface options
martians	definition	defines invalid destination addresses
snmp	protocol	enables reporting to SNMP
rip	protocol	enables RIP
hello	protocol	enables Hello protocol
redirect	protocol	removes routes installed by ICMP
egp	protocol	enables EGP
bgp	protocol	enables BGP

Table 7.3: gated Configuration Statements (continued)

Statement	Type	Function
static	static	defines static routes
accept	control	defines which routes are accepted
propagate	control	defines which routes are advertised

Just from the brief description above, you can see that the **gated** configuration language has many commands. The language provides configuration control for several different protocols and additional commands to configure the added features of **gated** itself. All of this can be confusing.

To avoid confusion don't try to understand the details of everything offered by **gated**. Your routing environment is probably a simple one. Many of the features available in **gated** are for handling very complex routing situations. Only those things that relate to your actual configuration need to be included in your configuration file. Don't expect all, or even most, of the commands to relate to your routing configuration. As you read this section, you can skip the things you don't need. For example, if you don't use the EGP protocol, don't study the egp statement. With this in mind, let's look at some sample configurations.

Sample gated.conf Configurations

The details in Appendix C may make **gated** configuration appear more complex than it is. The richness of the **gated** command language, its support for multiple protocols, and the fact that it often provides a few ways to do the same thing, can be confusing. But some examples will show that the language is simple to use.

The basis for the sample configurations is our imaginary network. We'll configure the host *peanut* to run RIP, the gateway's *filbert* and *pecan* to run RIP, and the gateway *almond* to run RIP and EGP.

Figure 7-2 shows part of our imaginary network. Combined with Figure 7-1, it gives a picture of how data is routed around our network. Subnet 1 (128.66.1.0) acts as a backbone network that interconnects the other subnets. This "backbone" structure is a very common way to implement a subnetted local area network. Most of the subnets shown in the figure have only one gateway through which they pass all data bound for remote networks, as well as for other subnets. Subnet 12 is the exception; it has two gateways. *pecan* provides subnet 12 with access to the other subnets, and *almond* provides it with access to the Internet.

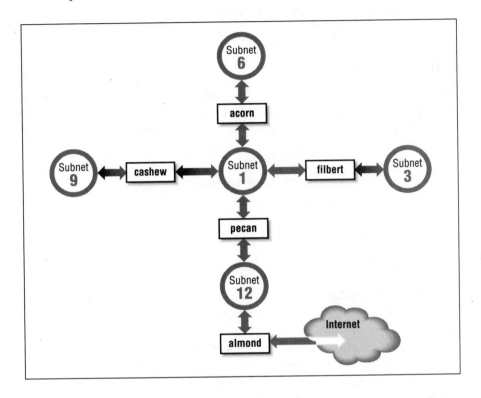

Figure 7.2: nuts-net Routing Configuration

The gateways *filbert, acorn,* and *cashew* all have the same type of configuration. To simplify things we'll look only at *filbert.* To hosts on subnet 3, *filbert* will advertise itself as the default gateway, because it is the only gateway that subnet 3 can access. On subnet 1, *filbert* will only advertise itself as the gateway to subnet 3.

pecan provides subnet 1 with access to subnet 12. By passing data through subnet 12, *pecan* also provides subnet 1 with access to the Internet. Because it provides access to the Internet, *pecan* will announce itself as the default gateway to the other systems on subnet 1. To the systems on subnet 12, *pecan* will only announce individual routes to the other subnets.

To systems on subnet 12, *almond* will announce itself as the default gateway, and it will announce to the Internet that it is the route to 128.66.0.0.

almond will receive subnet routes via RIP from *pecan*, and external routing information via EGP from its Milnet neighbors.

Let's look at each of these configurations.

A Host Configuration

The host routing configuration is very simple, containing only two configuration statements. This basic configuration should work for any system that runs RIP, and that has only one network interface. Here it is for *peanut*:

```
#
#        don't time-out the network interface
#
interface 128.66.12.2 passive ;
#
#        enable rip
#
rip yes ;
#
```

The keyword **passive** in the interface command is used here, just as we have seen it used before, to create a permanent static route that will not be removed from the routing table. In this case, the permanent route is through the directly attached network interface. Normally when **gated** thinks an interface is down, it removes it from the routing table to prevent a gateway from announcing that it can route data through a non-operational interface. Because our host has only one network interface, we don't want **gated** to remove that interface from the routing table, even if it does think the interface is down. That's why this configuration includes the statement, **interface 128.66.12.2 passive**.

Next, this configuration file enables RIP with a **rip yes** statement. This is not required because it is the default, but placing the explicit statement in the *gated.conf* file serves to document the configuration.

Interior Gateway Configurations

Gateway configurations are more complicated than the simple host configuration shown above. This is because gateways always have multiple interfaces and occasionally have multiple routing protocols. Our first sample configuration is for *filbert*, which is the gateway between subnet 3 and the central backbone. It uses RIP on both interfaces. Here's *filbert's* configuration:

```
#
#         enable rip
#
rip yes ;
#
#         using rip, announce subnet 3 via 128.66.1.2
#
propagate proto rip interface 128.66.1.2
{
      proto direct
      {
              announce 128.66.3.0 metric 0 ;
      } ;
} ;
#
#         using rip, announce via interface 128.66.3.1
#            all routes learned from 128.66.1.2
#
propagate proto rip interface 128.66.3.1
{
      proto rip interface 128.66.1.2
      {
              announce all ;
      } ;
} ;
```

This configuration file contains two propagate statements. The first one tells **gated** to announce, via the RIP protocol and interface 128.66.1.2, a direct route to subnet 128.66.3.0. That is, *filbert* tells 128.66.1.0 (the "backbone"), and hence the rest of *nuts-net*, that it is the route to 128.66.3.0 (its subnet). The second propagate statement announces to subnet 3, all routes learned from the backbone. This includes the subnet routes and the default route to the rest of the world.

Let's examine the first propagate statement more closely.* The first part of the propagate statement tells **gated** how to announce the routes. **proto rip** tells **gated** to use the RIP protocol, and **interface 128.66.1.2** tells **gated** to announce the routes out of that interface. The remainder of the statement tells **gated** what routes to announce. **proto direct** tells gated to announce the routes of all directly connected networks and **announce 128.66.3.0** limits the announcement to only the route to network 128.66.3.0. The metric used on the announce statement is a valid metric for the protocol used to advertise the route, which in this case is RIP.

---

*The propagate command is covered in detail in Appendix C.

This propagate statement was not required. By default **gated** announces every network that is directly connected to the gateway. The statement was explicitly entered in the configuration for two reasons. First, the statement documents what we think we're doing. It's nice to be able to go back to the configuration file and have it tell you what the configuration is. Second, the explicit statement avoids relying on defaults which may change in future releases.

In the second propagate statement, the clause **proto rip interface 128.66.1.2** tells **gated** to announce every route learned from RIP updates received via interface 128.66.1.2. This clause is so similar to the preceding clause, **proto rip interface 128.66.3.1**, that it can be confusing. Just remember that the first proto clause and the first interface clause in the propagate statement define the protocol and interface through which routes are *advertised*. Subsequent proto and interface clauses define the protocols and interfaces from which routes are *learned*.

This configuration can be used for any gateway that uses only RIP and that connects a single subnet to a larger network. Only the addresses need to be modified to use this exact configuration on the other sample gateways, *acorn* and *cashew*.

pecan's configuration is very similar to *filbert's*. Again the gateway only runs RIP, and again two propagate statements are used. However, *pecan* connects the backbone to subnet 128.66.12.0, which in turn provides the gateway to the outside world, so there are differences. The other gateways announced all routes to their subnets and announced only one subnet to the backbone. *pecan* announces the default route to the backbone, and it announces all of the individual subnet routes to subnet 128.66.12.0. In other words, *pecan* tells the other subnets that it can reach the rest of the world, and it tells subnet 12 the individual routes to the other subnets. Here's *pecan's* configuration:

```
#
#       enable rip
#
rip yes ;
#
#       using rip, announce all subnets via 128.66.12.3
#
propagate proto rip interface 128.66.12.3 metric 3
{
        proto rip interface 128.66.1.5
        {
                announce all ;
        } ;
```

```
} ;
#
#       using rip, announce default via 128.66.1.5
#
propagate proto rip interface 128.66.1.5
{
        proto rip interface 128.66.12.3
        {
                announce 0.0.0.0 ;
        } ;
} ;
```

The first propagate statement in this configuration explicitly directs **gated** to announce all of the routes it learns from interface 128.66.1.5, out though interface 128.66.12.3. The explicit **announce all** was not required because it is the default, but it makes the configuration file more understandable.

The format of this propagate statement varies slightly from the propagate statements we've seen before. The metric value is specified in the first part of the statement. In the other examples, the metric was defined in the announce clause. When used in the announce clause, the metric only applies to the specific route defined by the announce clause. When used near the beginning of the propagate statement, the metric value applies to every route announced via this protocol and interface. In our example, **metric 3** is used for every route announced over **interface 128.66.12.3** via **proto rip** (RIP).

Exterior Gateway Configuration

The configuration for *almond* is the most complex. This is because *almond* runs both RIP and EGP. *almond's* configuration is:

```
#       generate a default route
#
options gendefault ;
#
#       define the autonomous system number for EGP
#
autonomoussystem 249 ;
#
#       enable RIP
#
rip yes   ;
#
#       enable EGP with
#               hello interval 2 1/2 minutes, poll interval 10 minutes
#               neighbors 26.6.0.103 (ISI) and 26.20.0.72 (BBN)
#
egp yes
{
```

```
            packetsize 12288 ;
            group minhello 2:30 minpoll 10:00
            {
                    neighbor 26.6.0.103 ;
                    neighbor 26.20.0.72 ;
            } ;
    } ;
    #
    #        announce 128.66 to Milnet (AS 164)
    #
    propagate proto egp as 164 {
                    proto direct {
                            announce 128.66.0.0 metric 0 ;
                    } ;
    } ;
    #
    #        announce default via RIP with a cost of 3
    #
    propagate proto rip interface 128.66.12.1 {
                    proto default {
                            announce 0.0.0.0 metric 3 ;
                    } ;
    } ;
```

The first statement in this configuration, **options gendefault**, tells **gated** to generate a default route when the system acquires an EGP neighbor. The default route is used later in a propagate statement to advertise the default route to subnet 128.66.12.0.

This configuration enables both protocols, and sets certain protocol-specific parameters. EGP needs to know the AS number, which is 249 for *nuts-net*. The AS number is defined early in the configuration because **autonomoussystem** is a definition statement, and therefore must occur before the first protocol statement. Refer back to Table 7-3 for the various statement types.

EGP is enabled by the **egp yes** statement, which also defines a few additional EGP parameters:

- The **packetsize 12288** clause tells EGP to accept update packets up to 12288 bytes long. This is done because Milnet EGP update packets are very large.

- The **group** clause sets parameters for all of the EGP neighbors in the group. The EGP neighbors are indicated by the **neighbor** clauses.

- Because the Milnet core gateways are very busy, **minhello 2:30** is used to set the interval between the transmission of HELLO packets to two and a half minutes. For the same reason, **minpoll 10:00** is used to set the interval between polls to 10 minutes.

The first propagate statement directs **gated** to use EGP to advertise *nuts-net* (128.66.0.0) to the Internet. Notice that this is not a subnet address. It is the address of the entire class B network. It's also worth noting that the AS number specified in this statement, **as 164**, is not the AS number of *nuts-net*. 164 is the AS number of Milnet.* The first line of the propagate statement defines how routing information is being distributed. This information is being distributed via EGP to Milnet.

The second propagate statement is used to announce the default route to subnet 129.66.12.0 with a metric of 3. This metric makes it a very desirable route, but it allows enough flexibility for a host to define another default route if needed for some special purpose.

These few examples show that *gated.conf* files are usually very small, and frequently are quite simple to read. Use **gated** if you need to run a routing protocol on your computer. It allows you to use the same software and the same configuration language on all of your hosts, interior gateways, and exterior gateways.

The gated Command

The **gated** software is provided with some UNIX systems, but if possible you should obtain the latest version via anonymous **ftp** from *gated.cornell.edu*. **gated** is stored there in the */pub/gated* directory in a compressed **tar** file that contains the C source code and Makefile necessary to compile the software.

Once compiled, it is run using the **gated** command. There are many options on the **gated** command line, all of which are explained in detail in Appendix C. Some options trace the activity of the routing protocols; others are used to debug the **gated** configuration file. The most commonly used **gated** options are:

–t   Tells **gated** to log internal errors, external errors, and routing table changes to a trace file. If –t is used, the name of the trace file must be specified on the **gated** command line. The filename can be any name you wish. The events traced with this option are well chosen to provide the debugging information needed for most problems.

---

*Registered AS numbers are printed in the *Assigned Numbers* RFC.

−c   Tells **gated** to read the configuration file and check for syntax errors. When **gated** finishes reading the file, it terminates. The **−c** option turns on tracing; so specify a trace file, or the trace data will be displayed on your terminal. **gated** also produces a snapshot of its current state after it reads the configuration file and it writes the snapshot to */usr/tmp/gated_dump*. You don't need to be superuser or to terminate the active **gated** process to run **gated** when the **−c** option is used.

−n   Tells **gated** not to update the kernel routing table. This tests the routing configuration with real routing data without interfering with system operation.

−f *config_file* Tells **gated** to read the configuration from the file defined by *config_file* instead of from the default configuration file, */etc/gated.conf*. *config_file* can be any filename you choose. Used in conjunction with the **−c** option, this checks a new configuration without interfering with the currently running **gated** configuration.

Assume that a configuration file called *test.conf* has already been created. It is tested using **−c** on the command line, and the trace of the test is written to a file called *trace.test*.

```
% gated -c -f test.conf trace.test
```

The trace file (*trace.test*) can then be examined for errors and other information. When you're confident that the configuration is correct, become superuser and move your new configuration (*test.conf*) to */etc/gated.conf*.

Running gated at Startup

As with any routing software, **gated** should be included in your startup file. If you already have code in your startup file that runs **routed**, replace it with code to run **gated**. **gated** and **routed** should not be running at the same time.

Our imaginary gateway, *almond*, is a BSD system with code in the */etc/rc.local* file that starts **routed**. (This code was shown in the section on static routing.) We comment out those lines, and add these lines:

```
if [ -f /etc/gated -a -f /etc/gated.conf ]; then
     gated;      echo -n 'gated' > /dev/console
  fi
```

This code assumes that **gated** is installed in */etc* and that the configuration file is named */etc/gated.conf.* The code checks that **/etc/gated** is present, and that the configuration file */etc/gated.conf* exists. If both files are found, **gated** is started.

Some systems, SCO TCP/IP for example, come with the code to start **gated** included in the startup file. The */etc/tcp* file on an SCO system has code for both **routed** and **gated**. The code that starts **routed** checks for the *gated.conf* file. If it finds the file, **routed** is not started and **gated** is. You don't need to modify the startup file to run **gated**; just create a *gated.conf* file. */etc/tcp* will make sure the correct routing software is started.

The code checks for a configuration file because **gated** usually runs with one. If **gated** is started without a configuration file, it checks the routing table for a default route, and if it doesn't find one, it starts RIP; otherwise it just uses the default route. Create an */etc/gated.conf* file even if you only want to run RIP. The configuration file documents your routing configuration and protects you if the default configuration of **gated** changes in the future.

In this chapter:
• *BIND: UNIX Name
  Service*
• *Configuring the
  Resolver*
• *Configuring named*
• *Using nslookup*

8

Configuring DNS
Name Service

Congratulations! We have installed TCP/IP in the kernel, configured the network interface, and configured routing. At this point, we have completed all of the configuration tasks required to run TCP/IP on a UNIX system. While none of the remaining tasks are *required* for TCP/IP software to operate, they are necessary for making the network more friendly and useful. Perhaps the most important of these remaining tasks is configuring name service.

Strictly speaking, name service is not necessary for computers to communicate. It is, as the name implies, a service—specifically a service intended to make the network more user friendly. Computers are perfectly happy with IP addresses, but people prefer names. The importance of name service is indicated by the amount of coverage it has in this book. Chapter 3 discusses *why* name service is needed; this chapter covers *how* it is configured, and Appendix D covers the *details* of the name server configuration commands. This chapter provides sufficient information to show you how to configure BIND software to run on your system. But if you want to know more about why something is done, don't hesitate to refer to Appendix D and Chapter 3.

BIND: UNIX Name Service

In UNIX, DNS is implemented by the *Berkeley Internet Name Domain* (BIND) software. BIND is a client/server software system. The client side of BIND is called the *resolver.* It generates the queries for domain name information that are sent to the server. The DNS server software answers the resolvers' queries. The server side of BIND is a daemon called **named** (pronounced "name" "d").

This chapter covers three basic BIND configuration tasks:

- configuring the BIND resolver
- configuring the BIND name server (**named**)
- constructing the name server database files, called the *zone files*

The term *zone* is often used interchangeably with the word domain, but here we make a distinction between these terms. The term *zone* typically refers to the domain database file, while the term domain is used in more general contexts. In this book, a domain is part of the domain hierarchy identified by a domain name. A zone is a collection of domain information contained in a domain database file. The file that contains the domain information is called a zone file.

RFC 1033, the *Domain Administrators Operations Guide*, defines the standard records used to construct zone files. We'll use these records to construct the zone files used in this chapter. But how, or even if, you need to construct zone files on your system is controlled by the type of BIND configuration you decide to use.

BIND Configurations

BIND can be configured to run in several different ways. The common BIND configurations are resolver-only systems, caching-only servers, primary servers, and secondary servers.

The resolver is the code that asks name servers for domain information. On UNIX systems, it is implemented as a library, rather than a separate client program. Some systems, called resolver-only systems, only use the resolver; they don't run a name server. Resolver-only systems are very easy to configure: at most you need to set up the */etc/resolv.conf* file. However, UNIX resolver-only configurations are uncommon. They are typically used when some technical limitation prevents the system from running a name server locally.

The three other BIND configuration options are all for the **named** server software:

caching-only   A caching-only server runs the name server software, but keeps no name server database files. It learns the answer to every name server query from some remote server. Once it learns an answer, the server caches the answer and uses it to answer future queries for the same information. All name servers use cached information in this manner, but a caching-only server depends on this technique for all of its name server information. It is not considered an authoritative (or master) server,* because all of the information it provides is secondhand.

Only a cache file is required for a caching-only configuration. But the most common configuration also includes a loopback file. This is probably the most common name server configuration, and next to the resolver-only configuration, it is the easiest to configure.

primary   The primary name server is the authoritative source for all information about a specific domain. It loads the domain information from a locally maintained disk file that is built by the domain administrator. This file (the zone file) contains the most accurate information about a piece of the domain hierarchy over which this server has authority. The primary server is a master server, because it can answer any query about its domain with full authority.

Configuring a primary server requires a complete set of configuration files: zone files for the regular domain (*named.hosts*) and the reverse domain (*named.rev*), the boot file (*named.boot*), the cache file (*named.ca*), and the loopback file (*named.local*). No other configuration requires this complete set of files.

secondary   A secondary server transfers a complete set of domain information from the primary server. The zone file is transferred from the primary server and stored on the secondary server as a local disk file. This transfer is aptly called a *zone file transfer*. A secondary server keeps a complete copy of all domain information, and can answer

---

*The terms *master server* and *authoritative server* are used interchangeably.

queries about that domain with authority. Therefore, a secondary server is also considered a master server.

Configuring a secondary server does not require creating local zone files, because the zone files are downloaded from the primary server. However, the other files (a boot file, cache file, and loopback file) are required.

A server may be any one of these configurations or, as is often the case, it may combine elements of more than one type of configuration. However, all systems run the resolver, so let's begin by examining the configuration of the client side of the DNS software.

Configuring the Resolver

There are two ways to handle the resolver configuration. You either use the default configuration, or create a custom configuration using the *resolv.conf* file. The default configuration involves slightly less overhead because the resolver does not have to read a configuration file. The *resolv.conf* file provides slightly more configuration control because the configuration is directly controlled by commands you place in the file. We'll examine both configuration techniques.

The resolver is not a separate and distinct process; it is a library of routines called by network processes. If the *resolv.conf* file exists, it is read each time a process using the resolver starts. Because of this overhead, the file is usually not created unless it is required, and it is not required by systems that run **named**. Any system that runs **named**, the server side of DNS, can probably use the default resolver configuration.

The Default Resolver Configuration

The default configuration:

- Uses the local host as the default name server.
- Derives the default domain name from the string returned by the **host-name** command. It does this by removing the part of the string before the first dot, and using the remainder of the string as the domain name.

For the default configuration to work, the local host must run **named** and the host name must be properly defined. We discuss running **named** in a later section. The following examples explain the **hostname** command and illustrate how the resolver uses it.

hostname is a UNIX command used to check or set the host name of the local host. Only the superuser can set the host name, as in this example:

```
# hostname peanut.nuts.com
```

However, any user can check the host name by entering the **hostname** command without any other arguments:

```
% hostname
peanut.nuts.com
```

This example shows that the **hostname** command on *peanut* returns the string *peanut.nuts.com*. If no *resolv.conf* file is found, the resolver drops the first component of this host name (*peanut*) and uses the remainder (*nuts.com*) as the default domain name. This works properly only if a "fully qualified domain name" (FQDN) is used as the host name. If **hostname** simply returned the name *peanut*, a *resolv.conf* file containing a valid default domain name entry would be required.

Some systems that use the Network Information System (NIS) do this differently. They use the **hostname** command to set and check the host name, as on any UNIX system. However, they also have a **domainname** command that sets the name of the NIS domain.* These systems use the value returned by the **domainname** command as the default DNS domain when no *resolv.conf* file is found. Because of this, Sun recommends that the NIS and the DNS domains use the same name.

The Resolver Configuration File

If the local system does not run *named*, or if the domain name can't be derived from the hostname, you must use the *resolv.conf* file. The configuration file has some advantages over the default configuration. It defines the system's configuration clearly, and it allows you to name backup servers that are used if the default server doesn't respond. Therefore, despite the additional overhead, there are some situations in which a . *resolv.conf* file is desirable.

/etc/resolv.conf is a simple, human-readable file. There are system-specific variations in the commands used in the *resolv.conf*, but two entries are universally supported:

nameserver *address*

> The **nameserver** entries identify, by IP address, the servers that the resolver is to query for domain information. The name

---

Sun OS 4.1.1 uses the **domainname** command.

servers are queried in the order that they appear in the file. If no response is received from a server, the next server in the list is tried until the maximum number of servers are tried.* If no **nameserver** entries are contained in the *resolv.conf* file or no *resolv.conf* file exists, all name server queries are sent to the local host. However, if there is a *resolv.conf* file and it contains **nameserver** entries, the local host is *not* queried unless one entry points to the local host. On a host configured to run resolver-only, the *resolv.conf* file contains **nameserver** entries but no entry points to the local host.

domain *name*

The **domain** entry defines the default domain name. The resolver appends the default domain name to any host name that does not contain a dot.† It then uses the expanded host name in the query it sends to the name server. For example, if the host name *almond* (which does not contain a dot) is received by the resolver, the default domain name is appended to *almond* to construct the query. If the value for *name* in the **domain** entry is *nuts.com*, the resolver in our example would query for *almond.nuts.com*.

The most common *resolv.conf* configuration defines the default domain name, the local host as the first name server, and two backup name servers. An example of this configuration is shown below:

```
# Domain name resolver configuration file
#
domain nuts.com
# try yourself first
nameserver 127.0.0.1
# try almond next
nameserver 128.66.12.1
# finally try filbert
nameserver 128.66.1.2
```

This example is based on our imaginary network, so the default domain name is *nuts.com*. Other than providing for backup servers, this system could have used the default resolver configuration.

---

*Three is the maximum number of servers tried by most BIND implementations.

†This is the most common way that default domain names are used, but it is not the only way. See the section "Domain Names" in Chapter 3 for more details.

A Resolver-only Configuration

The resolver-only configuration is very simple. A sample *resolv.conf* file for a resolver-only system is shown below:

```
# Domain name resolver configuration file
#
domain nuts.com
# try almond
nameserver 128.66.12.1
# next try filbert
nameserver 128.66.1.2
```

This configuration tells the resolver to pass all queries to *almond*; if that fails, try *filbert*. Queries are never resolved locally. This simple *resolv.conf* file is all that is required for a resolver-only configuration.

Configuring named

While the resolver configuration requires, at most, one configuration file, several files are used to configure **named**. As noted earlier, the complete set of **named** configuration files are:*

named.boot	Sets general **named** parameters and points to the sources of domain database information used by this server. These sources can be local disk files or remote servers.
named.ca	Points to the root domain servers.
named.local	Used to locally resolve the loopback address.
named.hosts	The zone file that maps host names to IP addresses.
named.rev	The zone file for the reverse domain that maps IP addresses to host names.

In the following sections we'll look at how each of these files is used to configure **named**.

The named.boot File

The *named.boot* file points **named** to sources of DNS information. Some of these sources are local files; others are remote servers. You only need to create the files referenced in the primary and cache statements. We'll look at an example of each type of file you may need to create.

---

*The filenames shown here are generic names. You can choose any name you wish as long as you identify the file in the *named.boot* file.

Table 8-1 summarizes the configuration statements used in the *named.boot* file. It provides just enough information to help you understand the examples. Appendix D contains a full explanation of each command.

Table 8.1: named.boot Configuration Commands

Command	Function
directory	Defines a directory for all subsequent file references.
primary	Declares this server as primary for the specified zone.
secondary	Declares this server as secondary for the specified zone.
cache	Points to the cache file.
forwarders	Lists servers to which queries are forwarded.
slave	Forces the server to only use the forwarders.

The way in which you configure the *named.boot* file controls whether the name server acts as a primary server, a secondary server, or a caching-only server. The best way to understand these different configurations is to look at sample **named.boot** files. The next sections show examples of each type of configuration.

Configuring a Caching-only Name Server

A caching-only server configuration is simple. A *named.boot* file and a *named.ca* file are all that you need, though the *named.local* file is usually also used. The most common *named.boot* file for a caching-only server is:

```
;
;   a caching-only server configuration
;
primary          0.0.127.IN-ADDR.ARPA     /etc/named.local
cache                                     /etc/named.ca
```

The only line in this sample file required for a caching-only configuration is the **cache** statement. It tells **named** to maintain a cache of name server responses, and to initialize the cache with the contents of the file *named.ca*. The name of the cache initialization file can be any name you wish, but */etc/named.ca* is often used. The presence of a cache statement does not make this a caching-only configuration; a cache statement is used in almost every server configuration. It is the *absence* of primary and secondary statements that makes this a caching-only configuration.

But there is a primary statement in our sample *named.boot* file! In fact, you'll see this statement in almost every caching-only configuration. It defines the local server as the primary server for its own loopback domain, and it says that the information for the domain is stored in the file *named.local*. The loopback domain is an *in-addr.arpa* domain* that maps the address 127.0.0.1 to the name *localhost*. The idea of resolving your own loopback address makes sense to most people, so most *named.boot* files contain this entry.

These primary and cache statements are the only statements used in most caching-only server configurations, but other statements can be added. A directory statement, a forwarders statement, and even a slave statement can be used. None of these statements change a server from being a caching-only server. See Appendix D for more information about these less frequently used commands.

Primary and Secondary Server Configurations

The imaginary *nuts.com* domain is the basis for our sample primary and secondary server configurations. Here is the *named.boot* file to define *almond* as the primary server for the *nuts.com* domain:

```
;
;   nuts.com primary name server boot file.
;
directory                               /etc
primary     nuts.com                    named.hosts
primary     66.128.IN-ADDR.ARPA         named.rev
primary     0.0.127.IN-ADDR.ARPA        named.local
cache       .                           named.ca
```

The directory statement saves a few keystrokes on the subsequent filenames. It tells **named** that all filenames, no matter where they occur in the **named** configuration, are relative to the directory */etc*.

The first primary statement declares that this is the primary server for the *nuts.com* domain, and that the data for that domain is loaded from the file *named.hosts*. In our examples, we'll use the filename *named.hosts* as the zone filename, but you should choose a more descriptive filename. For example, a better name for the *nuts.com* zone file is *nuts.com.hosts*.

---

*See Chapter 4 for a description of *in-addr.arpa* domains.

The second primary statement points to the file that maps IP addresses from 128.66.0.0 to host names. This statement says that the local server is the primary server for the reverse domain *66.128.in-addr.arpa*, and that the data for that domain is loaded from the file *named.rev*. Again, the filename *named.rev* is just used as an example; use descriptive names in your actual configuration.

The format of a primary statement is the keyword **primary**, the domain name, and the name of the zone file from which the domain information is read. All primary statements have this simple format.

The final two statements in the sample configuration are the primary statement for the loopback domain and the cache statement. These statements are discussed earlier in the section about caching-only configurations. They have the same function in every configuration and are found in almost every configuration.

A secondary server's configuration differs from a primary's by using **secondary** instead of **primary** statements. Secondary statements point to remote servers as the source of the domain information instead of local disk files. Secondary statements begin with the keyword **secondary**, followed by the name of the domain, the address of the primary server for that domain, and finally the name of a local file where information received from the primary server will be stored. The following *named.boot* file configures *filbert* as a secondary server for the *nuts.com* domain:

```
;
;   nuts.com secondary name server boot file.
;
directory                                       /etc
secondary    nuts.com              128.66.12.1  nuts.com.hosts
secondary    66.128.IN-ADDR.ARPA   128.66.12.1  128.66.rev
primary      0.0.127.IN-ADDR.ARPA               named.local
cache        .                                  named.ca
```

The first secondary statement makes this a secondary server for the *nuts.com* domain. The statement tells **named** to download the data for the *nuts.com* domain from the server at IP address 128.66.12.1, and to store that data in the file */etc/nuts.com.hosts*. If the *nuts.com.hosts* file does not exist, **named** creates it, gets the zone data from the remote server, and writes the data in the newly created file. If the file does exist, **named** checks with the remote server to see if the remote server's data is different from the data in the file. If the data has changed, **named** downloads the updated data and overwrites the file contents with the new data. If the data has not changed, **named** loads the contents of the disk file and doesn't

bother with a zone transfer.* Keeping a copy of the database on a local
disk file makes it unnecessary to transfer the zone file every time the local
host is rebooted. It's only necessary to transfer the zone when the data
changes.

The next line in this configuration says that this local server is also a secondary server for the reverse domain *66.128.in-addr.arpa*, and that the data
for that domain should also be downloaded from 128.66.12.1. The reverse
domain data is stored locally in a file named *128.66.rev*, following the same
rules discussed above for creating and overwriting *nuts.com.hosts*.

Standard Resource Records

The configuration commands discussed above and listed in Table 8-1 are
only used in the *named.boot* file. All other files used to configure **named**
(*named.hosts*, *named.rev*, *named.local*, and *named.ca*) store domain database information. All of these files have the same basic format and use the
same type of records to define the domain database information. The
records they use are standard resource records, called RRs. Table 8-2 summarizes all of the standard resource records available in BIND. All of these
records are covered in detail in Appendix D.

Table 8.2: Standard Resource Records

Resource Record Text Name	Record Type	Function
Start of Authority	SOA	Marks the beginning of a zone's data, and defines parameters that affect the entire zone.
Name Server	NS	Identifies a domain's name server.
Address	A	Converts a host name to an address.
Pointer	PTR	Converts an address to a host name.
Mail Exchange	MX	Identifies where to deliver mail for a given domain name.
Canonical Name	CNAME	Defines an alias host name.

---

* Appendix D (in the SOA record section) discusses how **named** determines if data has been
updated.

Table 8.2: Standard Resource Records (continued)

Resource Record Text Name	Record Type	Function
Host Information	HINFO	Describes a host's hardware and OS.
Well Known Service	WKS	Advertises network services.

The resource records are defined in RFC 1033, the *Domain Administrators Operations Guide*. They are described in detail in Appendix D, but a little understanding of the structure of these records is necessary to read the sample configuration files used in this chapter. The format of DNS resource records is:

[*name*] [*ttl*] **IN** *type data*

name   This is the name of the domain object the resource record references. It can be an individual host or an entire domain. The string entered for *name* is relative to the current domain unless it ends with a dot. If the name field is blank, the record applies to the domain object that was named last. For example, if an A record has a *name* field containing the host name *peanut* and it is followed by an MX record with a blank *name* field, both the A record and the MX record apply to *peanut*.

ttl   Time-to-live defines the length of time, in seconds, that the information in this resource record should be kept in the cache. Usually this field is left blank and the default *ttl*, set for the entire zone in the SOA record, is used.*

IN   Identifies the record as an Internet DNS resource record. There are other classes of records, but they are not used by DNS.

type   Identifies what kind of resource record this is. Table 8-2 lists all record types under the heading "Record Type." You must specify one of these values in the *type* field.

data   The information specific to this type of resource record. For example, in an A record this is the field that contains the actual IP address.

---

*See the section on SOA records in Appendix D.

In the following sections we'll look at each of the remaining configuration files. As you look at the files, remember that all of the records in these files are standard resource records that follow the format described above.

The Cache Initialization File

The cache statement in *named.boot* points to a cache initialization file. Each server that maintains a cache has such a file. It contains the information needed to begin building a cache of domain data when the name server starts. The root domain is indicated on the cache statement by a single dot, and at a minimum the *named.ca* file contains the names and addresses of the root servers.

The basic *named.ca* file contains NS records that name the root servers, and A records that provide the addresses of the root servers. A basic *named.ca* file is shown below:

```
;
;               Servers for the root domain
;
.               99999999        IN      NS      TERP.UMD.EDU.
                99999999        IN      NS      AOS.BRL.MIL.
                99999999        IN      NS      C.NYSER.NET.
                99999999        IN      NS      NS.NASA.GOV.
                99999999        IN      NS      NS.NIC.DDN.MIL.
                99999999        IN      NS      A.ISI.EDU
                99999999        IN      NS      NIC.NORDU.NET.
;
;               Root servers by address
;
TERP.UMD.EDU.   99999999        IN      A       128.8.10.90
AOS.BRL.MIL.    99999999        IN      A       192.5.25.82
C.NYSER.NET.    99999999        IN      A       192.33.4.12
NS.NASA.GOV.    99999999        IN      A       192.52.195.10
NS.NIC.DDN.MIL. 99999999        IN      A       192.67.67.53
A.ISI.EDU.      99999999        IN      A       26.3.0.103
A.ISI.EDU.      99999999        IN      A       128.9.0.107
NIC.NORDU.NET.  99999999        IN      A       192.36.148.17
```

This file contains only name server and address records. First, we have a set of NS records that identify the name servers for the root (.) domain. After the NS records, are a group of A records that give the address of each root server. Though not required, the ttl for all of these records is traditionally 99999999—the largest possible value—because the root servers are never removed from the cache.

Keep accurate root server information in your cache. If your cache contains the name of a bogus root server, it could cause problems with your local server. An accurate list of root servers is available via anonymous **ftp** from *nic.ddn.mil* in the file *netinfo/root-servers.txt*. Download the *root-servers.txt* file about once a month; check it and make any changes necessary to your *named.ca* file. The data given above is correct as of publication, but could change at any time.

The *named.ca* file is sometimes called a "hints" file, because it contains hints **named** uses to initialize the cache. The hints file can contain more information than just the root servers. It is frequently used to store the addresses of other servers within the local server's domain, or the addresses of commonly requested hosts. The problem with adding your own hints is ensuring the reliability of the data stored in the cache. The reliability of the information in the *root-servers.txt* file is ensured by the people at the NIC. However, you're the only one who ensures the reliability of other hints placed in the cache, and inaccurate information can enter the domain name system in this way.

If your system is not connected to the Internet, it won't be able to communicate with the root servers. Initializing your cache with the servers listed in the *root-servers.txt* file would be pointless. In this case, initialize your cache with entries that point to the major name servers on your local network.

The named.local File

The *named.local* file is used to convert the address 127.0.0.1 (the "loopback address") into the name *localhost*. It's the zone file for the reverse domain 0.0.127.IN-ADDR.ARPA. Because all systems use 127.0.0.1 as the "loopback" address, this file is virtually identical on every server. Here's a typical *named.local* file, taken from *almond*:

```
@           IN   SOA    almond.nuts.com. jan.almond.nuts.com. (
                        1                ; serial
                        36000            ; refresh every 100 hours
                        3600             ; retry after 1 hour
                        3600000          ; expire after 1000 hours
                        36000            ; default ttl is 100 hours
                        )
            IN   NS     almond.nuts.com.
1           IN   PTR    localhost.
```

The SOA record's data fields and the NS record that contains the computer's host name, vary from system to system. The sample SOA record identifies *almond.nuts.com.* as the server originating this zone, and the e-mail address *jan.almond.nuts.com.* as the point of contact for any questions about the zone. (Note that in an SOA record, the @ that usually separates the recipient's name from the host name in an e-mail address is changed to a dot. The other fields remain the same.) Many systems do not even include the NS record. But when it is used, it contains the computer's host name. Change these three data fields and you can use this identical file on any host. In fact, since no other hosts will query your loopback domain, the SOA values and the NS record are just formalities. The *named.local* file does not need much thought to be properly configured.

The files discussed so far, *named.boot*, *named.ca*, and *named.local*, are the only files required to configure caching-only servers and secondary servers. Most of your servers will only use these files, and the files used will contain almost identical information on every server.

The simplest way to create these three files is to copy a sample file and modify it for your system. Most systems come with sample files. If your system doesn't, sample configuration files are available in the *master* directory* of the *bind.4.8.3.tar* file. This **tar** file can be obtained via anonymous **ftp** by downloading *networking/ip/dns/bind/bind.4.8.3.tar.Z* from *ftp.uu.net.*

The remaining **named** configuration files, *named.hosts* and *named.rev*, are more complex, but the number of servers that use these files is very small. Only the primary server needs all of the configuration files, and there should be only one primary server per domain.

The Reverse Domain File

The *named.rev* file is very similar in structure to the *named.local* file. Both of these files translate IP addresses into host names, so both files contain PTR records.

The *named.rev* file in our example is the zone file for the *66.128.in-addr.arpa* domain. The domain administrator creates this file on *almond*, and every other host that needs this information gets it from there.

```
;
;          Address to host name mappings.
;
@          IN      SOA      almond.nuts.com. jan.almond.nuts.com. (
```

---

*The sample *named.ca* file in this directory is called *root.cache*.

```
                          10099    ;    Serial
                          43200    ;    Refresh
                          3600     ;    Retry
                          3600000  ;    Expire
                          2592000 ) ;  Minimum
            IN      NS    almond.nuts.com.
            IN      NS    filbert.nuts.com.
            IN      NS    foo.army.mil.
1.12        IN      PTR   almond.nuts.com.
2.12        IN      PTR   peanut.nuts.com.
3.12        IN      PTR   pecan.nuts.com.
4.12        IN      PTR   walnut.nuts.com.
2.1         IN      PTR   filbert.nuts.com.
6           IN      NS    salt.plant.nuts.com.
            IN      NS    pecan.nuts.com.
```

Like all zone files, the *named.rev* file begins with an SOA record. The @ in the name field of the SOA record references the current domain. In this case it is the domain defined by the primary statement in our sample *named.boot* file:

```
primary   66.128.IN-ADDR.ARPA              named.rev
```

The @ in the SOA record allows the primary statement to define the zone file domain. This same SOA record is used on every zone file on *almond*; it always references the correct domain name because it references the domain defined for that particular zone file in *named.boot*. You'll see this same SOA format at the beginning of almost every zone file. Change the hostname (*almond.nuts.com.*) and the manager's mail address (*jan.almond.nuts.com.*), and use this SOA record in any of your zone files.

The NS records that follow the SOA record define the name servers for the domain. Generally the name servers are listed immediately after the SOA, before any other record has the chance to modify the domain name. Recall that a blank name field means that the last domain name is still in force. The SOA's domain reference is still in force because the following NS records have blank name fields.

PTR records dominate the *named.rev* file because they are used to translate addresses to host names. The PTR records in our example provide address to name conversions for hosts 12.1, 12.2, 12.3, 12.4, and 2.1 on network 128.66. Because they don't end in dots, the values in the name fields of these PTR records are relative to the current domain. For example, the value 3.12 is interpreted as *3.12.66.128.in-addr.arpa*. The host name in the data field of the PTR record is fully qualified to prevent it from being relative to the current domain name. Using the information in this PTR, **named** will translate *3.12.66.128.in-addr.arpa* into *pecan.nuts.com*.

The last two lines of this file are additional NS records. As with any domain, subdomains can be created in an *in-addr.arpa* domain. This is what the last two NS records do. These NS records point to *pecan* and *salt* as name servers for the subdomain *6.66.128.in-addr.arpa*. Any query for information in the *6.66.128.in-addr.arpa* subdomain is referred to them. NS records that point to the servers for a subdomain must be placed in the higher-level domain before you can use that subdomain.

Delegating *in-addr.arpa* subdomains is very common. Often this is done along subnet boundaries. A local organization is assigned an organizational subdomain name, a subnet number, and an *in-addr.arpa* subdomain that matches the subnet number. Even organizations that don't use real subnets often delegate groups of IP addresses and an *in-addr.arpa* subdomain to each organization that has its own subdomain name. The organization is then responsible for both the *in-addr.arpa* subdomain and the regular subdomain, so that it doesn't need approval for each host name and IP address assigned. The choice of how much should be delegated is based on the network size, and on the politics, structure, and style of the organization. Large networks need and use subnets and subdomains the most.

The named.hosts File

The *named.hosts* file contains most of the domain information. This file converts host names to IP addresses, so A records predominate, but it also contains MX, CNAME, and other records. The *named.hosts* file, like the *named.rev* file, is only created on the primary server. All others servers get this information from the primary server.

```
;
;        Addresses and other host information.
;
@       IN      SOA     almond.nuts.com. jan.almond.nuts.com. (
                                10118      ; Serial
                                43200      ; Refresh
                                3600       ; Retry
                                3600000    ; Expire
                                2592000 )  ; Minimum
;       Define the nameservers and the mail servers
                IN      NS      almond.nuts.com.
                IN      NS      filbert.nuts.com.
                IN      NS      foo.army.mil.
                IN      MX      10 almond.nuts.com.
                IN      MX      20 pecan.nuts.com.
;
;        Define localhost
;
localhost       IN      A       127.0.0.1
```

```
;
;       Define the hosts in this zone
;
almond          IN      A       128.66.12.1
                IN      MX      5 almond.nuts.com.
loghost         IN      CNAME   almond.nuts.com.
peanut          IN      A       128.66.12.2
                IN      MX      5 peanut.nuts.com.
goober          IN      CNAME   peanut.nuts.com.
pecan           IN      A       128.66.12.3
walnut          IN      A       128.66.12.4
filbert         IN      A       128.66.1.2
;       host table has BOTH host and gateway entries for 26.104.0.19
mil-gw .        IN      A       26.104.0.19
;
;    Glue records for servers within this domain
;
pack.plant      IN      A       128.66.18.15
acorn.sales     IN      A       128.66.6.1
;
;       Define sub-domains
;
plant           IN      NS      pack.plant.nuts.com.
                IN      NS      pecan.nuts.com.
sales           IN      NS      acorn.sales.nuts.com.
                IN      NS      pack.plant.nuts.com.
```

Like the *named.rev* file, the *named.hosts* file begins with an SOA record and a few NS records that define the domain and its servers, but the *named.hosts* file contains a wider variety of resource records than a *named.rev* file does. We'll look at each of these records in the order that they occur in the sample file, so that you can follow along using the sample file as your reference.

The first MX record identifies a mail server for the entire domain. This record says that *almond* is the mail server for *nuts.com* with a preference of 10. Mail addressed to *user***@nuts.com** is redirected to *almond* for delivery. Of course for *almond* to successfully deliver the mail, it must be properly configured as a mail server. The MX record is only part of the story. We look at configuring **sendmail** in Chapter 9.

The second MX record identifies *pecan* as a mail server for *nuts.com* with a preference of 20. Preference numbers let you define alternate mail servers. The lower the preference number, the more desirable the server. For example, our two sample MX records say "send mail for the *nuts.com* domain to *almond* first; if *almond* is unavailable, try sending the mail to *pecan*." Rather than relying on a single mail server, MX records allow you to create backup servers. If the main mail server is unreachable, the domain's mail will be sent to one of the backups instead.

These sample MX records redirect mail addressed to *nuts.com*, but mail addressed to *user*@**walnut.nuts.com** will still be sent directly to *walnut.nuts.com*—not to *almond* or *pecan*. This configuration allows simplified mail addressing in the form *user*@**nuts.com** for users that want to take advantage of it, but it continues to allow direct mail delivery to individual hosts for users that wish to take advantage of that.

The first A record in this example defines the address for *localhost*. This is the opposite of the PTR entry in the *named.local* file. It allows users within the *nuts.com* domain to enter the name *localhost* and have it resolved to the address 127.0.0.1 by the local name server.

The next A record defines the IP address for *almond*. (Note that the records that relate to a single host are grouped together, which is the most common structure used in zone files.) The A record is followed by an MX record and a CNAME record that both relate to *almond*. The *almond* MX record points back to the host itself, and the CNAME record defines an alias for the host name.

This host-specific MX records is provided as a courtesy to remote mailers. Some mailer implementations look for an MX record first, and then query for the host's address. Providing an MX record saves these mailers one additional name server query.

peanut's A record is also followed by an MX record and a CNAME record. However, *peanut*'s MX record serves a different purpose. It directs all mail addressed to *user*@**peanut.nuts.com** to *almond*. This MX record is required because the MX records at the beginning of the zone file only redirect mail if it is addressed to *user*@**nuts.com**. If you also want to redirect mail addressed to *peanut*, you need a "peanut-specific" MX record.

The name field of the CNAME record contains an alias for the official host name. The official name, called the canonical name, is provided in the data field of the record. Because of these records, *almond* can be referred to by the name *loghost*, and *peanut* can be referred to as *goober*. The *loghost* alias is a generic host name used to direct **syslogd** output to *almond*.* Host name aliases should *not* be used in other resource records.† For example, don't use an alias as the name of a mail server in an MX record. Use *only* the "canonical" (official) name that's defined in an A record.

---

*See chapter 3 for a further discussion of generic host names.

†See Appendix D for additional information about using CNAME records in the *named.hosts* file.

Your *named.hosts* file will be much larger than the sample file we've discussed, but it will contain essentially the same records. If you know the names and addresses of the hosts in your domain, you have most of the information necessary to create the **named** configuration. All in all, configuring **named** is a simple task.

Starting named

After you construct the *named.boot* file and the required zone files, start **named**. **named** is usually started at boot time from a startup script, but it can be started with the following command:

```
# named
```

The first time you run it, watch for error messages. **named** logs errors to the */usr/adm/messages* file. Once **named** is running to your satisfaction, use **nslookup** to query the name server to make sure it is providing the correct information.

Using nslookup

nslookup is a debugging tool provided as part of the BIND software package. It allows anyone to directly query a name server and retrieve any of the information known to the DNS system. It is helpful for determining if the server is running correctly and is properly configured, or for querying for information provided by remote servers.

The **nslookup** program is used to either resolve queries interactively or directly from the command line. From the command line **nslookup** is used to query for the IP address of a host. For example:

```
% nslookup almond.nuts.com
Server:   peanut.nuts.com
Address:  128.66.12.2

Name:     almond.nuts.com
Address:  128.66.12.1
```

Here a user asks **nslookup** to provide the address of *almond.nuts.com*. **nslookup** displays the name and address of the server used to resolve the query, and then it displays the answer to the query. This is useful, but **nslookup** is more often used interactively.

The real power of **nslookup** is seen in interactive mode. To enter interactive mode type **nslookup** on the command line without any other arguments. Terminate an interactive session by entering the **exit*** command at the (greater than) prompt. Redone in an interactive session, the query shown above is:

```
% nslookup
Default Server:  peanut.nuts.com
Address:  128.66.12.2

> almond.nuts.com
Server:  peanut.nuts.com
Address:  128.66.12.2

Name:     almond.nuts.com
Address:  128.66.12.1

> exit
```

By default, **nslookup** queries for A records but you can use the **set type** command to change the query to another resource record type, or to the special query type "ANY." ANY is used to retrieve all available resource records for the specified host.

The following example checks MX records for *almond* and *peanut*. Note that once the query type is set to MX, it stays MX. It doesn't revert to the default A type query. Another **set type** command is required to reset the query type.

```
% nslookup
Default Server:  peanut.nuts.com
Address:  128.66.12.2

> set type=MX
> almond.nuts.com
Server:  peanut.nuts.com
Address:  128.66.12.2

almond.nuts.com    preference = 5, mail exchanger = almond.nuts.com
almond.nuts.com    inet address = 128.66.12.1

> peanut.nuts.com
Server:  peanut.nuts.com
Address:  128.66.12.2

peanut.nuts.com    preference = 5, mail exchanger = peanut.nuts.com
peanut.nuts.com    inet address = 128.66.12.2
> exit
```

You can use the **server** command to control the server used to resolve queries. This is particularly useful for going directly to an authoritative

---

On SCO systems, use ^D to exit **nslookup**.

server to check some information. The following example does just that. In fact, this example contains several interesting commands:

- First we **set type=NS** and get the NS records for the *umd.edu* domain.

- From the information returned by this query, we select a server and use the **server** command to direct **nslookup** to use that server.

- Next, using the **set domain** command, we set the default domain to *umd.edu*. **nslookup** uses this default domain name to expand the host names in its queries, in the same way that the resolver uses the default domain name defined in *resolv.conf.*

- We set the query type to ANY. If the query type is not reset, **nslookup** still queries for NS records.

- Finally, we query for information about the host *mimsy.umd.edu*. Because the default domain is set to *umd.edu*, we simply enter *mimsy* at the prompt.

```
% nslookup
Default Server:  peanut.nuts.com
Address:  128.66.12.2

> set type=NS
> umd.edu
Server:  peanut.nuts.com
Address:  128.66.12.2

Non-authoritative answer:
umd.edu nameserver = NOC.UMD.EDU
umd.edu nameserver = NI.UMD.EDU
umd.edu nameserver = NAMESERVER.ARC.NASA.GOV
Authoritative answers can be found from:
NOC.UMD.EDU        inet address = 128.8.2.200
NI.UMD.EDU         inet address = 128.8.2.240
NAMESERVER.ARC.NASA.GOV inet address = 128.102.18.31
> server NOC.UMD.EDU
Default Server:  NOC.UMD.EDU
Address:  128.8.2.200

> set domain=umd.edu
> set type=any
> mimsy
Server:  NOC.UMD.EDU
Address:  128.8.2.200

mimsy.umd.edu    inet address = 128.8.128.8
mimsy.umd.edu    preference = 10, mail exchanger = mimsy.UMD.EDU
mimsy.umd.edu    CPU=VAX-11/785  OS=UNIX
mimsy.umd.edu    inet address = 128.8.128.8, protocol = 6
         7 21 23 25 79
```

```
mimsy.UMD.EDU   inet address = 128.8.128.8
> exit
```

The final example shows how to download an entire domain from an authoritative server, and examine it on your local system. The **ls** command requests a zone file transfer and displays the contents of the zone file it receives. If the zone file is more than a few lines long, redirect the output to a file, and use the **view** command to examine the contents of the file. (**view** sorts a file and displays it using the UNIX **more** command.) The combination of **ls** and **view** are helpful when tracking down a remote host name. In the following example the **ls** command retrieves the *big.com* zone and stores the information in *temp.file*. Then **view** is used to examine *temp.file*.

```
peanut% nslookup
Default Server:  peanut.nuts.com
Address:  128.66.12.2

> server minerals.big.com
Default Server:  minerals.big.com
Address:  199.82.20.1

> ls big.com > temp.file
[minerals.big.com]
########
Received 406 records.
> view temp.file
 acmite                      199.82.20.28
 adamite                     199.82.20.29
 adelite                     199.82.20.11
 agate                       199.82.20.30
 alabaster                   199.82.20.31
 albite                      199.82.20.32
 allanite                    199.82.20.20
 altaite                     199.82.20.33
 alum                        199.82.20.35
 aluminum                    199.82.20.8
 amaranth                    199.82.20.85
 amethyst                    199.82.20.36
 andorite                    199.82.20.37
 apatite                     199.82.20.38
 beryl                       199.82.20.23
 --More-- q
> exit
```

These examples show that **nslookup** allows you to:

- Query for any specific type of standard resource record.
- Directly query the authoritative servers for a domain.
- Get the entire contents of a domain into a file so you can view it.

Use **nslookup**'s **help** command to see its other features. Turn on debugging (with **set debug**) and examine the additional information this provides. As you play with this tool, you'll find many helpful features.

DNS is an important user service that should be used on every system connected to the Internet. In this chapter we have seen how to configure and test this service. In the next chapter we'll configure several other user services.

9

Network Applications

In this chapter our attention turns to configuring network applications. As with name service, applications are not strictly required for the network to operate, but they provide user services that are central to the network's purpose. Without the applications, the network serves no real purpose.

There are many network applications—many more than can be covered in this chapter. Fortunately, most of them require no special configuration. Once the network itself is set up, including the *etc/inetd.conf* file, you should be able to use applications like **ftp** and **telnet** without trouble. In this chapter, we discuss a few commonly used applications that *do* require some configuration.* These are:

- the UNIX **r** commands, including **rlogin**, **rsh**, and **rcp**
- the Network File System (NFS)
- the Network Information Service (NIS), formerly called the "Yellow Pages"

We begin with the UNIX **r** commands, which must be configured carefully to avoid compromising system security.

---

*Notable by its absence is **sendmail**. It requires so much discussion, it has its own chapter!

The r Commands

UNIX has its own set of networking applications, comparable to **ftp** and **telnet**. The most important ones are:

rlogin   Remote login provides interactive access to remote hosts. Its function is similar to **telnet**.

rcp   Remote copy allows files to be copied from or to remote systems. Its syntax is similar to copy (**cp**) except that the file path can include the name of a remote host. **rcp** is often compared to **ftp**. They both move files between hosts on a network, but **ftp** runs as an interactive program with many subcommands, while **rcp** runs with a simple command-line interface.

rsh   Remote shell passes a command to a remote host for execution. Standard output and standard error from the remote execution are returned to the local host. There is no parallel to **rsh** in the standard TCP/IP protocols.

These commands are easily demonstrated by a few examples. First, an **rlogin** example that shows a remote login from *peanut* to *almond*:

```
peanut% rlogin almond
Last login: Sat Sep 21 15:34:27 from peanut.nuts.com
SunOS Release 4.1.1 (JORDAN) #1: Thu Sep 12 14:42:54 EDT 1991
almond% logout
Connection closed.
```

The next example uses **rcp** to copy */etc/gated.conf* from *almond*, and store it in a file called *sample.conf*, in the current directory on *peanut*. Note how the host name *almond* is specified as part of the pathname of the file being retrieved. The colon (:) separates the host name from the filename.

```
peanut% rcp almond:/etc/gated.conf sample.conf
```

Finally we use **rsh** to send an **ls** command to *almond*, requesting the directory listing of */etc/named.boot*. The output of the **ls** command is sent to *peanut's* standard output.

```
peanut% rsh almond ls -l /etc/named.boot
-rw-r--r--  1 root           1496 Sep 12 09:05 /etc/named.boot
```

These commands are familiar to most UNIX users, so we won't elaborate on them here. If you need more details about any particular command, refer to the appropriate **man** pages. The purpose of presenting these commands is to discuss their configuration, not their use. There are several other **r** commands, but the configuration of **rlogin**, **rsh**, and **rcp** is the most critical, because these commands have serious security implications.

Securing the r Commands

None of the examples show the user being prompted for a password—not even the interactive login. Because these **r** commands bypass the normal password verification for logins, they can create security problems. If your network is isolated from the Internet and you trust the network's users, **r** command configuration may not be critical. But in the wide-open Internet, care must be taken to ensure that the **r** commands don't compromise system security. Improperly configured **r** commands can open access to your computer facilities to virtually everyone in the world.

Because of security, some sites eliminate the **r** commands by commenting them out of the */etc/inetd.conf* file.* You may wish to do the same if your site has strict security requirements. However, it is possible to keep the **r** commands and to force them to request passwords from all users by deleting the */etc/hosts.equiv* file, and making sure that users do not create personal ˜/.rhosts files. This is a less drastic solution than turning the **r** commands off entirely, because most **r** commands will work without these configuration files. When these files are removed, the **r** commands will require users to provide login information. The only problem is with **rcp**, which doesn't know how to ask for authentication information.

Most sites, however, like the convenience and power of the **r** commands, and of password-free access. They decide to keep them, taking care to properly configure the */etc/hosts.equiv* and *.rhosts* files that provide security for the **r** commands.

In place of password authentication, these commands use their own system based on trusted hosts and users. Trusted users on trusted hosts are allowed to access the local system without providing a password. Trusted hosts are also called "equivalent hosts" because the system assumes that users given access to a trusted host should be given equivalent access to the local host. The system assumes that user accounts with the same name on both hosts are "owned" by the same user. For example, a user logged in as *becky* on a trusted system is granted the same access as a user logged in as *becky* on the local system.

---

*Chapter 5 describes in detail how to disable network applications using */etc/inetd.conf*.

This authentication system requires databases that define the trusted hosts and the trusted users. The databases used to configure the **r** commands are:

- */etc/hosts.equiv*, which defines the trusted hosts and users for the entire system.
- *.rhosts*, which defines the trusted hosts and users for an individual user account.

The /etc/hosts.equiv File

The */etc/hosts.equiv* file defines the hosts and users that are granted "trusted" **r** command access to your system. This file can also define hosts and users that are explicitly denied trusted access. Not having trusted access doesn't necessarily mean that the a user is denied access; it just means that the user is required to supply a password.

The basic format of entries in the */etc/hosts.equiv* file is:

[+ | −][*hostname*] [*username*]

The *hostname* is the name of a "trusted" host, which may optionally be preceded by a plus (+) sign. The plus sign has no real significance, except when used alone. A + sign without a host name following it is a wildcard character that means "any host."

If a host is granted equivalence, users logged into that host are allowed access to like-named user accounts on your system without providing a password. (This is one good reason for administrators to observe uniform rules in handing out login names.) The optional *username* is the name of a user on the trusted host who is granted access to all user accounts. If *username* is specified, that user is not limited to like-named accounts, but is given access to all user accounts without being required to provide a password.*

The *hostname* may also be preceded by a minus sign (−). This explicitly says that the host is *not* an equivalent system. Users from that host must always supply a password when they use an **r** command to interact with your system. A *username* can also be preceded with a minus sign. This says that, whatever else may be true about that host, the user is "not trusted," and must always supply a password.

---

*The *root* account is not included.

The following examples show how entries in the *hosts.equiv* file are interpreted.

peanut	Allows password-free access from any user on *peanut* to a like-named user account on your local system.
–peanut	Denies password-free access from any user on *peanut* to accounts on your system.
peanut –david	Denies password-free access to the user *david*, if he attempts to access your system from *peanut*.
peanut +becky	Allows the user *becky* to access any account (except *root*) on your system, without supplying a password, if she logs in from *peanut*.
+ becky	Allows the user *becky* to access any account (except *root*) on your system without supplying a password, no matter what host she logs in from.

This last entry is an example of something that should never be used in your configuration. Don't use a standalone plus sign (+) in place of a host name. It allows access from any host anywhere, and can open up a big security hole. For example, if the entry shown above was in your *hosts.equiv* file, an intruder could create an account named *becky* on his system and gain access to every account on your system.

A simple typographical error could give you a standalone plus sign. For example, consider the entry:

```
+ peanut becky
```

The system administrator probably meant "give *becky* password-free access to all accounts when she logs in from *peanut*." However, with an extraneous space after the + sign, it means "allow users named *peanut* and *becky* password-free access from any host in the world." Don't use a plus sign in front of a host name, and always use care when working with the */etc/hosts.equiv* file to avoid security problems.

When configuring the */etc/hosts.equiv* file, only grant trusted access to the systems and users that you actually trust. Don't grant trusted access to every system attached to your local network. It is best only to trust hosts from your local network where you know the person responsible for that host, and where you know that the host is not available for public use. Don't grant trusted access by default—have some reason for conferring trusted status. Also, never begin your *hosts.equiv* file with a minus sign (–) as the first character. (This confuses some systems causing them to improperly grant access.) Always err on the side of caution when creating a *hosts.equiv* file. Adding trusted hosts as they are requested is much easier than recovering from a malicious intruder.

The .rhosts File

The *.rhosts* file grants or denies password-free **r** command access to a specific user's account. It is placed in the user's home directory and contains entries that define the trusted hosts and users. Entries in the *.rhosts* file use exactly the same format as entries in the *hosts.equiv* file, and function in almost the same way. The difference is the scope of access granted by entries in these two files. In the *.rhosts* file, the entries grant or deny access to a single user account; the entries in *hosts.equiv* control access to an entire system.

This functional difference can be shown in a simple example. Assume the following entry:

```
pecan anthony
```

In *almond's hosts.equiv* file, this entry means that the user *anthony* on *pecan* can access any account on *almond* without entering a password. In an *.rhosts* file in the home directory of user *resnick*, the exact same entry allows *anthony* to **rlogin** from *pecan* as *resnick* without entering a password, but it does not grant password-free access to any other accounts on *almond*.

Individuals use the *.rhosts* file to establish equivalence among the different accounts they own. The entry shown above would probably only be made if *anthony* and *resnick* are the same person. For example, I have accounts on several different systems and sometimes my user name is *hunt*, and sometimes it is *craig*. It would be nice if I had the same account name everywhere, but that is not always possible; the names *craig* and *hunt* are used by two other people on my local network. I want to be able to **rlogin** to my workstation from any host that I have an account on, but I don't want mistaken logins from the other *craig* and the other *hunt*. The *.rhosts* file gives me a way to control this problem.

For example, assume my username on *almond* is *craig*, but my username on *filbert* is *hunt*. Another user on *filbert* is *craig*. To allow myself password-free access to my *almond* account from *filbert*, and to make sure that the other user doesn't have password-free access, I put the following *.rhosts* file in my home directory.

```
filbert hunt
filbert -craig
```

If security is particularly important at your site, you should remember that the user can provide access with the *.rhosts* file even when the *hosts.equiv* file doesn't exist. The only way to prevent users from doing this is to periodically check for and remove the *.rhosts* files. Chapter 12 discusses one method of doing this.

Root Access

To understand the relationship of the *.rhosts* and *hosts.equiv* files, you need to know how they are processed. The *hosts.equiv* file is searched first, followed by the user's *.rhosts* file, if it exists. The first explicit match determines whether or not password-free access is allowed. Therefore, the *.rhosts* file cannot override the *hosts.equiv* file.

When a root user attempts to access a system via the **r** commands, the *hosts.equiv* file is not checked, only */.rhosts* is consulted. This allows root access to be more tightly controlled. If the *hosts.equiv* file was used for root access, entries that grant trusted access to hosts would give root users on those hosts root privileges. You can add trusted hosts to *hosts.equiv* without worrying that remote root users will get root access to your system.

The /usr/hosts Directory

The directory */usr/hosts* provides a shorthand method for using the **rlogin** and **rsh** commands. When links are created between */usr/ucb/rsh** and */usr/hosts* using host names as linknames, these host names can be used in place of the **rlogin** and **rsh** commands. This concept may be a bit confusing, but a sample configuration will make it clear.

Assume that users from *peanut* often use **rsh** and **rlogin** to access the host *almond*. To make this a bit easier, the superuser on *peanut* creates a link between **rsh** and *almond* in the */usr/hosts* directory as follows:

```
# cd /usr/hosts
# ln /usr/ucb/rsh almond
```

---

*On SCO systems, the links are created between */usr/bin/rcmd* and */usr/hosts*.

Users who want to use the new link add */usr/hosts* to their directory search path. Once this is done, the host name *almond* can be used as shorthand for **rlogin almond** as shown below:

```
peanut% almond
Last login: Thu Sep 26 14:57:05 from peanut.nuts.com
SunOS Release 4.1.1 (JORDAN) #1: Thu Sep 12 14:42:54 EDT 1991
almond% logout
Connection closed.
```

The link also serves as shorthand for the **rsh** command. Instead of entering **rsh** *hostname command*, the users can enter *hostname command*. For example, to remotely execute the command **ls -l /etc/gated.conf** on *almond*, the user from *peanut* enters:

```
peanut% almond ls -l /etc/gated.conf
-rw-r--r--  1 root          1496 Sep 12 09:05 /etc/gated.conf
```

The */usr/hosts* directory contains a script file called *MAKEHOSTS*.* The script reads */etc/hosts* and makes a link for every host in that file. This script is useful if you want to make a large number of links, and if the hosts you wish to link to are already in your */etc/hosts* file. Otherwise, it is simpler to create the individual links you need manually.

Network Information Service

The *Network Information Service* (NIS)† is an administrative database that provides central control and automatic dissemination of important administrative files. NIS converts several standard UNIX files into databases that can be queried over the network. The databases are called *NIS maps*. Some maps are created from files that you're familiar with from system administration, such as the password file (*/etc/passwd*) and the groups file (*/etc/group*). Others are derived from files related to network administration:

/etc/ethers   Creates the NIS maps, *ethers.byaddr* and *ethers.byname*. The */etc/ethers* file is used by RARP (Chapter 2).

/etc/hosts   Produces the two NIS maps, *hosts.byname* and *hosts.byaddr* (Chapter 3).

/etc/networks   Produces the the NIS maps, *networks.byname* and *networks.byaddr* (Chapter 3).

---

*SCO systems use */etc/mkhosts*.

†Formerly called the "Yellow Pages," or *yp*. Although the name has changed, the abbreviation *yp* is still used.

/etc/netmasks	Makes the *netmasks.byaddr* map. The */etc/netmasks* file contains subnet masks (Chapter 6).
/etc/protocols	Creates the two maps, *protocols.byname* and *protocols.byaddr* (Chapter 2).
/etc/services	Produces a single map called *services.byname* (Chapter 2).
/etc/aliases	Defines electronic mail aliases and produces the maps, *mail.aliases* and *mail.byaddr* (Chapter 10).
netgroup	Defines groups of hosts and users. This file produces two maps, *netgroup.byhost* and *netgroup.byuser.* These groups can then be referenced in the */etc/hosts.equiv*, the *.rhosts* file, and the NFS configuration. The *etc/netgroup* file is described in the next section.

The advantage of using NIS is that these important administrative files can be maintained on a central server, and yet be completely accessible to every workstation on the network. Remote access to the information is completely transparent and does not require the users to learn any new commands. All of the maps created from these files are stored on a master server that runs the NIS server process **ypserv**. The maps are queried remotely by client systems using the client process **ypbind**.

The NIS server and its clients are a *NIS domain*—a term NIS shares with DNS. Although NIS domains and DNS domains are distinct entities, Sun recommends using the DNS domain name as the NIS domain name to simplify administration and reduce confusion. NIS uses its domain name to create a directory within */var/yp* where the NIS maps are stored. For example, the DNS domain of our imaginary network is *nuts.com*, so we also use this as our NIS domain name. NIS will create a directory named */var/yp/nuts.com* and store the NIS maps in it.

The command **domainname** checks or sets the NIS domain name. The superuser on *almond* can make *nuts.com* the NIS domain name by entering:

```
# domainname nuts.com
```

The NIS domain name is normally configured at startup by placing the **domainname** command in one of the startup files. On SunOS 4.1.1 systems, the value for the NIS domain name is taken from the */etc/defaultdomain* file. This file is created by the installation script, and is used as input to a **domainname** command in the */etc/rc.local* file. As shown below, this file contains only the name of the NIS domain.

```
% cat /etc/defaultdomain
nuts.com
```

While NIS is a possible alternative to DNS for networks not connected to the Internet, networks connected to the Internet need DNS for name service. However, NIS provides more than simple name service, so you may want to use both NIS and DNS. In order to use both on a Sun OS 4.1.1 system, you must make a small change to the */var/yp/Makefile*. Near the beginning of the *Makefile* you'll see:

```
#B=-b
B=
```

Remove the comment mark (#) from the B=-b statement and make the statement B= into a comment, as shown below:

```
B=-b
#B=
```

To initialize the master server and build the initial maps, use **ypinit** with the **-m** option. There must be at least one server on each subnet, and *almond* is the master server on subnet 128.66.12.0. On *almond* the **ypinit** command creates a directory named */var/yp/nuts.com*. It reads the files in the */etc* directory and places maps created from them in the new */var/yp/nuts.com* directory. You'll be warned whenever **ypinit** attempts to create a map for which it can't find an input file in */etc*. This is only a warning—if you don't use those files, don't worry. To initialize *almond* as a master server:

```
# cd /var/yp
# /usr/etc/yp/ypinit -m
```

After initializing the maps, start the NIS server process **ypserv**.

```
# ypserv
```

Start the map transfer daemon, **ypxfrd**, that also runs on the master server. Remember to remove the comment mark from the line in */etc/rc.local* that starts this daemon, so that **ypxfrd** will start automatically at boot time.

```
# ypxfrd
```

Start the NIS client daemon, **ypbind**.

```
# ypbind
```

almond is now able to run both NIS and DNS, and both systems are using the domain name *nuts.com*. The clients on subnet 128.66.12.0 only need to define the correct domain name and to run the client software **ypbind**. To start *peanut* as a NIS client, enter:

```
# domainname nuts.com
# ypbind
```

The /etc/netgroup File

The */etc/netgroup* file defines groups of hosts and users that can be referenced wherever host names and user names are used. The */etc/netgroup*
file can only be used on systems running NIS, because it is only accessed
via its NIS maps, *netgroup.byhost* and *netgroup.byuser.* If your system does
not run NIS, skip this section.

The basic format of an entry in the netgroup file is:

    groupname member [*member*] . . .

groupname is any name you wish to assign to the group. *member* is an
item included in the group, and it can either be the name of another group
(i.e., another *groupname*) or the definition of an individual item. Individual
members of the group are defined by their host name, user name, and NIS
domain name—a form called a triple. The format of this triple is:

    (*hostname, username, domainname*)

The */etc/netgroup* entry to define a netgroup called *admin* that contains
two members is shown below. One member contains the host *almond* and
the user *kathy*, and the other member contains the host *peanut* and the
user *craig*:

```
admin   (almond,kathy,) (peanut,craig,)
```

Notice that the domainname field for each member is empty. *domainname*
is the name of the NIS domain in which this netgroup is valid. This field
either contains your local NIS domain name or it is empty. An empty field
is a wildcard value meaning that every possible value is included. You only
need to use your NIS domain name when multiple NIS domains exist on the
same network segment, and you need to define which NIS domain owns
the netgroup.

If the sample *admin* netgroup is used in situations that require host names,
the NIS software accesses the *netgroup.byhost* map and returns the values
almond and *peanut*. In situations that require user names, the *admin* netgroup provides the values *kathy* and *craig*, because NIS retrieves the values
from the *netgroup.byuser* map. A single reference to the netgroup provides
host names or user names, but not both. Which you get depends on the

context in which the netgroup is used. Because of this, most administrators prefer to define separate netgroups for hosts and users. For example:

```
adminhosts (almond,-,) (peanut,-,) (pecan,-,)
adminusers (-,kathy,) (-,sara,) (-,david,) (-,rebecca,)
```

These examples have fields that contain dashes (–). A dash means that no values are included in the set. All username fields in our *adminhosts* netgroup contain dashes, and all hostname fields in the *adminusers* netgroup contain dashes. So, if the *adminhosts* netgroup is used in a situation where user names are required, NIS returns a value indicating that no user names belong to this netgroup. The same null value is returned if the *adminusers* netgroup is used in a situation that calls for host names.

As an example of how netgroups are used in the *hosts.equiv* and *.rhosts* file, let's assume that *almond* has the following */etc/netgroup* file:

```
nuts sales research
research (almond,-,) (peanut,-,) (walnut,-,)
sales (-,sara,) (-,david,)
```

This file defines a netgroup called *nuts* that encompasses both of the other groups, *sales* and *research*. The netgroup called *research* contains the hosts *almond*, *peanut*, and *walnut*. The last entry is a netgroup called *sales* that contains the users *sara* and *david*.

The */etc/netgroup* entries created above can be referenced in *hosts.equiv* and *.rhosts* files. In either of these files, a netgroup name is always preceded by an at-sign (@). For example, if the *hosts.equiv* file contains **+@research**, it is the same as if the file contained these three entries:

```
almond
peanut
walnut
```

The netgroup entry and the three individual entries are equivalent. In both cases we are declaring that *almond*, *peanut*, and *walnut* are trusted hosts.

Likewise, the *.rhosts* entry **pecan +@sales** is the same as these two entries:

```
pecan sara
pecan david
```

In both of these examples, the netgroup entry and the individual entries, the *.rhosts* file grants *sara* and *david* password-free access to the account of the user who places the *.rhosts* file in his home directory.

Once groups are defined in the */etc/netgroup* file, they can be used to simplify creation of the *hosts.equiv* and *.rhosts* files. Netgroups are a shorthand way of referring to large groups of hosts and users on systems running NIS.

The information we have covered about NIS is very specific to Sun OS 4.1.1. Before installing NIS on your system, read your system's documentation. For more information about the Network Information Service, see the Nutshell Handbook, *Managing NFS and NIS*, by Hal Stern.

The Network File System

The Network File System (NFS) allows directories and files to be shared across a network. It was originally developed by Sun Microsystems, but is now supported by virtually all UNIX implementations, and many non-UNIX operating systems. Through NFS, users and programs can access files located on remote systems as if they were local files. In a perfect NFS environment, the user neither knows nor cares where files are actually stored.

NFS has several benefits:

- It reduces local disk storage requirements because a network can store a single copy of a directory, while the directory continues to be fully accessible to everyone on the network.

- NFS simplifies central support tasks, because files can be updated centrally, yet available throughout the network.

- NFS allows users to use familiar UNIX commands to manipulate remote files instead of learning new ones. There is no need to use **ftp** or **rcp** to copy a file between hosts on the network; **cp** works fine.

There are two sides to NFS—a client side and a server side. The client is the system that uses the remote directories as if they were part of its local filesystem. The server is the system that makes the directories available for use. Attaching a remote directory to the local filesystem (a client function) is called *mounting* a directory. Offering a directory for remote access (a server function) is called *exporting* a directory. Frequently a system will run both the client and the server NFS software. In this section we'll look at how to configure a system to export and mount directories.

This discussion is only an introduction to NFS. You should also be aware that NFS is not the only file-sharing system in existence. Two others are AT&T's RFS (remote file sharing), and the Andrew Filesystem (AFS). RFS has been available under System V for a number of years, but is not widely used. AFS is just making its way from the research environment to the commercial environment. There are only a few hundred AFS sites in the world, while there are hundreds of thousands of NFS sites. However, the popularity of AFS should increase in the next few years.

NFS Daemons

The Network File System is run by several daemons, some performing client functions and some performing server functions. Before we discuss the NFS configuration, let's look at the function of the daemons that run NFS:

nfsd [*nservers*]   The NFS daemon, **nfsd**, runs on NFS servers. This daemon services the client's NFS requests. The *nservers* option specifies how many daemons should be started. Eight is a commonly used number.

biod [*nservers*]   The block I/O daemon, **biod**, runs on NFS clients. This daemon handles the client side of the NFS I/O. *nservers* specifies the number of daemons to be run, and again eight is the commonly used number.

rpc.lockd   The lock daemon, **rpc.lockd**, handles file lock requests. Both clients and servers run the lock daemon. Clients request file locks, and servers grant them.

rpc.statd   The network status monitor daemon, **rpc.statd**, is required by **rpc.lockd** to provide monitoring services. In particular, it allows locks to be reset properly after a crash. Both clients and servers run **rpc.statd**.

rpc.mountd   The NFS mount daemon, **rpc.mountd**, processes the clients' mount requests. NFS servers run the mount daemon.

The daemons necessary to run NFS are started from the boot scripts. The following sample shows the type of code that is included in the startup file of a client. The code checks for the existence of the **biod**, **rpc.statd**, and **rpc.lockd** programs* and if they are present, starts eight copies of **biod** as well as a copy of **rpc.statd** and **rpc.lockd**.

```
#       start the NFS client software
#       biod, statd and lockd
#
if [ -f /usr/etc/biod -a -f /usr/etc/rpc.statd
     -a -f /usr/etc/rpc.lockd ]; then
     biod 8;               echo -n ' biod'
     rpc.statd &           echo -n ' statd'
     rpc.lockd &           echo -n ' lockd'
fi
```

---

*These programs may not be in */usr/etc* on your system, and the "rpc." prefix may not be used on the daemon names. Check your system's documentation.

NFS server systems run all of the daemons shown above,* plus the NFS server daemon, **nfsd**, and the mount server daemon, **rpc.mountd**. The type of code that starts the additional daemons necessary for an NFS server is shown below:

```
if [ -f /etc/exports ]; then
     > /etc/xtab
     exportfs -a
     nfsd 8 &                    echo -n ' nfsd'
     rpc.mountd
fi
```

This sample code first checks for the existence of */etc/exports*, which is the file that contains information about the directories the server exports to its NFS clients. If */etc/exports* is found, the code empties */etc/xtab* and runs **exportfs**. **exportfs** reads */etc/exports*, uses the information to export the specified directories, and lists information about the exported directories in the */etc/xtab* file. (The **–a** option tells **exportfs** to export *all* directories listed in */etc/exports*.)

Next, the sample code starts eight copies of **nfsd** and a copy of **rpc.mountd**. The mount daemon determines which directories it should process mount requests for, by reading the */etc/xtab* file created by **exportfs**. Figure 9-1 shows the flow of export information from the */etc/exports* file to **mountd**.

Each system may have a different technique for starting these daemons. If some of the daemons aren't starting, make sure your startup scripts are correct.

---

*It's not really necessary for servers to run **biod**, but many servers also act as clients.

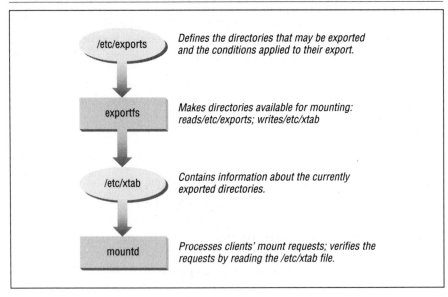

Figure 9.1: File Export Information for mountd

Exporting Filesystems

The first step in configuring a server is deciding which filesystems will be exported, and what restrictions will be placed on their export. Only filesystems that provide a benefit to the client should be exported. Before you export a filesystem, think about what purpose it will serve. Some common reasons for exporting filesystems are:

- to provide disk space to diskless clients;
- to prevent unnecessary duplication of the same data on multiple systems;
- to provide centrally supported programs and data;
- to share data among users in a group.

Once you've selected the filesystems you'll export, you must define them in the */etc/exports* file.

The /etc/exports File

The */etc/exports* file is the NFS server configuration file. It controls which files and directories are exported, which hosts can access them, and what kinds of access are allowed. A sample */etc/exports* file might contain these entries:

```
/usr/public
/usr/man          -rw=almond:pecan
/usr/local        -ro
/home/research    -access=peanut:almond:pecan:walnut
```

This sample file says that:

- */usr/public* can be mounted by any client on the network and used as if it were that client's local directory.

- */usr/man* can be mounted by any client, but it can only be written to by *almond* and *pecan*. Other clients have read-only access.

- */usr/local* can be mounted by any client, with read-only access.

- */home/research* can only be mounted by the hosts *peanut*, *almond*, *pecan*, and *walnut*. These four hosts have read-write access.

The options used in each of the entries in the */etc/exports* file determine what kinds of access are allowed. The information derived from the sample file is based on the options specified on each line in the file. The general format of the entries is:

directory [*–option*][,*option*] . . .

directory names the directory or file that is available for export, while each *option* specifies a condition for the export of that directory. The options used in the sample file are:

ro   Read-only prevents NFS clients from writing to this directory. Attempts by clients to write to a read-only directory fail with the message: "Read-only filesystem" or "Permission denied." If **ro** is not specified, clients are permitted to write to the directory as well as read from it.

rw[=*hostname*][:*hostname*] . . .

    Read-write permits clients to read and write to this directory. When specified without *hostname*, as simply **rw**, all clients are granted read-write access. (As noted above, this is the default.) If a *hostname* is specified, only the named host is given read-write permission. All other hosts are limited to read-only permission.

access=*hostname*[**:***hostname*] . . .

> **access** limits permission to mount this directory to those hosts speci-
> fied by *hostname*. No other hosts are permitted to mount this direc-
> tory. If the **access** option is not used, all hosts are allowed to mount
> the directory. Servers connected to the Internet should always use
> the **access** option; otherwise their filesystems will be exported to
> everyone on the Internet.

In any of these options a netgroup can be used in place of a host name.
For example, assume that the */etc/netgroup* file contains the following lines.
(This is the same sample *netgroup* file we used earlier.)

```
nuts sales research
research (almond,-,) (peanut,-,) (walnut,-,)
sales (-,sara,) (-,david,)
```

One of the sample */etc/exports* entries we saw above is:

```
/home/research  -access=peanut:almond:pecan:walnut
```

This entry can be rewritten, using the *research* netgroup, as:

```
/home/research  -access=research:pecan
```

The host names *peanut, almond,* and *walnut* are provided by the netgroup, and the host name *pecan* is explicitly defined. Both of these
/etc/exports statements perform the same function; i.e., they both limit
access to *peanut, almond, pecan,* and *walnut.*

If you're responsible for an NFS server for a large site, you should take care
in planning and implementing the NFS environment. The discussion in this
chapter tells how NFS is configured to run on a client and a server, but you
may want more details to design an optimal NFS environment. For a comprehensive treatment, see the Nutshell Handbook, *Managing NFS and NIS,*
by Hal Stern.

Mounting Remote Filesystems

You need some basic information before you can decide which NFS directories to mount on your system. You need to know which servers are connected to your network, and which directories are available from those
servers. A directory cannot be mounted unless it is first exported by a
server.

Your network administrator is a good source for this information. The
administrator can tell you what systems are providing NFS service, what
directories they are exporting, and what these directories contain. If you

are the administrator of an NFS server, you should develop this type of information for your users.

You can also obtain information about the exported directories directly from the servers by using the **showmount** command. The NFS servers are usually the same large, centrally supported systems that provide other services such as mail and domain name service. Select a likely server and query it with the command **showmount -e** *hostname*. In response to this command, the server will list the directories that it exports and the conditions applied to their export. For example, a **showmount –e** query to *filbert* produces the following output:

```
% showmount -e filbert
export list for filbert:
/usr/man            (everyone)
/usr/public         (everyone)
/home/research      peanut,almond,walnut,pecan
/usr/local          (everyone)
```

The export list shows the NFS directories exported by *filbert*, as well as who is allowed to access those directories. From this list, *peanut*'s administrator may decide to mount any of the directories offered by *filbert*. Our imaginary administrator decides to:

1. Mount */usr/man* from *filbert* instead of maintaining the **man** pages locally.
2. Mount */home/research* to more easily share files with other systems in the research group.
3. Mount the centrally maintained programs in */usr/local*.

These selections represent some of the most common motivations for mounting NFS directories. These are to:

- Save disk space.
- Share files with other systems.
- Maintain common files centrally.

The amount that you use NFS is a personal choice. Some people prefer the greater personal control you get from keeping files locally, while others prefer the convenience offered by NFS. Your site may have guidelines for how NFS should be used, which directories should be mounted, and which files should be centrally maintained. Check with your network administrator if you're unsure about how NFS is used at your site.

The mount Command

A client must mount an exported directory before using it. "Mounting" the directory attaches it to the client's filesystem hierarchy. Only directories named in the servers */etc/exports* file can be mounted, but any part of the exported directory, such as a subdirectory or a file, can be mounted.

NFS directories are mounted using the **mount** command. The general structure of the **mount** command is:

mount *hostname:remote-directory local-directory*

The *hostname* identifies an NFS server, and the *remote-directory* identifies all or part of a directory exported by that server. The **mount** command attaches that remote directory to the client's filesystem using the directory name provided for *local-directory*. The client's local directory, called the mount point, must be created before **mount** is executed. Once the mount is completed, files located in the remote directory can be accessed through the local directory exactly as if they were local files.

For example, assume that *filbert.nuts.com* is an NFS server and that it has the */etc/exports* file shown in the section above. Further assume that the administrator of *peanut* wants to access the */home/research* directory as a local directory. The administrator simply creates a local */home/research* directory, and mounts the remote */home/research* directory offered by *filbert* on this newly created mount point.

```
# mkdir /home/research
# mount filbert:/home/research /home/research
```

Once a remote directory is mounted, it stays attached to the local file system until it is explicitly dismounted or the local system reboots. To dismount a directory, use the **umount** command. On the **umount** command line, specify either the local or remote name of the directory that is to be dismounted. For example, the administrator of *peanut* can dismount the remote *filbert:/home/research* filesystem from the local */home/research* mount point, with either:

```
# umount /home/research
```

or:

```
# umount filbert:/home/research
```

Booting will also dismount NFS directories. Because clients frequently wish to mount the same directories every time they boot, NFS provides a system for automatically remounting directories after a boot.

The /etc/fstab File

The */etc/fstab* file provides information that is used to remount NFS directories after a system reboot. The file is very easy to build because the **mount** command **–p** option builds the file for you from existing mount information. Here's how.

Assume that the administrator of *peanut* wants to mount */usr/public*, */usr/man*, and */home/research* from *filbert*, and to ensure that these directories are remounted every time that *peanut* reboots. Assuming that all of the local mount point directories have already been created, the first step is to mount the remote directories.

```
# mount filbert:/usr/public /usr/public
# mount filbert:/usr/man /usr/man
# mount filbert:/home/research /home/research
```

Once the directories are mounted, the **mount** command is invoked with the **–p** option and the output from the command is directed to */etc/fstab*.

```
# mount -p > /etc/fstab
```

The */etc/fstab* file now contains information about the current NFS mounts. A **grep** of *fstab* shows this.*

```
% grep nfs /etc/fstab
filbert:/usr/spool/mail    /usr/spool/mail    nfs rw    0 0
filbert:/usr/man           /usr/man           nfs rw    0 0
filbert:/home/research     /home/research     nfs rw    0 0
```

Finally, code is placed in a boot script to mount the directories specified by the */etc/fstab* directory. Frequently, this startup code already exists in one of the boot scripts. If it doesn't, the following statement is added to the startup:

```
mount -vat nfs
```

The options on this command tell the system to mount all NFS-type directories found in the */etc/fstab* file. The **–v** option tells **mount** to display a message about each directory as it is being mounted. The **–a** option tells **mount** to mount all filesystems listed in the */etc/fstab* file, and the **–t** option followed by the **nfs** keyword limits the mount to only NFS-type filesystems. Our **grep** of the *fstab* file shows us that, on *peanut*, there are three **nfs**-type filesystems contained in that file. This code in the boot script causes **mount** to remount those three directories every time the system boots.

---

*grep is used because the *fstab* file contains other information not related to NFS.

This chapter discussed several of the network applications that require special configuration. In the next chapter we look at **sendmail**, the network application with the most complex configuration.

10

sendmail

Users have a love-hate relationship with e-mail; they love to use it, and hate when it doesn't work. It's the system administrator's job to make sure it does work. That is the job we tackle in this chapter.

sendmail is not the only mail transport program. MMDF (Multichannel Memorandum Distribution Facility) predates **sendmail** and is still used today; it is SCO's default mail transport program. There are also variations of basic **sendmail**, such as IDA sendmail, that are widely used. But plain **sendmail** is the most widely used mail transport program, and it's the one we cover.

This entire chapter is devoted to **sendmail**, and an entire book could easily be devoted to the subject. In part this is because of e-mail's importance, but it is also because **sendmail** has a complex configuration.

The variety of programs and protocols used for e-mail complicates configuration and support. SMTP sends e-mail over TCP/IP networks. Another program sends mail between users on the same system. Still another sends mail between systems on UUCP networks. Each of these mail systems—SMTP, UUCP, and local mail—has its own delivery program and its own mail addressing scheme. All of this can cause confusion for mail users and for system administrators.

sendmail's Function

sendmail eliminates some of the confusion caused by multiple mail delivery programs. It does this by routing mail for the user to the proper delivery program based on the e-mail address. It accepts mail from a user's mail program, interprets the mail address, rewrites the address into the proper form for the delivery program, and routes the mail to the correct delivery program. **sendmail** insulates the end user from these details. If the mail is properly addressed, **sendmail** will see that it is properly passed on for delivery. Likewise, for incoming mail **sendmail** interprets the address and either delivers the mail to a user's mail program or forwards it to another system.

Figure 10-1 illustrates **sendmail**'s special role in routing mail between the various mail programs found on UNIX systems.

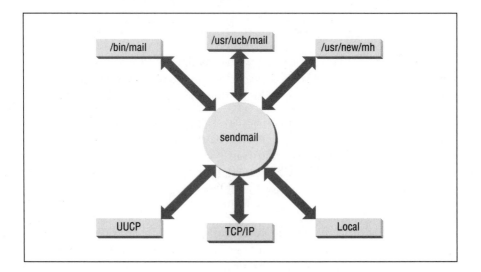

Figure 10.1: Mail is routed through sendmail

In addition to routing mail between user programs and delivery programs, **sendmail**:

- receives and delivers SMTP (internet) mail
- provides system-wide mail aliases, which allow mailing lists

Configuring a system to perform all of these functions properly is a complex task. In this chapter we discuss each of these functions, look at how they are configured, and examine ways to simplify the task. First, we'll see how **sendmail** is run to receive SMTP mail. Then we'll see how mail aliases are used, and how **sendmail** is configured to route mail based on the mail's address.

Running sendmail as a Daemon

To receive SMTP mail from the network, run **sendmail** as a daemon during system startup. The **sendmail** daemon listens to TCP port 25 and processes incoming mail. In most cases the code to start **sendmail** is already in one of your boot scripts. If it isn't, add the following code:

```
if [ -f /usr/lib/sendmail ]; then
        (cd /usr/spool/mqueue; rm -f lf*)
        /usr/lib/sendmail -bd -q1h; echo -n ' sendmail' > /dev/console
fi
```

First this code checks for the existence of the **sendmail** program. If the program is found, the code goes to the mail queue directory and removes any lock files found there. The mail queue directory holds mail that has not yet been delivered. It is possible that the system went down while the mail queue was being processed, so lock files may have been inadvertently left in that directory and should be removed during the boot.

Next the code starts **sendmail** with two command-line options. One option, the **–q** option, relates to the mail queue mentioned above. It tells **sendmail** how often to process the mail queue. In the sample code the queue is processed every hour (**–q1h**). This is a good setting for most systems. The exception to this is a central mail server that may need to process the queue more often—every 15 minutes (**–q15m**) or half hour (**–q30m**). Don't set this time too low. This can cause problems if the queue grows very large, due to a delivery problem such as a network outage.

The other option relates directly to internet mail. The option (**–bd**) tells **sendmail** to run as a daemon. This option causes **sendmail** to listen to TCP port 25 for incoming internet mail. Use this option if you want your system to accept incoming TCP/IP mail.

sendmail Aliases

It is almost impossible to exaggerate the importance of mail aliases. Without them, a **sendmail** system could not act as a central mail server. Mail aliases provide for:

- alternate names (nicknames) for individual users
- forwarding of mail to other hosts
- mailing lists

sendmail mail aliases are defined in the */etc/aliases* file.* The basic format of entries in the *aliases* file is:

alias: *recipient*[, *recipient*, ...]

alias is the name to which the mail is addressed, and *recipient* is the name to which the mail is delivered. *recipient* can be a user name, the name of another alias, or a full e-mail address containing both a user name and a host name. Including a host name allows mail to be forwarded to a remote host. Additionally there can be multiple recipients for a single alias. Mail addressed to that alias is delivered to all of the recipients. This creates a mailing list.

Aliases that define nicknames for individual users can be used to handle frequently misspelled names. You can also use aliases to deliver mail addressed to special names, such as *postmaster* or *root*, to the real users that do those jobs. Aliases can also be used to implement simplified mail addressing, especially when used in conjunction with MX records.† This *aliases* file from *almond* shows all of these uses:

```
# special names
postmaster: clark
root: norman
# accept first-initial_last-name@nuts.com
rhunt: becky@peanut
jmccafferty: jessie@walnut
aresnick: anthony@pecan
awright: andy@filbert
# a mailing list
admin: kathy, david@peanut, sara@pecan, becky@peanut, craig
        anna@peanut, jane@peanut, christy@filbert
owner-admin: craig
```

---

*Many systems use */usr/lib/aliases*.
†Chapter 8 discusses MX records.

The first two aliases are special names. Using these aliases, mail addressed to *postmaster* is delivered to the local user *clark*, and mail addressed to *root* is delivered to *norman*.

The second set of aliases is in the form of *first-initial* and *last-name*. The first alias in this group is *rhunt*. Mail addressed to *rhunt* is forwarded from *almond* and delivered to *becky@peanut*. Combine this alias with an MX record that names *almond* as the mail server for *nuts.com*, and mail addressed to *rhunt@nuts.com* is delivered to *becky@peanut.nuts.com*. This type of addressing scheme allows each user to advertise a consistent mailing address that does not change just because the user's account moves to another host. Additionally, if a remote user knows that this *first-initial-last-name* addressing scheme is used at *nuts.com*, he can address mail to Rebecca Hunt as *rhunt@nuts.com* without knowing her real e-mail address.

The last two aliases are for a mailing list. The alias *admin* defines the list itself. If mail is sent to *admin*, a copy of the mail is sent to each of the recipients (*kathy, david, sara, becky, craig, anna, jane,* and *christy*). Note that the mailing list continues across multiple lines. A line that starts with a blank or a tab is a continuation line.

The *owner-admin* alias is a special form used by **sendmail**. The format of this special alias is **owner–***listname* where *listname* is the name of a mailing list. The person specified on this alias line is responsible for the list identified by *listname*. The *owner-admin* alias defines *craig* as the person responsible for maintaining the mailing list *admin*. If **sendmail** has problems delivering mail to any of the recipients in the *admin* list, an error message is sent to *craig*.

sendmail does not use the *aliases* file directly. The *aliases* file must first be processed by the **newaliases** command.* **newaliases** creates the **dbm** database files that are used by **sendmail** when it is searching for aliases. You should invoke **newaliases** after updating the *aliases* file to make sure that **sendmail** will be able to use the new aliases.†

***newaliases** is equivalent to **sendmail –bi**. The **–bi** option causes **sendmail** to create the aliases database from *aliases*.
†If the D option is used (see Table 10-4), **sendmail** automatically rebuilds the aliases database—even if **newaliases** is not run.

Personal Mail Forwarding

In addition to the mail forwarding provided by *aliases*, **sendmail** allows individual users to define their own forwarding. The user defines his personal forwarding in the *.forward* file in his home directory. **sendmail** checks for this file after using the *aliases* file and before making final delivery to the user. If the *.forward* file exists, **sendmail** delivers the mail as directed by that file. For example, say that user *kathy* has a *.forward* file in her home directory that contains *kathy@podunk.edu*. The mail that **sendmail** would normally deliver to the local user *kathy* is forwarded to *kathy's* account at *podunk.edu*.

Use the *.forward* file for temporary forwarding. Modifying *aliases* and rebuilding the database takes more effort than modifying a *.forward* file, particularly if the forwarding change will be short-lived. Additionally, the *.forward* file puts the user in charge of his own mail forwarding.

Mail aliases and mail forwarding are handled by the *aliases* file and the *.forward* file. Everything else about the **sendmail** configuration is handled in the */etc/sendmail.cf* file.

The sendmail.cf File

The **sendmail** configuration file is */etc/sendmail.cf.** It contains most of the **sendmail** configuration, including the information required to route mail between the user mail programs and the mail delivery programs. The *sendmail.cf* file has three main functions:

* It defines the **sendmail** environment.
* It rewrites addresses into the appropriate syntax for the receiving mailer.
* It maps addresses into the instructions necessary to deliver the mail.

Several commands are necessary to perform all of these functions. Macro definitions and option commands define the environment. Rewrite rules rewrite e-mail addresses. Mailer definitions define the instructions necessary to deliver the mail. The terse syntax of these commands makes most system administrators reluctant to read a *sendmail.cf* file, let alone write one! Fortunately, you can avoid writing your own *sendmail.cf* file, and we'll show you how.

---

*Many systems use the file */usr/lib/sendmail.cf*.

Locating a Sample sendmail.cf File

There is rarely any good reason to write a *sendmail.cf* file from scratch. Locate an existing file with a configuration similar to your system's, modify it, and store it in */etc/sendmail.cf*. That's how you configure **sendmail**, and that's what we discuss in this section. Sample configuration files are delivered with most systems' software and others can be downloaded with the *sendmail.tar* file. The **tar** file can be downloaded via anonymous **ftp** from *ftp.uu.net*, in the file *mail/sendmail/sendmail.5.65.tar.Z*.

Even if your UNIX system comes with its own version of **sendmail**, it can be worthwhile to obtain the **tar** file from *ftp.uu.net*. It contains very useful sample configuration files and documentation. In particular *Sendmail: An Internetwork Mail Router* and *Sendmail Installation and Operation Guide*, both by Eric Allman, are important references for serious students of **sendmail**. With Eric's permission, the **sendmail** material in this chapter is largely derived from these two sources. Additionally, the examples used here are directly derived from the sample configuration files found in the **tar** file's *sendmail.5.65/cf/cf* directory.

The *sendmail.5.65/cf/cf* directory contains several sample configuration files. Three of these are prototype files designed to be easily modified and used in different network environments. The three prototype files are:

tcpuucpproto.cf   For systems that have both direct TCP/IP and UUCP network connections.

tcpproto.cf   For systems that have direct TCP/IP network connections and no direct UUCP connections.

uucpproto.cf   For systems that have direct UUCP network connections and no direct connections to TCP/IP networks.

These configuration files are almost identical. The few differences occur at the beginning and end of the files. Most of the items that require custom configuration are located in the first two sections of the files. You can ignore the bulk of the configuration and concentrate on the few items that may need customizing.

General sendmail.cf Structure

Many *sendmail.cf* files have, more or less, the same structure because most are descendants of a few original files. Therefore, the files provided with your system may be similar to the ones used in our examples. Some systems use a different structure, but the functions of the sections described here will be found somewhere in most *sendmail.cf* files.

The prototype file, *tcpuucpproto.cf*, is our example of *sendmail.cf* file structure. *tcpuucpproto.cf* supports direct UUCP and TCP/IP connections, so it's a good general example. The section labels from the prototype file are used here to provide an overview of the *sendmail.cf* structure. These sections will be described in greater detail when we modify a sample configuration. The sections are:

Local Information

> Defines the information that is specific to the individual host. For example in the *tcpuucpproto.cf* file, Local Information defines the Internet host name, the UUCP host name, and the local UUCP connections. This section is usually customized during configuration.

General Macros

> Defines the information that is specific to this local network. In our sample file General Macros defines the domain name, the "official" host name,* and the mail relay hosts. This section is usually modified during configuration.

Classes

> Defines groups of host names or domain names used for special mail routing. Modifications are usually not required.

Version Number

> Identifies the version number of the *sendmail.cf* file. Increase the version number each time you modify the configuration.

Special Macros

> Defines some special macros used by **sendmail**. In the *tcpuucpproto.cf* file, the Special Macros section contains such things as the name that **sendmail** uses to identify itself when it returns error messages, and the message that **sendmail** displays during an SMTP login. This section is not modified.

Options

> Defines the **sendmail** options. This section usually requires no modifications.

Message Precedence

> Defines the various message precedence values used by **sendmail**. This section is not modified.

---

*The official host name is usually the full host name including the domain name part.

Trusted Users

> Defines the users who are trusted to override the sender address when they are sending mail. This section is not modified. Adding users to this list is a potential security problem.

Format of Headers

> Defines the format of the headers that **sendmail** inserts into mail. This section is not modified.

Rewriting Rules

> Defines the rules used to rewrite mail addresses. Rewriting Rules contains the general rules called by **sendmail** or other rewrite rules. This section is not modified during the initial **sendmail** configuration. Rewrite rules are usually only modified to correct a problem or to add a new service.

Mailers

> Defines the instructions used by **sendmail** to invoke the mail delivery programs. The specific rewrite rules associated with each individual mailer are also defined in this section. The mailer definitions are usually not modified.

Rule Set Zero

> Defines a special rewrite rule set, called *rule set zero*, that is applied to the delivery address. This section is not modified. The part of rule set zero that is modified has its own section heading.

Machine-dependent Part of Rule Set Zero

> Defines those parts of rule set zero that are specific to this configuration. This section varies slightly based on the mailers configured for the system. A system that can directly deliver UUCP and SMTP mail will have different rewrite rules in this section than a system that can only directly deliver UUCP mail. You probably won't have to modify this section if you select a sample **sendmail** configuration file that matches your network configuration.

The section labels in the sample file delivered with your system are probably different from these. However, the structure of your sample file is probably similar to the structure discussed above in these ways:

- The information that is customized for each host is probably at the beginning of the file.
- Similar types of commands, e.g., option commands, header commands, etc., are usually grouped together.
- The bulk of the file consists of rewrite rules.
- The last part of the file probably contains mailer definitions intermixed with the rewrite rules that are associated with the individual mailers.

Look at the comments in your *sendmail.cf* file. Sometimes these comments provide valuable insight into the file structure and the things that are necessary to configure a system.

It's important to realize how little of *sendmail.cf* needs to be modified for a typical system. If you pick the right sample file to work from, you may only need to modify a few lines in the first two sections. From this perspective, **sendmail** configuration appears to be a trivial task. So why are system administrators so intimidated by the **sendmail** configuration? In large part it is because of the difficult syntax of the *sendmail.cf* configuration language.

sendmail Configuration

Every time it starts up, **sendmail** reads *sendmail.cf*. For this reason, the syntax of the *sendmail.cf* commands is designed to be easy for **sendmail** to parse—not necessarily easy for humans to read. As a consequence, **sendmail** commands are very terse, even by UNIX standards. The commands and variables are each only one character long. It's easy to confuse a single character command and a single character variable!

This terse syntax can be very hard to decipher, but it helps to remember that the first character on the line is always the command. From this single character you can determine what the command is and therefore its structure. Table 10-1 lists the *sendmail.cf* commands and their syntax.

Table 10.1: sendmail Configuration Commands

Command	Syntax	Meaning
Define Macro	**D***xvalue*	Set macro *x* to *value*.
Define Class	**C***cword1*[*word2*] . . .	Set class *c* to *word1 word2* . . .
Define Class	**F***cfile*	Load class *c* from *file*.
Set Option	**O***ovalue*	Set option *o* to *value*.
Trusted Users	**T***user1*[*user2* . . .]	Trusted users are *user1 user2* . . . .
Set Precedence	**P***name=number*	Set *name* to precedence *number*.
Define Mailer	**M***name, {field=value}*	Define mailer *name*.
Define Header	**H**[?*mflag*?]*name:format*	Set header format.

Table 10.1: sendmail Configuration Commands (continued)

Command	Syntax	Meaning
Set Ruleset	**S***n*	Start ruleset number *n*.
Define Rule	**R***lhs rhs comment*	Rewrite *lhs* patterns to *rhs* format.

The configuration command is not separated from its variable or value by any spaces. This "run together" format makes the commands hard to read. Figure 10-2 illustrates the format of a command. In the figure, a define macro command assigns the value *nuts.com* to the macro D.

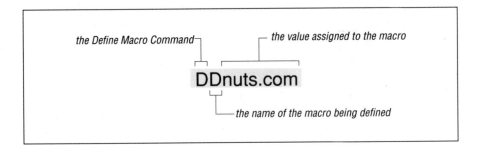

Figure 10.2: A sendmail.cf Configuration Command

The following sections describe each configuration command in more detail.

The Define Macro Command

The define macro command (**D**) defines a macro and stores a value in it. Once the macro is defined, it is used to provide the stored value to other *sendmail.cf* commands and directly to **sendmail** itself. This allows **sendmail** configurations to be shared by many systems, simply by modifying a few system-specific macros.

A macro name can be any single ASCII character. Lowercase letters are used as names for **sendmail**'s own internal macros. User-created macros use uppercase letters as names. This does not mean that you won't be called upon to define a value for a macro with a lowercase name. Some of **sendmail**'s internal macros *must* be defined in the *sendmail.cf* file. These macros are listed in Table 10-2. All of the macros listed in Table 10-2 are defined in a configuration file, but only the value assigned to macro j is usually modified.

*Table 10.2: Required sendmail Macros**

Macro	Value Assigned This Macro	Example
e	SMTP entry message	De$j Sendmail $v ready at $b
j	site's official domain name	Dj$w.$D
l	format of the UNIX from line	DlFrom $g $d
n	name used in error messages	DnMAILER-DAEMON
o	set of operators in addresses	Do.:%\@!^=/
q	default sender address format	Dqg?x ($x)$.

To retrieve the value stored in a macro, reference it as $x, where x is the macro name. For example, the code below defines the macros w, D, and j. After this code executes, $w returns *almond*, $D returns *nuts.com*, and $j returns *almond.nuts.com*. This sample code defines j as containing the value of w ($w), plus a literal dot, plus the value of D ($D). If the value assigned to a macro contains references to other macros, the references are expanded when the macro is used.

```
Dwalmond
DDnuts.com
Dj$w.$D
```

In this example D is a user-created macro, while j and w are macros with specific internal meanings to **sendmail**. We know this because D is upper-case, and w and j are lowercase. Table 10-3 provides a complete list of **sendmail**'s internal macros.† Compare this to the much shorter list in Table 10-2. The values of most internal macros are not set in the *send-mail.cf* file; they are assigned internally by **sendmail**.

---

*Table 10-2 is taken from *Sendmail Installation and Operation Guide*, page 17.
†Table 10-3 is from *Sendmail Installation and Operation Guide*, page 18.

Table 10.3: sendmail's Internal Macros

Name	Function
a	origination date in RFC 822 format
b	current date in RFC 822 format
c	hop count
d	date in UNIX (ctime) format
e	SMTP entry message
f	sender "from" address
g	sender address relative to the recipient
h	recipient host
i	queue id
j	"official" domain name for this site
l	format of the UNIX from line
n	name of the daemon (for error messages)
o	set of "operators" in addresses
p	sendmail's pid
q	default format of sender address
r	protocol used
s	sender's host name
t	numeric representation of the current time
u	recipient user
v	version number of sendmail
w	hostname of this site
x	full name of the sender
z	home directory of the recipient

When customizing your *sendmail.cf* file, it will probably be necessary to modify some macro definitions. The macros that usually require modification define site-specific information, such as host names and domain names.

Conditionals

One of the macro definitions in Table 10-2, the definition of macro q, deserves special comment. It is different from the other definitions because it contains a conditional. Here's the code for macro q shown in the table:

```
Dq$g$?x ($x)$.
```

The **D** is the define macro command; q is the macro being defined; and $g says to use the value stored in macro g. But what does **$?x ($x)$.** mean? The construct **$?x** is a conditional. It tests whether macro x has a value set. If the macro has been set, the text following the conditional is interpreted. The **$.** construct ends the conditional.

Given this, the assignment of macro q is interpreted as follows: q is assigned the value of g; and if x is set, it is also assigned a literal blank, a literal left parenthesis, the value of x, and a literal right parenthesis. So if g contains *chunt@nuts.com* and x contains *Craig Hunt*, q will contain:

```
chunt@nuts.com (Craig Hunt)
```

The conditional can be used with an "else" construct, which is **$|**. The full syntax of the conditional is:

$?x *text1* **$|** *text2* **$.**

This is interpreted as:

- *if* ($?) *x* is set;
- use *text1*;
- else ($|); use *text2*;
- end if ($.).

The Define Class Command

Two commands, **C** and **F**, define **sendmail** classes. A class is an array of values. Classes are used for anything with multiple values that are handled in the same way, such as multiple names for the local host or a list of **uucp** host names. Classes allow **sendmail** to compare against a list of values, instead of against a single value. Special pattern matching symbols are used with classes. The **$=** symbol matches any value in a class, and the **$~** symbol matches any value not in a class. (More on pattern matching later.)

Like macros, classes have single character names, and user-created classes use uppercase letters for names. Class values can be defined on a single line, on multiple lines, or loaded from a file. For example, class V is often used to define local UUCP connections. To assign class V the values *bronson* and *ora*, you can enter the values on a single line:

```
CVbronson ora
```

Or you can enter the values on multiple lines:

```
CVbronson
CVora
```

You can also use the **F** command to load the class values from a file. The **F** command reads a file and stores the words found there in a class variable. For example, to define class w and assign it all of the strings found in */etc/sendmail.cw*, use:

```
Fw/etc/sendmail.cw
```

You may need to modify a few class definitions when creating your *sendmail.cf* file. Frequently information relating to **uucp**, to alias host names, and to special domains for mail routing is defined in class statements. If your system has a **uucp** connection as well as a TCP/IP connection, pay particular attention to the class definitions. But in any case, check the class definitions carefully and make sure they apply to your configuration.

Here we **grep** the sample configuration file for lines beginning with **C** or **F**:

```
% grep '^[CF]' tcpuucpproto.cf
Fw/usr/lib/sendmail.cw
CUYOUR_UUCP_ALIASES_GO_HERE
CV      YOUR
CV      UUCP
CV      NEIGHBORS
CV      GO
CV      HERE
CIUUCP BITNET CSNET
```

This **grep** shows that *tcpuucpproto.cf* defines classes w, U, V, and I. w contains the host's name and its aliases. In this sample, it is read from a file. U holds the host's UUCP aliases. V holds the UUCP connections, and I holds the fake domains used for mail routing. In our sample file, most of the values are not yet configured. After configuration, **grep** would show something different:

```
% grep '^[CF]' tcpuucpproto.cf
CUlos
CVbronson
CVora
CVgenly
CVbabss
CVm10
CIUUCP BITNET
```

Notice that the **F** command is gone. This example assumes that the system doesn't read its host name from */etc/sendmail.cw*; it gets the correct host name internally from **sendmail**. The system's only UUCP name is *los*. The system's UUCP connections are *bronson, ora, genly, babss,* and *m10*. The fake mail domains were changed to delete CSNET. The values used for these classes had to come from the system administrator's knowledge of his system and its network connections.

Remember that your system will be different. The uppercase letters used for these class names mean that they are user-created classes. These same class names may be used for other purposes on your system, and are only presented here as an example. Carefully read the comments in your *sendmail.cf* file for guidance as to how classes and macros are used in your configuration.

The Set Option Command

Set option commands (**O**) assign values to **sendmail** options. These are internal options set inside the *sendmail.cf* file. They are not the same as the command-line arguments, which are documented later in Table 10-9.

Use the **O** command to set values appropriate for your installation. The value assigned to an option is a string, an integer, a boolean, or a time interval, as appropriate for the individual option. All options define values used directly by **sendmail**.

There are no user-created options. The meaning of each **sendmail** option is defined within **sendmail** itself. Table 10-4 lists the meaning and use of each option, and there are plenty of them.*

Table 10.4: sendmail Options

Name	Function
A*file*	Define the name of the alias file.
a*N*	Wait *N* minutes for @:@; then rebuild the alias file.
B*c*	Define the blank substitution character.
c	Queue mail for expensive mailers.
D	Rebuild the alias database.
db	Deliver in background mode.

*Table 10-4 is taken from *Sendmail Installation and Operations Guide*, Appendix B.

Table 10.4: sendmail Options (continued)

Name	Function
di	Deliver interactively.
dq	Deliver during the next queue run.
ee	Mail error messages and always return 0 exit status.
em	Mail back error messages.
ep	Print error messages.
eq	Just return exit status, not error messages.
ew	Write back error messages.
F*n*	Set permissions for temporary files to *n*.
f	Retain Unix-style "From" lines.
g*n*	Set the default group id for mailers to *n*.
H*file*	Define the name of the SMTP help file.
I	Use the BIND name server to resolve all host names.
i	Ignore dots in incoming messages.
L*n*	Set the level of logging to *n*.
M*xval*	Set macro *x* to *val*.
m	Send to me, too.
N*net*	Define the name of the home network.
o	Accept old format headers.
Q*dir*	Define the name of the queue directory.
q*n*	Define a factor *n* used to decide when to queue jobs.
r*t*	Set interval *t* for read timeout.
S*file*	Define the name of the statistics log file.
s	Always create the queue file before attempting delivery.
T*t*	Set the queue timeout to *t*.
u*n*	Set the default userid for mailers to *n*.
v	Run in verbose mode.
W*pass*	Define password used for remote debugging
X*l*	Refuse SMTP connections if load average exceeds *l*.
x*l*	Queue messages if load average exceeds *l*.
Y	Deliver each queued job in a separate process.
y*n*	Lower priority of jobs by *n* for each recipient.
Z*n*	Decrease a job's priority by *n* each time it is run.
z*n*	Factor used with precedence to determine message priority.

A few sample options from the *tcpuucpproto.cf* file are shown below. The
A option defines the name of the **sendmail** *aliases* file as */usr/lib/aliases*.
If you wanted to put the *aliases* file elsewhere, you would change this

option. The F option defines the default file mode as 0600 for temporary files created by **sendmail** in */var/spool/mqueue*. The T option sets the timeout interval for undeliverable mail, here set to three days (3d). These options show the kind of general configuration parameters set by the option command.

```
# location of alias file
OA/usr/lib/aliases
# temporary file mode
OF0600
# default timeout interval
OT3d
```

From Table 10-4 it's easy to see that most of the options have specialized, narrow meanings. Most of the options defined in a sample file don't require modification for any type of configuration. The options in the configuration file that came with your system are almost certainly correct.

Defining Trusted Users

The **T** command defines a list of users who are trusted to override the sender address using the mailer **–f** flag.* Normally the trusted users are defined as *root*, *uucp*, and *daemon*. Be careful if you extend this list. Trusted users can provide a false sender name. In the hands of the wrong users, this authority may cause security problems or embarrassment to your organization.

Trusted users can be specified as a list of user names on a single command line, or on multiple command lines. The users must be valid user names from the */etc/passwd* file. The most commonly defined trusted users are:

```
Troot
Tdaemon
Tuucp
```

Most sites do not need to modify this list.

Defining Mail Precedence

Precedence is one of the factors used by **sendmail** to assign priority to messages entering its queue. The **P** command defines the message precedence values available to **sendmail** users. The higher the precedence number, the greater the precedence of the message. The default

---

*Mailer flags are listed in Table 10-5.

precedence of a message is 0. Negative precedence numbers indicate especially low priority mail. Error messages are not generated for mail with a
negative precedence number, making low priorities attractive for mass
mailings. Some commonly used precedence values are:

```
Pfirst-class=0
Pspecial-delivery=100
Pbulk=-60
Pjunk=-100
```

To specify the precedence he desires, a user adds a **Precedence** header to
his message. He uses the text name from the **P** command in the **Precedence** header to set the specific precedence of the message. Given the
precedence definitions shown above, a user who wanted to avoid receiving
error messages for a large mailing could select a message precedence of -60
by including the following header line in his mail:

```
Precedence: bulk
```

The four precedence values shown above are probably more than you'll
ever need.

Defining Mail Headers

The **H** command defines the format of header lines that **sendmail** inserts
into messages. The format of the header command is the **H** command,
optional header flags enclosed in question marks, a header name, a colon,
and a header template. The header template is a combination of literals
and macros that are included in the header line. Macros in the header template are expanded before the header is inserted in a message.

The header flags often arouse more questions than they merit. The function of the flags is very simple. The header flags control whether or not the
header is inserted into mail bound for a specific mailer. If no flags are
specified, the header is used for all mailers. If a flag is specified, the header
is used only for a mailer that has the same flag set in the mailer's definition.
(Mailer flags are listed in Table 10-6.) Header flags only control header
insertion. If a header is received in the input, it is passed to the output,
regardless of the flag settings.

The header definitions from our sample file are:

```
H?P?Return-Path: <$g>
HReceived: $?sfrom $s $.by $j ($v/$Z)
H?D?Resent-Date: $a
H?D?Date: $a
H?F?Resent-From: $q
```

```
H?F?From: $q
H?x?Full-Name: $x
HSubject:
H?M?Resent-Message-Id: <$t.$i@$j>
H?M?Message-Id: <$t.$i@$j>
```

These headers are sufficient for most installations, and it's unlikely you'll ever need to change them.

Defining Mailers

The **M** commands define the mail delivery programs used by **sendmail**. The syntax of the command is:

Mname, {field=value}

name is an arbitrary name used internally by **sendmail** to refer to this mailer. The name doesn't matter as long as it is used consistently within the *sendmail.cf* file to refer to this mailer. For example, the mailer used to deliver SMTP mail within the local domain might be called *tcpld* on one system, and it might be called *ether* on another system. The function of both mailers is the same, only the names are different.

There are two exceptions to this freedom of choice. The mailer that delivers local mail to users on the same machine must be called *local*, and the mailer that delivers mail to programs must be called *prog*.

The mailer name is followed by a comma-separated list of *field=value* pairs that define the characteristics of the mailer. Table 10-5 shows the single character *field* identifiers and the contents of the *value* field associated with each of them.* Most mailers don't require all of these fields.

Table 10.5: Mailer Definition Fields

Field	Meaning	Contents	Example
P	Path	Path of the mailer	P=/bin/mail
F	Flags	sendmail flags for this mailer	F=lsDFMe
S	Sender	Ruleset for sender addresses	S=10
R	Recipient	Ruleset for recipient addresses	R=20
A	Argv	The mailer's argument vector	A=sh -c $u

---

*Table 10-5 is taken from *Sendmail Installation and Operation Guide*, page 16.

Table 10.5: Mailer Definition Fields (continued)

Field	Meaning	Contents	Example
E	Eol	End-of-line string for the mailer	E=\r\n
M	Maxsize	Maximum message length	M=100000

The Path (P) fields contain either the path to the mail delivery program or the literal string [IPC] that stands for interprocess communication. Mailer definitions that specify P=[IPC] use **sendmail** to deliver mail via SMTP. The path to a mail delivery program will vary from system to system depending on where the systems store the programs. Make sure you know where the programs are stored before you modify the Path field. If you use a sample configuration from another computer, such as the samples we use in this chapter, make sure that the mailer paths are valid for your system.

The Flags (F) field contains the **sendmail** flags used for this mailer. These are the mailer flags referenced above in the *Define Header* section, but these flags do more than just control header insertion. The flags and their functions are listed in Table 10-6.*

Table 10.6: sendmail Mailer Flags

Name	Function
C	Add *@domain* to addresses that do not have an @.
D	The mailer wants a Date: header line.
E	Add > to message lines that begin with From:.
e	This an expensive mailer. See **sendmail** option c.
F	The mailer wants a From: header line.
f	The mailer accepts a -f flag from trusted users.
h	Preserve uppercase in host names.
I	The mailer will be speaking SMTP to another sendmail.
L	Limit the line lengths as specified in RFC821.
l	This is a local mailer.
M	The mailer wants a Message-Id: header line.
m	The mailer can send to multiple users in one transaction.
n	Don't insert a UNIX-style From: line in the message.
P	The mailer wants a Return-Path: line.

*Table 10-6 is taken from *Sendmail Installation and Operations Guide, Appendix C.*

Table 10.6: sendmail Mailer Flags (continued)

Name	Function
R	Use the MAIL FROM: return-path rather than the return address.
r	The mailer accepts a -r flag from trusted users.
S	Don't reset the userid before calling the mailer.
s	Strip quotes off of the address before calling the mailer.
U	The mailer wants Unix-style From: lines.
u	Preserve uppercase in user names.
X	Prepend a dot to lines beginning with a dot.
x	The mailer wants a Full-Name: header line.

The Sender (S) and the Recipient (R) fields identify the rulesets used to rewrite the sender and recipient addresses for this mailer. Each ruleset is identified by its number. We'll have more to say about rulesets later in this chapter.

The Argv (A) field defines the argument vector passed to the mailer. It contains, among other things, macro expansions that provide the recipient user name ($u),* the recipient host name ($h), and the sender's from address ($f). These macros are expanded before the argument vector is passed to the mailer.

The last two fields have very simple functions. The End-of-line (E) field defines the characters used to mark the end of a line. A newline is the default. Maxsize (M) defines, in bytes, the longest message that this mailer will handle. These two fields are used infrequently.

Some Common Mailer Definitions

The following mailer definitions are from *tcpuucpproto.cf.*

```
Mlocal, P=/bin/mail,   F=rlsDFMmn,  S=10, R=20, A=mail -d $u
Mprog,  P=/bin/sh,     F=lsDFMe,    S=10, R=20, A=sh -c $u
Mtcpld, P=[IPC],       F=mDFMueXLC, S=17, R=27, A=IPC $h, E=\r\n
Mtcp,   P=[IPC],       F=mDFMueXLC, S=14, R=24, A=IPC $h, E=\r\n
Muucp,  P=/usr/bin/uux, F=DFMhuU,   S=13, R=23, M=100000,
        A=uux - -r -z -a$f -gC $h!rmail ($u)
```

---

*In the *prog* mailer definition, $u actually passes a program name in the argument vector.

This example contains the following common mailer definitions:

- A definition for local mail delivery, always called *local*. This definition is required by **sendmail**.
- A definition for delivering mail to programs, always called *prog*. This definition is also required by **sendmail**.
- A definition for TCP/IP mail to the local domain, here called *tcpld*.
- A definition for TCP/IP mail to the Internet, here called *tcp*.
- A definition for **uucp** mail, usually called *uucp*.

A close examination of the fields in one of these mailer entries, for example the entry for the *uucp* mailer, shows the following:

Muucp   A mailer, arbitrarily named *uucp*, is being defined.

P=/usr/bin/uux

> The path to the program used for this mailer is */usr/bin/uux.*

F=DFMhuU

> The **sendmail** flags for this mailer say that Date, From, and Message-Id headers are needed; that uppercase should be preserved in host names and user names; and that UNIX-style "From" lines are used. Refer to Table 10-5.

S=13   All sender addresses are processed through ruleset 13.

R=23   All recipient addresses are processed through ruleset 23.

M=100000

> This mailer will not handle messages greater than 100,000 bytes long.

A=uux - -r -z -a$f -gC $h!rmail ($u)

> The meaning of each option in this argument vector is exactly as defined on the **man** page for **uux**. The macros are expanded to provide the sender's from address ($f), the recipient host ($h) on which the **rmail** command is executed, and the recipient user ($u). After the macros are expanded, the vector is passed to **/usr/bin/uux**.

Despite this long discussion, there is no need for you to worry about mailer definitions. The sample configuration file that comes with your system will contain the correct mailer definitions to run **sendmail** in a TCP/IP network environment. You shouldn't need to modify any mailer definitions.

Rewriting the Mail Address

Rewrite rules are the heart of the *sendmail.cf* file. Rulesets are groups of individual rewrite rules used to parse e-mail addresses from user mail programs and rewrite them into the form required by the mail delivery programs. Each rewrite rule is defined by an **R** command. The syntax of the **R** command is:

R*pattern   transformation   comment*

The fields in an **R** command are separated by tab characters. The *comment* field is ignored by the system, but good comments are vital if you want to have any hope of understanding what's going on. The *pattern* and *transformation* fields are the heart of this command.

Pattern Matching

Rewrite rules match the input address against the pattern, and if a match is found, rewrite the address in a new format using the rules defined in the transformation. A rule may process the same address several times because, after being rewritten, the address is again compared against the pattern. If it still matches, it is rewritten again. The cycle of pattern matching and rewriting continues until the address no longer matches the pattern.

The pattern is defined using macros, classes, literals, and special metasymbols. The macros, classes, and literals provide the values against which the input is compared, and the metasymbols define the rules used in matching the pattern. Table 10-7 shows the metasymbols used for pattern matching.*

Table 10.7: Pattern Matching Symbols

Symbol	Meaning
$*	Match zero or more tokens.
$+	Match one or more tokens.
$-	Match exactly one token.
$=x	Match any token in class x.
$~x	Match any token not in class x.
$x	Match all tokens in macro x.

---

*From *Sendmail Installation and Operation Guide*, page 19.

Table 10.7: Pattern Matching Symbols (continued)

Symbol	Meaning
$%*x*	Match any token in the NIS map named in macro *x*.*
$!*x*	Match any token not in the NIS map named in macro *x*.*
$%y	Match any token in the NIS hosts.byname map.*

All of the metasymbols request a match for some number of tokens. A token is a string of characters in an e-mail address delimited by an operator. The operators are the characters defined in macro *o*.† Operators are also counted as tokens when an address is parsed. For example:

```
becky@peanut.nuts.com
```

This e-mail address contains seven tokens: becky, @, peanut, ., nuts, ., and com. This address would match the pattern:

```
$-@$+
```

The address matches the pattern because:

- It has exactly one token before the @ that matches the requirement of the $– symbol.
- It has an @ that matches the pattern's literal @.
- It has one or more tokens after the @ that match the requirement of the $+ symbol.

Many addresses, *hostmaster@nic.ddn.mil*, *chunt@nist.gov*, etc., match this pattern, but other addresses do not. For example, *hunt%nbsenh@almond.nuts.com* does not match because it has three tokens: hunt, %, and nbsenh, before the @. Therefore, it fails to meet the requirement of exactly one token specified by the $– symbol. Using the metasymbols, macros and literals, patterns can be constructed to match any type of e-mail address.

When an address matches a pattern, the strings from the address that match the metasymbols are assigned to *indefinite tokens*. The matching strings are called indefinite tokens because they may contain more than one token value. The indefinite tokens are identified numerically according to the

---

*This symbol is specific to Sun OS systems.
†See Table 10-2.

relative position in the pattern of the metasymbol that the string matched. In other words, the indefinite token produced by the match of the first metasymbol is called $1; the match of the second symbol is called $2; the third is $3 and so on. For example, when the address *becky@pea-nut.nuts.com* matched the pattern $–@$+, two indefinite tokens were created. The first is identified as $1 and contains the single token *becky* that matched the $– symbol. The second indefinite token is $2 and contains the five tokens: peanut, ., nuts, ., and com that matched the $+ symbol. The indefinite tokens created by the pattern matching can then be referenced by name ($1, $2, etc.) when rewriting the address.

Transforming the Address

The transformation field, from the right-hand side of the rewrite rule, defines the format used for rewriting the address. It is defined with the same things used to define the pattern: literals, macros, and special metasymbols. Literals in the transformation are written into the new address exactly as shown. Macros are expanded and then written. The metasymbols perform special functions. The transformation metasymbols and their functions are shown in Table 10-8.*

Table 10.8: Transformation Metasymbols

Symbol	Meaning
$n	Substitute indefinite token *n*.
$[*name*$]	Substitute canonical *name*.
$>n	Call ruleset *n*.
$@	Terminate ruleset.
$:	Terminate rewrite rule.

The $n symbol, where *n* is a number, is used for the indefinite token substitution discussed above. The indefinite token is expanded and written to the "new" address. The following example demonstrates how indefinite tokens are used.

---

*Table 10-8 is from *Sendmail Installation and Operation Guide*, page 19.

Addresses are always processed by several rewrite rules. No one rule tries to do everything. Assume the input address *hunt@nbsenh.bitnet* has been through some preliminary processing and now is:

```
hunt<@nbsenh.bitnet>
```

Assume the current rewrite rule is:

```
R$+<@$+.bitnet>    $1%$2<@$B>    Use the Bitnet relay
```

The address matches the pattern because it contains one or more tokens before the literal <@, one or more tokens after the <@, and then the literal string .bitnet>. The pattern match produces two indefinite tokens that are used in the transformation to rewrite the address.

The transformation contains the indefinite token $1, a literal %, indefinite token $2, a literal <@, the macro B, and the literal >. After the pattern matching, $1 contains hunt and $2 contains nbsenh. Assume that the macro B was defined elsewhere in the *sendmail.cf* file as *cunyvm.cuny.edu*, a major Bitnet relay host. In this case the input address is rewritten as:

```
hunt%nbsenh<@cunyvm.cuny.edu>
```

Figure 10-3 illustrates this specific address rewrite. It shows the tokens derived from the input address, and how those tokens are matched against the pattern. It also shows the indefinite tokens produced by the pattern matching, and how the indefinite tokens, and other values from the transformation, are used to produce the rewritten address.

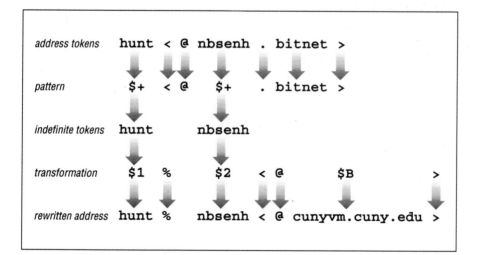

Figure 10.3: Rewriting an Address

After rewriting, the address is again compared to the pattern. This time it fails to match the pattern because it no longer contains the literal string .bit-net>. So, no further processing is done by this rewrite rule and the address is passed to the next rule in line. This example shows that indefinite token substitution is essential for flexible address rewriting. Without it, values could not be easily moved from the input address to the rewritten address.

The **$[***name***$]** symbol converts a host's nickname or its IP address to its canonical name by passing the value *name* to the name server for resolution.* For example, using the *nuts.com* name servers, $[mil-gw$] returns *almond.nuts.com* and $[[128.66.12.2]$] returns *peanut.nuts.com.*

The **$>***n* symbol calls ruleset *n* and passes the address defined by the remainder of the transformation to ruleset *n* for processing. For example:

```
$>9$1%$2
```

This transformation calls ruleset 9 ($>9), and passes the contents of $1, a literal %, and the contents of $2 to ruleset 9 for processing. When ruleset 9 finishes processing, it returns a rewritten address to the calling rule. The returned e-mail address is then compared again to the pattern in the calling rule. If it still matches, ruleset 9 is called again.

The recursion built into rewrite rules creates the possibility for infinite loops. The last two metasymbols shown in Table 10-8 are used to prevent loops. The **$@** and the **$:** symbols are used to control processing. If the transformation begins with the **$@** symbol, the entire ruleset is terminated and the remainder of the transformation is the value returned by the ruleset. If the transformation begins with the **$:** symbol, the individual rule is executed only once. Use **$:** to prevent recursion and to prevent loops when calling other rulesets. Use **$@** to exit a ruleset at a specific rule.

There is a special rewrite rule syntax that is only used in ruleset 0. Ruleset 0 defines the triple (*mailer, host, user*) that specifies the mail delivery program, the recipient host, and the recipient user. The special transformation syntax used to do this is:

```
$#mailer$@host$:user
```

---

*Sun has two versions of **sendmail**; */usr/lib/sendmail.mx* uses DNS name service.

An example of this syntax taken from the *tcpuucpproto.cf* sample file is:

```
# resolve SMTP traffic
R$*<@$+>$*     $#tcpld$@$2$:$1<@$2>$3  user@host.domain
```

Assume the e-mail address *david<@filbert.nuts.com>* is processed by this rule. The address matches the pattern $*<@$+>$* because:

- The address has zero or more tokens (the token david) that match the first $* symbol.
- The address has a literal <@.
- The address has one or more tokens (the five tokens filbert.nuts.com) that match the requirement of the $+ symbol.
- The address has a literal >.
- The address has zero or more, in this case zero, tokens that match the requirement of the last $* symbol.

This pattern match produces two indefinite tokens. Indefinite token $1 contains david and $2 contains filbert.nuts.com. No other matches occurred, so $3 is null. These indefinite tokens are used to rewrite the address into the following triple:

```
$#tcpld$@filbert.nuts.com$:david<@filbert.nuts.com>
```

The components of this triple are:

$#tcpld   *tcpld* is the internal name of the mailer that delivers the message.

$@filbert.nuts.com   *filbert.nuts.com* is the recipient host.

$:david<@filbert.nuts.com>   *david<@filbert.nuts.com>* is the recipient user.

There is one special variant of this syntax, also used only in ruleset 0, that passes error messages to the user:

$#error$:*message*

message is the text of an error message returned to the user, for example:

```
R@      $#error$:Invalid address
```

This rule returns the message "Invalid address" if the address matches the pattern.

The Set Ruleset Command

Rulesets are groups of associated rewrite rules that can be referenced by number. The **S** command marks the beginning of a ruleset and identifies it with a number. In the **S***n* command syntax, *n* is the number that identifies the ruleset. Normally, numbers in the range of 0 to 29 are used.

Rulesets can be thought of as subroutines, or functions, designed to process e-mail addresses. They are called from mailer definitions, from individual rewrite rules, or directly by **sendmail**. Five rulesets have special functions and are called directly by **sendmail**. These are:

- Ruleset 3, the largest and most complicated ruleset, is the first ruleset applied to addresses. It converts an address to the canonical form: *local-part@host.domain*.

  In specific circumstances the *@host.domain* part is added by **sendmail** after ruleset 3 terminates. This happens only if the mail has been received from a mailer with the C flag set.* In our sample configuration files, only the SMTP mailers use this flag. If that flag is set, the sender's *@host.domain* is added to all addresses in the mail that have only a *local-part*. This processing is done after ruleset 3 and before rulesets 1 and 2. (This function is represented in Figure 10-4 by the box marked D.)

- Ruleset 0 is applied to the addresses used to deliver the mail. Ruleset 0 is applied after ruleset 3, and only to the recipient addresses actually used for mail delivery. It resolves the address to the triple (*mailer, host, user*) composed of the name of the mailer that will deliver the mail, the recipient host name, and the recipient user name.

- Ruleset 1 is applied to all sender addresses in the message.

- Ruleset 2 is applied to all recipient addresses in the message.

- Ruleset 4 is applied to all addresses in the message and is used to translate internal address formats into external address formats.

Figure 10-4 shows the flow of the message and addresses through these rulesets. The D box does not symbolize a ruleset. It is the internal **sendmail** process described above. The S and R symbols do stand for rulesets. They have numeric names just like all normal rulesets, but the numbers are not fixed as is the case with rulesets 0, 1, 2, 3, and 4. The S and R ruleset numbers are identified by the S and R fields in the mailer definition. Each

---

*See Table 10-6

mailer may specify its own S and R rulesets for mailer-specific cleanup of the sender and recipient addresses just before the message is delivered.

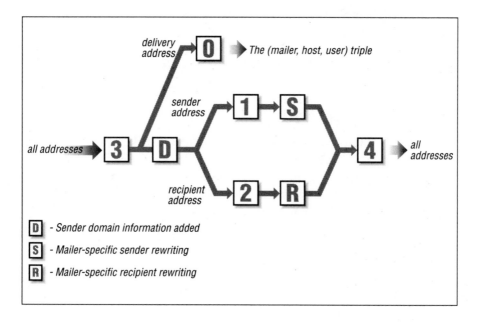

Figure 10.4: Sequence of Rulesets

There are, of course, many more rulesets in most *sendmail.cf* files. These rulesets provide additional address processing and are called by existing rulesets using the **$>***n* construct.* The rulesets provided in any sample *sendmail.cf* file will be adequate for delivering SMTP mail to the internet. It's unlikely you'll have to add to these rulesets.

Modifying a sendmail.cf File

In this section we put into practice everything we discussed about sample configuration files—their structure and the commands used to build them. We'll modify the prototype configuration file, *tcpproto.cf*, for use on *peanut.nuts.com*. We've chosen to modify this file, because unlike a vendor's *sendmail.cf* file, *tcpproto.cf* is available to everyone. Also the *tcpproto.cf* configuration is closest to the configuration we need for *peanut.nuts.com*.

---

*See Table 10-8.

peanut is a workstation on a TCP/IP Ethernet, and it uses SMTP mail. The *tcpproto.cf* configuration is just right for this type of system.

The full text of the modified file is shown in *Appendix E*. The following sections are titled according to the sections of the file, and they describe the modifications we'll make to the file, section by section. Remember other *sendmail.cf* files will probably use different section titles, but the basic information provided in the configuration will be the same.

Modifying Local Information

The first section of the file contains a single line that defines class w. The command reads the host's nicknames from a file called */usr/lib/sendmail.cw* and stores the nicknames in class w. On most systems, **sendmail** is able to correctly define the value for w internally. The w class is only defined if the system is known by more than one host name.

In our sample, we comment out this **F** command and let **sendmail** define the value for w internally. This is the most common method.

Another approach is to replace the **F** command with a **C** command that contains the system's nicknames directly on the command line. When a class contains only a few values, it is just as easy to enter the values directly on the command line. Also, because the */usr/lib* directory is shared, it's not a good place for the *sendmail.cw* file. Generally *sendmail.cw* is not used. The value for *w* is either defined internally by **sendmail** or directly in the *sendmail.cf* file.

Modifying the General Macros

We must also modify the next section of the sample file. This section, General Macros, defines site-specific values, and it does not contain the correct values for our configuration. The sample file contains the following lines that are really instructions for modifying the file:

```
# local domain name
DDYOUR_DOMAIN_GOES_HERE
# UUCP relay host
DRYOUR_UUCP_RELAY_GOES_HERE
# csnet relay host
DCYOUR_CSNET_RELAY_GOES_HERE
# bitnet relay host
DBYOUR_BITNET_RELAY_GOES_HERE
# my official hostname
Dj$w
```

We'll modify these lines using the domain name *nuts.com* for the D macro, the well-known UUCP relay *uunet.uu.net* for the R macro, and the well-known Bitnet relay *cunyvm.cuny.edu* for the B macro.* Alas CSNET, one of the great network services, is no longer in business, so we'll comment out macro C. Here is our new code:

```
# local domain name
DDnuts.com
# UUCP relay host
DRuunet.uu.net
# csnet relay host
#DCYOUR_CSNET_RELAY_GOES_HERE
# bitnet relay host
DBcunyvm.cuny.edu
# my official hostname
Dj$w
```

No modification is necessary for the j macro definition, because the w macro is used to initialize the j macro. We're running DNS name service, so **sendmail** obtains a fully qualified domain name as the value for the w macro. Macro w is an internal **sendmail** macro that holds the local system's host name. On some systems this is a fully qualified domain name; on other systems it is just the host name without the domain extension. If w contains the full name, it can be used to initialize j. If it doesn't contain the full name, initialize j with **Dj$w.$D**. See Table 10-2 for a description of these macros, and see Appendix E for more details about the General Macros section of the sample file.

Modifying the Classes

The next section defines class I. In our sample, class I stores the names of some special mail routing domains. These fake domain names allow users who are not on the Internet to be addressed with Internet style e-mail addresses. For example, mail addressed from an Internet user to a Bitnet user normally uses the format *user%bitnet-host@bitnet-relay*. This address format is affectionately known as the "% kludge." Using the fake Bitnet domain, mail can be addressed to *user@bitnet-host.BITNET*. **sendmail** detects the fake Bitnet domain and rewrites the address into the correct form, using the % kludge and the relay host defined by the B macro in the General Macros section.

---

*If you have local hosts that can relay mail to these networks, use the local hosts as your relay hosts.

The fake domains are also designed to deliver UUCP mail. Mail can be addressed using the normal UUCP "bang" syntax, e.g., *ora!los!craig*. Or it can be addressed in a pseudo-Internet format, e.g., *craig@los.ora.uucp*. These mail routing domains simplify the address that the user enters, and route the mail to the correct mail relay host.

The class I definition in *tcpproto.cf* does not *require* any modification. However, with the demise of CSNET, we decide to edit the class I definition and delete the CSNET entry. The original code is:

```
CIUUCP BITNET CSNET
```

We change it to:

```
CIUUCP BITNET
```

Modifying the Version Number

The version number also doesn't *require* modification, but it's a good idea to keep track of the changes you make to your **sendmail** configuration and this is the place to do it. Each time you modify the configuration, change the version number. At the same time, enter a comment in the file describing the changes you made. Usually this is the last change made to the files so the comments reflect all changes. For example, the original version number section in the *tcpproto.cf* file is:

```
######################
#   Version Number    #
######################

DZ1.34
```

After we have finished all of our modifications, it will contain:

```
######################
#   Version Number    #
######################
#  2.0  modified for peanut by Craig
#         - modified local info and general macros
#         - changed path for aliases and sendmail.st
#         - removed all references to CSNET and to .arpa
#  2.1  added macro A for MX mail domain
#         - modified S14 and S24 to delete class N and use macro A

DZ2.1
```

Modifying Options

The next section, *Special Macros*, requires no modification, but the *Options* section may be modified. The *Options* section defines all of the **sendmail** options. Some of these options specify the file paths used by **sendmail**. In the *tcpproto.cf* file, the options that define file paths are:

```
# location of alias file
OA/usr/lib/aliases
# location of help file
OH/usr/lib/sendmail.hf
# queue directory
OQ/usr/spool/mqueue
# status file
OS/usr/lib/sendmail.st
```

If these paths are correct for your system, don't modify them. On *peanut* we want to keep the *aliases* file and the *sendmail.st* file in the */etc* directory, so we modify two of the paths as follows:

```
# location of alias file
OA/etc/aliases
# status file
OS/etc/sendmail.st
```

We modify option t that defines the time zone names. This option is not used by current versions of **sendmail**, so it can be commented out or just ignored. However, if it is not commented out, it is cleaner to modify it to the correct time zone names for your region. For *peanut* these are Eastern Standard Time (EST) and Eastern Daylight Time (EDT), so we modify the code as follows:

```
# time zone names (V6 only)
OtEST,EDT
```

Option W is used to store the "wizard password." This password allows remote debug access into the **sendmail** program, if **sendmail** was compiled with the debug option. **sendmail**'s debug access is a known security problem that can be exploited by an intruder, so we want to make sure it is unavailable. Check that debugging is not enabled as follows:

```
% telnet localhost 25
Trying 127.0.0.1 ...
Connected to localhost.
Escape character is '^]'.
220 peanut.nuts.com Sendmail 4.1/1.36 ready at Mon, 15 Jun 92 09:51:31 EDT
debug
500 Command unrecognized
quit
221 peanut.nuts.com closing connection
Connection closed by foreign host.
```

The error message shows that debug access is not permitted. If you're prompted for a password when you run this test, you have a problem. Contact your vendor, notify them of your problem, and get the latest version of **sendmail** that does not allow remote debugging.

In our sample configuration, we delete option W because we're not going to allow remote debugging. Deleting unused options creates a cleaner configuration.

Modifying the Rewrite Rules

The next few sections of the *tcpproto.cf* file define the messages' precedences, the trusted users, and the headers. None of these sections are modified. After these sections, come the rewrite rules and the mailers. This material is the bulk of the file and the heart of the configuration. This configuration is designed to allow mail delivery to the Internet, so we assume no modifications are *required*. But because this sample file was originally written in 1989, we make a few small changes before beginning testing, just to clean up the configuration.

One modification we made to the rewrite rules was to comment out all rules that mentioned CSNET. We made this change because, with the demise of CSNET, it is cleaner not to reference it in the configuration. Similarly we comment out all rewrite rules that reference *.arpa* because that domain should no longer be used. With these small changes our configuration is "ready."

Now that we have the configuration ready, we want to test it before copying it into *sendmail.cf*. We'll save it in a temporary configuration file, *test.cf*, and use the troubleshooting features of **sendmail** to test it.

Testing sendmail.cf

sendmail provides powerful tools for configuration testing and debugging. These test tools are invoked on the **sendmail** command line using some of the many **sendmail** command-line arguments. Table 10-9 summarizes all of the arguments.*

---

*Table 10-9 is taken from *Appendix A* of *Sendmail Installation and Operation Guide*.

Table 10.9: sendmail Command-line Arguments

Argument	Function
–f *addr*	Sender's machine address is *addr*.
–r *addr*	Obsolete form of **-f**.
–h *cnt*	Drop mail if forwarded *cnt* times.
–F*name*	Sets the full name of this user to *name*.
–n	Don't do aliasing or forwarding.
–t	Send to everyone listed in To:, Cc:, and Bcc:.
–bm	Deliver mail (default).
–ba	Run in arpanet mode.*
–bs	Speak SMTP on input side.
–bd	Run as a daemon.
–bt	Run in test mode.
–bv	Verify addresses; don't collect or deliver mail.
–bi	Initialize the alias database.
–bp	Print the mail queue.
–bz	Freeze the configuration file.
–q[*time*]	Process queued mail. Repeat at interval *time*.
–C*file*	Use *file* as the configuration file.
–d*level*	Set debugging level.
–o*xvalue*	Set option *x* to the specified *value*.
–e	Defines how errors are returned.
–i	Ignore dots in incoming messages.
–m	Send to me, too.
–v	Run in verbose mode.
–s *addr*	Alternate form of **–f**.

Some of the command-line arguments are used to verify address processing and to gain confidence in the new configuration. Once you think your configuration will work, choose friends at a variety of sites, and send them mail using the **–C** argument to read the test configuration file and the **–v** argument to display the details of the mail delivery. **–v** displays the complete SMTP exchange between the two hosts.

---

*Reads the header From: line to find the sender. Uses three digit reply codes, and ends error lines with <CRLF>.

By observing if your mailer properly connects to the remote mailer and formats the addresses correctly, you'll get a good idea of how the configuration is working. The following example is a test from *peanut* using the *test.cf* configuration file we just created:

```
peanut# /usr/lib/sendmail -Ctest.cf -t -v
To: hunt@nbsenh.bitnet
From: craig
Subject: Sendmail Test

Becky, please reply if you get this.  Thanks.  Craig
^D
hunt@nbsenh.bitnet... Connecting to cunyvm.cuny.edu via tcp...
Trying 128.228.1.2... connected.
220 CUNYVM.CUNY.EDU on Wed, 30 Oct 91 16:53:23 EST
>>> HELO peanut.nuts.com
250 CUNYVM.CUNY.EDU is my domain name.
>>> MAIL From:<craig%peanut.nuts.com@>
250 OK
>>> RCPT To:<hunt%nbsenh.BITNET@cunyvm.cuny.edu>
250 OK
>>> DATA
354 Enter mail body.  End by new line with just a '.'
>>> .
250 Mail Delivered
>>> QUIT
221 CUNYVM.CUNY.EDU closing connection
hunt@nbsenh.bitnet... Sent
```

We entered everything before the control-D (^D). Everything after the ^D was displayed by **sendmail**. Figure 10-5 highlights some of the important information in this display, and notes the **sendmail** macros that relate to the highlighted material.

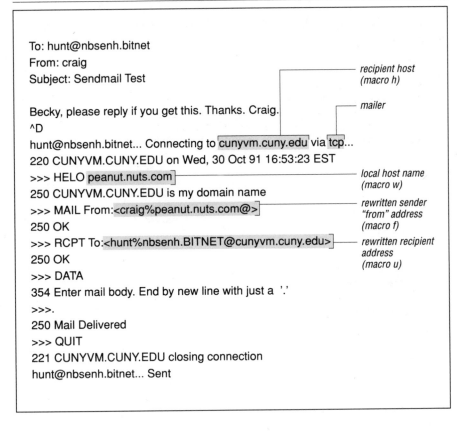

To: hunt@nbsenh.bitnet
From: craig
Subject: Sendmail Test ————————————————————— recipient host
                                                         (macro h)

Becky, please reply if you get this. Thanks. Craig. ——— mailer
^D
hunt@nbsenh.bitnet... Connecting to cunyvm.cuny.edu via tcp...
220 CUNYVM.CUNY.EDU on Wed, 30 Oct 91 16:53:23 EST
>>> HELO peanut.nuts.com ————————————————————— local host name
                                                         (macro w)
250 CUNYVM.CUNY.EDU is my domain name
>>> MAIL From:<craig%peanut.nuts.com@> ——————— rewritten sender
                                                         "from" address
250 OK   (macro f)
>>> RCPT To:<hunt%nbsenh.BITNET@cunyvm.cuny.edu> — rewritten recipient
                                                         address
250 OK   (macro u)
>>> DATA
354 Enter mail body. End by new line with just a '.'
>>>.
250 Mail Delivered
>>> QUIT
221 CUNYVM.CUNY.EDU closing connection
hunt@nbsenh.bitnet... Sent

Figure 10.5: Verbose Mail Output

This test attempts to deliver mail to Bitnet using the fake *.bitnet* domain. The **sendmail** output shows that *peanut* successfully connected to the Bitnet relay host *cunyvm.cuny.edu* via the *tcp* mail delivery program, and that the recipient address is properly formatted with the % kludge. So far, so good! But examining the From: address shows a problem; *craig%peanut.nuts.com@* is clearly an incorrect address. **sendmail** provides additional debugging tools that can help us fix this problem.

Testing Rewrite Rules

The problem in the address is caused by a bad rewrite rule. The From: address went into **sendmail** as *craig*, and it came out as *craig%peanut.nuts.com@*. Obviously it has been rewritten incorrectly. It looks like the system has attempted to rewrite the sender address into the % kludge format and failed to add a relay host after the @. To get more information, we run **sendmail** with the **–bt** option that tests rewrite rules. Using **–bt**, we can debug the rewrite rules as follows:

```
# /usr/lib/sendmail -bt -Ctest.cf
ADDRESS TEST MODE
Enter <ruleset> <address>
> 0 hunt@nbsenh.bitnet
rewrite: ruleset  3    input: "hunt" "@" "nbsenh" "." "bitnet"
rewrite: ruleset  8    input: "hunt" "@" "nbsenh" "." "bitnet"
rewrite: ruleset  8 returns: "hunt" "@" "nbsenh" "." "bitnet"
       .
       .
       .
rewrite: ruleset  6    input: "hunt" "<" "@" "nbsenh" "." "bitnet" ">"
rewrite: ruleset  6 returns: "hunt" "<" "@" "nbsenh" "." "bitnet" ">"
rewrite: ruleset  0 returns: $# "tcp" $@ "cunyvm" "." "cuny" "." "edu"
       $: "hunt" "<" "@" "nbsenh" "." "BITNET" ">"
> 1,14,4 craig
rewrite: ruleset  3    input: "craig"
rewrite: ruleset  8    input: "craig"
rewrite: ruleset  8 returns: "craig"
rewrite: ruleset  3 returns: "craig"
rewrite: ruleset  1    input: "craig"
rewrite: ruleset  1 returns: "craig"
rewrite: ruleset 14    input: "craig"
rewrite: ruleset 14 returns: "craig" "%" "peanut" "." "nuts" "." "com"
       "<" "@" ">"
rewrite: ruleset  4    input: "craig" "%" "peanut" "." "nuts" "." "com"
       "<" "@" ">"
rewrite: ruleset  4 returns: "craig" "%" "peanut" "." "nuts" "." "com"
       "@"
> ^D
```

When **sendmail** is invoked with the **–bt** option, it prompts for input using the greater than symbol (>). At the prompt, enter a ruleset number and an e-mail address. The address is the test data, and the ruleset number is the ruleset to be tested. The address is easy to select; it is the one that was improperly rewritten. But how do you know which ruleset to specify?

Ruleset 3 is the first ruleset applied to all addresses, and in address test mode it is assumed to be the first ruleset for every test. No matter what ruleset you specify, the address is first processed by ruleset 3 and then by the rulesets you select. Therefore, don't enter ruleset 3 when prompted by **sendmail**. Use Figure 10-4 to determine which rulesets to enter.

Figure 10-4 shows that the delivery address is resolved through rulesets 3 and 0. To find out which mailer delivered the test mail, process the recipient address through ruleset 0. (Remember ruleset 3 is called by default.) In our example, the recipient address is *hunt@nbsenh.bitnet*. So we enter **0 hunt@nbsenh.bitnet** at the > prompt. The first field in the value returned by ruleset 0 is the mailer name. It tells us that this mail is delivered through the *tcp* mailer.* Knowing the mailer, we can determine the rulesets called to process the sender From: address.

Again, refer back to Figure 10-4. It shows that the sender address goes through ruleset 3, ruleset 1, the ruleset specified by S, and ruleset 4. The mailer definition for *tcp* in our sample configuration defines its S ruleset as ruleset 14. Therefore, the rulesets that process this sender address are 3, 1, 14, and 4. In address test mode ruleset 3 is called by default, so we enter **1,14,4 craig** to test the sender address.

The test shows that the sender address goes wrong in ruleset 14. A line-by-line inspection of that ruleset shows two lines that reference information not defined in our configuration—class N and macro A:

```
R$+<@$=N.$D>      $@$1<@$2.$D>        nic-reg hosts are ok
R$+<@$*.$D>       $@$1%$2.$D<@$A>     else -> u%h@gateway
```

The comments on these rules give us some clues as to what they are doing. Obviously class N is related to NIC-registered hosts. This was important in 1989, but now we're using DNS name service and we don't need to worry about the NIC host table. So we comment out all occurrences of this rule. It's common for the same rule to be used in multiple rulesets, and this rule occurs in both rulesets 14 and 24 of our test file.

The next rule appears to be more closely related to our problem. It appears to be a rule for writing the sender address into the % kludge format, *user%host@relay*. This rule existed because, at one time, a host that wasn't in the old NIC host table had to deliver mail to the Internet through a mail relay. We don't need to include a mail relay host in the sender address because MX records are now used to direct remote hosts to the correct mail delivery host, and *peanut* can directly address the Internet. So we can comment out this rule in rulesets 14 and 24. However, instead of removing this rule, another approach is to modify it so it can be used for our own purposes. We'll use this rule to rewrite the sender address to direct return mail to the MX mail delivery host. To do this, we define macro A and

---

*This can also be determined from the words *via tcp* contained in the first message displayed by **sendmail** during the delivery test.

assign it the value of the *nuts.com* MX mail domain. This is done in the General Macros section of the test configuration as follows:

```
#  MX mail domain
DAnuts.com
```

Next we modify the troublesome rule in rulesets 14 and 24 to the following form:

```
R$+<@$*.$D>        $@$1<@$A>          else -> user@domain
```

This should now rewrite the sender mail address for any mail that uses the *tcp* mailer into the form *user@domain*. For example, the address *craig* will be rewritten to *craig@nuts.com*. The *tcp* mailer is used for non-local SMTP mail, so only this type of mail will be rewritten to the *user@domain* form. Local mail will not be rewritten. This is exactly what we want.

Creating the Frozen sendmail Configuration

Rerunning the mail test shows that the updated configuration works and produces the correct address. The corrected configuration is saved as */etc/sendmail.cf* to be used as *peanut's* **sendmail** configuration until another problem comes up that needs to be corrected. If you want to, you can create a memory image of the configuration that eliminates the need to parse the configuration file when **sendmail** starts up. To create the file, enter:

```
# /usr/lib/sendmail -bz
```

The **–bz** option writes the memory image of the configuration to the file */etc/sendmail.fc.** This file is called the "frozen configuration" file. It cannot be changed directly. To modify this file, the change must first be made to the *sendmail.cf* file and then **sendmail** must be run with the **–bz** option. The advantage of the frozen configuration is that **sendmail** will start up faster. The disadvantage is that you add another step to the configuration. Most people use it, but it is not required.

Debugging the **sendmail** configuration is an iterative process. Don't expect everything to be right from the start. By using the **sendmail** troubleshooting features, you should be able to gradually improve your configuration until you have what you want. Encourage users to report problems as soon as they see them. It's better to know about and correct problems as soon as they occur than it is to have users develop their own special workarounds.

---

*Many systems use the file */usr/lib/sendmail.fc*.

In this chapter we discussed troubleshooting the **sendmail** configuration. In the next chapter, we look at troubleshooting a wide range of network problems.

11

Troubleshooting TCP/IP

Network administration tasks fall into two very different categories: configuration and troubleshooting. Configuration tasks prepare for the expected; they require detailed knowledge of command syntax but are usually simple and predictable. Once a system is properly configured, there is rarely any reason to change it. The configuration process is repeated each time a new operating system release is installed, but usually with very few changes.

In contrast, network troubleshooting deals with the unexpected. Troubleshooting frequently requires knowledge that is conceptual rather than detailed. Network problems are usually unique and sometimes difficult to resolve. Troubleshooting is an important part of maintaining a stable, reliable network service.

In this chapter we discuss the tools used to ensure that the network is in good running condition. However, good tools are not enough. No troubleshooting tool is effective if applied haphazardly. Effective troubleshooting requires a methodical approach to the problem, and a basic understanding of how the network works. So we'll start our discussion by looking at ways to approach a network problem.

Approaching a Problem

To approach a problem properly, you need a basic understanding of TCP/IP. The first few chapters of this book discuss the basics of TCP/IP, and provide enough background information to troubleshoot most network problems. Knowledge of how TCP/IP routes data through the network, between individual hosts, and between the layers in the protocol stack, is important for understanding a network problem, but detailed knowledge of each protocol usually isn't necessary. The fine details of the protocols are rarely needed in debugging, and when they are used, they should be looked up in a definitive reference—not recalled from memory.

Not all TCP/IP problems are alike, and not all problems can be approached in the same manner. But the key to solving any problem is understanding what the problem is. This is not as easy as it may seem. The "surface" problem is sometimes misleading, and the "real" problem is frequently obscured by many layers of software. When the true nature of the problem is understood, the solution to the problem is often obvious.

First, gather detailed information about exactly what's happening. When the problem is reported, talk to the user. Find out which application failed. What is the remote host's name and IP address? What is the user's host name and address? What error message was displayed? If possible, verify the problem by having the user run the application while you talk him through it. If possible, duplicate the problem on your own system.

Testing from the user's system, and other systems, find out:

- Does the problem occur in other applications on the user's host, or is only one application having trouble? If only one application is involved, the application may be misconfigured or disabled on the remote host. Because of rising security concerns, more and more systems are disabling some services.

- Does the problem occur with only one remote host, all remote hosts, or only certain "groups" of remote hosts? If only one remote host is involved, the problem could easily be with that host. If all remote hosts are involved, the problem is probably with the user's system (particularly if no other hosts on your local network are experiencing the same problem). If only hosts on certain subnets or external networks are involved, the problem may be related to routing.

- Does the problem occur on other local systems? Make sure you check other systems on the same subnet. If the problem only occurs on the user's host, concentrate testing on that system. If the problem affects every system on a subnet, concentrate on the router for that subnet.

Once you know the symptoms of the problem, visualize each protocol and device that handles the data. Visualizing the problem will help you avoid oversimplification, and keep you from assuming that you know the cause even before you start testing. Using your TCP/IP knowledge, narrow your attack to the most likely causes of the problem, but keep an open mind.

Troubleshooting Hints

There are several useful troubleshooting hints you should know. These are not a troubleshooting methodology; just good ideas to keep in mind. Here they are, listed in no particular order:

- Approach problems methodically. Allow the information gathered from each test to guide your testing. Don't jump into another test scenario, based on a hunch, without ensuring that you can pick up your original test scenario where you left off.

- Keep good records of the tests you have completed and their results. Keep a historical record of the problem in case it reappears.

- Keep an open mind. Don't assume too much about the cause of the problem. Don't assume a problem seen at the application level is not caused by a problem at a lower level. Some people assume their network is always at fault, while others assume the remote end is always the problem. Some people are so sure they know the cause of a problem that they ignore the evidence of the tests. Don't fall into these traps. Test each possibility and base your actions on the evidence of the tests.

- Pay attention to error messages. Error messages are often vague, but they frequently contain important hints for solving the problem.

- Duplicate the reported problem yourself. Don't rely too heavily on the user's problem report. The user has probably only seen this problem from the application level. If necessary, obtain the user's data files to duplicate the problem. Even if you cannot duplicate the problem, log the details of the reported problem for your records.

- Most problems are caused by human errors. You can prevent some of them by providing information and training on network configuration and usage.

- Keep your users informed. This reduces the number of duplicated trouble reports, and the duplication of effort when several system administrators work on the same problem without knowing others are already working on it. If you're lucky, someone may have seen the problem before and have a helpful suggestion about how to resolve it.

- Don't speculate about the cause of the problem while talking to the user. Save your speculations for discussions with your networking colleagues. Your speculations may be accepted by the user as gospel, and become rumors. These rumors can cause users to avoid using legitimate network services and may undermine confidence in your network. Users want solutions to their problems; they're not interested in speculative techno-babble.

- Stick to a few simple troubleshooting tools. For most TCP/IP software problems, the tools discussed in this chapter are sufficient. You could spend more time learning how to use a new tool than it would take to resolve the problem with an old familiar tool.

- Thoroughly test the problem at your end of the network before locating the owner of the remote system to coordinate testing with him. The greatest complication of network troubleshooting is that you do not always control the systems at both ends of the network. In many cases, you may not even know who does control the remote system.* The more information you have about your end, the simpler the job will be when you have to contact the remote administrator.

- Don't neglect the obvious. A loose Ethernet cable is a very common network problem. Check plugs, connectors, cables, and switches. Small things can cause big problems.

Diagnostic Tools

Because most problems have a simple cause, developing a clear idea of the problem often provides the solution. Unfortunately this is not always true, so in this section we begin to discuss the tools that can help you attack the most intractable problems. Many diagnostic tools are available, ranging from commercial systems with specialized hardware and software that may cost thousands of dollars, to free software that is available from the Inter-

---

*Chapter 13 explains how to find out who is responsible for a remote network.

net. Many tools are provided with your UNIX system. This book emphasizes free or "built-in" diagnostic tools that run on UNIX systems.

There are a few reasons for this emphasis. First, a commercial system that costs thousands of dollars should be fully documented. Second, many administrators can't buy commercial diagnostic tools, but everyone has access to the free tools. Finally, most network problems can be solved using the free diagnostic software. Large networks probably need a commercial network analyzer, or at least a hardware tester such as a time domain reflectometer (TDR), but many smaller networks can make do with the publicly available diagnostic software.

The tools used in this chapter, and many more, are described in RFC 1147, *FYI on a Network Management Tool Catalog: Tools for Monitoring and Debugging TCP/IP Internets and Interconnected Devices*. A catchy title, and a very useful RFC! Here are the tools listed in that catalog and discussed in this book:

ifconfig Provides information about the basic configuration of the interface. It is useful for detecting bad IP addresses, incorrect subnet masks, and improper broadcast addresses. **ifconfig** is covered in detail in Chapter 6. This tool is provided with the UNIX operating system.

arp Provides information about Ethernet/IP address translation. It can be used to detect systems on the local network that are configured with the wrong IP address. **arp** is covered in this chapter, and is used in an example in Chapter 2. **arp** is delivered as part of UNIX.

netstat Provides a variety of information. It is commonly used to display detailed statistics about each network interface, network sockets, and the network routing table. **netstat** is used repeatedly in this book, most extensively in Chapters 2, 6, and 7. **netstat** is delivered as part of UNIX.

ping Indicates whether a remote host can be reached. **ping** also displays statistics about packet loss and delivery time. **ping** is discussed in Chapter 1 and used in Chapter 7. **ping** also comes as part of UNIX.

nslookup Provides information about the DNS name service. **nslookup** is covered in detail in Chapter 8. It comes as part of the BIND software package.

dig   Also provides information about name service, and is similar to **nslookup**. **dig** is available via anonymous **ftp** from *venera.isi.edu* in the file *pub/dig.2.0.tar.Z.*

ripquery   Provides information about the contents of the RIP update packets being sent or received by your system. It is provided as part of the **gated** software package, but it does not require that you run **gated**. It will work with any system running RIP.

traceroute   Tells you which route packets take going from your system to a remote system. Information about each hop is printed. It is available via anonymous **ftp** from *ftp.ee.lbl.gov* in the file *traceroute.tar.Z.*

etherfind   Analyzes the individual packets exchanged between hosts on a network. **etherfind** is a TCP/IP protocol analyzer that can examine the contents of packets, including their headers. It is most useful for analyzing protocol problems. It is the SunOS version of a program called **tcpdump**. **tcpdump** is available via anonymous **ftp** from *ftp.ee.lbl.gov.*

Each of these tools, even those covered earlier in the text, are used in this chapter. We start with **ping**, which is used in more troubleshooting situations than any other diagnostic tool.

Testing Basic Connectivity

The **ping** command tests whether a remote host can be reached from your computer. This simple function is extremely useful for testing the network connection, independent of the application in which the original problem was detected. **ping** allows you to determine whether further testing should be directed toward the network connection (the lower layers) or the application (the upper layers). If **ping** shows that packets can travel to the remote system and back, the user's problem is probably in the upper layers. If packets can't make the round-trip, lower protocol layers are probably at fault.

Frequently a user reports a network problem by stating that he can't **telnet** (or **ftp**, or send e-mail, or whatever) to some remote host. He then immediately qualifies this statement with the announcement that it worked before. In cases like this, where the ability to connect to the remote host is in question, **ping** is a very useful tool.

Using the host name provided by the user, **ping** the remote host. If your **ping** is successful, have the user **ping** the host. If the user's **ping** is also successful, concentrate your further analysis on the specific application that the user is having trouble with. Perhaps the user is attempting to **telnet** to a host that only provides anonymous **ftp**. Perhaps the host was down when the user tried his application. Have the user try it again, while you watch or listen to every detail of what he is doing. If he is doing everything right and the application still fails, detailed analysis of the application with **etherfind** and coordination with the remote system administrator may be needed.

If your **ping** is successful and the user's **ping** fails, concentrate testing on the user's system configuration, and on those things that are different about the user's path to the remote host, when compared to your path to the remote host.

If your **ping** fails, or the user's **ping** fails, pay close attention to any error messages. The error messages displayed by **ping** are helpful guides for planning further testing. The details of the messages may vary from implementation to implementation, but there are only a few basic types of errors:

unknown host

The remote host's name cannot be resolved by name service into an IP address. The name servers could be at fault (either your local server or the remote system's server), the name could be incorrect, or something could be wrong with the network between your system and the remote server. If you know the remote host's IP address, try to **ping** that. If you can reach the host using its IP address, the problem is with name service. Use **nslookup** or **dig** to test the local and remote servers, and to check the accuracy of the host name the user gave you.

network unreachable

The local system does not have a route to the remote system. If the numeric IP address was used on the **ping** command line, re-enter the **ping** command using the host name. This eliminates the possibility that the IP address was entered incorrectly, or that you were given the wrong address. If a routing protocol is being used, make sure it is running and use **netstat** to check the routing table. If RIP is being used, use **ripquery** to check the contents of the RIP updates being received. If a static default route is being used, re-install it. If everything seems fine on the host, check its default gateway for routing problems.

no answer

> The remote system did not respond. Most network utilities have some version of this message. Some **ping** implementations print the message "100% packet loss." **telnet** prints the message "Connection timed out" and **sendmail** returns the error "cannot connect." All of these errors mean the same thing. The local system has a route to the remote system, but it receives no response from the remote system to any of the packets it sends.

> There are many possible causes of this problem. The remote host may be down. Either the local or the remote host may be configured incorrectly. A gateway or circuit between the local host and the remote host may be down. The remote host may have routing problems. Only additional testing can isolate the cause of the problem. Carefully check the local configuration using **netstat** and **ifconfig**. Check the route to the remote system with **traceroute**. Contact the administrator of the remote system and report the problem.

All of the tools mentioned here will be discussed later in this chapter. However, before leaving **ping**, let's look more closely at the command and the statistics it displays.

The ping Command

The basic format of the **ping** command is:*

ping *host* [*packetsize*] [*count*]

host
: The host name or IP address of the remote host being tested. Use the host name or address provided by the user in the trouble report.

packetsize
: Defines the size in bytes of the test packets. This field is only required if the *count* field is going to be used. Use the default *packetsize* of 56 bytes.

count
: The number of packets to be sent in the test. Use the *count* field, and set the value low. Otherwise, the **ping** command continues to send test packets until you interrupt it, usually by pressing control-C (^C). Sending excessive numbers of test packets is not a good use of network bandwidth and

---

****ping** varies slightly on each system. Check your system's documentation.

system resources. Usually five packets are sufficient for a test.

To check that *uunet.uu.net* can be reached from *peanut,* we send five 56-byte packets with the following command:

```
% ping -s uunet.uu.net 56 5
PING uunet.uu.net: 56 data bytes
64 bytes from uunet.UU.NET (137.39.1.2): icmp_seq=0. time=14. ms
64 bytes from uunet.UU.NET (137.39.1.2): icmp_seq=1. time=14. ms
64 bytes from uunet.UU.NET (137.39.1.2): icmp_seq=2. time=13. ms
64 bytes from uunet.UU.NET (137.39.1.2): icmp_seq=3. time=12. ms
64 bytes from uunet.UU.NET (137.39.1.2): icmp_seq=4. time=15. ms

----uunet.UU.NET PING Statistics----
5 packets transmitted, 5 packets received, 0% packet loss
round-trip (ms)  min/avg/max = 12/13/15
```

The **–s** option is included because *peanut* is a Sun workstation, and we want packet-by-packet statistics. Without the **–s** option, Sun's **ping** command would only print a summary line saying "uunet.uu.net is alive." Other **ping** implementations do not require the **–s** option; they display the statistics by default.

This test shows an extremely good wide area network link to *uunet.uu.net* with no packet loss and fast response. The round-trip between *peanut* and *uunet.uu.net* is taking only an average of 13 milliseconds. A small packet loss, and the round-trip times an order of magnitude higher, would be more normal for a connection made across a wide area network. The statistics displayed by the **ping** command can indicate low-level network problems. The key statistics are:

- The sequence in which the packets are arriving, as shown by the ICMP sequence number (icmp_seq) displayed for each packet.
- How long it takes a packet to make the round-trip, which is displayed in milliseconds after the string time=.
- The percentage of packets lost, which is displayed in a summary line at the end of the **ping** output.

If the packet loss is high, the response time is very slow, or packets are arriving out of order, there could be a network hardware problem. If you see these conditions when communicating great distances on a wide area network, there is nothing to worry about. TCP/IP was designed to deal with unreliable networks, and some wide area networks suffer a lot of packet loss. But if these problems are seen on a local area network, they indicate trouble.

On a local network cable segment the round-trip time should be near zero, there should be no little or no packet loss, and the packets should arrive in order. If these things are not true, there is a problem with the network hardware. On an Ethernet the problem could be improper cable termination, a bad cable segment, or a bad piece of "active" hardware, such as a repeater or transceiver. Check the cable terminations first. It's easy to check; either there is a terminating resistor or there isn't, and it's a common problem, particularly if the cable ends in a work area where users have access to it.

A helpful tool for checking cable hardware problems is a time domain reflectometer (TDR). A TDR sends a signal down the cable and listens for the echoes that the signal produces. These echoes are displayed on a small screen on the front of the tester. If the cable is not terminated, the signal display jumps to the top of the screen. If the cable is shorted, the signal jumps to the bottom of the screen. A normal display shows only small spikes where the transceivers tap into the network. With a TDR it's easy to detect a cable problem.

The results of a simple **ping** test, even if the test is successful, can help you direct further testing toward the most likely causes of the problem. But other diagnostic tools are needed to examine the problem more closely and find the underlying cause.

Troubleshooting Network Access

The "no answer" and "cannot connect" errors indicate a problem in the lower layers of the network protocols. If the preliminary tests point to this type of problem, concentrate your testing on routing and on the network interface. Use the **ifconfig**, **netstat**, and **arp** commands to test the Network Access Layer.

Troubleshooting with the ifconfig Command

ifconfig checks the network interface configuration. Use this command to verify the user's configuration if the user's system has been recently configured, or if the user's system cannot reach the remote host while other systems on the same network can.

When **ifconfig** is entered with an interface name and no other arguments, it displays the current values assigned to that interface. For example, checking interface le0 on *peanut* gives this report:

```
% ifconfig le0
le0: flags=63<UP,BROADCAST,NOTRAILERS,RUNNING>
        inet 128.66.12.2 netmask ffff0000 broadcast 128.66.0.0
```

The **ifconfig** command displays two lines of output. The first line of the display shows the interface's name and its characteristics. Check for these characteristics:

UP   The interface is enabled for use. If the interface is "down," have the system's superuser bring the interface "up" with the **ifconfig** command (e.g., **ifconfig le0 up**). If the interface won't come up, replace the interface cable and try again. If it still fails, have the interface hardware checked.

RUNNING   This interface is operational. If the interface is not "running," the driver for this interface may not be properly installed. The system administrator should review all of the steps necessary to install this interface, looking for errors or missed steps.

The second line of **ifconfig** output shows the IP address, the subnet mask (written in hexadecimal), and the broadcast address. Check these three fields to make sure the network interface is properly configured.

Two common interface configuration problems are misconfigured subnet masks and incorrect IP addresses. A bad subnet mask is indicated when the host can reach other hosts on its local subnet and remote hosts on distant networks, but it cannot reach hosts on other local subnets. **ifconfig** quickly reveals if a bad subnet mask is set.

An incorrectly set IP address can be a subtle problem. If the network part of the address is incorrect, every **ping** will fail with the "no answer" error. In this case, using **ifconfig** will reveal the incorrect address. However, if the host part of the address is wrong, the problem can be more difficult to detect. A small system, such as a PC that only connects out to other systems and never accepts incoming connections, can run for a long time with the wrong address without its user noticing the problem. Additionally, the system that suffers the ill effects may not be the one that is misconfigured. It is possible for someone to accidentally use your IP address on his system, and for his mistake to cause your system intermittent communications problems. An example of this problem is discussed later. This type of configuration error cannot be discovered by **ifconfig**, because the error is on a remote host. The **arp** command is used for this type of problem.

Troubleshooting with the arp Command

The **arp** command is used to analyze problems with IP to Ethernet address translation. The **arp** command has three useful options for trouble-shooting:

–a   Display all ARP entries in the table.

–d *hostname*   Delete an entry from the ARP table.

–s *hostname ether-address*   Add a new entry to the table.

With these three options you can view the contents of the ARP table. Delete a problem entry, and install a corrected entry. The ability to install a corrected entry is useful in "buying time" while you look for the permanent fix.

Use **arp** if you suspect that incorrect entries are getting into the address resolution table. One clear indication of problems with the ARP table is a report that the "wrong" host responded to some command, like **ftp** or **tel-net**. Intermittent problems that affect only certain hosts can also indicate that the ARP table has been corrupted. ARP table problems are usually caused by two systems using the same IP address. The problems appear intermittent, because the entry that appears in the table is the address of the host that responded quickest to the last ARP request. Sometimes the "correct" host responds first, and sometimes the "wrong" host responds first.

If you suspect that two systems are using the same IP address, display the address resolution table with the **arp –a** command. Here's an example:

```
% arp -a
peanut (128.66.12.2) at 8:0:20:b:4a:71
almond (128.66.12.1) at 8:0:20:e:aa:40
pecan (128.66.12.3) at 0:0:93:e0:80:b1
```

It is easiest to verify that the IP and Ethernet address pairs are correct if you have a record of each host's correct Ethernet address. For this reason you should record each host's Ethernet and IP address when it is added to your network. If you have such a record, you'll quickly see if anything is wrong with the table.

If you don't have this type of record, the first three bytes of the Ethernet address can help you to detect a problem. The first three bytes of the address identify the equipment manufacturer. A list of these identifying prefixes is found in the *Assigned Numbers* RFC, in the section entitled "Ethernet Vendor Address Components."

Table 11-1 lists several equipment manufacturers and their assigned prefixes. Using this information, we see that the first two ARP entries displayed in our example are Sun systems (8:0:20). If *pecan* is also supposed to be a Sun, the 0:0:93 Proteon prefix indicates that a Proteon router has been mistakenly configured with *pecan's* IP address.

Table 11.1: Vendor Ethernet Prefixes

Prefix	Manufacturer	Prefix	Manufacturer
00:00:0C	Cisco	08:00:0B	Unisys
00:00:0F	NeXT	08:00:10	AT&T
00:00:10	Sytek	08:00:11	Tektronix
00:00:1D	Cabletron	08:00:14	Excelan
00:00:65	Network General	08:00:1A	Data General
00:00:6B	MIPS	08:00:1B	Data General
00:00:77	MIPS	08:00:1E	Apollo
00:00:89	Cayman Systems	08:00:20	Sun
00:00:93	Proteon	08:00:25	CDC
00:00:A2	Wellfleet	08:00:2B	DEC
00:00:A7	NCD	08:00:38	Bull
00:00:A9	Network Systems	08:00:39	Spider Systems
00:00:C0	Western Digital	080:04:6	Sony
00:00:C9	Emulex	080:04:7	Sequent
00:80:2D	Xylogics Annex	08:00:5A	IBM
00:AA:00	Intel	08:00:69	Silicon Graphics
00:DD:00	Ungermann-Bass	08:00:6E	Excelan
00:DD:01	Ungermann-Bass	08:00:86	Imagen/QMS
02:07:01	MICOM/Interlan	08:00:87	Xyplex terminal servers
02:60:8C	3Com	08:00:89	Kinetics
08:00:02	3Com (Bridge)	08:00:8B	Pyramid
08:00:03	ACC	08:00:90	Retix
08:00:05	Symbolics	AA:00:03	DEC
08:00:08	BBN	AA:00:04	DEC
08:00:09	Hewlett-Packard		

If neither checking a record of correct assignments nor checking the manufacturer prefix helps you identify the source of the errant ARP, try using **telnet** to connect to the IP address shown in the ARP entry. If the device supports **telnet**, the login banner might help you identify the incorrectly configured host.

ARP Problem Case Study

Recently a user called in asking if the server was down, and reported the following problem. The user's workstation, called *cashew*, appeared to "lock up" for minutes at a time when certain commands were used, while other commands worked with no problems. The network commands that involved the NIS name server all caused the lock-up problem, but some unrelated commands, such as **calendartool**, also caused the problem. The user reported seeing the error message:

```
NFS getattr failed for server almond: RPC: Timed out
```

The server *almond* was providing *cashew* with NIS and NFS services. The commands that failed on *cashew* were commands that required NIS service, or that were stored in the centrally maintained */usr/local* directory exported from *almond*. The commands that ran correctly were installed locally on the user's workstation. No one else reported a problem with the server, and we were able to **ping** *cashew* from *almond* and get good responses.

We had the user check the */usr/adm/messages* file for recent error messages, and she discovered this:

```
Mar  6 13:38:23 cashew vmunix: duplicate IP address!!
        sent from ethernet address: 0:0:c0:4:38:1a
```

This message indicates that the workstation detected another host on the Ethernet responding to its IP address. The "imposter" used the Ethernet address 0:0:c0:4:38:1a in its ARP response. The correct Ethernet address for *cashew* is 8:0:20:e:12:37.

We checked *almond's* ARP table and found that it had the incorrect ARP entry for *cashew*. We deleted the bad *cashew* entry with the **arp –d** command, and installed the correct entry with the **–s** option, as shown below:

```
# arp -d cashew
cashew (128.66.180.130) deleted
# arp -s cashew 8:0:20:e:12:37
```

ARP entries received via the ARP protocol are temporary. The values are held in the table for a finite lifetime and are deleted when that lifetime expires. New values are then obtained via the ARP protocol. Therefore, if some remote interfaces change, the local table adjusts and communications continue. Usually this is a good idea, but if someone is using the wrong IP address, that bad address can keep reappearing in the ARP table even if it is deleted. However, manually entered values are permanent; they stay in the table and can only be deleted manually. This allowed us to install a correct entry in the table, without worrying about it being immediately overwritten by a bad address.

This quick fix resolved *cashew's* immediate problem, but we still needed to find the culprit. We checked the */etc/ethers* file to see if we had an entry for Ethernet address 0:0:c0:4:38:1a, but we didn't. From the first three bytes of this address, 0:0:c0, we knew that the device was a Western Digital card. Since our network has only UNIX workstations and PCs, we assumed the Western digital card was installed in a PC. We also guessed that the problem address was recently installed because the user had never had the problem before. We sent out an urgent announcement to all users asking if anyone had recently installed a new PC, reconfigured a PC, or installed TCP/IP software on a PC. We got one response. When we checked his system, we found out that he had entered the address 128.66.180.130 when he should have entered 128.66.180.138. The address was corrected and the problem did not recur.

Nothing fancy was needed to solve this problem. Once we checked the error messages, we knew what the problem was and how to solve it. Involving the entire network user community allowed us to quickly locate the problem system and to avoid a room-to-room search for the PC. Reluctance to involve users and make them part of the solution is one of the costliest, and most common, mistakes made by network administrators.

Checking the Interface with netstat

If the preliminary tests lead you to suspect that the connection to the local area network is unreliable, the **netstat -i** command can provide useful information. The example below shows the output from the **netstat –i** command:

```
% netstat -i
Name Mtu  Net/Dest Address     Ipkts  Ierrs Opkts  Oerrs Collis Queue
le0  1500 nuts.com almond      442697 2     633424 2     50679  0
lo0  1536 loopback localhost   53040  0     53040  0     0      0
```

The line for the loopback interface, lo0, can be ignored. Only the line for the real network interface is significant, and only the last five fields on that line provide significant troubleshooting information.

Let's look at the last field first. There should be no packets queued (*Queue*) that cannot be transmitted. If the interface is up and running, and the system cannot deliver packets to the network, suspect a bad drop cable or a bad interface. Replace the cable and see if the problem goes away. If it doesn't, call the vendor for interface hardware repairs.

The input errors (*Ierrs*) and the output errors (*Oerrs*) should be close to zero. Regardless of how much traffic has passed through this interface, 100 errors in either of these fields is high. High output errors could indicate a saturated local network or a bad physical connection between the host and the network. High input errors could indicate that the network is saturated, the local host is overloaded, or there is a physical network problem. Tools, such as **ping** statistics or a TDR, can help you determine if it is a physical network problem. Evaluating the collision rate can help you determine if the local Ethernet is saturated.

A high value in the collision field (*Collis*) is normal, but if the percentage of output packets that result in a collision is too high, it indicates that the network is saturated. Collision rates greater than 5% bear watching. If high collision rates are seen consistently, and are seen among a broad sampling of systems on the network, you may need to subdivide the network to reduce traffic load.

Collision rates are a percentage of output packets. Don't use the total number of packets sent and received; just use *Opkts* and *Collis* when determining the collision rate. For example, the output in the **netstat** sample above shows 50679 collisions out of 633424 outgoing packets. That's a collision rate of 8%. This sample network could be overworked; check the statistics on other hosts on this network. If the other systems also show a high collision rate, consider subdividing this network.

Subdividing an Ethernet

To reduce the collision rate, you must reduce the amount of traffic on the network segment. A simple way to do this is to create multiple segments out of the single segment. Each segment will have fewer hosts and, supposedly, less traffic. We'll see that it's not quite this simple.

A simple and effective way to subdivide a cable segment is to cut the cable and join it back together through a router or a bridge. A *router* is a device that filters traffic based on the IP address. (Routers, also called *gateways*, are discussed extensively in this book.) This approach creates two separate subnets, and uses IP routing to filter the traffic between them. The other device that can filter traffic between the two new cable segments is a bridge. A *bridge* filters the traffic based on the Ethernet address. The network remains a single subnet, but the subnet is made up of two physically separate Ethernets.

Generally, routers are used to build large networks, and bridges are used to connect cable segments. Bridges are more popular for subdividing Ethernets because:

- Bridges are generally less expensive then routers, unless, of course, you already have the router hardware.

- Bridges do not require changes to the IP addresses of the hosts. It is possible that using a router to create a new subnet may require that some hosts change their IP addresses.

- Bridges forward packets faster than routers because they only process the packets through the lowest layers; routers process the packets up to the IP level.

Figure 11-1 shows a simple network divided in two different ways. In the first example an existing router is used. In the second case, a bridge is inserted. This illustration hints at the major problem you must plan for when subdividing a network. Where do you put the central services? If all of the services are on one side of the bridge, traffic may not be significantly reduced. Demand for the services could cause the bridge to become a bottleneck. Before inserting a bridge you must evaluate what services are in demand, and develop a plan for locating those services that reduces the amount of traffic flowing over the bridge.* Try to balance the services evenly on both sides of the bridge; locate the primary users of a service on the same side of the bridge as the service they use.

---

*NFS, particularly with diskless clients, is a demanding service. See the Nutshell Handbook, *Managing NFS and NIS*, by Hal Stern, for specific information about properly locating NFS servers on your network.

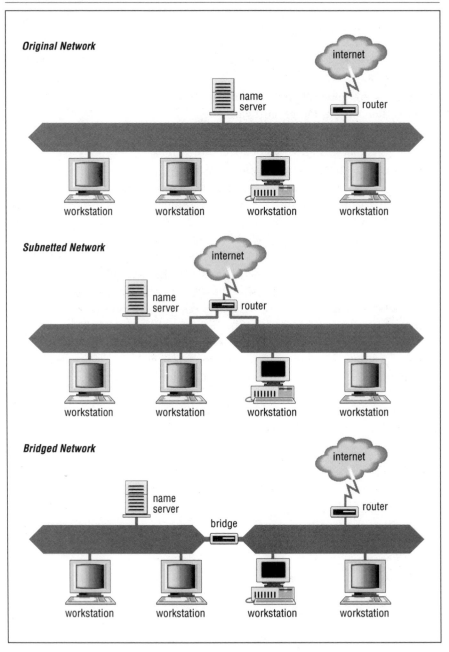

Figure 11.1: *Subdividing a Network with Bridges and Routers*

Network Hardware Problems

Some of the tests discussed in this section can show a network hardware problem. If a hardware problem is indicated, contact the people responsible for the hardware. If the problem appears to be in a leased telephone line, contact the telephone company. If the problem appears to be in a wide area network, contact the management of that network. Don't sit on a problem expecting it to go away. It could easily get worse.

If the problem is in your local area network, you will have to handle it yourself. Some tools, such as the TDR described above, can help. But frequently the only way to approach a hardware problem is by brute force. The "binary search method" is sometimes your only choice. Start by dividing the network into separate segments. Hopefully you'll have some convenient point, a repeater or bridge, where this can be done. It's a good idea to pre-plan this when you're installing your cable, so that you have it installed with connectors that allow it to be easily divided.

Determine which segment still has the problem and further divide that segment until you have the smallest segment possible. It may then be necessary to remove the devices from that segment one at a time until the problem disappears. If you identify a device causing the problem, repair or replace it. Remember the problem can be the cable itself, rather than any particular device; in this case, you have to isolate and replace the faulty cable segment.

Checking Routing

The "network unreachable" error message clearly indicates a routing problem. If the problem is in the local host's routing table, it is easy to detect and resolve. First, use **netstat –nr** and **grep** to see whether or not a valid route to your destination is installed in the routing table. This example checks for a specific route to network 128.8.0.0:

```
% netstat -nr | grep '128\.8\.0'
128.8.0.0    26.20.0.16    UG    0   37    std0
```

This same test, run on a system that did not have this route in its routing table, would return no response at all. For example, a user reports that the "network is down" because he cannot **telnet** to *nic.ddn.mil*, and a **ping** test returns the following results:

```
% ping -s nic.ddn.mil 56 2
PING nic.ddn.mil: 56 data bytes
sendto: Network is unreachable
ping: wrote nic.ddn.mil 64 chars, ret=-1
sendto: Network is unreachable
ping: wrote nic.ddn.mil 64 chars, ret=-1

----nic.ddn.mil PING Statistics----
2 packets transmitted, 0 packets received, 100% packet loss
```

Based on the "network unreachable" error message, check the user's routing table. In our example, we're looking for a route to *nic.ddn.mil*. The IP address* of nic.ddn.mil is 192.112.36.5, which is a class C address. Remember that routes are network oriented. So we check for a route to network 192.112.36.0:

```
% netstat -nr | grep '192.112.36.0'
%
```

This test shows that there is no *specific* route to 192.112.36.0. If a route was found, **grep** would display it. Since there's no specific route to the destination, remember to look for a default route. This example shows a successful check for a default route:

```
% netstat -nr | grep def
default       128.66.12.1     UG    0    101277    1e0
```

If **netstat** shows the correct specific route, or a valid default route, the problem is not in the routing table. In that case, use **traceroute**, as described later in this chapter, to trace the route all the way to its destination.

If **netstat** doesn't return the expected route, it's a local routing problem. There are two ways to approach local routing problems, depending on whether the system uses static or dynamic routing. If you're using static routing, install the missing route using the **route add** command. Remember, most systems that use static routing rely on a default route, so the missing route could be the default route. Make sure that the startup files add the needed route to the table whenever the system reboots. See Chapter 7 for details about the **route add** command.

---

*nslookup** can be used to find the IP address if you don't know it. **nslookup** is discussed later in this chapter.

If you're using dynamic routing, make sure that the routing program is running. For example, the command below makes sure that **gated** is running:

```
% ps `cat /etc/gated.pid`
  PID TT STAT  TIME COMMAND
27711 ?  S    304:59 gated -tep /etc/log/gated.log
```

If the correct routing daemon is not running, restart it and specify tracing. Tracing allows you to check for problems that might be causing the daemon to terminate abnormally.

Checking RIP Updates

If the routing daemon is running and the local system receives routing updates via Routing Information Protocol (RIP), use **ripquery** to check the updates received from your RIP suppliers. For example, to check the RIP updates being received from *almond* and *pecan*, the *peanut* administrator enters the following command:

```
% ripquery -n -r almond pecan
44 bytes from almond.nuts.com(128.66.12.1):
      0.0.0.0, metric 3
      26.0.0.0, metric 0
264 bytes from pecan.nuts.com(128.66.12.3):
      128.66.5.0, metric 2
      128.66.3.0, metric 2
              .
              .
              .
      128.66.12.0, metric 2
      128.66.13.0, metric 2
```

After an initial line identifying the gateway, **ripquery** shows the contents of the incoming RIP packets, one line per route. The first line of the report above indicates that **ripquery** received a response from *almond*. That line is followed by two lines for the two routes advertised by *almond*. *almond* advertises the default route (destination 0.0.0.0) with a metric of 3, and its direct route to Milnet (destination 26.0.0.0) with a metric of 0. Next, **ripquery** shows the routes advertised by *pecan*. These are the routes to the other *nuts-net* subnets.

The two **ripquery** options used in this example are:

–n   Causes **ripquery** to display all output in numeric form. **ripquery** attempts to resolve all IP addresses to names if the **–n** option is not specified. It's a good idea to use the **–n** option; it produces a cleaner display, and you don't waste time resolving names.

−r   Directs **ripquery** to use the RIP REQUEST command, instead of the RIP POLL command, to query the RIP supplier. RIP POLL is not universally supported. You are more likely to get a successful response if you specify **−r** on the **ripquery** command line.

The routes returned in these updates should be the routes you expect. If they are not, or if no routes are returned, check the configuration of the RIP suppliers. Routing configuration problems cause RIP suppliers to advertise routes that they shouldn't, or to fail to advertise the routes that they should. You can detect these problems only by applying your knowledge of your network configuration. You must know what is right to detect what is wrong. Don't expect to see error messages or strange garbled routes. For example, assume that in the test above *pecan* returned the following update:

```
264 bytes from pecan.nuts.com(128.66.12.3):
      0.0.0.0, metric 2
      128.66.3.0, metric 2
              .
              .
              .
      128.66.12.0, metric 2
      128.66.13.0, metric 2
```

This update shows that *pecan* is advertising itself as a default gateway with a lower cost (2 versus 3) than *almond*. This would cause every host on this subnet to use *pecan* as its default gateway. If this is not what you wanted, the routing configuration of *pecan* should be corrected.*

Tracing routes

If the local routing table and RIP suppliers are correct, the problem may be occurring some distance away from the local host. Remote routing problems can cause the "no answer" error message, as well as the "network unreachable" error message. But the "network unreachable" message does not always mean a routing problem. It can literally mean that the remote network cannot be reached because something is down between the local host and the remote destination. **traceroute** is the program that can help you locate these problems.

traceroute traces the route of UDP packets from the local host to a remote host. It prints the name (if it can be determined) and IP address of each gateway along the route to the remote host.

---

*Correct routing configuration is discussed in Chapter 7.

traceroute uses two techniques, small *ttl* (time-to-live) values and an invalid port number, to trace packets to their destination. **traceroute** sends out UDP packets with small *ttl* values to detect the intermediate gateways. The *ttl* values start at one and increase in increments of one for each group of three UDP packets sent. When a gateway receives a packet, it decrements the *ttl*. If the *ttl* is then zero, the packet is not forwarded and an ICMP "Time Exceeded" message is returned to the source of the packet. **traceroute** displays one line of output for each gateway from which it receives a "Time Exceeded" message. Figure 11-2 shows a sample of the single line of output that is displayed for a gateway, and it shows the meaning of each field in the line.

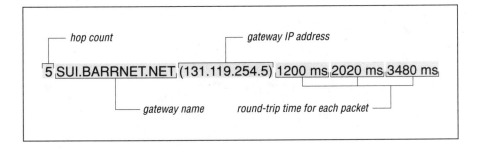

Figure 11.2: traceroute Output

When the destination host receives a packet from **traceroute**, it returns an ICMP "Unreachable Port" message. This happens because **traceroute** intentionally uses an invalid port number (33434) to force this error. When **traceroute** receives the "Unreachable Port" message, it knows that it has reached the destination host, and it terminates the trace. In this way, **traceroute** is able to develop a list of the gateways, starting at one hop away and increasing one hop at a time, until the remote host is reached. Figure 11-3 illustrates the flow of packets tracing to a host three hops away.

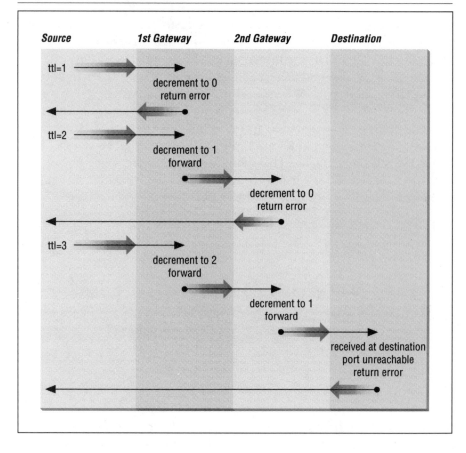

Figure 11.3: Flow of traceroute Packets

The following example shows a **traceroute** to *nic.ddn.mil* from a system hanging off SURAnet. **traceroute** sends out three packets at each *ttl* value. If no response is received to a packet, **traceroute** prints an asterisk (*). If a response is received, **traceroute** displays the name and address of the gateway that responded, and the packet's round-trip time in milliseconds.

```
% traceroute nic.ddn.mil
traceroute to nic.ddn.mil (192.112.36.5), 30 hops max, 40 byte packets
 1  * pgw (129.6.80.254)  4 ms  3 ms
 2  129.6.1.245 (129.6.1.245)  4 ms  4 ms  3 ms
 3  129.6.2.252 (129.6.2.252)  5 ms  5 ms  4 ms
 4  128.167.122.1 (128.167.122.1)  50 ms  6 ms  6 ms
 5  * 192.80.214.247 (192.80.214.247)  96 ms  18 ms
 6  129.140.9.10 (129.140.9.10)  18 ms  25 ms  15 ms
 7  nsn.sura.net (192.80.214.253)  21 ms  18 ms  23 ms
 8  GSI.NSN.NASA.GOV (128.161.252.2)  22 ms  34 ms  27 ms
 9  NIC.DDN.MIL (192.112.36.5)  37 ms  29 ms  34 ms
```

This trace shows that eight intermediate gateways are involved, that packets are reliably making the trip, and that round-trip travel time for packets from this host to *nic.ddn.mil* is about 33 ms.

Variations and bugs in the implementation of ICMP on different types of gateways, and the unpredictable nature of the path a datagram can take through a network, can cause some odd displays. For this reason, you shouldn't examine the output of **traceroute** too closely. The most important things in the **traceroute** output are:

- Did the packet get to its remote destination?
- If not, where did it stop?

Below we show another trace of the path to *nic.ddn.mil*. This time the trace does not go all the way through to the NIC.

```
% traceroute nic.ddn.mil
traceroute to nic.ddn.mil (192.112.36.5), 30 hops max, 40 byte packets
 1  * pgw (129.6.80.254)   3 ms   3 ms
 2  129.6.1.245 (129.6.1.245)   4 ms   4 ms   4 ms
 3  129.6.2.252 (129.6.2.252)   5 ms   5 ms   4 ms
 4  128.167.122.1 (128.167.122.1)   6 ms   6 ms   10 ms
 5  enss.sura.net (192.80.214.248)   9 ms   6 ms   8 ms
 6  t3-1.cnss58.t3.nsf.net (140.222.58.2)   10 ms   15 ms   13 ms
 7  t3-0.enss145.t3.nsf.net (140.222.145.1)   13 ms   12 ms   12 ms
 8  GSI.NSN.NASA.GOV (128.161.252.2)   22 ms   26 ms   21 ms
 9  * * *
10  * * *
        .
        .
        .
29  * * *
30  * * *
```

When **traceroute** fails to get packets through to the remote end-system, the trace trails off, displaying a series of three asterisks at each hop count until the count reaches 30. If this happens, contact the administrator of the remote host you're trying to reach, and the administrator of the last gateway displayed in the trace. Describe the problem to them; they may be able to help.* In our example, the last gateway that responded to our packets was GSI.NSN.NASA.GOV. We would contact this system administrator, and the administrator of *nic.ddn.mil*.

---

*Chapter 13 explains how to find out who is responsible for a specific computer.

Checking Name Service

Name server problems are indicated when the "unknown host" error message is returned by the user's application. Name server problems can usually be diagnosed with **nslookup** or **dig**. **nslookup** is discussed in detail in Chapter 8. **dig** is an alternative tool with similar functionality that is discussed in this chapter. Before looking at **dig**, let's take another look at **nslookup** and see how it is used to troubleshoot name service.

The three features of **nslookup** covered in Chapter 8 are particularly important for troubleshooting remote name server problems. These features are its ability to:

- locate the authoritative servers for the remote domain using the NS query;
- obtain all records about the remote host using the ANY query;
- browse all entries in the remote zone using **nslookup**'s **ls** and **view** commands.

When troubleshooting a remote server problem, directly query the authoritative servers returned by the NS query. Don't rely on information returned by non-authoritative servers. If the problems that have been reported are intermittent, query all of the authoritative servers in turn and compare their answers. Intermittent name server problems are sometimes caused by the remote servers returning different answers to the same query.

The ANY query returns all records about a host, thus giving the broadest range of troubleshooting information. Simply knowing what information is (and isn't) available can solve a lot of problems. For example, if the query returns an MX record but no A record, it is easy to understand why the user couldn't **telnet** to that host! Many hosts are accessible to mail that are not accessible by other network services. In this case, the user is confused and is trying to use the remote host in an inappropriate manner.

If you are unable to locate any information about the host name that the user gave you, perhaps the host name is incorrect. Given that the host name you have is wrong, looking for the correct name is like trying to find a needle in a haystack. However, **nslookup** can help. Use **nslookup**'s **ls** command to dump the remote zone file, and redirect the listing to a file. Then use **nslookup**'s **view** command to browse through the file, looking for names similar to the one the user supplied. Many problems are caused by a mistaken host name.

All of the **nslookup** features and commands mentioned here are used in Chapter 8. However, some examples using these commands to solve real name server problems will be helpful. The three examples that follow are based on actual trouble reports.*

Some Systems Work, Others Don't

A user reported that she could resolve a certain host name from her workstation, but could not resolve the same host name from the central system. However, the central system could resolve other host names. We ran several tests and found that we could resolve the host name on some systems and not on others. There seemed to be no predictable pattern to the failure. So we used **nslookup** to check the remote servers.

```
% nslookup
Default Server:  almond.nuts.com
Address:  128.66.12.1

> set type=NS
> foo.edu.
Server:  almond.nuts.com
Address:  128.66.12.1

foo.edu          nameserver = gerbel.foo.edu
foo.edu          nameserver = red.big.com
foo.edu          nameserver = shrew.foo.edu
gerbel.foo.edu   inet address = 198.97.99.2
red.big.com   inet address = 184.6.16.2
shrew.foo.edu   inet address = 198.97.99.1
> set type=ANY
> server gerbel.foo.edu
Default Server:  gerbel.foo.edu
Address:  198.97.99.2

> hamster.foo.edu
Server:  gerbel.foo.edu
Address:  198.97.99.2

hamster.foo.edu          inet address = 198.97.99.8
> server red.big.com
Default Server:  red.big.com
Address:  184.6.16.2
```

---

*The host and server names are fictitious, but the problems were real.

```
> hamster.foo.edu
Server:  red.big.com
Address:  184.6.16.2
```

```
*** red.big.com can't find hamster.foo.edu: Non-existent domain
```

This sample **nslookup** session contains several steps. The first step is to locate the authoritative servers for the host name in question (*hamster.foo.edu*). We set the query type to NS to get the name server records, and queried for the domain (*foo.edu*) in which the host name is found. This returns three names of authoritative servers: *gerbel.foo.edu*, *red.big.com*, and *shrew.foo.edu*.

Next, we set the query type to ANY to look for any records related to the host name in question. Then we set the server to the first server in the list, *gerbel.foo.edu*, and queried for *hamster.foo.edu*. This returns an address record. So server *gerbel.foo.edu* works fine. We repeated the test using *red.big.com* as the server, and it fails. No records are returned.

The next step is to get SOA records from each server and see if they are the same:

```
> set type=SOA
> foo.edu.
Server:  red.big.com
Address:  184.6.16.2

foo.edu          origin = gerbel.foo.edu
      mail addr = amanda.gerbel.foo.edu
        serial=10164, refresh=43200, retry=3600, expire=3600000,
        min=2592000
> server gerbel.foo.edu
Default Server:  gerbel.foo.edu
Address:  198.97.99.2

> foo.edu.
Server:  gerbel.foo.edu
Address:  198.97.99.2

foo.edu          origin = gerbel.foo.edu
      mail addr = amanda.gerbel.foo.edu
        serial=10164, refresh=43200, retry=3600, expire=3600000,
        min=2592000

> exit
```

If the SOA records have different serial numbers, perhaps the zone file, and therefore the host name, has not yet been downloaded to the secondary server. If the serial numbers are the same and the data is different, as in this case, there is a definite problem. Contact the remote domain administrator and notify her of the problem. The administrator's mailing address is shown in the "mail addr" field of the SOA record. In our example, we would send mail to *amanda@gerbil.foo.edu* reporting the problem.

The Data is Here and the Server Can't Find It!

This problem was reported by the administrator of one of our secondary name servers. The administrator reported that his server could not resolve a certain host name in a domain for which his server was a secondary server. The primary server was, however, able to resolve the name. The administrator dumped his cache (more on dumping the server cache in the next section), and he could see in the dump that his server had the correct entry for the host. But his server still would not resolve that host name to an IP address!

The problem was replicated on several other secondary servers. The primary server would resolve the name; the secondary servers wouldn't. All servers had the same SOA serial number and a dump of the cache on each server showed that they all had the correct address records for the host name in question. So why wouldn't they resolve the host name to an address?

Visualizing the difference between the way primary and secondary servers load their data, made us suspicious of the zone file transfer. Primary servers load the data directly from local disk files. Secondary servers transfer the data from the primary server via a zone file transfer. Perhaps the zone files were getting corrupted. We displayed the zone file on one of the secondary servers and it showed the following data:

```
% cat /usr/etc/sales.nuts.com.hosts
PCpma       IN      A         129.6.64.159
            IN      HINFO     "pc" "n3/800salesnutscom"
PCrkc       IN      A         129.6.64.155
            IN      HINFO     "pc" "n3/800salesnutscom"
PCafc       IN      A         129.6.64.189
            IN      HINFO     "pc" "n3/800salesnutscom"
accu        IN      A         129.6.65.27
cmgds1      IN      A         132.163.130.40
cmg         IN      A         132.163.130.30
PCgns       IN      A         129.6.64.167
            IN      HINFO     "pc" "(3/800salesnutscom"
gw          IN      A         129.6.65.254
zephyr      IN      A         129.6.64.188
            IN      HINFO     "Sun" "sparcstation"
ejw         IN      A         129.6.65.17
PCecp       IN      A         129.6.64.193
            IN      HINFO     "pc" "n^Lsparcstationstcom"
```

Notice the odd display in the last field of the HINFO statement for each PC.*
This data might have been corrupted in the transfer or it might be bad on
the primary server. We used **nslookup** to check that.

```
% nslookup
Default Server:  almond.nuts.com
Address:  128.66.12.1

> server acorn.sales.nuts.com
Default Server:  acorn.sales.nuts.com
Address:  128.66.6.1

> set query=HINFO
> PCwlg.sales.nuts.com
Server:  acorn.sales.nuts.com
Address:  128.66.6.1

PCwlg.sales.nuts.com     CPU=pc  OS=ov
packet size error (0xf7fff590 != 0xf7fff528)
> exit
```

In this **nslookup** example, we set the server to *acorn.sales.nuts.com*,
which is the primary server for *sales.nuts.com*. Next we queried for the
HINFO record for one of the hosts that appeared to have a corrupted record.
The "packet size error" message clearly indicates that **nslookup** was even
having trouble retrieving the HINFO record directly from the primary server.
We contacted the administrator of the primary server and told him about
the problem, pointing out the records that appeared to be in error. He
discovered that he had forgotten to put an operating system entry on some
of the HINFO records. He corrected this, and it fixed the problem.

Cache Corruption

The problem described above was caused by having the name server cache
corrupted by bad data. Cache corruption can occur even if your system is
not a secondary server. Sometimes the root server entries in the cache
become corrupted. Dumping the cache can help diagnose these types of
problems.

For example, a user reported intermittent name server failures. She had no
trouble with any host names within the local domain, or with some names
outside the local domain, but names in several different remote domains
would not resolve. **nslookup** tests produced no solid clues, so the name
server cache was dumped and examined for problems. The root server

---

*See Appendix D for a detailed description of the HINFO statement.

entries were corrupted, so **named** was reloaded to clear the cache and reread the *named.ca* file. Here's how it was done.

The SIGINT signal causes **named** to dump the name server cache to the file */usr/tmp/named_dump.db*. The following command passes **named** this signal:

```
# kill -INT `cat /etc/named.pid`
```

The process id of **named** can be obtained from */etc/named.pid*, as in the example above, because **named** writes its process id in that file during startup.

Once SIGINT causes **named** to snapshot its cache to the file, we can then examine the first part of the file to see if the names and addresses of the root servers are correct. For example:

```
# head -10 /usr/tmp/named_dump.db
; Dumped at Wed Sep 18 08:45:58 1991
; --- Cache & Data ---
$ORIGIN .
        .       80805   IN      SOA     NS.NIC.DDN.MIL. HOSTMASTER.NIC.DDN.MIL. (
                        910909 10800 900 604800 86400 )
                479912  IN      NS      NS.NIC.DDN.MIL.
                479912  IN      NS      AOS.BRL.MIL.
                479912  IN      NS      A.ISI.EDU.
                479912  IN      NS      C.NYSER.NET.
                479912  IN      NS      TERP.UMD.EDU.
```

The cache shown above is clean. If intermittent name server problems lead you to suspect a cache corruption problem, examine the cache and check the names and addresses of all the root servers. Things that might indicate a problem with the root server cache are:

- Incorrect root server names. The section on */etc/named.ca* in Chapter 8 explains how you can locate the correct root server names. The easiest way to do this is to get the file */netinfo/root-servers.txt* from the NIC.

- No address or an incorrect address for any of the servers. Again the correct addresses are in */netinfo/root-servers.txt*.

- A name other then root (.) in the name field of the first root server NS record, or the wildcard character (*) occurring in the name field of a root or top-level name server. The structure of NS records is described in Appendix D.

A "bad cache" with multiple errors might look like this:

```
# head -10 /usr/tmp/named_dump.db
; Dumped at Wed Sep 18 08:45:58 1991
; --- Cache & Data ---
$ORIGIN .
arpa    80805   IN    SOA    SRI-NIC.ARPA.  HOSTMASTER.SRI-NIC.ARPA. (
                910909 10800 900 604800 86400 )
        479912  IN    NS     NS.NIC.DDN.MIL.
        479912  IN    NS     AOS.BRL.MIL.
        479912  IN    NS     A.ISI.EDU.
        479912  IN    NS     C.NYSER.NET.
        479912  IN    NS     TERP.UMD.EDU.
*       479912  IN    NS     NS.FOO.MIL.
```

This contrived example has three glaring errors. The "arpa" entry in the first field of the SOA record is invalid, and is the most infamous form of cache corruption. The last NS record is also invalid. NS.FOO.MIL. is not a valid root server, and an asterisk (*) in the first field of a root server record is not normal.

If you see problems like these, force **named** to reload its cache with the SIGHUP signal as shown below:

```
# kill -HUP `cat /etc/named.pid`
```

This clears the cache and reloads the valid root server entries from your *named.ca* file.

dig, an Alternative to nslookup

An alternative to **nslookup** for making name service queries is **dig**. **dig** queries are usually entered as single-line commands, while **nslookup** is usually run as an interactive session. But the **dig** command performs essentially the same function as **nslookup**. Which you use is mostly a matter of personal choice. They both work well.

As an example, we'll use **dig** to ask the root server *terp.umd.edu* for the NS records for the *mit.edu* domain. To do this, enter the following command:

```
% dig @terp.umd.edu mit.edu ns
```

In this example, *@terp.umd.edu* is the server that is being queried. The server can be identified by name or IP address. If you're troubleshooting a problem in a remote domain, specify an authoritative server for that domain. In this example we're asking for the names of servers for a top-level domain (*mit.edu*), so we ask a root server.

If you don't specify a server explicitly, **dig** uses the local name server, or the name server defined in the */etc/resolv.conf* file. (Chapter 8 describes *resolv.conf.*) Optionally, you can set the environment variable LOCALRES to the name of an alternate *resolv.conf* file. This alternate file will then be used in place of */etc/resolv.conf* for **dig** queries. Setting the LOCALRES variable will only affect **dig**. Other programs that use name service will continue to use */etc/resolv.conf.*

The last item on our sample command line is *ns*. This is the query type. A query type is a value that requests a specific type of DNS information. It is similar to the value used in **nslookup**'s **set type** command. Table 11-2 shows the possible **dig** query types and their meanings.

Table 11.2: dig Query Types

Query Type	DNS Record Requested
a	Address records
any	Any type of record
mx	Mail Exchange records
ns	Name Server records
soa	Start of Authority records
hinfo	Host Info records
axfr	All records in the zone
txt	Text records

Notice that the function of **nslookup**'s **ls** command is performed by the query type **axfr**, and that query type **txt**, which is not supported by BIND 4.8.1, is also included in the list.

dig also has an option that is useful for locating a host name when you only have an IP address. If you only have the IP address of a host, you may want to find out the host name because numeric addresses are more prone to typos. Having the host name can reduce the user's problems. The *in-addr.arpa* domain converts addresses to host names, and **dig** provides a simple way to enter *in-addr.arpa* domain queries. Using the **–x** option, you can query for a number to name conversion without having to manually reverse the numbers and add "in-addr.arpa." For example, to query for the host name of IP address 18.72.0.3, simply enter:

```
% dig -x 18.72.0.3
; <<>> DiG 2.0 <<>> -x
;; ->>HEADER<<- opcode: QUERY , status: NOERROR, id: 6
;; flags: qr aa rd ra ; Ques: 1, Ans: 1, Auth: 0, Addit: 0
;; QUESTIONS:
;;      3.0.72.18.in-addr.arpa, type = ANY, class = IN
;; ANSWERS:
3.0.72.18.in-addr.arpa. 21600   PTR     BITSY.MIT.EDU.
;; Sent 1 pkts, answer found in time: 445 msec
;; FROM: peanut.nuts.com to SERVER: default -- 0.0.0.0
;; WHEN: Sat Nov 16 10:47:37 1991
;; MSG SIZE  sent: 40  rcvd: 67
```

The answer to our query is BITSY.MIT.EDU, but **dig** displays lots of other output. The first five lines and the last four lines provide information and statistics about the query. For our purposes, the only important information is the answer.*

Analyzing Protocol Problems

Problems caused by bad TCP/IP configurations are much more common than problems caused by bad TCP/IP protocol implementations. Most of the problems you encounter will succumb to analysis using the simple tools we have already discussed. But on occasion, you may need to analyze the protocol interaction between two systems. In the worst case, you may need to analyze the packets in the data stream bit by bit.

Tools called network analyzers, or protocol analyzers, can help you do this. Despite the fact that the terms "network analyzer" and "protocol analyzer" are used interchangeably, there is a distinction. *Network analyzers* usually combine hardware and software. The special hardware in these analyzers gives them the ability to detect physical network problems, and it gives them higher performance than software-only analyzers. But the additional hardware adds to the cost of the analyzer. Software-based *protocol analyzers* are usually less expensive, and some are even free. For example, **netwatch** is a free package for DOS systems that is available from the FTP site *windom.ucar.edu*, and **tcpdump** is a free program for UNIX systems that is available from *ftp.ee.lbl.gov*. Software based protocol

---

*To see a single-line answer to this query, pipe **dig**'s output to **grep**; e.g., **dig -x 18.72.0.3 | grep PTR**.

analyzers usually cannot analyze physical network problems. They're used to analyze protocol problems, which is just what we'll use them for here.

etherfind and **tcpdump** are the tools we'll use. **etherfind** is provided as part of SunOS. **tcpdump** is available free, as noted above, and will be included in the BSD 4.4 release. A VMS version is included as part of the commercial Multinet software. Although we use **etherfind** in all of our examples, the concepts introduced in this section should be applicable to the analyzer that you use, because most protocol analyzers function in basically the same way. Protocol analyzers allow you to select, or filter, the packets you want to examine, and to examine those packets byte by byte. We'll discuss both of these functions.

Protocol analyzers watch all the packets on the network. Therefore, you only need *one* system that runs analyzer software on the affected part of the network. One PC with **netwatch**, or one Sun with **etherfind**, can monitor the network traffic and tell you what the other hosts are (or aren't) doing.

Packet Filters

etherfind reads all the packets on an Ethernet. It does this by placing the Ethernet interface into *promiscuous mode*. Normally, an Ethernet interface only passes packets up to the higher layer protocols that are destined for the local host. In promiscuous mode, all packets are accepted and passed to the higher layer. This allows **etherfind** to view all packets and to select packets for analysis, based on a filter you define. Filters can be defined to capture packets from, or to, specific hosts, protocols, and ports, or combinations of all these. As an example, let's look at a very simple **etherfind** filter. The following **etherfind** command displays all packets sent between the hosts *almond* and *peanut*:

```
# etherfind between peanut almond
Using interface le0
                                          icmp type
    lnth proto     source       destination   src port    dst port
      60  arp       peanut        almond
      60  arp       almond        peanut
      98  icmp      peanut        almond      echo
      98  icmp      almond        peanut      echo reply
      60  tcp       peanut        almond      1023        login
      60  tcp       almond        peanut      login       1023
^C
```

The filter "between peanut almond" selects only those packets that are from *peanut* to *almond*, or from *almond* to *peanut*. The filter is constructed from a set of primitives, and associated host names, protocol names, and port numbers. The primitives can be modified and combined with the operators **and**, **or**, and **not**. For **etherfind**, the filter is not optional, because there is no default. For **tcpdump**, the filter may be omitted; this causes **tcpdump** to display all packets from the network.

Table 11-3 shows the primitives used to build the filters. The primitives are identical for **etherfind** and the VMS version of **tcpdump**. The UNIX version of **tcpdump** differs slightly. The variations for UNIX **tcpdump** are shown in the third column of the table.

Table 11.3: Expression Primitives

Primitive	Matches Packets	UNIX tcpdump
dst *destination*	To *destination* host	**dst** *destination*
src *source*	From *source* host	**src** *source*
host *host*	To or from *host*	**host** *host*
between *host1 host2*	To or from *host1* or *host2*	**host** *h1* **and host** *h2*
dstnet *destination*	To *destination* network	**dst net** *destination*
srcnet *source*	From *source* network	**src net** *source*
dstport *destination*	To *destination* port	**dst port** *destination*
srcport *source*	From *source* port	**src port** *source*
proto *protocol*	Of *protocol* type (**icmp**, **udp**, or **tcp**)	**ip proto** *protocol*

Using these primitives with the operators **and** and **or**, complex filters can be constructed. However, filters are usually simple. Capturing the traffic between two hosts is probably the most common filter. You may further limit the data captured to a specific protocol, but often you're not sure which protocol will reveal the problem. Just because the user sees the problem in **ftp** or **telnet** does not mean that is where the problem actually occurs. Analysis must often start by capturing all packets, and can only be narrowed after test evidence points to some specific problem.

Modifying Analyzer Output

The example in the previous section shows that **etherfind** displays two header lines. The first line identifies the network interface being used, and the other lists headings for each of the fields that will be displayed. The headings are:

lnth   Total length of the packet in bytes.

proto   Protocol type of the packet.

source   Source address of the packet. **etherfind** has a **–n** option that prevents converting the address to a host name.

destination   Destination address of the packet. Again, this is converted to a host name unless the **–n** option is used.

icmp type   ICMP message type is displayed if this is a packet whose protocol type (proto) is icmp.

src port   Source port of the packet is displayed if the protocol type is *not* icmp.

dst port   Destination port of the packet is displayed if the protocol type is *not* icmp.

By default, **etherfind** displays a single line of output for each packet received. Each line of output provides only the information indicated by the headings. This information may be sufficient to gain insight into how packets flow between two hosts. However, troubleshooting protocol problems requires more detailed information about each packet. **etherfind** has options that give you control over what information is displayed.

To display the actual contents of the packets, use the **–x** option. This option causes the entire contents of the packet to be dumped in hex. In most cases, you don't need to see the entire packet; usually, the headers are sufficient to troubleshoot a protocol problem. To limit the number of bytes dumped for each packet, use the option **–l** *length*.*

To determine what value should be used for *length*, remember that all of the headers are contiguous bytes located at the beginning of the packet, and that **etherfind** starts the hex dump with the 14 byte Ethernet header.† The *length* value of the **–l** option is set to the number of TCP/IP header bytes you wish to view, plus 14 for the Ethernet header. Chapter 1 describes the TCP/IP headers. Figure 1-5 shows that the IP datagram header is no more than six 32-bit words long, and Figure 1-9 shows that the TCP Segment header is also six words long. Therefore, to see both the IP header and the TCP header, set **–l** to 62 bytes; that is, 14 bytes, plus six words, plus six words.

---

*By default **tcpdump** dumps 96 bytes. **tcpdump** uses **–s** to change the number of bytes dumped.
†Some analyzers do not display the Ethernet header. Check your documentation.

The following example shows the first and last packets dumped by **ether-find** when monitoring a **telnet** session. The **–x** causes the packets to be dumped, and the **–l** limits the dump to 64 bytes for each packet. Each packet's summary line is still printed, and the header lines are still displayed.

```
# etherfind -x -1 64 between peanut pecan
Using interface le0
                                           icmp type
  lnth proto          source      destination  src port   dst port
    60  tcp           peanut        pecan       telnet       4180
  08 00 20 0e 12 37 00 00 93 e0 80 b1 08 00 45 00
  00 2c 19 fb 00 00 1b 06 21 11 81 06 12 32 81 06
  50 82 00 17 10 54 fb d8 36 01 75 d9 ec 01 60 12
  80 00 04 e1 00 00 02 04 10 08 00 04
            .
            .
            .
    60  tcp           peanut        pecan       telnet       4180
  08 00 20 0e 12 37 00 00 93 e0 80 b1 08 00 45 10
  00 28 1a c8 00 00 1b 06 20 38 81 06 12 32 81 06
  50 82 00 17 10 54 fb d8 3b a3 75 d9 ec 58 50 10
  7f ff 20 fb 00 00 3d 3d 3d 3d 3d 3d
```

Since the Ethernet header occupies the first 14 bytes of the dump, the 15th byte of each packet is the first byte of the IP header. In both of these packets, this byte contains the value 45 (hex). The first byte of an IP header contains four bits for the version number and four bits for the header length.* Therefore, in this example, the IP version number is 4, and the IP header length is five words. Knowing the IP header length, we can locate the start of the TCP segment header. If the next five words (20 bytes) are the IP header, then the 21st byte after the start of the IP header is the first byte of the TCP segment header. That's the 35th byte from the start of each packet in this example. The first two bytes of the TCP segment header are the source port. In both of these packets, the source port is hex 0017 (decimal 23), which is the well-known port number of **telnet**. Therefore, we're looking at packets from a TELNET session.

Figure 11-4 should help clarify the structure of this packet. It shows the data from the packet marked off into the three header areas: Ethernet, IP, and TCP. Above the data representation, the figure has a block diagram that shows the fields in each of the three headers. Perhaps this will save

---

*Figure 11-4 shows the format of these headers. These headers are also discussed in Chapter 1 and Appendix F.

you from flipping back to Chapter 1 when we discuss a protocol problem in the following section.

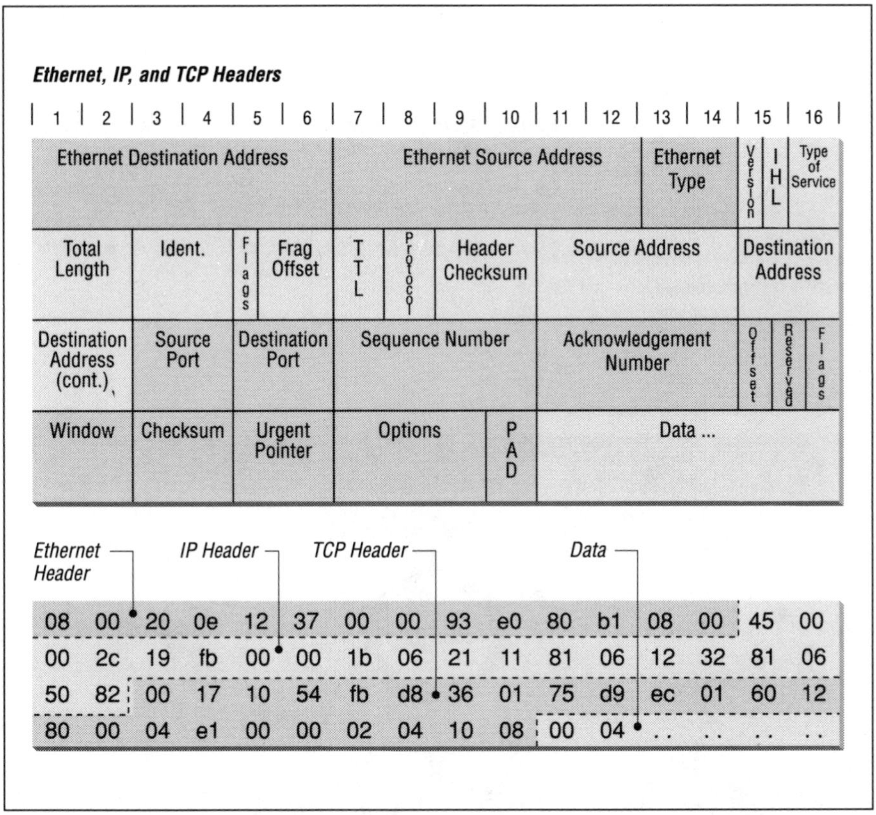

Ethernet, IP, and TCP Headers

| 1 | 2 | 3 | 4 | 5 | 6 | 7 | 8 | 9 | 10 | 11 | 12 | 13 | 14 | 15 | 16 |

Ethernet Destination Address			Ethernet Source Address		Ethernet Type	Version	IHL	Type of Service
Total Length	Ident.	Flags	Frag Offset	TTL	Protocol	Header Checksum	Source Address	Destination Address
Destination Address (cont.)	Source Port	Destination Port	Sequence Number		Acknowledgement Number		Offset	Reserved	Flags
Window	Checksum	Urgent Pointer	Options		PAD	Data ...		

Ethernet Header — IP Header ⌐ TCP Header ⌐   Data ⌐

08	00	20	0e	12	37	00	00	93	e0	80	b1	08	00	45	00
00	2c	19	fb	00	00	1b	06	21	11	81	06	12	32	81	06
50	82	00	17	10	54	fb	d8	36	01	75	d9	ec	01	60	12
80	00	04	e1	00	00	02	04	10	08	00	04	..	..	..	..

Figure 11.4: Packet Header Structure

Protocol Case Study

This example is an actual case that was solved by protocol analysis. The problem was reported as an occasional **ftp** failure with the error message:

```
netout: Option not supported by protocol
421 Service not available, remote server has closed connection
```

Only one user reported the problem, and it occurred only when transferring large files from a workstation to the central computer, via our token-ring backbone network.

We obtained the user's data file and were able to duplicate the problem from other workstations, but only when we transferred the file to the same central system via the backbone network. Figure 11-5 graphically summarizes the tests we ran to duplicate the problem.

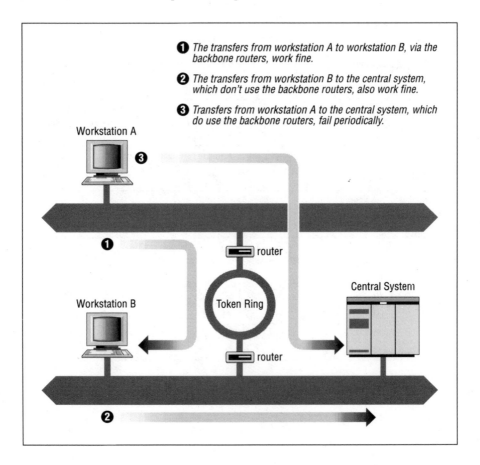

① The transfers from workstation A to workstation B, via the backbone routers, work fine.

② The transfers from workstation B to the central system, which don't use the backbone routers, also work fine.

③ Transfers from workstation A to the central system, which do use the backbone routers, fail periodically.

Figure 11.5: FTP Test Summary

We notified all users of the problem. In response, we received reports that others had also experienced it, but again only when transferring to the central system, and only when transferring via the backbone. They had not reported it, because they rarely saw it. But the additional reports gave us some evidence that the problem did not relate to any recent network changes.

Because the problem had been duplicated on other systems, it probably was not a configuration problem on the user's system. The **ftp** failure could also be avoided if the backbone routers and the central system did not interact. So we concentrated our attention on those systems. We checked the routing tables and ARP tables, and ran **ping** tests on the central system and the routers. No problems were observed.

Based on this preliminary analysis, the **ftp** failure appeared to be a possible protocol interaction problem between a certain brand of routers and a central computer. We made that assessment because the transfer routinely failed when these two brands of systems were involved, but never failed in any other circumstance. If the router or the central system were misconfigured, they should fail when transferring data to other hosts. If the problem was an intermittent physical problem, it should occur randomly regardless of the hosts involved. Instead, this problem occurred predictably, and only between two specific brands of computers. Perhaps there was something incompatible in the way these two systems implemented TCP/IP.

Therefore, we used **etherfind** to capture the TCP/IP headers during several **ftp** test runs. Reviewing the dumps showed that all transfers that failed with the *netout* error message had an ICMP Parameter Error packet near the end of the session, usually about 50 packets before the final close. No successful transfer had this ICMP packet. Note that the error did *not* occur in the last packet in the data stream, as you might expect. It is common for an error to be detected, and for the data stream to continue for some time before the connection is actually shut down. Don't assume that an error will always be at the end of a data stream.

Here are the headers from the key packets. First, the IP header of the packet from the backbone router that caused the central system to send the error:

```
  566 tcp          fs2      bnos        1176     ftp-data
  08 00 25 30 06 51 00 00 93 e0 a0 bf 08 00 45 00
  02 28 8a 22 00 00 39 06 ff ff 81 06 50 03 84 a3
  a0 01
```

And this is the ICMP Parameter Error packet sent from the central system in response to that packet:

```
   70 icmp          bnos      fs2          parameter problem
  00 00 93 e0 a0 bf 08 00 25 30 06 51 08 00 45 00
  00 38 00 0c 00 00 3b 01 8a 0b 84 a3 a0 01 81 06
  50 03 0c 00 0d 9f 0a 00 00 00 45 00 02 28 8a 22
  00 00 39 06 00 00 81 06 50 03 84 a3 a0 01
```

Remember that the first 14 bytes of the dump are the Ethernet header, that the IP header starts in the 15th byte, and that the first byte of the IP header contains the header length that allows us to determine the start of the ICMP header. Just as in the previous example, the header is five words long.* Therefore, the ICMP header starts 20 bytes after the start of the IP header, which is the 35th byte of this packet dump. Figure 11-6 shows the format of the ICMP header.

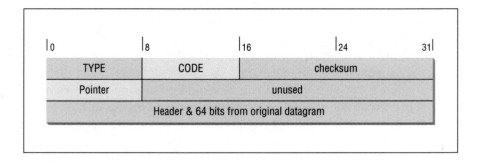

Figure 11.6: ICMP Header Format

Each packet was broken out bit-by-bit and mapped to the appropriate TCP/IP header fields. Table 11-4 shows the breakout of the data in the IP header from the router, and Table 11-5 shows how we interpreted the ICMP Parameter Error packet. Appendix F contains material excerpted from the RFCs that explains the fields in the IP, TCP, UDP, and ICMP headers.

Table 11.4: Breakout of the Router's Packet

Header Field	Packet Value	Header Field	Packet Value
Version	4	Fragment Offset	000 (none)
IP Header Length	5	Time-to-Live	39
Type-of-Service	00 (routine)	Protocol	06 (TCP)
Total Length	0228 (552 decimal)	IP Checksum	ffff
Identification	8a22	source	81065003
			(129.6.80.3)
Flags	0 (none)	destination	84a3a001
			(132.163.160.1)

---

*The first byte of this IP header contains the value 45. The version number is 4, and the header length is 5.

Table 11.5: Breakout of the ICMP Packet

Header Field	Packet Value	Header Field	Packet Value
Version	4	Protocol	01 (ICMP)
IP Header Length	5	IP Checksum	8a0b
Type-of-Service	00 (routine)	source	84a3a001
			(132.163.160.1)
Total Length	0038 (56 decimal)	destination	81065003
			(129.6.80.3)
Identification	000c	ICMP Type	0c (12-Parameter
			Problem)
Flags	0 (none)	ICMP Code	00 (Pointer
			indicates error)
Fragment Offset	000 (none)	Checksum	0d9f
Time-to-Live	3b	ICMP Pointer	0a (10th byte
			is error)

From this detailed analysis of each packet, we saw that the router issued an IP Header Checksum of 0xffff, and that the central system objected to this checksum. We know that the central system objected to the checksum because it returned an ICMP Parameter Error with a Pointer of 10. The Parameter Error indicates that there is something wrong with the data the system has just received, and the Pointer identifies the specific data that the system thinks is in error. The tenth byte of the router's IP header is the IP Header Checksum. The data field of the ICMP error message returns the header that it believes is in error. Notice that when the central system returned the header, the checksum field was "corrected" to 0000. Clearly the central system disagreed with the router's checksum calculation.

Occasional checksum errors will occur. They can be caused by transmission problems, and are intended to detect these types of problems. Every protocol suite has a mechanism for recovering from checksum errors. So how should they be handled in TCP/IP?

To determine the correct protocol action in this situation, turn to the authoritative sources—the RFCs. RFC 791, *Internet Protocol*, provided information about the checksum calculation, but the best source for this particular problem was RFC 1122, *Requirements for Internet hosts—communication layers*, by R. Braden. This RFC provided two specific references that define the action to be taken. These two quotes are taken from page 29 of RFC 1122:

> In the following, the action specified in certain cases is to "silently discard" a received datagram. This means that the datagram will be discarded without further processing and that the host will not send any ICMP error message (see Section 3.2.2) as a result. . . .
>
> . . . A host MUST verify the IP header checksum on every received datagram and silently discard every datagram that has a bad checksum.

Therefore, when a system receives a packet with a bad checksum, it is not supposed to do anything with it. The packet should be discarded, and the system should wait for the next packet to arrive. The system should not respond with an error message. A system cannot respond to a bad IP header checksum, because it cannot really know where the packet came from. If the header checksum is in doubt, how do you know if the addresses in the header are correct? And if you don't know for sure where the packet came from, how can you respond to it?

IP relies on the upper layer protocols to recover from these problems. If TCP is used (as it was in this case), the sending TCP eventually notices that the recipient has never acknowledged the segment, and it sends the segment again. If UDP is used, the sending application is responsible for recovering from the error. In neither case does recovery rely on an error message returned from the recipient.

Therefore, for an incorrect checksum, the central system should have simply discarded the bad packet. The vendor was informed of this problem and, much to their credit, they sent us a fix for the software within two weeks. Not only that, the fix worked perfectly!

Not all problems are resolved so cleanly. But the technique of analysis is the same no matter what the problem.

12

Network Security

Hosts attached to a network, particularly the worldwide Internet, are exposed to a wider range of security threats than unconnected hosts. Network security reduces the risks of connecting to a network. But by their natures, network access and computer security work at cross purposes. A network is a data highway designed to increase access to computer systems, while security is designed to control access. Providing network security is a balancing act between open access and security.

The highway analogy is very appropriate. Like a highway, the network provides equal access for all—welcome visitors as well as unwelcome intruders. At home, you provide security for your possessions by locking your house, not by blocking the streets. Likewise, network security generally means providing adequate security on individual host computers, not providing security directly on the network.

In very small towns, where people know each other, doors are often left unlocked. But in big cities, doors have dead-bolts and chains. In the last decade, the Internet has grown from a small town of a few thousand users to a big city of millions of users. Just as the anonymity of a big city turns neighbors into strangers, the growth of the Internet has reduced the level of trust between network neighbors. The ever increasing need for computer security is an unfortunate side effect. Growth, however, is not all bad. In the same way that a big city offers more choices and more services, the expanded network provides increased services. For most of us, security consciousness is a small price to pay for network access.

Network break-ins have increased as the network has grown and become more impersonal, but it is easy to exaggerate the real extent of these break-ins. Overreacting to the threat of break-ins may hinder the way you use the network. Don't make the cure worse than the disease. The best advice about network security is to use common sense. RFC 1244, *Site Security Handbook*, by Holbrook, Reynold, et. al., states this principle very well:

> Common sense is the most appropriate tool that can be used to establish your security policy. Elaborate security schemes and mechanisms are impressive, and they do have their place, yet there is little point in investing money and time on an elaborate implementation scheme if the simple controls are forgotten.

This chapter emphasizes the simple controls that can be used to increase your network's security. A reasonable approach to security, based on the level of security required by your system, is the most cost effective—both in terms of actual expense and in terms of productivity.

Security Planning

One of the most important network security tasks, and probably one of the least enjoyable, is developing a network security policy. Most computer people want a technical solution to every problem. We want to find a program that "fixes" the network security problem. Few of us want to write a paper on network security policies and procedures. However, a well thought-out security plan will help you decide what needs to be protected, how much you are willing to invest in protecting it, and who will be responsible for carrying out the steps to protect it.

Assessing the Threat

The first step toward developing an effective network security plan is to assess the threat that connection presents to your systems. The *Site Security Handbook*, RFC 1244, identifies three distinct types of security threats usually associated with network connectivity:

- *Unauthorized access*—a break-in by an unauthorized person.
- *Disclosure of information*—any problem that causes the disclosure of valuable or sensitive information to people who should not have access to the information.
- *Denial of service*—any problem that makes it difficult or impossible for the system to continue to perform productive work.

Assess these threats in relation to the number of users who would be affected, as well as to the sensitivity of the information that might be compromised. For some organizations, break-ins are an embarrassment that can undermine the confidence that others have in the organization, and intruders tend to target government and academic organizations that will be the most embarrassed by the break-in. But for most organizations, unauthorized access is not a major problem unless it involves one of the other threats: disclosure of information or denial of service.

Assessing the threat of information disclosure depends on the type of information that could be compromised. No system with highly classified information should ever be directly connected to the Internet, but there are other types of sensitive information which do not necessarily prohibit connecting the system to a network. Personnel information, medical information, corporate plans, credit records—all of these things have a certain type of sensitivity and must be protected. In most cases, this information can be adequately protected by standard UNIX file security procedures. However, in some cases, the risk of liability if this information is disclosed may be sufficient to keep the host that stores the information from being connected to the Internet.

Denial of service can be a severe problem if it impacts many users or a major mission of your organization. Some systems can be connected to the network with little concern. The benefit of connecting individual workstations and small servers to the Internet generally outweighs the chance of having service interrupted for the individuals and small groups served by these systems. Other systems may be vital to the survival of your organization. The threat of losing the services of a mission-critical system must be evaluated seriously before connecting such a system to the network.

Network threats are, of course, not the only threats to computer security, or the only reasons for denial of service. Natural disasters and internal threats (threats from people who have legitimate access to a system) are also serious. Network security has had a lot of publicity lately, so it's a fashionable thing to worry about; but more computer time has probably been lost because of fires than has ever been lost because of network security problems. Similarly, more data has probably been improperly disclosed by authorized users than by unauthorized break-ins. This book naturally emphasizes network security, but network security is only part of a larger security plan that includes physical security and disaster recovery plans.

Many traditional (non-network) security threats are handled, in part, by physical security. Don't forget to provide an adequate level of physical security for your network equipment and cables. Again, the investment in physical security should be based on your realistic assessment of the threat.

Distributed Control

One approach to network security is to distribute responsibility for, and control over, segments of a large network to small groups within the organization. This approach involves a large number of people in security, and runs counter to one school of thought that seeks to increase security by centralizing control. However, distributing responsibility and control to small groups can create an environment of small networks composed of trusted hosts. Using the analogy of small towns and big cities, it is similar to creating a neighborhood watch to reduce risks by giving people connection with their neighbors, mutual responsibility for one another, and control over their own fates.

Additionally, distributing security responsibilities formally recognizes one of the realities of network security—most security actions take place on individual systems. The managers of these systems must know that they are responsible for security, and that their contribution to network security is recognized and appreciated. If people are expected to do a job, they must be empowered to do it.

Use Subnets to Distribute Control

Subnets are a powerful tool for distributing network control. A subnet administrator should be appointed when a subnet is created. The administrator is then responsible for the security of the network and is empowered to assign IP addresses for the devices connected to the networks. Assigning IP addresses gives the subnet administrator some control over who connects to the subnet. It also helps to ensure that the subnet administrator knows each system that is assigned an address and who is responsible for that system. When the subnet administrator assigns a system an IP address, he also assigns certain security responsibilities to the system's administrator. Likewise, when the system administrator grants a user an account, the user is assigned certain security responsibilities.

The hierarchy of responsibility flows from the network administrator, to the subnet administrator, to the system administrator, and finally to the user. At each point in this hierarchy the individuals are given responsibilities and the power to carry them out. To support this structure, it is important for users to know what they are responsible for, and how to carry out that responsibility. The network security policy, described in the next section, provides this information.

Use Mailing Lists to Distribute Information

If your site adopts distributed control, you must develop a system for disseminating security information to each group. Mailing lists for each administrative level can be used for this purpose. The network administrator receives security information from outside authorities, filters out irrelevant material, and forwards the relevant material to the subnet administrators. Subnet administrators forward the relevant parts to their system administrators, who in turn forward what they consider important to the individual users. The filtering of information at each level ensures that individuals get the information they need, without receiving too much information. If too much unnecessary material is distributed, users begin to ignore everything they receive.

At the top of this information structure is the information that the network administrator receives from outside authorities. In order to receive this, the network administrator should join the appropriate mailing lists. A few mailing lists that pertain directly to computer security are the following:*

- Computer Emergency Response Team (CERT) Advisories. The CERT advisory list distributes information about known security problems, and the fixes to these problems. To join this mailing list, send mail to *cert@cert.sei.cmu.edu,* and specify that you wish to join the CERT advisory mailing list. Old advisories can be retrieved via anonymous **ftp** from *cert.sei.cmu.edu* in the directory */pub/cert_advisories.*

- DDN Security Bulletins. These bulletins are very similar in content to the CERT advisories, though DDN bulletins do occasionally add information of specific interest to Milnet users. DDN bulletins and CERT advisories deal primarily with network security threats. To join this list, send mail to *nic@nic.ddn.mil* and ask to be placed on the security bulletins mailing list. Past bulletins can be retrieved via anonymous **ftp** from the *scc* directory on *nic.ddn.mil.*

- Risks Forum. The risks forum discusses the full range of computer security risks. To join this list, send mail to *risks-request@csl.sri.com* and ask to be placed on the risks forum mailing list.

---

*There are many mailing lists. See Chapter 13 for details about how to obtain the "list of lists," an enormous catalog of mailing lists.

- Computer Virus Information. The VIRUS-L list deals primarily with computer viruses—a threat usually associated with PCs. To join, send mail to *listserv%lehiibm1.bitnet@mitvma.mit.edu* with a single line of text in the body of the message that says: SUB VIRUS-L *your full name.*

Writing a Security Policy

Security is largely a "people problem." People, not computers, are responsible for implementing security procedures, and people are responsible when security is breached. Therefore, network security is ineffective unless people know their responsibilities. It is important to write a security policy that clearly states what is expected, and who it is expected from. A network security policy should define:

The network user's security responsibilities

> The policy may require users to change their passwords at certain intervals, to use passwords that meet certain guidelines, or to perform certain checks to see if their accounts have been accessed by someone else. Whatever is expected from users, it is important that it be clearly defined.

The system administrator's security responsibilities

> The policy may require that specific security measures, login banner messages, and monitoring and accounting procedures, be used on every host. It might list applications that should not be run on any host attached to the network.

The proper use of network resources

> Define who can use network resources, what things they can do, and what things they should not do. If your organization takes the position that e-mail, files, and histories of computer activity are subject to security monitoring, tell the users very clearly that this is the policy.

The actions taken when a security problem is detected

> What should be done when a security problem is detected? Who should be notified? It is easy to overlook things during a crisis, so you should have a detailed list of the exact steps that a system administrator, or user, should take when a security breach has been detected. This could be as simple as telling the users to "touch nothing, and call the network security officer." But even these simple actions should be in the policy so that they are readily available.

Connecting to the Internet brings with it certain security responsibilities. RFC 1281, *A Guideline for the Secure Operation of the Internet*, provides guidance for users and network administrators on how to use the Internet in a secure and responsible manner. Reading this RFC will provide insight into the information that should be in your security policy.

A great deal of thought is necessary to produce a complete network security policy. The outline shown above describes the contents of a network policy document, but if you are personally responsible for writing a policy, you may want more detailed guidance. I also recommend that you read RFC 1244. It is a very good guide for developing a security plan.

Security planning (assessing the threat, assigning security responsibilities, and writing a security policy) is the basic building block of network security, but a plan must be implemented before it can have any effect. In the remainder of this chapter, we'll turn our attention to implementing basic security procedures.

Passwords

Good passwords are the simplest, and most important, part of network security. The CERT estimates that 80% of all network security problems are caused by bad passwords.* The mythology of the network says that network security breaches are caused by sophisticated security crackers, who exploit software security holes to break into computer systems. But in reality, most intruders enter systems simply by guessing passwords. These are a few things that make it easy to guess passwords:

- Accounts that use the account name as the password. Accounts with this type of trivial password are called *joe accounts*.
- Guest or demonstration accounts that require no password, or use a well-publicized password.
- System accounts with default passwords. (This is primarily a VMS problem.)

Guessing these kinds of passwords requires no skill, just lots of spare time!

A more sophisticated form of password guessing is *dictionary guessing*. Dictionary guessing uses a program that encrypts each word in a dictionary (e.g., */usr/dict/words*) and compares each encrypted word to the encrypted password in the */etc/passwd* file. Dictionary guessing is not limited to words from a dictionary. Things known about you (your name, initials, telephone number, etc.) are also run through the guessing program when

---

*This estimate is according to RFC 1244, *Site Security Handbook*, page 8.

trying to guess the password for your account. Because of dictionary guessing, you must protect the */etc/passwd* file. Make sure it cannot be retrieved via anonymous **ftp** or **tftp**.* A simple test to see if */etc/passwd* is accessible via **tftp** is:

```
% tftp localhost
tftp> get /etc/passwd
Error code 1: File not found
tftp> quit
```

In this example, we access the local host via **tftp** and attempt to get the */etc/passwd* file. Thankfully, we receive an error message instead of the file. If you are able to transfer the */etc/passwd* file via **tftp**, disable **tftp** by commenting it out of the *inetd.conf* file, and assume that your password file has been compromised. If the */etc/passwd* file has been compromised, change every password on your system. In general, you should not run the **tftp** daemon on your system unless it is absolutely required, and then only if it can be run in a secure mode (**tftp -s**) that restricts **tftp** access to a specific directory.

Some systems use a *shadow password file* to hide the encrypted passwords from potential intruders. Shadow password files have restricted permissions that prevent them from being read by intruders. The encrypted password is only stored in the shadow password file and not in the */etc/passwd* file. Hiding encrypted passwords greatly reduces the risk of password guessing. If your system has a shadow password facility, use it.

Changing your password frequently is an additional deterrent to password guessing. However, if you choose good passwords, don't change them so often that it is hard to remember them. Many security experts recommend that passwords should be changed about every 3 to 6 months.

The encryption algorithm used for passwords has not been broken. No intruder can take the encrypted password and decrypt it back to its original form, but encrypted passwords can be compared against encrypted dictionaries. If bad passwords are used, they can be easily guessed. Take care to choose good passwords and protect the */etc/passwd* file.

---

*See Chapter 12 for information on setting up anonymous **ftp**.

Choosing a Password

No security measure is more effective than a good password. Choosing a good password boils down to this, don't choose a password that can be guessed using the techniques described above. Some guidelines for choosing a good password are:

- Don't use your login name.
- Don't use the name of anyone or anything.
- Don't use any English, or foreign language, word or abbreviation.
- Don't use any personal information associated with the owner of the account. For example, don't use initials, phone number, social security number, job title, organizational unit, etc.
- Don't use keyboard sequences, e.g., qwerty.
- Don't use any of the above things spelled backwards, or in caps, or otherwise disguised.
- Don't use an all numeric password.
- Don't use a sample password, no matter how good, that you've gotten from a book that discusses computer security.
- *Do* use a mixture of numbers and mixed-case letters.
- *Do* use at least six characters.
- *Do* use a seemingly random selection of letters and numbers.

Common suggestions for constructing seemingly random passwords are:

1. Use the first letter of each word from a line in a book, song, or poem. For example: "Where are the strong? Who are the trusted?"* would produce Wats?Watt?

2. Use the output from a random password generator. Select a random string that can be pronounced and is easy to remember. For example, the random string "adazac" can be pronounced a-da-zac, and you can remember it by thinking of it as "A-to-Z." Add uppercase letters to create your own emphasis, e.g., aDAzac.†

3. Use two short words connected by punctuation, e.g., wRen%Rug.

4. Use numbers and letters to create an imaginary vanity license plate password, e.g., 2hot4U?.

---

*Elvis Costello, "(What's So Funny 'Bout) Peace, Love and Understanding."
†A VMS system password generator was used to create this password.

A common theme of these suggestions is that the password should be easy to remember. Avoid passwords that must be written down to be remembered. If unreliable people gain access to your office and find the password you have written down, the security of your system will be compromised.

However, don't assume that you will not be able to remember a random password. It may be difficult the first few times you use the password, but any password that is used often enough is easy to remember. If you have an account on a system that you rarely use, you may have trouble remembering a random password. But in that case, the best solution is to get rid of the account. Unused and under-utilized accounts are prime targets for intruders. They like to attack unused accounts because there is no user to notice changes to the files or strange *Last login:* messages. Remove all unused accounts from your systems.

Password Software

How do you ensure that this guidance for creating new passwords will be followed? The most important step is to make sure that every user knows these suggestions and the importance of following them. This information should be covered in your network security plan, and periodically reinforced through newsletter articles and online system bulletins.

It is also possible to use programs that force users to follow specific password selection guidelines. The programs **npasswd** and **passwd+** do exactly that.

npasswd

npasswd is a program that forces passwords to meet a specific set of rules before they are added to the */etc/passwd* file. **npasswd** is not a random password generator. It allows users to choose their own passwords, but the passwords they choose must meet certain criteria. The passwords are checked:

- For a minimum number of characters. Passwords that are too short are rejected. As a corollary of this length check, passwords that are too long are accepted, but a warning message is sent to the user. On most UNIX systems, only the first eight characters of the password are encrypted and stored in */etc/passwd*. Therefore, the password "Aberdeen/PGrnd8" could easily be guessed by dictionary guessing, because it is really only the password "Aberdeen." The warning helps make users aware of this problem.

- For illegal characters. Certain control characters or repeated characters (e.g., "aaa") cause the password to be rejected. This is done to eliminate trivial passwords such as "aaaaaa," and to avoid the terminal problems sometimes caused by special characters in the password.

- For mixed case. Password that are all uppercase or all lowercase are rejected.

- Against personal information. The password is compared to the login name, host name, user's first and last names, and to various information about the user returned by the **finger** command. Various permutations of this information, e.g., spelling forward and backward, are also checked. If any matches are found, the password fails.

- Against a dictionary. The password is searched for in a list of dictionaries. If the password is found in any dictionary, it is rejected.

If a password meets all of these criteria, it is encrypted and placed in the */etc/passwd* file. These criteria are controlled by the system administrator via the */usr/adm/checkpasswd.cf* file. Table 12-1 shows the configuration commands available in *checkpasswd.cf.*

Table 12.1: checkpasswd Configuration Commands

Command	Function
dictionary *filename*	Define a dictionary file to be searched.
singlecase yes | **no**	Allow single case. Default is **no**.
minlength *n*	Minimum password length is *n* characters.
maxlength *n*	Maximum password length is *n* characters.
printonly yes | **no**	Allow only ASCII printable characters.
badchars "*list*"	Replace characters that can't be used with *list*.
badchars +"*list*"	Add *list* to characters that can't be used.

npasswd is available via anonymous **ftp** from *ftp.cc.utexas.edu* in the compressed **tar** file *pub/npasswd/npasswd.tar.Z.*

passwd+

Like **npasswd**, **passwd+** also subjects a password to a series of tests before adding it to the */etc/passwd* file, but it provides a more flexible set of possible tests than **npasswd**. With this increased flexibility comes increased complexity, so **passwd+** has a complex configuration language.

passwd+ is configured by placing password tests in */etc/password.test*. This configuration can be as simple as copying the *pwsample* file, which comes with **passwd+**, to */etc/password.test*, or as complicated as constructing each individual password test by hand. For most sites, the configuration in *pwsample* is sufficient. If you have special password test requirements that are not addressed by **npasswd** or **passwd+**, see Appendix G for the **passwd+** configuration language details. That language is flexible enough to handle any reasonable password test.

Password Aging

A password aging mechanism defines a lifetime for each password. When a password reaches the end of its lifetime, the password aging mechanism notifies the user to change the password. If it is not changed in some specified period, the password is removed from the system and the user is blocked from using his account.

Some systems provide a standard mechanism for password aging, but many do not. If your system provides a standard procedure for password aging, use it. If it doesn't, it is easy to set up your own password aging system. The following steps implement a simple manual system:

1. Make an historical copy of */etc/passwd*, and store it in some place safe from intruders (for example, on a tape locked in a cabinet).

2. After 60 days, compare the historical *passwd* file to the current file. Send every user who has *not* changed his password a message saying that he must change his password within 30 days.

3. Three weeks later, compare the current file and the historical file. Send users who have still not changed passwords a warning that they must change their passwords within one week or be locked out of their accounts.

4. One week later compare the files again, and change all unchanged passwords to asterisks (*). You should not retain the deactivated accounts on the system for very long. Inactive accounts are favorite targets of intruders. Check with the user of each inactive account. If the

user does not need the account, or does not respond to your queries, remove the account.

5. Go back to step 1 and start another 90-day cycle.

The longest period that a password can remain unchanged is slightly less than two full cycles. Therefore, using this plan, no passwords will be kept more than 6 months, and an "average" password will be changed every 3 months. Change the length of the cycle to suit your installation.

Other Precautions

Having good passwords is the most important security measure you can take. If you don't do anything else, make sure that everyone on your network uses good passwords. However, using good passwords isn't the only thing that you can do to improve the security of your computer and your network. In this section we'll look at several things that can be done to improve security.

Check Application Security

Some applications use their own security mechanisms. Make sure that the security for these applications is configured properly. In particular check:

- The UNIX *r* commands. The *r* commands use the */etc/hosts.equiv* and *˜/.rhosts* files for security. Check these files, and */etc/hosts.lpd*, to make sure that none of them contain a plus-sign (+) entry. Remember to check the *.rhosts* file in every user's home directory. (See Chapter 9 for a detailed discussion of properly configuring the *r* commands.)

- UUCP. This is not a book about UUCP, but DDN Bulletin 9124 suggests the following UUCP security precautions:

  - Remove any unneeded commands from *L.cmds*.

  - Change *L.cmds* ownership to *root*. The following command will take care of this: **chown root L.cmds**

  - Change the *L.sys* file's ownership to *uucp* with permission 600. The command **chown uucp L.sys ; chmod 600 L.sys** will take care of this.

- **sendmail**. Unless you are actually using them, remove the aliases *uudecode* and *decode* from the */etc/aliases* file. (See Chapter 9 for details about configuring the */etc/aliases* file.)

- NFS. On an NFS server, the */etc/exports* file controls which filesystems the server exports and who has access to them. Use the **–access** keyword to limit filesystem access to clients who truly need it. In addition, avoid using the **-root** keyword, which grants remote systems root access to the exported filesystem. (See Chapter 9 for details about configuring NFS.)

Remove Unnecessary Secure Terminals

The root user may login from any "secure" terminal. A terminal is considered secure if the keyword **secure** appears in the terminal's entry in the */etc/ttys* or */etc/ttytab* file. For example, a few lines from the */etc/ttytab* file might be:

```
#
# @(#)ttytab 1.6 89/12/18 SMI
#
# name   getty                        type      status  comments
#
console "/usr/etc/getty std.9600"     sun       on  local secure
ttya    "/usr/etc/getty std.9600"     unknown   on  local secure
ttyb    "/usr/etc/getty std.9600"     unknown   on  local secure
tty00   "/usr/etc/getty std.9600"     unknown   on  local secure
tty01   "/usr/etc/getty std.9600"     unknown   on  local secure
```

Every configuration line in this sample file ends with the keyword **secure**, indicating that the root user can log in from any of these terminals. To increase security, limit root logins to the console by removing the keyword **secure** from every configuration line except the console line (the first line in the example). After editing */etc/ttytab*, pass the hangup signal (-HUP) to the **init** process to force it to reload */etc/ttytab*. Assuming the sample file shown above, the following commands accomplish this task:

```
# mv /etc/ttytab /etc/ttytab.org
# cat /etc/ttytab.org | sed '7,$s/secure//' > /etc/ttytab
# kill -HUP 1
```

An even more secure configuration is to remove the **secure** keyword from all lines, even the line defining the console. This prevents direct logins as root. To access the root account, the user must first log in with his own account and then use **su** to become root.

Remove Unnecessary Software

Any software that allows an incoming connection from a remote site has the potential of being exploited by an intruder, but some programs are a greater security threat than others. Security experts recommend you remove **systat**, **tftp**, and **link** from the */etc/inetd.conf* file unless you absolutely need them. (Configuring the *inetd.conf* files is discussed in Chapter 6, with explicit examples of removing **tftp** from service.)

Some security-conscious sites also remove the UNIX *r* commands, the **finger** daemon, and in extreme cases the **ftp** and **telnet** daemons. In these extreme cases, these functions are only allowed on the firewall machine. (Firewalls will be explained in a later section.) For most sites, extreme restrictions are unnecessary and can be counterproductive.

Keep Software Updated

Vendors frequently release new versions of network software for the express purpose of improving network security. Use the latest version of the network software offered by your vendor. DDN Security Bulletin 9124, available from *nic.ddn.mil* in the file */scc/ddn-security-9124*, lists a few programs that are particularly important to keep updated:

sendmail   Make sure that you are using the latest **sendmail**, Berkeley version 5.65 or later.

fingerd   Make sure that the version of **finger** running on your system closes the security hole exploited by the Morris Internet worm.* These fixes were incorporated in **fingerd** in November 1988.

ftpd   Make sure that your system is running a version of **ftp** that incorporates all of the latest security fixes. According to the DDN Bulletin, the latest version of **ftp** is Berkeley version 5.60 created in July 1990.

Checking the version of the software packages on your system may not be easy. Many vendors provide their own version numbers that cannot be directly compared to the Berkeley version numbers referenced above. Additionally, using **ls** to look at the creation date of an executable can only provide negative evidence. For example, if an **ls** of **fingerd** returns a creation date before November 1988, you know you need a new version of **fingerd**. But if the date is more recent than November 1988, you still don't know if the necessary fixes were incorporated. Contact your vendor for authoritative information about the latest version of these programs.

Keep yourself aware of the latest information about all fixes for your system. Contact your vendor and find out what services they provide for distributing security fixes. Make sure that the vendor knows that security is important to you.

---

*The Internet worm is the Internet's most notorious security incident. See *Attack of the Giant Worm* in the Nutshell Handbook, *Computer Security Basics*, by Deborah Russell and G. T. Gangemi.

Security Monitoring

A key element of effective network security is security monitoring. Good security is an ongoing process. Following the security guidelines discussed above is just the start. You must also monitor the systems to detect unauthorized user activity, and to locate and close security holes. Over time a system will change—active accounts become inactive; file permissions are changed. You need to detect and fix these problems as they arise.

Know Your System

Network security is monitored by examining the files and logs of individual systems on the network. To detect unusual activity on a system, you must know what normal activity is. What processes are normally running? Who is usually logged in? Who commonly logs in after hours? You need to know this, and more, about your system in order to develop a "feel" for how things should be. Some common UNIX commands—**ps**, **who**, and **ls**—can help you learn what normal activity is for your system.

The **ps** command displays the status of currently running processes. Run **ps** regularly to gain a clear picture of what processes run on the system at different times of the day, and who runs them. The BSD **ps –aux** command, or the **ps -ef** System V command, displays the user and the command that initiated each process. This should be sufficient information to learn who runs what, and when they run it. If you notice something unusual, investigate it. Make sure you understand how your system is being used.

The **who** command provides information about who is currently logged into your system. It displays who is logged in, what device they are using, when they logged in and, if applicable, what remote host they logged in from. (The **w** command, a variation of **who** available on some systems, also displays the currently active process started by each user.) The **who** command helps you learn who is usually logged in, as well as what remote hosts they normally log in from. Investigate any variations from the norm.

You can use the **ls –lR** command to create a master checklist that shows the ownership, permissions, creation date, and size of every file on your system. Periodically create a new list and compare it, using **diff**, against the master list to check for unusual and unwanted changes in the filesystem. If the new checklist is acceptable, it becomes the new master checklist until the next periodic check. In this way the master list is constantly updated and the filesystem remains under close scrutiny.

If any of these routine checks gives you reason to suspect a security problem, examine the system for unusual or modified files, and for unusual login activity. This close examination of the system can also be made using everyday UNIX commands. Not every command or file we discuss will be available on every system. But every system will have some tools that help you keep a close eye on how your system is being used.

Looking for Trouble

Intruders often leave behind files or shell scripts to help them re-enter the system or gain root access. Use the **ls –a | grep** ´^\.´ command to check for files with names that begin with a dot (.). Intruders particularly favor names such as *.mail, .xx,* ... (dot, dot, dot),* .. (dot, dot, space), or ..^G (dot, dot, control-G).

If any files with names like these are found, suspect a break-in. (Remember that one file named . and one file named .. is in every directory.) Examine the contents of any suspicious files and follow your normal incident-reporting procedures.

You should also examine certain key files if you suspect a security problem:

/etc/inetd.conf

> Check the names of the programs started from the */etc/inetd.conf* file. In particular, make sure that it does not start any shell programs (e.g., */bin/csh*). Also check the programs that are started by **inetd** to make sure the programs have not been modified. */etc/inetd.conf* should not be world-writable.

r command security files

> Check */etc/hosts.equiv, /etc/hosts.lpd,* and the *.rhosts* file in each user's home directory to make sure they have not been improperly modified. In particular, look for any plus-sign (+) entries, and any entries for hosts outside of your local trusted network. These files should not be world-writable.

/etc/passwd

> Make sure that the */etc/passwd* file has not been modified. Look for new user names, and changes to the UID or GID of any account. */etc/passwd* should not be world-writable.

---

*Morris code!

files run by **cron** or **at**

> Check all of the files run by **cron** or **at**, looking for new files or unexplained changes. Sometimes intruders use procedures run by **cron** or **at** to re-admit themselves to the system, even after they have been kicked off.

executable files

> Check all executable files, binaries, and shell files, to make sure they have not been modified by the intruder. The master checklist, mentioned in the previous section, is helpful for this. Executable files should not be world-writable.

If you find any problems, even if you suspect any problems, follow your reporting procedure and let people know about the problem. This is particularly important if you are connected to a local area network. A problem on your system could spread to other systems on the network.

Checking Files with find

The **find** command is a powerful tool for detecting potential filesystem security problems because it can search the entire filesystem for files based on file permissions. Intruders often leave behind setuid programs to grant themselves root access. The following command searches for these files, recursively, starting from the root directory:

```
# find / -user root -perm -4000 -print
```

This **find** command starts searching at the root (/) for files owned by the user root (–user root) that have the setuid permission bit set (–perm –4000). All matches found are displayed at the terminal (-print). If any filenames are displayed by **find**, closely examine the individual files to make sure that these permissions are correct. As a general rule, shell scripts should not have setuid permission.

You can use the **find** command to check for other problems that might open security holes for intruders. The other common problems that **find** checks for are world-writable files (**–perm –2**), setgid files (**–perm –2000**), and unowned files (**–nouser –o –nogroup**). Unowned files, files that are not owned by a valid user, should be removed. World-writable and setgid files should be checked to make sure that these permissions are appropriate. As a general rule, files with names beginning with a dot (.) should not be world-writable, and setgid permission, like setuid, should be avoided for shell scripts.

Checking Login Activity

Strange login activity, at odd times of the day or from unfamiliar locations, can indicate attempts by intruders to gain access to your system. We have already used the **who** command to check who is currently logged into the system. To check who has logged into the system in the past, use the **last** command.

The **last** command displays the contents of the */usr/adm/wtmp* file. It is useful for learning normal login patterns and detecting abnormal login activity. The */usr/adm/wtmp* file keeps a historical record of who logged into the system, when they logged in, what remote site they logged in from, and when they logged out.

Figure 12-1 shows a single line of **last** command output. The figure highlights the fields that show the user who logged in, the device, the remote location from which the login originated (if applicable), the day, the date, the time logged in, the time logged out (if applicable), and the elapsed time.

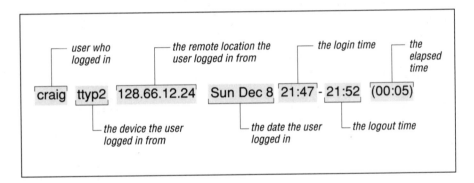

Figure 12.1: last Command Output

Simply typing **last** produces a large amount of output because every login stored in */usr/adm/wtmp* is displayed.* To limit the output, specify a user name or tty device on the command line. This limits the display to entries for the specified user name or terminal. It is also useful to use **grep** to

---

*On some systems, SCO is an example, this file is */etc/wtmp*.

search **last**'s output for certain conditions. For example, the command below checks for logins that occur on Saturday or Sunday:

```
% last | grep 'S[au]' | more
craig      console                       Sun Dec 15 10:33    still logged in
reboot     ~                             Sat Dec 14 18:12
shutdown   ~                             Sat Dec 14 18:14
craig      ttyp3    modems.nuts.com      Sat Dec 14 17:11 - 17:43  (00:32)
craig      ttyp2    128.66.12.24         Sun Dec  8 21:47 - 21:52  (00:05)
           .
           .
           .
--More--
```

The next example searches for root logins that did not originate from the console. If you didn't know who made the two logins reported in this example, you should be suspicious:

```
% last root | grep -v console
root      ttyp3    peanut.nuts.com    Tue Oct 29 13:12 - down   (00:03)
root      ftp      almond.nuts.com    Tue Sep 10 16:37 - 16:38  (00:00)
```

While the **last** command is a major source of information about previous login activity, it is not the only source. The */usr/adm/messages* file records logins to the root account, failed logins, and use of the **su** command.* Failed logins and root logins at odd times or from odd places are suspicious. The following **grep** command checks */usr/adm/messages* for root logins and **su root** activity:

```
% grep -i root /usr/adm/messages
Dec 16 08:40:44 almond su: 'su root' succeeded for kathy on /dev/ttyp0
Dec 16 14:48:04 almond su: 'su root' succeeded for kathy on /dev/ttyp0
Dec 16 15:51:33 almond login: ROOT LOGIN ttyp0 FROM pecan.nuts.com
Dec 17 08:53:29 almond su: 'su root' failed for kathy on /dev/ttyp0
Dec 17 09:21:47 almond su: 'su root' succeeded for kathy on /dev/ttyp0
Dec 17 21:08:18 almond su: 'su root' succeeded for kathy on /dev/ttyp0
Dec 18 09:51:14 almond login: ROOT LOGIN ttyp0 FROM pecan.nuts.com
Dec 19 07:41:44 almond login: ROOT LOGIN ttyp0 FROM pecan.nuts.com
```

Report any security problems that you detect, or even suspect. Don't be embarrassed to report a problem because it might turn out to be a false alarm. Don't keep quiet because you might get "blamed" for the security breach. Your silence will only help the intruder.

---

*Some systems, SCO is an example, don't log **su** activity and root logins in the */usr/adm/messages* file.

COPS

COPS (Computer Oracle Password and Security) is a collection of programs that automate many of the computer monitoring procedures discussed in the previous sections. As with any monitoring system, COPS detects potential problems; it does not correct them. COPS does not replace personal monitoring by the system administrator, but it does provide additional tools to help the administrator perform monitoring tasks.

The tools in the COPS package check:

- permissions for files, directories, and devices;
- contents of */etc/passwd* and */etc/group* files;
- contents of */etc/hosts.equiv* and `~/.rhosts` files;
- changes in SUID status.

After completing these checks, COPS mails a report of the results to the system administrator.

COPS can be obtained via anonymous **ftp** from *cert.sei.cmu.edu* in the compressed **tar** file *pub/cops/cops.tar.Z*. The **tar** file contains instructions for "making" COPS. Once COPS is made, edit the COPS shell file so that the variable SECURE points to the directory that contains the COPS programs, and the variable SECURE_USERS contains the e-mail address of the person who should receive the COPS report.

The great advantage of COPS is that it is simple. COPS removes the hassles from security monitoring, making it more likely that these tasks will be performed. To run COPS, simply enter:

```
% cops
```

Here's a sample report:

```
ATTENTION:
Security Report for Wed Dec 18 17:35:30 EST 1991
from host peanut.nuts.com

Warning!  A "+" entry in /etc/hosts.equiv!
Warning!  "." (or current directory) is in roots path!
Warning!  Directory /usr/spool/mail is _World_ writable!
Warning!  File /etc/motd is _World_ writable!
Warning!  File /etc/mtab is _World_ writable!
Warning!  File /etc/remote is _World_ writable!
Warning!  File /etc/sm is _World_ writable!
Warning!  File /etc/sm.bak is _World_ writable!
Warning!  File /etc/state is _World_ writable!
Warning!  File /etc/syslog.pid is _World_ writable!
```

```
Warning!  File /etc/tmp is _World_ writable!
Warning!  File /etc/utmp is _World_ writable!
Warning!  File /etc/motd (in /etc/rc*) is _World_ writable!
Warning!  User uucp's home directory /var/spool/uucppublic is mode
     03777!
Warning!  Password file, line 2, negative user id:
     nobody:*:-2:-2::/:
Warning!  Password file, line 11, no password:
     sync::1:1::/:/bin/sync
Warning!  Password file, line 12, user sysdiag has uid = 0 and is not
     root
     sysdiag:*:0:1:System
     Diagnostic:/usr/diag/sysdiag:/usr/diag/sysdiag/sysdiag
Warning!  YPassword file, line 282, no password:
     dim::99:10:dim screen:/usr/spool/uucppublic:/usr/local/bin/dim
```

Look at each line in the report you receive. Some lines might indicate major problems, such as the first line in our sample report that indicates */etc/hosts.equiv* contains a plus-sign (+) entry. Other lines might indicate conditions that are not problems for your system. In our example, we decide to leave */etc/tmp* with world-write permission. Evaluate each line of the report and correct anything that needs correcting. Rerun COPS and examine the new report. It should only report the problems that you are willing to accept.

Once you're satisfied with your system's security, schedule COPS to run at regular intervals. New problems can always be introduced into your system over time. It's better to have the COPS discover the problem than to have the "robbers" discover it!

Limiting Access

For many sites, well-informed users and administrators, good password security, and good system monitoring provide adequate network security. But for some security-conscious sites, more may be desired. That "more" is usually some technique for limiting access between systems connected to the network, or for limiting access to the data the network carries.

Encryption

Encryption is a technique for limiting access to the data carried on the network. Encryption encodes the data in a form that can only be read by systems that have the "key" to the encoding scheme. The original text, called the "clear text," is encrypted using an encryption device (hardware or software) and an encryption key. This produces encoded text, which is called the cipher. To recreate the "clear text," the cipher must be decrypted using the same type of encryption device and key.

Largely because of spy novels and World War II movies, encryption is one of the first things that people think of when they think of security. However, encryption is not always applicable to network security. Encrypting data for transmission across a network requires that the same encryption equipment, or software, be used at both ends of the data exchange. Unless you control both ends of the network, and can ensure that the same encryption device is available, it is difficult to use end-to-end data encryption. For this reason, encryption is most commonly used in places where the entire system is under the control of a single authority, such as military networks, private networks, isolated local networks, or individual systems.

When is Encryption Needed?

Before using encryption, decide why you want to encrypt the data, whether or not the data should be protected with encryption, and whether or not the data should even be stored on a networked computer system.

A few valid reasons for encrypting data are:

- To prevent casual browsers from viewing sensitive data files.
- To prevent accidental disclosure of sensitive data.
- To prevent privileged users (e.g., system administrators) from viewing private data files.
- To complicate things for intruders who attempt to search through a system's files.

Encryption is not a substitute for good computer security. Encryption can protect sensitive or personal information from casual snooping, but it should never be the sole means of protecting critical information. Encryption systems can be broken, and encrypted data can be deleted or corrupted just like any other data. So don't let encryption lull you into a false sense of security. Some information is so sensitive or critical that it should not be stored on a networked computer system, even if it is encrypted. Encryption is only a small part of a complete security system. That said, let's look at how data is encrypted on UNIX systems.

des and crypt

Two widely used UNIX encryption commands are **crypt** and **des**. **des** is a UNIX implementation of the Data Encryption Standard, a relatively modern encryption technique developed in the 1970s. **crypt** implements an old encryption technique based on the German Enigma machine. (The Enigma was a code machine used by the Germans in World War II.) Of these two commands, **des** produces the more securely encrypted files. Techniques for breaking **crypt**'s coding scheme are widely known. Use **des** if it is available for your system.

Both encryption programs are simple to use and have similar command lines. They both read from standard input and write to standard output, and both **des** and **crypt** require a unique key to encrypt data. If no key is provided on the command line, both programs prompt the user to provide one.

The encryption key is a string similar to a password. Like a good password, a good encryption key is not easy to guess but is easy to remember. Apply the same rules to choosing an encryption key that you apply to choosing a password.

In the following example, **des** is used to encrypt a file named *data.file*, and to store the encrypted text in a file called *encoded.file*. The encryption key, indicated by the **–k** option, is the string *aDAzac*. The **–e** option tells **des** to encrypt the file:*

```
% des -k aDAzac -e data.file encoded.file
```

Once the file is encrypted, it no longer contains plain ASCII text. You must treat it as a binary file if you transfer it over the network. Displaying the encrypted file shows the type of data it contains:†

```
% cat encoded.file
4MH-[rJ]EG/R6
```

To read the file again, it must be decrypted using the same encryption software and the same key (**–k aDAzac**). In our example, we use the **des** command with the **-d** (decrypt) option. Because no output file is specified

---

*Several different implementations of **des** are available. Our examples use the **des** implementation available via anonymous **ftp** from *kampi.hut.fi* in the compressed **tar** file *alo/des-dist.tar.Z*. Other **des** implementations will have different command-line options.

†Naturally, unprintable characters don't show up in this example.

on the command line, the decrypted text is displayed to the standard output:

```
% des -k aDAzac -d encoded.file
Mary had a little lamb, little lamb, little lamb.
```

Let's repeat the process of encrypting and decrypting the file, but this time let's use the **crypt** command. Here is the **crypt** command that encrypts *data.file* using the key *aDAzac*, and stores the result in *encoded.file*:

```
% crypt  aDAzac <data.file >encoded.file
```

The **crypt** command to decrypt *encoded.file* and display it to standard output is:

```
% crypt aDAzac <encoded.file
```

Because files encrypted with **crypt** can easily be decrypted by code-breaking programs, you may want to **tar** the sensitive file together with some binary files, and compress the resultant **tar** file before encrypting it. The fact that the compressed **tar** file will be binary data makes the job of decrypting the file much more complex. However, it also makes your task of encrypting and decrypting the file more burdensome. If you have files that require this much protection, perhaps they should not be kept on a networked computer.

Firewalls

Many recent computer security discussions refer to firewall systems. The term "firewall" implies protection from danger, and just as the firewall in your car protects the passengers' compartment from the car's engine, a firewall computer system protects your network from the outside world. A firewall computer provides strict access control between your systems and the outside world.

The concept of a firewall is quite simple. A firewall system replaces an IP router with a multi-homed host that does not forward packets. By not forwarding IP packets between networks, firewalls effectively sever the connection between the networks.* To provide the network behind the firewall with some level of network connectivity, the firewall performs certain unique functions discussed in the next section.

---

*The role that IP routers, also called gateways, play in gluing the Internet together is covered extensively in earlier chapters.

Figure 12-2 shows a comparison between an IP router and a firewall. A router handles packets up through the IP layer. The router forwards each packet based on the packet's destination address, and the route to that destination indicated in the routing table. A host, on the other hand, does not forward packets, and the firewall system is just a special type of multi-homed host.* Just like any host, the firewall accepts packets that are addressed to it, and processes those packets through the Application Layer. The firewall ignores packets that are not addressed to it.

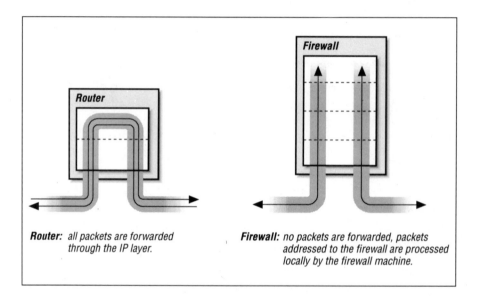

Router: all packets are forwarded through the IP layer.

Firewall: no packets are forwarded, packets addressed to the firewall are processed locally by the firewall machine.

Figure 12.2: Firewalls versus Routers

This definition of a firewall, as a device completely distinct from an IP router, is not universally accepted. Some people refer to routers with special security features as firewalls, but this is really just a matter of semantics. In this book, routers with special security features are called secure routers or secure gateways. Firewalls, on the other hand, are not routers because they do not forward packets, even when they are used in place of routers.

---

*See the IPFORWARDING parameter in Chapter 5 for information on how to prevent a multi-homed host from forwarding packets.

Because firewalls are used in place of routers, they are usually thought of as a way to separate an internal network from the external world. However, isolating an entire network behind a firewall may not be required. Even at sites that need a firewall, most workstations and desktop computers may not contain information or applications that need this level of protection. Frequently, only a limited set of computers contain truly sensitive data or processes critical to the operation of the organization.

One way to limit the impact of a firewall on the operation of a network is to use an internal firewall that isolates selected critical systems, while allowing all other systems to operate in a normal manner. Figure 12-3 illustrates networks using both internal and external firewalls. The difficulty of identifying all sensitive systems, and the fear of making a mistake that could compromise critical information, causes many security-conscious sites to prefer an external firewall, or even a combination of internal and external firewalls. However, if sensitive systems can be identified and isolated, the majority of users benefit from a more user friendly network because the entire network is not isolated behind an external firewall.

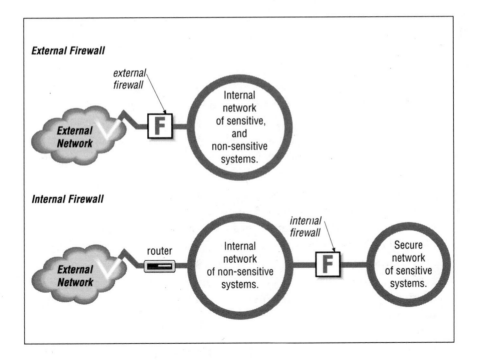

Figure 12.3: Internal and External Firewalls

Functions of the Firewall

With a firewall in place, an intruder cannot mount a direct attack on any of the systems behind the firewall. Packets destined for hosts behind the firewall are simply not delivered. The intruder must instead mount an attack directly against the firewall machine. Because the firewall machine can be the target of break-in attacks, it employs very strict security guidelines. But because there is only one firewall machine versus many machines on the local network, it is easier to enforce strict security on that system.

The disadvantage of a firewall system is obvious. In the same manner that it restricts access from the outside into the local network, it restricts access from the local network to the outside world. To minimize the inconvenience caused by the firewall, the system must do many more things than a router does. The firewall must provide:

- DNS name service for the outside world. Full name service for the internal network is provided by an internal system. The firewall provides limited name service for the outside world. It provides only an MX record that points to the firewall itself, and the external address of the firewall system. The firewall name server does not provide name or address information about any internal host.

- E-mail forwarding. On the firewall system, **sendmail** is configured to deliver mail to every user on all internal systems. Each user is identified by an alias to obscure the user's actual login name. Mail destined for the outside world is rewritten to reflect the user's alias, and to indicate the firewall system as the origin of the mail. Login names and internal host names are not provided in mail delivered to external sites.

- **ftp** service. All **ftp** transfers take place from the firewall system. Files are first moved to the firewall system before they are moved into, or out of, the local network. Internal users log into the firewall system to get files from, or send files to, remote sites. If anonymous **ftp** is offered at all, it is only offered on the firewall system.

- **telnet** or **rlogin** service. All remote terminal access takes place from the firewall machine. To **telnet** or **rlogin** to, or from, a remote site, the user first logs into the firewall system.

Only the minimal services listed above should be provided on a firewall system. Other common network services (NIS, NFS, **rsh**, **rcp**, **finger**, etc.) should generally not be provided. Services are limited to decrease the number of holes through which an intruder can gain access. On firewall systems, security is more important than service.

ftp service and remote terminal service are the biggest problems for the firewall machine. To maintain a high level of security, user accounts are discouraged on the firewall machine, but at the same time users must log in to the firewall system to have access to **ftp** and remote terminal services. This problem is usually handled by creating a special user account for **ftp**, and one for **telnet**, that are shared by all internal users. Group accounts are generally viewed as security problems, but if these accounts are carefully designed and properly restricted, they can be reasonably secure.

Because a firewall must be constructed with great care to be effective, and because there are many configuration variables for setting up a firewall machine, vendors are beginning to offer special firewall software for their systems. Some vendors sell special-purpose machines designed specifically for use as firewall systems. Before setting up your own firewall, investigate the options available from your hardware vendor.

Firewall systems are useful to some sites that have special security needs, but for many other sites they are not appropriate. The restrictions that they place on individual users are not acceptable to many organizations, and the restrictions can drive independent-minded users to find other ways to handle their communications needs.

Routing Control

A firewall system works by interrupting routing between the protected system and the rest of the world. A carefully modified static routing table can be used to provide a similar type of protection.

As we discussed in the chapters on routing and troubleshooting, it is necessary for your system to have a routing table entry for every network that it will communicate with. This can be either an explicit route for an individual network, or a default route for all networks. Without the proper routes your system cannot communicate with remote networks, and the remote networks cannot communicate with your system. Regardless of how the remote site sets up its routing, it cannot communicate with your host if your host does not have a route back to the remote site. Because of this, you can control which remote sites are able to communicate with your system by controlling the contents of the routing table.

For example, assume that the *nuts.com* personnel department is on subnet 128.66.9.0, and that the router for their subnet is 128.66.9.1. They only want to talk to other hosts on their subnet and to a management system named *hickory.nuts.com* (128.66.18.7). To implement this policy with the routing table, each host administrator on the personnel subnet:

1. Makes sure that no routing protocol is running, and that none is started automatically at boot time.

2. Makes sure that there is no default route in the routing table, and that a default route is not added automatically at boot time.

3. Adds a host specific route to 128.66.18.7 (*hickory.nuts.com*), and makes sure that this static route is added each time the system boots.

Using **netstat** to display this limited routing table on host 128.66.9.14 shows the following:

```
# netstat -nr
Routing tables
Destination    Gateway        Flags    Refcnt Use    Interface
127.0.0.1      127.0.0.1      UH       2      7126   lo0
128.66.18.7    128.66.9.1     UGH      1      1285   le0
128.66.9.0     128.66.9.14    U        30     89456  le0
```

The display shows the loopback route, a route to the local subnet (128.66.9.0), and a host route to hickory.nuts.com (128.66.18.7). There are no other routes, so there are no other locations that this host can communicate with. Therefore, if an intruder launched an attack against this system, he would receive no response.

This security technique is less restrictive than a firewall, because it only affects the systems that contain the data or processes that are being protected. This technique is easy to implement and does not require special equipment or software. However, it is also less secure than a firewall. If any of these systems is successfully attacked, all of the systems could be compromised. Each system being protected this way must be properly configured, while one firewall can protect a group of systems. But if you don't need all of the protection of a firewall, this is a possible alternative.

Access Control

Another technique for limiting access that is less restrictive than a firewall is called *access control*. Routers and hosts that use access control check the address of a host requesting a service against an *access control list*. If the list says that the remote host is permitted to use the requested service, the access is granted. If the list says that the remote host is not permitted to access the service, the access is denied. Access control does not bypass any normal security checks. It adds a check to validate the source of a service request, and retains all of the normal checks to validate the user.

Access control systems are common in terminal servers, and are provided by some routers. For example, CISCO has an access control facility. New secure routers that provide sophisticated access control systems are also beginning to enter the market. The Eagle Secure Gateway is one example. Access control software is also available for UNIX hosts. One such package is the *wrapper* program. Clearly, there are a variety of ways to implement access controls. In this section we use wrapper.

wrapper

The wrapper package performs two basic functions: it logs requests for internet services, and provides an access control mechanism for UNIX systems. Logging requests for specific network services is a useful monitoring function, especially if you are looking for possible intruders. If this were all it did, wrapper would be a useful package. But the real power of wrapper is its ability to control access to network services.

The wrapper software is available via anonymous **ftp** from *cert.sei.cmu.edu* in the file *pub/network_tools/tcp_wrapper.shar.* The file contains the C source code and Makefile necessary to build the wrapper daemon **tcpd**.*

Make **tcpd** and install it in the same directory as the other network daemons. Edit */etc/inetd.conf* and replace the path to each network service daemon that you wish to place under access control with the path to **tcpd**. The only field in the */etc/inetd.conf* entry affected by **tcpd** is the sixth field, which contains the path to the network daemon. For example, assume that the entry for the **finger** daemon in */etc/inetd.conf* is:

```
finger  stream  tcp  nowait  nobody  /usr/etc/in.fingerd  in.fingerd
```

---

*Read the instructions that come with *wrapper* carefully. There are special instructions for Ultrix and Apollo UNIX.

The value in the sixth field is */usr/etc/in.fingerd*. To monitor access to the **finger** daemon, replace this value with */usr/etc/tcpd*, as in the following entry:

```
finger   stream  tcp  nowait  nobody  /usr/etc/tcpd   in.fingerd
```

Now when **inetd** receives a request for **fingerd**, it starts **tcpd** instead. **tcpd** then logs the **fingerd** request, checks the access control information, and, if permitted, starts the real **finger** daemon to handle the request.

Make a similar change for every service you want to place under access control. Good candidates for access control are **ftpd**, **tftpd**, **telnetd**, **rshd**, **rlogind**, **rexecd**, and **fingerd**. Obviously, **tcpd** cannot control access for daemons that are not started by **inetd**, such as **sendmail** and NFS.

tcpd Access Control Files

The information **tcpd** uses to control access is in two files, */etc/hosts.allow* and */etc/hosts.deny*. Each file's function is obvious from its name. *hosts.allow* contains the list of hosts that are allowed to access the network's services, and *hosts.deny* contains the list of hosts that are denied access. If the files are not found, **tcpd** permits every host to have access and simply logs the access request. Therefore, if you only want to monitor access, don't create these two files.

If the files are found, **tcpd** checks the *hosts.allow* file first, followed by the *hosts.deny* file. It stops as soon as it finds a match for the host and the service in question. Therefore, access granted by *hosts.allow* cannot be overridden by *hosts.deny*.

The format of entries in both files is the same:

> *service-list* **:** *host-list* [**:** *shell-command*]

The *service-list* is a list of network services, separated by commas. These are the services to which access is being granted (*hosts.allow*) or denied (*hosts.deny*). Each service is identified by the process name used in the seventh field of the */etc/inetd.conf* entry. This is simply the name that immediately follows the path to **tcpd** in *inetd.conf*. (See Chapter 5 for a description of the *arguments* field in the */etc/inetd.conf* entry.) Again, let's use **finger** as an example. We changed its *inetd.conf* entry to read:

```
finger   stream  tcp  nowait  nobody  /usr/etc/tcpd   in.fingerd
```

Therefore, we would use **in.fingerd** as the service name in a *hosts.allow* or *hosts.deny* file.

The *host-list* is a comma-separated list of host names, domain names, internet addresses, network numbers, or netgroups.* The systems listed in the *host-list* are granted access (*hosts.allow*) or denied access (*hosts.deny*) to the services specified in the *service-list*. A host name or an internet address matches an individual host. For example, *peanut* is a host name and 128.66.12.2 is an internet address. Both match a particular host. A domain name matches every host within that domain; e.g., *.nuts.com* matches *almond.nuts.com*, *peanut.nuts.com*, *pecan.nuts.com*, and any other hosts in the domain. When specified in a **tcpd** access control list, domain names always start with a dot (.). A network number matches every IP address within that network's address space. For example, 128.66. matches 128.66.12.1, 128.66.12.2, 128.66.5.1, and any other address that begins with 128.66. Network addresses in a **tcpd** access control list always end with a dot (.).

A completed *hosts.allow* entry that grants FTP and TELNET access to all hosts in the *nuts.com* domain is shown below:

```
ftpd,telnetd : .nuts.com
```

Two special keywords can be used in *hosts.allow* and *hosts.deny* entries. The keyword ALL can be used in the *service-list* to match all network services, and in the *host-list* to match all host names and addresses. The second keyword, LOCAL, can only be used in the *host-list*. It matches all local host names. **tcpd** considers a host name "local" if it contains no embedded dots. Therefore, the host name *peanut* would match on LOCAL, but the host name *peanut.nuts.com* would not match. The following entry affects all services and all local hosts:

```
ALL : LOCAL
```

The final field that can be used in these entries is the optional *shell-command* field. The shell command specified in this field will execute whenever a match occurs. The command is executed in addition to the normal functions of the access list match. In other words, if a match occurs for an entry that has an optional shell command, **tcpd** logs the access, grants or denies access to the service, and then passes the shell command to the shell for execution.

A more complete example of how **tcpd** is used will help you understand these entries. First, assume that you wish to allow every host in your local domain (*nuts.com*) to have access to all services on your system, but you

---

*Netgroups are NIS-specific structures. See Chapter 9 for details.

want to deny access to every service to all other hosts. Make an entry in */etc/hosts.allow* to permit access to everything by everyone in the local domain:

```
ALL : LOCAL, .nuts.com
```

The keyword ALL in the services-list indicates that this rule applies to all network services. The colon (:) separates the services-list from the *host-list*. The keyword LOCAL indicates that all local host names without a domain extension are acceptable, and the *nuts.com* domain name extension is also acceptable. To prevent access from everyone else, make an entry in the */etc/hosts.deny* file:

```
ALL : ALL
```

Every system that does not match the entry in */etc/hosts.allow* is passed on to */etc/hosts.deny*. Here the entry denies access to everyone, regardless of what service they are asking for. Remember, even with ALL in the services-list field, only services started by **inetd**, and only those services whose entries in *inetd.conf* have been edited to invoke **tcpd**, are affected. This does not provide security for any other service.

Words to the Wise

I am not a security expert; I am a network administrator. In my view, good security is good system administration and vice versa. Most of this chapter is just common-sense advice. It is probably sufficient for most circumstances, but certainly not for all.

Make sure that you know if there is an existing security policy that applies to your network or system. Find out if your security situation is governed by regulations or laws. If there are policies, regulations, or laws governing your situation, make sure to obey them. Never do anything to undermine the security system established for your site.

No system is completely secure. No matter what you do, you will have problems. Realize this and prepare for it. Prepare a disaster recovery plan and do everything necessary, so that when the worst does happen, you can recover from it with the minimum possible disruption.

If you want to read more about security I recommend the following:

- RFC 1244, *Site Security Handbook*, P. Holbrook, J. Reynold, et al., July 1991.
- RFC 1281, *Guidelines for the Secure Operation of the Internet*, R. Pethia, S. Crocker and B. Fraser, November 1991.

- *Improving the Security of Your UNIX System*, David A. Curry, ITSTD-721-FR-90-21, SRI International, Information and Telecommunications Science and Technology Division, April 1990.
- *Practical UNIX Security*, Simson Garfinkel and Gene Spafford, O'Reilly and Associates, 1991.
- *Computer Security Basics*, Deborah Russell and G. T. Gangemi Sr., O'Reilly & Associates, 1991.

13

Internet Information Resources

Now that our network is configured, debugged, and secure, how will we use it? The classic applications **telnet**, **ftp**, and **sendmail**, are still the most popular. But increasingly the network is used not merely as a delivery link between two hosts, but as a path to information resources. Information servers, file repositories, databases, and information directories are available throughout the Internet, but with over 1,000,000 devices connected to the Internet, finding these services can be a daunting task.*

This chapter explores various ways to avail yourself of this storehouse of information. We look at how information is retrieved from network servers, how you can configure your system as an anonymous **ftp** server, and some recent developments that make it easier to locate that information.

---

*If you're not connected to the Internet, your access to these resources is limited. In itself, that's a good reason for connecting.

Anonymous ftp

Throughout this book, we have mentioned anonymous **ftp** for retrieving publicly available files and programs from the many **ftp** servers around the Internet. Anonymous **ftp** is simply an **ftp** session in which you log into the remote server using the user name *anonymous* and, by convention, your real user name as the password.* The anonymous **ftp** example below should make this simple process clear:

```
% ftp ftp.nisc.sri.com
Connected to phoebus.NISC.SRI.COM.
220 phoebus FTP server (SRI Version 1.98 Fri Apr 19 11:57:54 PDT 1991)
ready.
Name (FTP.NISC.SRI.COM:kathy): anonymous
331 Guest login ok, send ident as password.
Password:
230 Guest login ok, access restrictions apply.
ftp> cd netinfo
250 CWD command successful.
ftp> binary
200 Type set to I.
ftp> get interest-groups.Z
200 PORT command successful.
150 Opening BINARY mode data connection for interest-groups.Z (328085
bytes).
226 Transfer complete.
local: interest-groups.Z remote: interest-groups.Z
328085 bytes received in 49 seconds (6.5 Kbytes/s)
ftp> quit
221 Be Excellent to one another!
```

In this example, the user logs into the server *ftp.nisc.sri.com* using the user name *anonymous* and the password *kathy*, which is her real user name. With anonymous FTP, she can log in even though she doesn't have an account on *ftp.nisc.sri.com*. Of course what she can do is restricted, but she can retrieve certain files from the system, and that's just what she does. She changes to the *netinfo* directory, and gets the compressed file *netinfo/interest-groups.Z*. The file is retrieved in binary mode because it is a compressed file.

---

*Some **ftp** servers request your full e-mail address as a password.

Creating an ftp Server

Using the anonymous **ftp** service offered by a remote server is very simple. However, setting up an anonymous **ftp** service on your own system is a little more complicated. Here are the steps to set up an anonymous FTP server:

1. Add user *ftp* to the */etc/passwd* file.

2. Create an *ftp* home directory owned by ftp that cannot be written to by anyone.

3. Create a *bin* directory under the *ftp* home directory that is owned by *root*, and that cannot be written to by anyone. The **ls** program should be placed in this directory and changed to mode 111 (execute-only).

4. Create an *etc* directory in the *ftp* home directory that is owned by *root*, and that cannot be written to by anyone. Create special *passwd* and *group* files in this directory, and change the mode of both files to 444 (read-only).

5. Create a *pub* directory in the *ftp* home directory that is owned by ftp and is mode 777 (read, write, and execute). This is the only directory where anonymous **ftp** users can store files. If you don't want to allow remote users to store files on your server, change the mode of this directory to 444 (read-only).

The following examples show each of these steps. First, create the *ftp* home directory and the required subdirectories. In our example, we create the *ftp* directory under the */usr* directory.

```
# mkdir /usr/ftp
# cd /usr/ftp
# mkdir bin
# mkdir etc
# mkdir pub
```

Then copy **ls** to */usr/ftp/bin*, and set the correct permissions.

```
# cp /bin/ls /usr/ftp/bin
# chmod 111 /usr/ftp/bin/ls
```

Create a group that will only be used by anonymous **ftp**, a group that has no other members. In our example we create a group called *anonymous*.

An entry for this new group is added to the */etc/group* file, and a file named */usr/ftp/etc/group* is created that contains only this single entry.

```
anonymous:*:15:
```

Create a user named *ftp* by placing an entry for that user in the file */etc/passwd*. Also create a file named */usr/ftp/etc/passwd* that contains only the **ftp** entry. Here's the entry we used in both files:

```
ftp:*:15:15:Anonymous ftp:/home/ftp:
```

These examples use a gid of 15 and a uid of 15. These are only examples; pick a uid and gid that aren't used for anything else on your system.

A **cat** of the newly created */usr/ftp/etc/passwd* and */usr/ftp/etc/group* files shows the following:

```
% cat /usr/ftp/etc/passwd
ftp:*:15:15:Anonymous ftp:/home/ftp:
% cat /usr/ftp/etc/group
anonymous:*:15:
```

After the edits are complete, set both files to mode 444.

```
# chmod 444 /usr/ftp/etc/passwd
# chmod 444 /usr/ftp/etc/group
```

Set the correct ownership and mode for each of the directories. The ownership of */usr/ftp/bin* and */usr/ftp/etc* do not need to be changed because the directories were created by *root*.

```
# cd /usr/ftp
# chown ftp pub
# chmod 777 pub
# chmod 555 bin
# chmod 555 etc
# cd ..
# chown ftp ftp
# chmod 555 ftp
```

For most UNIX systems, the installation is complete. But if you have a Sun system, a few more steps are necessary. The dynamic linking used in Sun OS 4.x, requires that the *ftp* home directory contains:

1. the runtime loader
2. the shared C library
3. */dev/zero*

These Sun-specific steps are shown in the following examples. First create the directory */usr/ftp/usr/lib*, then copy the files *ld.so* and *libc.so.** into the new directory, and set the file permissions:

```
# cd /usr/ftp
# mkdir usr
# mkdir usr/lib
# cp /usr/lib/ld.so usr/lib
# cp /usr/lib/libc.so.* usr/lib
# chmod 555 libc.so.*
# chmod 555 usr/lib
# chmod 555 usr
```

Next, create the *ftp/dev* directory, and run **mknod** to create *dev/zero*:

```
# cd /usr/ftp
# mkdir dev
# cd dev
# mknod zero c 3 12
# cd ..
# chmod 555 dev
```

Now you can copy the files you wish to make publicly available into *˜/ftp/pub*. To prevent these files from being overwritten by remote users, set the mode to 644, and make sure they are not owned by user *ftp*.

After completing the configuration steps necessary for your system, test it thoroughly before announcing the service. Make sure that your server provides the anonymous **ftp** service you want, without providing additional "services" that you don't want (such as allowing anonymous users access to files outside of the *ftp* home directory). Anonymous **ftp** is a potential security risk. If you offer this service at all, limit the number of systems at your site that provide it (one is usually enough), and take care to ensure that the installation is done properly.

Retrieving RFCs

Throughout this book, we have referred to many RFCs. These are the Internet documents used for everything from general information to the definitions of the TCP/IP protocols standards. As a network administrator, there are several important RFCs that you'll want to read. In this section we describe how you can obtain them.

The most common method for obtaining an RFC is via anonymous **ftp**. RFCs are stored at many different sites around the world. Table 13-1 lists just a few of these repositories. They store the RFCs with filenames in the form *rfcnnnn.txt* or *rfcnnnn.ps*—where *nnnn* is the RFC number, and *txt* or *ps* indicates whether the RFC is ASCII text or PostScript. These files are usually kept in a directory named *rfc*. Therefore, to retrieve RFC 1122, **ftp** to one of the listed repositories and enter **get rfc/rfc1122.txt** at the ftp> prompt.

Table 13.1: RFC Repositories

Host Name	Location	Host Name	Location
nic.ddn.mil	US (eastern)	*munnari.oz.au*	Australia
ftp.nisc.sri.com	US (western)	*funet.fi*	Finland
nisc.jvnc.net	US (eastern)	*sunic.sunet.se*	Sweden
nnsc.nsf.net	US (eastern)	*chalmers.se*	Sweden

There are three files that can help you get a handle on the large number of RFCs. They are all located in the *netinfo* directory of *nic.ddn.mil*:

rfc-index.txt   a complete index of all RFCs by RFC number
rfc-by-title.txt   an alphabetical listing of RFCs by title
rfc-by-author.txt   an alphabetical listing of RFCs by author name

In the following example, we retrieve *rfc-index.txt* from *netinfo* on *nic.ddn.mil*, storing it in the local file *rfc.index*:

```
% ftp nic.ddn.mil
Connected to nic.ddn.mil.
220 nic FTP server (SunOS 4.1) ready.
Name (nic.ddn.mil:craig): anonymous
331 Guest login ok, send ident as password.
Password:
230 Guest login ok, access restrictions apply.
ftp> get netinfo/rfc-index.txt rfc.index
200 PORT command successful.
150 ASCII data connection for rfc-index.txt (128.66.12.2,1265) (154112
bytes).
226 ASCII Transfer complete.
local: rfc.index remote: rfc-index.txt
157982 bytes received in 14 seconds (11 Kbytes/s)
ftp> quit
221 Goodbye.
```

The newly created file, *rfc.index*, can now be searched for references to the RFC you're interested in. In this example we're searching for any RFC about BGP.

```
% grep BGP rfc.index
1163 Lougheed, K.; Rekhter, Y. Border Gateway Protocol (BGP). 1990 June;
1105 Lougheed, K.; Rekhter, Y. Border Gateway Protocol (BGP). 1989 June;
```

You can then retrieve the specific RFC directly from *nic.ddn.mil*, and keep the RFC index for later use. You'll only need to get a new RFC index occasionally. Most of the time, the RFC you're looking for has been in publication for some time and is already listed in the index. If you need to be informed about the latest RFCs as soon as they become available, join the *rfc@nic.ddn.mil* mailing list. (Details about mailing lists and how to join them are covered in a later section.)

Retrieving RFCs by Mail

While anonymous **ftp** is the fastest and most commonly used way to get an RFC, it is not the only way. You can also obtain RFCs through electronic mail.

Retrieving RFCs through e-mail, unfortunately, is not as well standardized as anonymous **ftp**. Some systems use the "Subject:" line of the e-mail message to request the RFC, and some use the body of the text. An example of each approach, one using a server located on the East Coast of the U.S. (*nisc.jvnc.net*), and the other using a server on the West Coast (*nisc.sri.com*), is shown below:

```
% mail sendrfc@nisc.jvnc.net
Subject: RFC 1261
^D
Null message body; hope that's ok
```

The first example requests a copy of RFC 1261 from *nisc.jvnc.net*. The mail is sent to the RFC mail server at *jvnc.net*, which is *sendrfc@jvnc.net*. The mail server at *jvnc.net* expects the RFC request in the "Subject:" line. The *null message* complaint comes from the local system, and does not cause any problems for the RFC retrieval.

```
% mail mail-server@nisc.sri.com
Subject:
send rfc1258
^D
```

In this example, we request RFC 1258. Here the RFC mail server is addressed as *mail-server@nisc.sri.com*. The "Subject:" line is blank, and the name of the requested RFC is in the body of the e-mail text, preceded by the keyword **send**.

Both techniques work very well. In the time it took to type these paragraphs, the requested RFCs were already in my mailbox.

Mailing Lists

Mailing lists provide a service for the Internet that is similar to the service provided to USENET by **news**. In fact, some mailing lists are digests of newsgroups. Like **news**, Internet mailing lists bring together people with similar interests to exchange information and ideas. However, most mailing lists run under stricter supervision and tighter usage guidelines than newsgroups do. Mailing lists are more often used as places to report problems and get solutions, or to receive announcements, than as places for unrestricted discussion.

There are an enormous number of mailing lists. The *list-of-lists* contains information about many of the mailing lists available to Internet users.* The list-of-lists can be obtained via anonymous **ftp** from *nisc.sri.com* in the compressed file *netinfo/interest-groups.Z*. The **ftp** example in the "Anonymous ftp" section of this chapter shows this file being retrieved.

Once the list-of-lists has been retrieved and **uncompress**'d, it can be searched for mailing lists that interest you. When you find a list you wish to join, don't send mail directly to the list asking to be enrolled. Instead, send the enrollment request to *list-name*-**request@***host* where *list-name* is the actual name of the list, and is followed by the literal string **-request**. The **-request** extension is almost universally used as the address for administrative requests, such as being added to or dropped from a list. For example, to join the *rfc@nic.ddn.mil* mailing list, send your enrollment request to *rfc-request@nic.ddn.mil*. All other correspondence is sent directly to the list.

A few lists readers of this book might be interested in are:

gated-people@gated.cornell.edu
> Provides announcements of new **gated** releases and fixes for the current release. It also provides a place to discuss technical questions about **gated**.

namedroppers@nic.ddn.mil
> Provides a forum for technical discussions of Domain Name Service.

---

*Despite its large size, not every mailing list is contained in the list-of-lists. You hear about some lists by word-of-mouth.

bind@ucbarpa.berkeley.edu
> Provides announcements of fixes and new releases for BIND.

tcp-ip@nic.ddn.mil
> Provides a forum for general discussion of technical TCP/IP questions.

Resource Discovery Programs

Anonymous **ftp** requires detailed knowledge from the user. To retrieve a file, you must know the **ftp** server and the directory where the file is located. When the network was small, this was not a major problem. There were a limited number of important **ftp** servers, and they were well stocked with files. You could always **ftp** to a major server, like *uunet.uu.net*, and search through some directories using **ftp**'s **ls** command. This old approach is not compatible with a large and expanding Internet for two reasons:

- There are now several hundred major anonymous **ftp** servers. Knowing them all is difficult.
- There are now millions of Internet users. They cannot all rely on a few well-known servers. The servers would quickly be overwhelmed with **ftp** requests.

One approach to this problem is to provide network users with access to a large list of available **ftp** servers. At present, this list is available via anonymous **ftp** from *pilot.njin.net* in the file *pub/ftp-list/ftp.list*.* With this information, it is hoped that users will access the **ftp** servers closest to them on the network and not converge on a few well-known servers. This approach, however, still puts the responsibility for searching for a specific file on the network user.

The rapid growth of the Internet has spurred interest in programs that can locate the desired network resource for you—saving your time and the Internet's resources. A few of the programs that perform the search function for the user are **archie** from McGill University, **gopher** from the University of Minnesota, and WAIS (pronounced "ways") from Thinking Machines Corporation. Of these three programs, **archie** is the one most frequently used to provide information about anonymous **ftp** sites.

---

*The people who maintain the **ftp** list encourage the use of **archie** and plan to discontinue updates to the list.

archie

archie is a powerful new service that greatly expands the usefulness of anonymous **ftp**. This service helps you locate the file, program, or other information that you are looking for, by using information servers that maintain databases containing information about hundreds of **ftp** servers, and thousands of files and programs throughout the Internet.

archie's primary database is a listing of files and the servers from which the files can be retrieved. In the simplest sense, you tell **archie** which file you're looking for, and **archie** tells you which **ftp** servers the file is available from.

archie can be used in three different ways: interactively, through electronic mail, or from an **archie** client. To use **archie** interactively **telnet** to one of the **archie** servers. (There are currently four: *archie.mcgill.ca*, *archie.sura.net*, *archie.funet.fi*, and *archie.au*.) Log in using the user name *archie* and no password. At the *archie>* prompt, type *help* to get a full set of interactive **archie** commands.

There are many interactive **archie** commands, but the basic function of **archie** can be reduced to two commands. These are:

prog *pattern*   Display all files in the database with names that match the specified *pattern*.

mail *address*   Mail the output of the last command to *address*, which is normally your own e-mail address.

The following example uses both of these commands to interactively search for *gated-2.0.1.14.tar.Z*, and then mail the results of the search to *craig@peanut.nuts.com*.

```
% telnet archie.sura.net
Trying 128.167.254.179 ...
Connected to nic.sura.net.
Escape character is '^]'.
SunOS UNIX (nic.sura.net)
login: archie
Last login: Fri Nov 22 17:08:06 from helios.ece.arizo
SunOS Release 4.1.1 (CTHULHU) #1: Wed May 29 11:30:09 EDT 1991
        Welcome to the ARCHIE server at SURAnet
If you need further instructions type help at the archie> prompt.
archie> prog gated-2.0.1.14.tar.Z
# matches / % database searched:   13 / 96%
Host theta.iis.u-tokyo.ac.jp   (130.69.48.4)
Last updated 23:22 11 Nov 1991
    Location: /network
      FILE  rw-rw-r--  442743  Sep 26 03:12 gated-2.0.1.14.tar.Z
```

```
         .
         .
         .
archie> mail craig@peanut.nuts.com
# mailing results of "prog gated-2.0.1.14.tar.Z" to craig@peanut.nuts.com
# Mail command for "prog gated-2.0.1.14.tar.Z" completed successfully
archie> quit
```

The **archie** output provides all of the information you need to initiate an anonymous **ftp** transfer:

- the name of the server (*theta.iis.u-tokyo.ac.jp* in our example);
- the directory on the server that contains the file (*/network* in our example);
- the full name of the file (*gated-2.0.1.14.tar.Z* in our example).

You can also use **archie** by sending e-mail to *archie* at any one of the **archie** servers; for example, *archie@archie.mcgill.ca*. The text of the mail message must contain a valid **archie** e-mail command. To get a complete list of **archie** e-mail commands, send mail containing the *help* command to one of the servers. In the example below the e-mail help file is requested from *archie.mcgill.ca*.

```
% mail archie@archie.mcgill.ca
Subject:
help
^D
```

While these two methods of accessing **archie** work fine, the best way to use **archie** is through an **archie** client. Using an **archie** client reduces the load on the **archie** servers and is more responsive for the user. If you believe that your users may access **archie** frequently, set up an **archie** client.

archie Client Software

archie client software is available via anonymous **ftp** from the **archie** servers. The software is stored in the *pub/archie/clients* directory. The README file in this directory provides a short description of each type of client. There are at least three different client software packages for UNIX: an X windows client, and two command-line clients, one written in C* and the other written in **perl**. Check the **archie** servers for the latest developments in client software.

---

*Versions of the C-based **archie** client are available for VMS and DOS systems.

This section uses the command-line **archie** client written in C as an example. This software can be retrieved from *archie.sura.net* in the compressed **tar** file *pub/archie/clients/c-archie-1.2.tar.Z*. The C code and the instruction to **make** the **archie** client are all contained in this file. Once the client has been made and installed, it is invoked using this command:

```
% archie [options] string
```

The *string* is the name of the file that you are asking **archie** to find. It can be the exact filename, a substring of the name, or a regular expression.

The *options* control how the *string* is interpreted. The **–e** option searches for a filename that exactly matches the string; the **–s** option matches on any record that contains the string as any part of the filename; and the **–r** option interprets the string as a UNIX regular expression when looking for matches.

The following example uses the **archie** client to search for sites from which the **ppp** software can be retrieved. The search uses a regular expression that will match any compressed **tar** file with a name that starts with **ppp**.

```
% archie -r '^ppp.*\.tar\.Z' > ppp.locations
```

Our example stores **archie**'s output in the file *ppp.locations*. You can then examine *ppp.locations* to find the closest **ftp** server that has the latest version of the **ppp** tar file. Redirecting the output to a file is usually a good idea because **archie** often produces a lot of output. By default, the **archie** client will return as many as 95 matches to the search. To limit the number of matches returned, use the option **–m**n, where n is the maximum number of matches **archie** should return. For example, **–m**5 limits the search to five matches.

archie specializes in providing information about anonymous **ftp** servers. Using it, you can locate almost any file you might want to obtain through anonymous **ftp**. Another resource discovery program, **gopher**, provides a different type of information.

gopher

gopher is document retrieval software that provides a menu-driven interface to aid the user in searching for documents. It not only facilitates the search, **gopher** retrieves the selected information.

Like **archie**, **gopher** uses a client/server structure. Hundreds of information servers exist and more are being added all the time. To take full advantage of **gopher**, install the **gopher** client on your system. The client software is available via anonymous **ftp** from *boombox.micro.umn.edu*, in the directory *pub/gopher/Unix*. As of this writing, the current version of the UNIX software is available in the compressed **tar** file *gopher0.9.tar.Z*. This file contains the Makefile and C code necessary to build both the **gopher** client and server.

Once the **gopher** client is built, run it by typing **gopher** on the command line. When it is running, **gopher** is controlled by making menu selections. The sample below shows a typical first menu:

```
              Internet Gopher Information Client v0.9
                          Root Directory
      -->     1.  Information About Gopher/
              2.  Computer Information/
              3.  FTP Searches/
              4.  Fun & Games/
            . 5.  Libraries/
              6.  Mailing Lists/
              7.  News/
              8.  Other Gopher and Information Servers/
              9.  Phone Books/
              10. Search lots of places at the U of M  <?>
              11. UofM Campus Information/
      Press ? for Help, q to Quit, u to go up
      Page: 1/1
```

The **gopher** menu system is largely self-explanatory. Selections are made by number, or by moving the selection arrow up or down on the menu list. Table 13-2 shows the **gopher** commands that can be used when a menu is displayed.

Table 13.2: gopher Commands

Command	Action
carriage-return	Select current item.
number	Move pointer to item *number.*
k or ^p	Move pointer up one item.
j or ^n	Move pointer down one item.
u	Move up to the previous menu.
Q	Exit gopher.

Table 13.2: gopher Commands (continued)

Command	Action
O	Change gopher options.
?	Display the help screen.

A menu item that ends in a dot (.) is a file; one that ends in a slash (/) is a directory; and one that ends with the enclosed question mark (<?>) is an index. When you select a file from the menu, it is displayed on the screen and you can print it on your local printer. When you select a directory, **gopher** displays a new menu showing the contents of that directory. Finally, if you select an index, **gopher** prompts for a search string. It then searches that index looking for all files containing data that match the string.

For example, if we select the directory listed as item 8 in the menu above, **gopher** displays a second menu:

```
             Internet Gopher Information Client v0.9
                Other Gopher and Information Servers
     -->     1.  Europe/
             2.  Middle East/
             3.  North America/
             4.  Pacific/
             5.  Terminal Based Information/
             6.  WAIS Based Information/
  Press ? for Help, q to Quit, u to go up
  Page: 1/1
```

If we select 3 from this menu, we see another menu listing **gopher** servers in North America. At this writing there are more than 50 servers in the "North America" menu. If we select one of the servers listed in that menu, we are presented with another menu listing the information available from that server. In this way, we move from server to server until we find the information we're interested in.

Notice item 6 in the menu above. That item points to WAIS information servers. WAIS is another, very powerful information service.

Wide Area Information Server

The Wide Area Information Server (WAIS) software is an information retrieval service similar to **gopher**. Like **gopher**, WAIS helps you find and retrieve documents and other information. But there are definite differences between the two packages.

The **gopher** command-line client uses a menu-driven interface. The typical **gopher** user browses through the servers looking for interesting information. **gopher** is a powerful tool for the new user who doesn't know exactly what he wants, but who needs access to network information.

The WAIS system is a very powerful tool for the user who *does* know what he wants, but does not necessarily know where to find it. WAIS has the ability to locate the correct document based on the contents of the document. WAIS can search for keywords or strings of information contained in the body of the document, and WAIS has access to a huge reservoir of information. At this writing there are more than 200 WAIS servers.

WAIS has a command-line interface that uses keywords to search for and locate the desired information. However, the real power of WAIS is best appreciated using the more flexible X windows based client, **xwais**. **xwais** presents multiple windows that allow you to control the sources of information searched, and the exact combination of information searched for. The documents that match the search criteria are displayed in a subwindow of the "XWAIS Question" window. If you select one of the documents, its contents is then displayed in its own window. Through refinements of the search question, you can locate exactly the information you desire.

Unlike **ftp**, where you need to know the name and location of the document you want to retrieve, or even **gopher** where you must make assumptions about the contents of a document based on its name, **xwais** allows you to select a document by the information that the document contains. This is a powerful tool!

WAIS can be obtained via anonymous **ftp** from *quake.think.com*; get the compressed **tar** file *pub/wais/wais-8-b4.1.tar.Z*. This file contains the source for the WAIS client and server software, as well as extensive documentation. WAIS is currently the best documented of the three software packages—**archie**, **gopher**, and WAIS.

Whether or not **archie**, **gopher**, and WAIS all survive to become important Internet services, I am sure that some information services like these will continue to develop and grow in importance for the Internet.

The White Pages

archie provides information about **ftp** servers; **gopher** and **xwais** provide information about documents. **whois** provides information about people. One of the most important pieces of information in a network is who is in charge at the other end. In Chapter 11, we pointed out that it is important to know who is responsible for the other end of the link when troubleshooting a network problem. **whois** is a tool that helps you find this out.

whois obtains the requested information from the Internet white pages. The white pages is a database of information about users and responsible people that is maintained at *nic.ddn.mil.* To register yourself in the NIC white pages, fill in the **whois** registration form shown in *Appendix B* and send the completed form to *registrar@nic.ddn.mil.* When you register, you're issued a *NIC handle*, which is the index of your personal record in the white pages database.

When you request an official network number or domain name, you are asked to provide your NIC handle. If you don't have a NIC handle, the NIC assigns you one and automatically registers you in the white pages. Because of this, everyone who is responsible for an official network or domain has an entry in the white pages, and that entry can be retrieved by anyone who needs to contact them.

Many UNIX systems provide a **whois** command that can be used to query the NIC white pages. The general form of this command is:

```
% whois [-h server] name
```

The *server* field is the name of a system containing the NIC white pages (use *nic.ddn.mil*).* The *name* field is the information to be searched for in the white pages database.

In the following example, we search for an entry for *Craig Hunt.* An individual's name is entered in the white pages as: *last-name, first-name initial.* So we ask to search for *Hunt, Craig.*†

```
% whois 'Hunt, Craig'
Hunt, Craig W. (CWH3)                   Hunt@ENH.NIST.GOV
    National Institute of Standards and Technology
    Computer Systems and Communications Division
    Technology Building, Room A151
```

---

*Define the **alias whois 'whois -h nic.ddn.mil'** to direct all queries to *nic.ddn.mil.*
†**whois hunt** would return more than 130 matches. Be as specific as possible to reduce the number of matches.

```
     Gaithersburg, MD 20899
     (301) 975-3827 (FTS) 879-3827
     MILNET TAC user

     Record last updated on 03-Dec-90.
```

If multiple matches are returned, as in the case below, follow with a query for the individual's NIC handle to get the full information display. For example, a query for Norman Hunt returns four answers:

```
% whois 'Hunt, Norman'
Hunt, Norman (NKH6)            foo!nhunt@TACO.AF.MIL
                              (DSN) 555-3419
Hunt, Norman A. (NAH42)       NAH@RICH.ARMY.MIL
                              (301) 555-5406
                              (DSN) 555-5406
Hunt, Norman A. (NAH41)       log286@FOO.AF.MIL
                              (405) 555-5958
                              (DSN) 555-5958
Hunt, Norman A. (NAH36)       nhunt@FOO.ARMY.MIL
                              (201) 555-6312
                              (DSN) 555-6312
To single out one record, look it up with "!xxx", where xxx is the
handle, shown in parenthesis following the name, which comes first.
```

We then query for the NIC handle, which is the field enclosed in parentheses directly following the user name. The message at the end of the sample output implies that handles are entered as !xxx. This is true for users logged in directly to *nic.ddn.mil*, but the UNIX **whois** command does not use the ! syntax. For example, there are three different users named Norman A. Hunt; their NIC handles are NAH36, NAH41, and NAH42. To get more details about NAH36, enter:

```
% whois nah36
Hunt, Norman A. (NAH36)          nhunt@FOO.ARMY.MIL
    Army Research Development Center
    Attn: Norman Hunt B/1
    Big Arsenal, NJ 07006
    (201) 555-6312 (DSN) 555-6312
Record last updated on 09-Oct-90.
```

Most of the users registered in the white pages are Milnet users. This is natural because *nic.ddn.mil* is the Milnet's network information center. This user information is generally only useful if you want to send a Milnet e-mail and you don't know his or her address. But the NIC white pages database contains several other kinds of records, a few of which are very helpful for locating the people responsible for network, domains, and hosts throughout the Internet. These record types are:

Domain   Provides detailed contact information for the people responsible for the specified domain.

Host   Provides the information necessary to contact the system administrator of the specified host.

Network   Provides detailed information for the contacts for the specified network.

These record types can be used in the **whois** query to speed processing and limit the amount of output. All of the record types shown above can be abbreviated to their first two letters.

A sample query for the domain *ora.com* produces the following results:

```
% whois 'do ora.com'
O'Reilly and Associates (ORA-DOM1)
    90 Sherman Street
    Cambridge, MA 02140
Domain Name: ORA.COM
Administrative Contact:
        O'Reilly, Tim   (TO24)   tim@ORA.COM
        (617) 354-5800
Technical Contact,, Zone Contact:
        Love, William J.   (WJL4)   LOVE@CAMB.COM
        (617) 868-1111
Record last updated on 30-Apr-91.

Domain servers in listed order:
    RUBY.ORA.COM            140.186.65.25
    CCA.CAMB.COM            140.186.64.1
    NIC.CENT.NET            140.186.1.4
To see this host record with registered users, repeat the command with
a star ('*') before the name; or, use '%' to show JUST the registered
users.
```

The query displays the name, address, and telephone number of the administrative and technical contacts for the domain, as well as a list of hosts providing authoritative name service for the domain.

To query the host record for a specific host, in this case one of the name servers listed above, simply query the desired host name. For example, to find out who is responsible for *ruby.ora.com*, enter:

```
% whois 'host ruby.ora.com'
O'Reilly and Associates (RUBY-ORA)
    Hostname: RUBY.ORA.COM
    Address: 140.186.65.25
    System: ? running ?
    Coordinator:
        Love, William J.      (WJL4)   love@ORA.COM
        (617) 354-5800
    Domain Server
    Record last updated on 18-Apr-91.
To see this host record with registered users, repeat the command with
```

a star ('*') before the name; or, use '%' to show JUST the registered users.

This query displays the host name, IP address, and the system configuration. The name of the system administrator and the fact that this is an authoritative name server are also displayed.

Finally, to query for the point of contact for the specific network to which the host is connected, enter a **whois** query with the network number. In our example the IP address is 140.186.64.1. This is a class B address, so the network number is 140.186.0.0. The query is constructed as shown in the example below:

```
% whois 'net 140.186.0.0'
International Lisp Associates, Inc. (NET-CENTNET)
    114 Mount Auburn Street
    Cambridge, MA 02138
Netname: CENTNET
Netnumber: 140.186.0.0
Coordinator:
        Adams, Glenn A., Jr.  (GAA)  glenn@ILA.COM
        (617) 864-9745
Domain System inverse mapping provided by:
    NIC.CENT.NET               140.186.1.4
    NIC.NEAR.NET               192.52.71.4
Record last updated on 03-Jan-91.
To see this host record with registered users, repeat the command with
a star ('*') before the name; or, use '%' to show JUST the registered
users.
```

This query could also be done by network name, *centnet* in our example, but frequently you won't know the network name until you get the response from your query. In addition to the network name and number, this query tells you who is responsible for this network, and what name servers provide *in-addr.arpa* domain service for this network.

With the information from these queries, we could contact the domain administrator, the system administrator of the domain server, and the network administrator. From these key contacts, we could learn about the administrators of individual systems in their domain or on their network. This information could put us directly in touch with the other system administrator we need to talk to when debugging a network problem.

Not all systems have a local **whois** command. If your system doesn't, **telnet** to *nic.ddn.mil* and enter **whois** at the @ prompt. You'll then be prompted with *Whois:*. At this prompt enter any name you wish to search for, or enter *help* for more information.

X.500

whois and the NIC white pages are being replaced by a new directory system. This system is based on the OSI standard directory service, X.500. The current project to replace **whois** and make X.500 widely available is called the Field Operational X.500 (FOX) project.

Several X.500 directory servers are available. Perhaps the largest X.500 pilot project is the PSI white pages project. This online directory can be accessed via **telnet** at *wp.psi.com*. Log in as *fred*. No password is required.

fred is a user interface to the PSI directory service. **fred** emulates the **whois** syntax so that experienced Internet users are familiar with the commands necessary to use the new directory service. The following example shows a simple **fred** query:

```
% telnet wp.psi.com
    .
    .
    .
login: fred
    .
    .
    .
Welcome to the PSI White Pages Pilot Project

Try   "help" for a list of commands
      "whois" for information on how to find people
      "manual" for detailed documentation
      "report" to send a report to the white pages manager
To find out about participating organizations, try
      "whois -org *"

  accessing service, please wait...

fred> whois smoe
2 matches found.
  1. David Smoe                        smoe@foo.com
  2. Joe Smoe                          joe@foo.com
fred> whois !2
Joe Smoe (2)                           joe@foo.com
    .
    .
    .
Modified: Tue Oct  2 19:05:09 1990
        by: Manager, Performance Systems International,
           US (3)
fred> quit
Connection closed by foreign host.
```

At the fred> prompt, we entered **whois smoe**. This query asks **fred** to search for any names that contain the string "smoe." Two matches were found; each match is identified numerically. The numeric identifier is used to see more details about a match. That is what we are doing in the second query, *whois !2*. (This is similar to the way we used the NIC handle in the **whois** examples.)

The purpose of the FOX project is not simply to replicate the function already available in **whois**. X.500 is intended to provide a wider range of information, available on a broader base of servers. The X.500 database is a distributed system, while the **whois** database is a single large database. The most important information in the **whois** database is the information about who is responsible for specific network resources—hosts, networks, and domains. The user information is dominated by Milnet entries, and therefore has a limited applicability outside of Milnet. The new X.500 white pages should have a broader applicability because it uses a distributed structure that is designed to draw information from many organizations. The importance of this service will increase as more organizations add directory databases to the system.

fred, **whois**, **archie**—all of the services discussed in this chapter—are not presented for you to learn the details of how to use them.* They are presented so that you can learn the possibilities of the network. There is a world of information available on the network. To take full advantage of it, you must be willing to explore, and learn about the new services as you go.

More Reading

There is a wealth of printed material available through the network. Much of the available material provides information about TCP/IP and networking that can help you "learn more about it." The RFCs are, of course, a great source of information, but many RFCs are not written for beginners. It can be difficult determining which RFCs to read first. To help you make that decision, some RFCs that provide general information are identified as FYIs (For Your Information). To obtain a list of the FYIs, get the file *netinfo/fyi-index.txt* from *nic.ddn.mil* via anonymous **ftp**. The index will

---

*If you want more details about these services see the Nutshell Handbook, *The Whole Internet User's Guide & Catalog*, by Ed Krol.

list the small set of RFCs that are also FYIs. Select a few interesting RFCs from this list, and start reading. A few likely choices are:

- Martin, J. *There's Gold in them thar Networks! or Searching for Treasure in all the Wrong Places.* RFC 1290, December 1991; 27 pages.
- Bowers, K.L.; LaQuey, T.L.; Reynolds, J.K.; Roubicek, K.; Stahl, M.K.; and Yuan, A. *FYI on Where to Start: A Bibliography of Internetworking Information.* RFC 1175, August 1990; 42 pages.
- Malkin, G. and Marine, A. *FYI on Questions and Answers—Answers to Commonly Asked "New Internet User" Questions.* RFC 1325, May 1992; 42 pages.
- Malkin, G.S.; Marine, A.N.; and Reynolds, J.K. *FYI on Questions and Answers: Answers to Commonly Asked "Experienced Internet User" Questions.* RFC 1207, February 1991; 15 pages.

RFCs are not the only sources of information. There are many books and papers published about networking. An extensive list of information sources for TCP/IP, UNIX, and Ethernet has been compiled by Charles Spurgeon at the University of Texas at Austin. His paper, *Network Reading List: TCP/IP, UNIX, and Ethernet*, is available via anonymous **ftp** from *ftp.sura.net* in the directory *pub/networking*. The PostScript file is *network-reading-list.ps* and the ASCII file is *network-reading-list.txt*.

Perhaps the most complete reference to Internet information resources is the Nutshell Handbook, *The Whole Internet User's Guide & Catalog*, by Ed Krol. Not only does it explain how to use the information retrieval tools introduced in this chapter, it provides a well organized catalog of many of the information sources available on the network.

As you explore these information sources, you'll see that there is much more to the network than can ever be covered in one book. This book has been your launching pad; helping you connect your system to the network. Now that your system is up and running, use it as a tool to expand your information horizons.

Network Contacts

This appendix provides information from the NNSC's Network Provider Referral List. NNSC is the NSF Network Service Center, and the Network Provider Referral List is a list of several organizations that provide Internet access. The list provides the phone number and name of a contact at each network organization, as well as information about what part of the U.S. is serviced by each network provider. If an organization provides international service, that is also indicated.

If you can send e-mail to the Internet, request the latest copy of the Network Provider Referral List from the NNSC's information server by sending mail to *info-server@nnsc.nsf.net*. Place the following two lines in the body of the mail message:

> Request: nsfnet
> Topic: referral-list

NNSC can be reached directly via e-mail at *nnsc@nnsc.nsf.net*, via telephone at (617)873-3400, or via postal mail at the following address:

> NSF Network Service Center
> 10 Moulton Street
> Cambridge, MA 02138

Internet Contacts

Table A-1 lists the contacts for the network service providers that provide Internet access within the United States. This information is from the NNSC's Network Provider Referral List dated November, 1992.

Table A.1: U.S. Network Providers

Network	Service Area	Contact	Phone
Alternet	Entire US	UUNET	(800)4UUNET3
ANS	Entire US	Joel Maloff	(313)663-7610
BARRNET	Bay Area	Paul Baer	(415)723-7520
CERFnet	West	CERFnet Hotline	(800)876-2373
CICnet	Midwest	John Hankins	(313)998-6102
CO Supernet	Colorado	Ken Harmon	(303)273-3471
CONCERT	North Carolina	Joe Ragland	(919)248-1404
INet	Indiana	Dick Ellis	(812)855-4240
JVNCnet	East	Sergio Heker	(800)35TIGER
Los Nettos	Los Angeles	Ann Cooper	(310)822-1511
MichNet/Merit	Michigan	Jeff Ogden	(313)764-9430
MIDnet	Mid US	Dale Finkelson	(402)472-5032
MRnet	Minnesota	Dennis Fazio	(612)342-2570
MSEN	Michigan	Owen Medd	(313)998-4562
NEARnet	Northeast	John Curran	(617)873-8730
netILLINOIS	Illinois	Joel Hartman	(309)677-3100
NevadaNet	Nevada	Don Zitter	(702)784-6133
NorthwestNet	Northwest	Eric Hood	(206)562-3000
NYSERnet	New York	Jim Luckett	(315)443-4120
OARnet	Ohio	Alison Brown	(614)292-8100
PACCOM	Hawaii	Torben Nielsen	(808)956-3499
PREPnet	Pennsylvania	Thomas Bajzek	(412)268-7870
PSCNET	East	Eugene Hastings	(412)268-4960
PSINet	Entire US	PSI, Inc.	(800)82PSI82
Sesquinet	Texas	Farrell Gerbode	(713)527-4988
SDSCnet	San Diego	Paul Love	(619)534-5043
SURAnet	Southeast	Deborah Nunn	(301)982-4600
THEnet	Texas	Tracy Parker	(512)471-2444
VERnet	Virginia	James Jokl	(804)924-0616
Westnet	West	Pat Burns	(303)491-7260

Table A.1: U.S. Network Providers (continued)

Network	Service Area	Contact	Phone
WiscNet	Wisconsin	Tad Pinkerton	(608)262-8874
WVNET	West Virginia	Harper Grimm	(304)293-5192

Table A-2 lists all of the network service providers from the Network Providers Referral List that provide international access to Internet.

Table A.2: International Network Providers

Network	Contact	Phone	E-mail Address
AARNet	AARNet Support	+61 6 249-3385	aarnet@aarnet.edu.au
Alternet	UUNET	(800)4UUNET3	alternet-info@uunet.uu.net
ANS	Joel Maloff	(313)663-7610	info@ans.net
CERFnet	CERFnet Hotline	(800)876-2373	help@cerf.net
EUnet	EUnet Support	+31 20 592-5124	glenn@eu.net
ICM	Robert Collet	(703)940-2230	rcollet@icm1.icp.net
JVNCnet	Sergio Heker	(800)35TIGER	market@jvnc.net
PACCOM	Torben Nielsen	(808)956-3499	torben@hawaii.edu
Pipex	Richard Nuttall	+44-223-424616	sales@pipex.net
PSINet	PSI, Inc.	(800)82PSI82	info@psi.com
SprintLink	Bob Doyle	(703)904-2230	bdoyle@icm1.icp.net
UKnet	UKnet Support	+44-227-475497	postmaster@uknet.ac.uk

Table A-3 lists the Canadian network service providers from the Network Providers Referral List.

Table A.3: Canadian Network Providers

Network	Service Area	Contact	Phone
ARnet	Alberta	Walter Neilson	(403)450-5188
BCnet	British Columbia	Mike Patterson	(604)822-3932
MBnet	Manitoba	Gerry Miller	(204)474-8230
NB*net	New Brunswick	David MacNeil	(506)453-4573
NLnet	Newfoundland/Labrador	Wilf Bussey	(709)737-8329
NSTN	Nova Scotia	Michael Martineau	(902)468-NSTN

Table A.3: Canadian Network Providers (continued)

Network	Service Area	Contact	Phone
ONet	Ontario	Andy Bjerring	(519)661-2151
PEINet	Prince Edward Island	Jim Hancock	(902)566-0450
RISQ	Quebec	Bernard Turcotte	(514)340-5700
SASK#net	Saskatchewan	Dean C. Jones	(306)966-4860

B

Forms, Forms, Forms

This appendix contains the forms required for registering information about networks, domains, and users. These forms have been slightly edited to make them more suitable for book form; in particular we have deleted lists of applicable RFCs, because they are discussed elsewhere in this book. However, all instructions for completing the forms have been left intact.

In addition to the forms printed here, there are two other important forms that allow Bitnet sites and sites connected via UUCP to register Internet-style domain names. The forms cannot be obtained from the NIC, but they can be obtained by following these instructions:

UUCP Domain Name Registration

All UUCP sites can register a domain name with the Internet. To obtain the necessary form, send a request to *uunet!postmaster*. When you have completed the form, send it to *uunet!domain-request* or to the postal address shown on the form. Instructions for completing this application come with the form.

Bitnet Domain Name Registration

Bitnet sites can also register domain names with the Internet. The necessary form is available from NETSERV at BITNIC, in the file *domain guide*. To retrieve this form, send e-mail to *netserv@bitnic* with the command get domain guide in the body of the message. Instructions for completing the form will be sent with it. Return the form via e-mail to *domains@bitnic*.

The list below shows the forms that are included in this appendix, what they are used for, who uses them, where the latest version is stored, and where to send the completed form. If you have access to FTP, all of these forms can be obtained from the NIC via anonymous **ftp**; therefore, we have also included the filename for each form.

Whois Registration

Users wishing to register an e-mail address in the NIC white pages should complete this form. It is stored at *nic.ddn.mil* in the file *netinfo/user-template.txt*. Send the completed form by e-mail to *registrar@nic.ddn.mil*, or by postal mail to the NIC.

Network Number Assignment

Network administrators submit this form to obtain an official network number. It is in the file *netinfo/internet-number-template.txt*. Send the completed form to *hostmaster@nic.ddn.mil*.

Internet Domain Name Registration

Organizations connected to the Internet complete this form to register their domain names. It is stored in the file *netinfo/domain-template.txt*. E-mail the completed form to *hostmaster@nic.ddn.mil*.

IN-ADDR.ARPA Registration

Organizations connected to the Internet use this form to register their in-addr.arpa domains. It is in the file *netinfo/in-addr-template.txt*. Send completed forms to *hostmaster@nic.ddn.mil*.

Autonomous System Number Application

Sites using BGP or EGP use this form to obtain an official autonomous system number. It is in the file *netinfo/asn-template.txt*. Submit completed forms to *hostmaster@nic.ddn.mil*.

You can request all of the forms mentioned above from the NIC and return them to the NIC's postal address:

> DDN Network Information Center
> 14200 Park Meadow Drive
> Suite 200
> Chantilly, VA 22021

You can also reach the NIC via telephone at 1-800-365-3642 or 1-703-802-4535.

Whois Registration

[netinfo/user-template.txt]   [10/91]

PROCEDURE FOR "WHOIS" REGISTRATION

This file contains information for individual users wishing to
register in the WHOIS database maintained by the DDN Network
Information Center (DDN NIC) on the host NIC.DDN.MIL (192.112.36.5).
The user registration template below has been created to standardize
the registration procedure and help insure that the DDN NIC will
receive complete information about each user. Below are the
 1) instructions for filling in the User Registration template; 2)
instructions for sending the template to the DDN NIC; 3) a sample
template, and 4) a blank template for you to fill in.

Any user with electronic mail access to the Internet may be included
in the NIC WHOIS database. If you are sending the template to
the DDN NIC in order to be added to a NIC mailing list, please
specify which list you'd like to join when you return the template.

I.   HOW TO FILL IN THE USER REGISTRATION TEMPLATE

Using an editor of your choice, create a file containing the blank
template at the end of this file, and fill in all relevant fields.
Each field should begin on a new line. Detailed instructions for
the format of each section are given below under SPECIFIC INSTRUCTIONS
FOR EACH TEMPLATE FIELD.

II.   WHERE TO SEND THE COMPLETED TEMPLATE

The completed template should be sent online to REGISTRAR@NIC.DDN.MIL.

III.   SPECIFIC INSTRUCTIONS FOR EACH TEMPLATE FIELD AND SAMPLE TEMPLATE

    FULL NAME:

The name may be entered in any of the following formats:

        Lastname, Firstname I.
        Lastname, Firstname
        Lastname, I. Middlename
        Lastname, Firstname I., Jr.
        Lastname, Firstname I., III

    where "I." = an initial

    Do not include military rank or professional titles.

    U.S. MAIL ADDRESS - some standard procedures:

Line 1: The name of your organization; do not use acronyms.
Line 2: Information such as the department name, code, or attention line.

Line 3: (optional) The building name or number, room number.
Line 4: Your street address or Post Office Box.
Line 5: City, state and zip code. If you commonly use a 9 digit zip
      code, enter that.

DO NOT USE ANY ABBREVIATIONS OR ACRONYMS, with the exception of:

```
Incorporated.......Inc.
Limited............Ltd.
Corporation........Corp.
Company............Co.
Post Office Box....P.O. Box
```

Separate lines of the address by a carriage return.

PHONE:

Up to four phone numbers are allowed. Acceptable formats are:

U.S. numbers

```
(123) 456-7890
(123) 456-7890 ext 123
(123) 456-7890 (DSN) 567-7890
(123) 456-7890 (DSN) 567-7890 (FTS) 667-7890
(123) 456-7890 or 456-0987 (DSN) 567-7890 or 567-0987
```

Overseas numbers

```
+49 711-123456 or (DSN) 420-1234 or (M) 8765-1234
(For overseas numbers, specify the country code with a plus symbol
 in front of the number.)
```

AUTHORIZING HOST:

This is the name of the user's "home" host. Enter the OFFICIAL
HOSTNAME rather than an approved nickname.

PRIMARY LOGIN NAME:

This is the primary login name/username/directory name of the
user on the authorizing host.

If the login name is a part of the security system on your host
and therefore should be kept secret, do not enter it in this
field.

The primary login name may be a group directory name if it is the
only one the individual uses.

PRIMARY NETWORK MAILBOX:

This is the mailbox where this individual prefers to receive
mail. This may or may not be his or her primary login name on

the host. If mail addresses are case dependent on your host,
specify the mailbox string accordingly. Otherwise enter the
string in upper case.

Separate the username and hostname parts of the mailbox by "@".

Format: USERNAME@HOSTNAME
Example: SMITH@NIC.DDN.MIL

For those hosts whose official hostname is a Fully Qualified
Domain Name (FQDN), enter the FQDN in the hostname part of the
mailbox. The FQDN is preferred.

Example: Smith@AI.AI.MIT.EDU

TERMINATION DATE:

The DEROS date (Date Eligible for Return from Overseas) for
military users, estimated date of graduation for students,
estimated elapse date for temporary users.

This field was requested for use on military hosts. Other users
do not have to fill in the field.

Format: MO/YR
Example: 10/87

===
SAMPLE USER REGISTRATION TEMPLATE
===

FULL NAME: McCollum, Bob
U.S. MAIL ADDRESS: Network Information Systems Center
14200 Park Meadow Dr., Suite 200200
Chantilly, VA 22021
PHONE: (703) 802-4535
AUTHORIZING HOST: NIC.DDN.MIL
PRIMARY LOGIN NAME: bobm
PRIMARY NETWORK MAILBOX: bobm@NIC.DDN.MIL
MILNET TAC ACCESS (Y/N):
TERMINATION DATE:
DELETE (Y/N):

===
BLANK REGISTRATION TEMPLATE -- YOU MAY USE THIS FORM TO SEND TO THE NIC
===

FULL NAME:
U.S. MAIL ADDRESS:
PHONE:
AUTHORIZING HOST:
PRIMARY LOGIN NAME:
PRIMARY NETWORK MAILBOX:

```
MILNET TAC ACCESS (Y/N):
TERMINATION DATE:
DELETE (Y/N):
```

Network Number Request

[netinfo/internet-number-template.txt]   [12/91]

This form must be completed as part of the application process for
obtaining an Internet Protocol (IP) Network Number. To obtain an
Internet number, please provide the following information online, via
electronic mail, to HOSTMASTER@NIC.DDN.MIL. If electronic mail is not
available to you, please mail hardcopy to:

> DDN Network Information Center
> 14200 Park Meadow Dr., Suite 200
> Chantilly, VA   22021

Once the NIC receives your completed application we will send you an
acknowledgement, via electronic or postal mail. PLEASE ALLOW AT LEAST 8
WORKING DAYS FOR PROCESSING YOUR REQUEST.

NOTE: This application is solely for obtaining a legitimate IP network
number assignment. If you're interested in officially registering a
domain please complete the domain application found in
netinfo/domain-template.txt. If FTP is not available to you, please
contact HOSTMASTER@NIC.DDN.MIL or phone the NIC at (800) 365-3642 for
further assistance.

YOUR APPLICATION MUST BE TYPED.

1) If the network will be connected to the Internet, you must provide
the name of the governmental sponsoring organization, and the name,
title, mailing address, phone number, net mailbox, and NIC Handle (if
any) of the contact person (POC) at that organization who has authorized
the network connection. This person will serve as the POC for
administrative and policy questions about authorization to be a part of
the Internet. Examples of such sponsoring organizations are: DISA DNSO,
the National Science Foundation (NSF), or similar military or government
sponsors.

NOTE: If the network will NOT be connected to the Internet, then you do
not need to provide this information.

```
     1a.  Sponsoring Organization:
     1b.  Contact name (Lastname, Firstname):
     1c.  Contact title:
     1d.  Mail Address :

     1e.  Phone :
     1f.  Net mailbox :
     1g.  NIC handle (if known):
```

2) Provide the name, title, mailing address, phone number, and organization of the technical POC. The online mailbox and NIC Handle (if any) of the technical POC should also be included. This is the POC for resolving technical problems associated with the network and for updating information about the network. The technical POC may also be responsible for hosts attached to this network.

       2a. NIC handle (if known):
       2b. Technical POC name (Lastname, Firstname):
       2c. Technical POC title:
       2d. Mail address :

       2e. Phone :
       2f. Net Mailbox :

3) Supply the short mnemonic name for the network (up to 12 characters). This is the name that will be used as an identifier in internet name and address tables.

       3. Network name:

4) Identify the network geographic location and the responsible organization establishing the network.

       4a. Postal address for main/headquarters network site:

       4b. Name of Organization:

5) Question #5 is for MILITARY or DOD requests, ONLY.

If you require that this connected network be announced to the NSFNET please answer questions 5a, 5b, and 5c.

5a. Do you want MILNET to announce your network to the NSFNET? (Y/N):

5b. Do you have an alternate connection, other than MILNET, to the NSFNET? (please state alternate connection if answer is yes):

5c. If you've answered yes to 5b, please state if you would like the MILNET connection to act as a backup path to the NSFNET? (Y/N):

6) Estimate the number of hosts that will be on the network:

       6a. Initially:
       6b. Within one year:
       6c. Within two years:
       6d. Within five years:

7) Unless a strong and convincing reason is presented, the network (if it qualifies at all) will be assigned a class C network number. If a class C network number is not acceptable for your purposes state why.

(Note: If there are plans for more than a few local networks, and more than 100 hosts, you are strongly urged to consider subnetting. [See RFC 950])

    7. Reason:

8) Networks are characterized as being either Research, Defense, Government - Non Defense, or Commercial, and the network address space is shared between these four areas. Which type is this network?

    8. Type of network:

9) What is the purpose of the network?

    9. Purpose:

PLEASE ALLOW AT LEAST 8 WORKING DAYS FOR PROCESSING THIS APPLICATION

For further information contact the DDN Network Information Center (NIC):

Via electronic mail:	HOSTMASTER@NIC.DDN.MIL
Via telephone:	(800) 365-3642
Via postal mail:	DDN Network Information Center
	14200 Park Meadow Dr., Suite 200
	Chantilly, VA 22021

Internet Domain Name Registration

[NETINFO:DOMAIN-TEMPLATE.TXT]   [10/90 DM]

To establish a domain, the following information must be sent to the NIC Domain Registrar (HOSTMASTER@NIC.DDN.MIL). Questions may be addressed to the NIC Hostmaster by electronic mail at the above address, or by phone at (703) 802-4535 or (800) 365-3642.

NOTE: The key people must have electronic mailboxes and NIC "handles," unique NIC database identifiers. If you have access to "WHOIS", please check to see if you are registered and if so, make sure the information is current. Include only your handle and any changes (if any) that need to be made in your entry. If you do not have access to "WHOIS", please provide all the information indicated and a NIC handle will be assigned.

(1) The name of the top-level domain to join
    (EDU, COM, MIL, GOV, NET, ORG).

    1. Top-level domain:

(2) The name of the domain (up to 12 characters). This is the name that will be used in tables and lists associating the domain with the domain server addresses. [While, from a technical standpoint, domain

names can be quite long we recommend the use of shorter, more user-friendly names.]

    2.   Complete Domain Name:

(3) The name and address of the organization establishing the domain.

    3a.   Organization name:
    3b.   Organization address:

(4) The date you expect the domain to be fully operational.

    4.   Date operational:

(5) The NIC handle of the administrative head of the organization or this person's name, mailing address, phone number, organization, and network mailbox. This is the contact point for administrative and policy questions about the domain. In the case of a research project, this should be the principal investigator.

NOTE: Both the Administrative and the Technical/Zone contact of a domain MUST have a network mailbox, even if the mailbox is to be within the proposed domain.

    Administrative Contact

  5a.   NIC Handle (if known) :
  5b.   Name (Last, First) :
  5c.   Organization:
  5d.   Mail Address:

  5e.   Phone Number:
  5f.   Net Mailbox :

(6) The NIC handle of the technical contact for the domain -- or the person's name, mailing address, phone number, organization, and network mailbox. This is the contact point for problems concerning the domain or zone, as well as for updating information about the domain or zone.

    Technical and Zone Contact

  6a.   NIC Handle (if known):
  6b.   Name (Last, First) :
  6c.   Organization:
  6d.   Mail Address:

  6e.   Phone Number:
  6f.   Net Mailbox :

(7) Domains must provide at least two independent servers
    on Government-sponsored networks that provide the domain
    service for translating names to addresses for hosts in
    this domain.

* If you are applying for a domain and a network number assignment
simultaneously and a host on your proposed network will be used
as a server for the domain, you must wait until you receive your
network number assignment and have given the server(s) a netaddress
before sending in the domain application. Sending in the domain
application without complete information in Sections 7 and 8 of
this template will result in the delay of the domain registration.

Also, establishing the servers in physically separate locations
and on different PSNs and/or networks is strongly recommended.

NOTE: All new hosts acting as servers will appear in the DNS root
      servers but will not appear in the HOSTS.TXT file
      unless otherwise requested.

   Primary Server: HOSTNAME, NETADDRESS, HARDWARE, SOFTWARE

   7a. Primary Server Hostname:
   7b. Primary Server Netaddress:
   7c. Primary Server Hardware:
   7d. Primary Server Software:

(8) The Secondary server information.

   8a. Secondary Server Hostname:
   8b. Secondary Server Netaddress:
   8c. Secondary Server Hardware:
   8d. Secondary Server Software:

(9) If any currently registered hosts will be renamed into the new
    domain, please specify old hostname, netaddress, and new hostname.

   For example:

      BAR-FOO2.XYZ.COM (26.8.0.193) -> FOO2.BAR.COM
      BAR-FOO3.XYZ.COM (192.7.3.193) -> FOO3.BAR.COM
      BAR-FOO4.ARPA (34.6.0.193) -> FOO4.BAR.COM

   NOTE: Hostname changes to MILNET hosts must be approved by the
         MILNET Manager - MILNETMGR@DDN-CONUS.DDN.MIL.

(10) Please describe your organization briefly.

   For example: Our Corporation is a consulting
   organization of people working with UNIX and the C language in an
   electronic networking environment. It sponsors two technical
   conferences annually and distributes a bimonthly newsletter.

PLEASE ALLOW AT LEAST 8 WORKING DAYS FOR PROCESSING THIS APPLICATION

For further information contact the DDN/INTERNET Network Information Center (NIC):

Via electronic mail: HOSTMASTER@NIC.DDN.MIL
Via telephone: (800) 365-3642 or (703) 802-4535
Via postal mail: DDN Network Information Center
                      14200 Park Meadow Dr., Suite 200
                      Chantilly, VA 22021

IN-ADDR.ARPA Registration

[netinfo/in-addr-template.txt]   [9/90]

The Internet uses a special domain to support gateway location and Internet address to host mapping. The intent of this domain is to provide a guaranteed method to perform host address to host name mapping, and to facilitate queries to locate all gateways on a particular network in the Internet.

IN-ADDR.ARPA Registration

The following information is needed for delegation of registered networks in your domain for inclusion in the IN-ADDR.ARPA zone files:

        * the IN-ADDR.ARPA domain
        * the Network name
        * the Hostnames of the two hosts on networks
           that will be acting as IN-ADDR servers

IN-ADDR domains are represented using the network number in reverse. For example, network 123.45.67.0's IN-ADDR domain is represented as 67.45.123.IN-ADDR.ARPA.

        For example:

        IN-ADDR domain   Network Name   IN-ADDR Servers
                                             (Hostname)
                                             (NetAddress)
                                             (CPUType/OpSys)

        41.192.IN-ADDR.ARPA NET-TEST-ONE   BAR.FOO.EDU
                                             123.45.67.89
                                             VAX-II/VMS
                                             ONE.ABC.COM
                                             98.76.54.32
                                             SUN/UNIX

- -

NOTE: Unless specified, new hosts registered as IN-ADDR servers will
be registered in the root servers only and will not appear in the
HOSTS.TXT file.

Please have the Network Coordinator complete and return the following
information for those networks needing IN-ADDR registration.

```
         IN-ADDR domain        Network Name    IN-ADDR Servers
         ==============        ============    ===============
```

- -

Completed templates and questions can be directed to Hostmaster at
HOSTMASTER@NIC.DDN.MIL, or mailed to:

> DDN Network Information Center
> 14200 Park Meadow Dr., Suite 200
> Chantilly, VA 22021

PLEASE ALLOW EIGHT WORKING DAYS FOR PROCESSING THIS TEMPLATE

Autonomous System Number Application

[netinfo/asn-template.txt]   [10/90]

Registering for an Autonomous System Number implies that you plan to
implement one or more gateways and use them to connect networks in the
DDN-Internet. Please provide us with further details about your plans,
and with information about the administrative authority you have for
participating in the Internet.

It is strongly advised that you follow the development of
inter-autonomous systems protocols in the IAB task forces.

Send the completed application online to HOSTMASTER@NIC.DDN.MIL.
Or, if electronic mail is not available to you, please mail paper
copy to:

> DDN Network Information Center
> 14200 Park Meadow Dr., Suite 200
> Chantilly, VA 22021

Questions may be addressed to the NIC Hostmaster by electronic mail at
the above address, or by phone at (800) 365-3642 or (703) 802-8400.

To obtain an Autonomous System Number the following information
must be provided:

NOTE: The key people must have electronic mailboxes and NIC
"Handles," unique NIC database identifiers. If you have access to
WHOIS, please check to see if you are registered and if so, make
sure the information is current. Include only your Handle and any
changes (if any) that need to be made in your entry. If you do not
have access to WHOIS, or are not registered in the NIC WHOIS
database, please provide all the information requested and a NIC
Handle will be assigned.

1) The name, title, mailing address, phone number, and organization
of the administrative head of the organization. This is the
contact point for administrative and policy questions about the
autonomous system. In the case of a research project this should
be the Principal Investigator. The online mailbox and NIC Handle
(if any) of this person should also be included.

Example:

Administrator

> | | |
> |---|---|
> | Organization | Network Solutions, Inc. |
> | | Network Information Center |
> | Name | Lastname, Firstname |
> | Title | Principal Investigator |
> | Mail Address | Government Systems, Inc. |
> | | 14200 Park Meadow Dr., Suite 200 |
> | | Chantilly, VA 22021 |
> | Phone Number | (XXX) XXX-XXXX |
> | Net Mailbox | pi@NIC.DDN.MIL |
> | NIC Handle | BB34 |

2) The name, title, mailing address, phone number, and organization
of the technical contact. The online mailbox and NIC Handle (if
any) of the technical contact should also be included. This is the
contact point for problems with the autonomous system and for
updating information about the autonomous system. Also, the
technical contact may be held responsible for the behavior of
gateways in this autonomous system.

Example:

Technical Contact

Organization	Network Solutions, Inc.
	Network Information Center
Name	Lastname, Firstname
Title	Computer Scientist
Mail Address	Network Information Center
	14200 Park Meadow Dr., Suite 200
	Chantilly, VA 22021
Phone Number	(XXX) XXX-XXXX
Net Mailbox	cs@NIC.DDN.MIL
NIC Handle	CC56

3) The name of the autonomous system (up to 12 characters). This is the name that will be used in tables and lists associating autonomous systems and numbers.

Example: ALPHA-BETA

4) A description of the gateway that implements the inter-autonomous system protocol for interaction with other autonomous systems. Currently the exterior gateway protocol (EGP) is being used for this purpose (RFC 904). This gateway should comply with RFC 1009, Requirements for Internet Gateways.

Example: This is a new gateway developed by the XYZ Group at the ABC Corporation.

or

Example: This is an instance of the well known IJK company gateway, but set up as a distinct autonomous system.

5) A description of the gateway hardware, including CPU and interfaces.

Example: DEC PDP-11/23, ARPANET Interface by ACC, Ethernet Interfaces by 3COM.

6) A description of the gateway software, including operating system and languages.

Example: The gateway is implemented using language "C" and runs Berkeley 4.2 Unix.

7) The deployment schedule for the autonomous system.
   (a) initially,
   (b) within one year,
   (c) two years, and
   (d) five years.

Example:

(a) initially   =   1
(b) one year   =   3
(c) two years   =   5
(d) five years = 10

8) What networks will be interconnected by these gateways? What are the internet addresses of each gateway?

Example: One gateway, interconnecting MILNET and LEWIS-PRNET2, with address 26.7.0.159 on MILNET and 128.108.12.10 on LEWIS-PRNET2.

PLEASE ALLOW AT LEAST 8 WORKING DAYS FOR PROCESSING THIS APPLICATION

For further information contact the DDN Network Information Center (NIC):

Via electronic mail: HOSTMASTER@NIC.DDN.MIL
Via telephone: 1-800-365-3642
Via postal mail: DDN NIC
                       14200 Park Meadow Dr., Suite 200
                       Chantilly, VA 22021

C

A gated Reference

This appendix covers the syntax of the **gated** command and the **gated** configuration language. As a reference to the **gated** configuration language, this appendix stands on its own. But to fully understand how to configure **gated**, use this reference in conjunction with the sample configuration files in Chapter 7.

gated is constantly being improved. As **gated** is upgraded, the command language changes. Refer to the latest **man** pages for the most recent information about **gated**.

The gated Command

The syntax of the **gated** command is:

gated [–c] [–n] [–t *trace_options*] [–f *config_file*] [*trace_file*]

The first two command-line options debug the routing configuration file without impacting the network or the kernel routing table. Frequently, these debugging options are used with a test configuration identified by the **−f** *config_file* option:

−c   Tells **gated** to read the configuration file and check for syntax errors. The **−c** option turns on **−tierk** tracing. When **gated** finishes reading the configuration file, it produces a snapshot of its status and then terminates. It writes the snapshot to */usr/tmp/gated_dump*. Running **gated** with the **−c** option does not require superuser privilege, and it is not necessary to terminate the active **gated** process.

−n   Tells **gated** not to update the kernel routing table. This is used to test the routing configuration with real routing data without interfering with system operation.

−f *config_file*   Tells **gated** to read the configuration from *config_file* instead of from the default configuration file, */etc/gated.conf*. Used in conjunction with the **−c** option, **−f** checks a new configuration without interfering with the currently running **gated** configuration.

The command-line arguments, *trace_options* and *trace_file*, are used for protocol tracing. The *trace_file* argument is the filename to which the trace output is written. If a file is not specified, the trace is written to the standard output. Tracing frequently produces a large amount of output.

The options used for tracing are:

−t This option turns on tracing. If **−t** is specified with no other trace options, **gated** traces internal errors (**i**), external errors (**e**), and routing table changes (**r**). To control which events are traced, specify other trace flags after the **−t** option. The options referred to in the command syntax as *trace_options* can be used in conjunction with the **−t** flag. These are:

A   *All* turns on every possible trace option. This generates an enormous amount of output.*

i   *Internal* turns on tracing of internal informational and error messages. Tracing errors is helpful for debugging.

e   *External* turns on tracing of all external errors. Again, tracing errors is usually helpful.

---

*The names of the trace flags used here are the keyword names used with the **traceoptions** command discussed later in this appendix.

k   *Kernel* turns on tracing of changes to the kernel's routing table. The kernel table is the table actually used by IP to make routing decisions.*

r   *Route* turns on tracing of **gated** routing table changes. This differs from the **k** trace option because **gated** maintains its own internal routing table. This table, which is distinct from the kernel routing table, is used by **gated** when choosing the best route. It is not used directly by IP.

m   *Mark* outputs a message to the trace file every ten minutes. This flag does not turn on any tracing; the message to the trace file just indicates that **gated** is running.

t   *Nostamp* tells **gated** not to timestamp messages written to the trace file. Normally trace file messages include a timestamp. This flag reduces the length of trace file messages by preventing **gated** from adding a timestamp. Because this flag modifies the trace messages produced by other *trace_options*, use it only in conjunction with some other trace flag.

P   *Protocol* turns on tracing of BGP and EGP protocol machine state transitions. The RFCs describe these protocols using *finite state machine* (FSM) diagrams or tables. The protocols transition from one state to another based on the occurrence of certain events. For example, the state might change from *idle* to *connect* when a *connection open* event occurs. This is a highly specialized trace flag, only useful to those who have a thorough understanding of the protocols involved. Use this flag with the **p** flag to trace EGP state transitions or with the **B** flag to trace BGP transitions.

M   *SNMP* turns on tracing of *Simple Network Management Protocol* (SNMP) updates. SNMP is a network management protocol—not a routing protocol. This flag traces the updates of **gated** status sent to the SNMP software. If used in conjunction with the **u** flag, the entire contents of the update are written to the trace file.

R   *RIP* turns on tracing of the RIP packets sent and received. If used with **u** the entire contents of the RIP packets is written to the trace file.

---

*The kernel routing table is sometimes called the *forwarding table*.

H *Hello* turns on tracing of Hello packets. Again the trace can be modified by the **u** flag.

C *ICMP* turns on tracing of the ICMP Redirect packets received. The contents of the packet is traced if the **u** flag is used.

p *EGP* turns on tracing of the EGP packets sent and received. If used with **u**, the contents of the packet is traced; if used with the **P** flag, the machine state transitions are traced.

B *BGP* turns on tracing of the BGP packets sent and received. This flag can also be used with the **u** and **P** flags to modify the trace output.

u *Update* turns on tracing of the contents of the protocol packet. This flag is used in conjunction with one or more of the flags **M**, **R**, **H**, **C**, **p**, or **B**.

Most of these flags require that you have a good understanding of the protocols you are monitoring. **gated** provides the kind of debugging support that is very important to the networking experts who run the large national networks. For the rest of us, tracing errors is usually enough. The default trace options (**–tier**) are well designed to provide the debugging information needed for most problems.

Signal Processing

gated processes the following signals:

SIGHUP Tells **gated** to re-read the configuration file. The new configuration replaces the one that **gated** is currently running. SIGHUP loads the new configuration file without interrupting **gated** service. SIGHUP is available for quick configuration changes.

    At most sites the routing configuration changes infrequently. The few times you need to change to a new configuration, terminate **gated** and rerun it with the new configuration. This is a more accurate test of how things will run at the next boot.

SIGINT Tells **gated** to snap-shot its current state to the file */usr/tmp/gated_dump*.

SIGTERM Tells **gated** to shutdown gracefully. All protocols are shut down following the rules of that protocol. For example, EGP sends a CEASE message and waits for it to be confirmed. SIGTERM removes from the kernel routing table all routes learned via the exterior routing protocols. If you need to preserve those routes while **gated** is out of operation, use SIGKILL or SIGQUIT.

SIGKILL/SIGQUIT   Tells **gated** to terminate immediately and dump core. Routes are not removed from the routing table, and no graceful shutdown is attempted.

SIGUSR1   Tells **gated** to toggle tracing. If no trace flags are set, SIGUSR1 has no effect. But if tracing is enabled, the first SIGUSR1 causes **gated** to toggle off tracing and to close the trace file. The next SIGUSR1 turns tracing back on and opens the trace file. When the trace file is closed, it can be moved or removed without interfering with the operation of **gated**. Use this to periodically empty out the trace file to prevent it from becoming too large.

The following is an example of **gated** signal handling. First the SIGUSR1 signal is passed to the **gated** process using the process id obtained from the */etc/gated.pid* file.

```
# kill -USR1 `cat /etc/gated.pid`
```

Next the old trace file (*/usr/tmp/gated.log* in this case) is removed, and **gated** is passed another SIGUSR1 signal.

```
# rm /usr/tmp/gated.log
# kill -USR1 `cat /etc/gated.pid`
```

After receiving the second signal, **gated** opens a fresh trace file (still named */usr/tmp/gated.log*). An **ls** shows that the new file has been created.

```
# ls -l /usr/tmp/gated.log
-rw-rw-r--  1 root           105 Jul  6 16:41 /usr/tmp/gated.log
```

The gated Configuration Language

The **gated** configuration language is a highly structured language similar to C in appearance. Comments either begin with a #; or they begin with / * and end with * /. **gated** configuration statements end with a semicolon, and groups of associated statements are enclosed in curly braces. The language structure is familiar to most UNIX system administrators, and the structure makes it easy to see which parts of the configuration are associated with each other. This is important when multiple protocols are configured in the same file.

The configuration language is composed of six types of statements. Two statement types, *directive statements* and *trace statements*, can occur anywhere in the *gated.conf* file and do not directly relate to the configuration of any protocol. These statements provide instructions to the parser and control tracing from within the configuration file. The other four statement types are *definition statements, protocol statements, static statements,* and *control statements*. These statements must appear in the configuration file in the correct order. Definition statements appear first, then protocol statements, then static statements, and finally control statements. Entering a statement out of order causes an error when parsing the file.

The remainder of this appendix provides a description of all commands in the **gated** configuration language, organized by statement type.

Directive Statements

Directive statements provide direction to the **gated** command language parser about "include" files. An include file is an external file whose contents is parsed into the configuration as if it were part of the original *gated.conf* file. Include files can contain references to other include files, and these references can be nested up to ten levels deep.

The two directive statements are:

%include *filename*
> Identifies an include file. The contents of the file is "included" in the *gated.conf* file at the point in the *gated.conf* file where the **%include** directive is encountered. *filename* is any valid UNIX filename. If *filename* is not fully qualified, i.e., does not begin with a /, it is considered to be relative to the directory defined in the **%directory** directive.

%directory *pathname*
> Defines the directory where the include files are stored. When it is used, **gated** looks in the directory identified by *pathname* for any include file that does not have a fully qualified filename.

Unless you have a very complex routing configuration, avoid using include files. In a complex environment, segmenting a large configuration into smaller, more easily understood segments can be helpful, but most **gated** configurations are very small. One of the great advantages of **gated** is that it combines the configuration of several different routing protocols into a single file. If that file is small and easy to read, segmenting the file unnecessarily complicates things.

Trace Statements

Trace statements allow you to control the trace file and its contents from within the *gated.conf* file. The two trace statements are:

tracefile *filename* [**replace**] ;

> Identifies the file that will receive the trace output. It has exactly the same function as the *trace_file* argument on the **gated** command line. A nice feature of this command is that you can choose to replace the existing trace file by specifying the keyword **replace**. If you do not use this keyword, the trace output is appended to the current contents of the file.

traceoptions *traceoption* [*traceoption*] [. . .] ;

> Defines the events that will be traced by **gated**. Most of the trace options available here were explained in the discussion of the **gated** command line. Here each trace option is defined by a keyword name instead of a single letter as it was on the command line. For example, the command-line trace option **a** is specified in a trace options statement with the keyword **all**.

gated provides the flexibility for you to choose where you want to control tracing—on the command line or in the configuration file. By and large, the same trace options can be set on the **gated** command line or in the configuration file. However, there are some additional trace options that can only be set from inside the *gated.conf* file. Table C-1 shows the name used to identify each trace option, the letter used to define the equivalent command-line option, and a short description of the events that are traced when the option is specified. The trace options without a value in the "Option Letter" field can only be set from inside the *gated.conf* file. Refer to the section on the **gated** command line for a description of setting trace options on the command line.

Table C.1: Trace Options

Keyword	Option Letter	Events Traced to the Log
none		turns off all tracing
all	A	all options except nostamp
general		same as internal, external, and route
internal	i	internal errors
external	e	external errors
nostamp	t	turn off timestamps

Table C.1: Trace Options (continued)

Keyword	Option Letter	Events Traced to the Log
mark	m	post an "up" message every ten minutes
task		tasks, signals, packet reception
timer		timer scheduling
lex		lexical objects from *gated.conf*
parse		tokens from *gated.conf*
config		correctly parsed configuration statements
route	r	**gated** routing table updates
kernel	k	kernel routing table updates
bgp	B	BGP packets, modified by "update"
egp	p	EGP packets, modified by "update"
rip	R	RIP packets, modified by "update"
hello	H	Hello packets, modified by "update"
icmp	C	ICMP packets, modified by "update"
snmp	M	SNMP packets, modified by "update"
protocol	P	state transitions; use with "bgp" or "egp"
update	u	packet contents

Definition Statements

Definition statements are general configuration statements that relate to all of **gated** or to more than one protocol. If you use them, definition statements must appear before any other type of configuration statement in *gated.conf.* The four definition statements are:

options *options_list* ;

> Directs **gated** to do special internal processing. The *options_list* can be either or both of the following keywords:

> **noinstall** When **noinstall** is specified, routes are not installed in the kernel. This is the same as the **–n** command line option. I prefer using **–n** because after running with **noinstall** to verify the configuration file, the file must be re-edited to remove **noinstall** before it can be used. If **–n** is used to check out the file, there is no need to re-edit a clean file before using it. However, some people prefer **noinstall** because it ensures that the test file

cannot accidentally be loaded into **gated**. Both work equally well. The one you use is a matter of personal choice.

gendefault A default route is generated when **gated** peers with an EGP or BGP neighbor, if you specify **gendefault**. The gateway in the generated route is the system itself. This default route is not installed in the kernel table; it is only used to advertise this system as a default gateway. Whether or not the system actually advertises the route is controlled by another statement later in the configuration file.

autonomoussystem *as_number* **;**

Defines the AS number used by both EGP and BGP. *as_number* is the official autonomous system number assigned to you by the NIC.

interface *interface_list options_list* **;**

Defines configuration options for the network interfaces. The *interface_list* defines the interfaces affected by the options defined in the *options_list*. The interfaces are identified by interface name (e.g., le0), by IP address, or by the keyword **all** which refers to every interface on the system. Most system administrators prefer to use the IP address to identify an interface. After all, IP addresses are inherently a part of TCP/IP, and it's TCP/IP routing that this file configures. Additionally, remote systems know this interface by its IP address, not its interface name. Finally, there is no guarantee that the interface name will not change in a future operating system release.

The *interface_options* that can be applied to the interfaces are:

metric *metric*

Sets a metric for the interface. The metric is used by RIP or Hello and is similar to the metric set by **ifconfig**. Set the metric here, instead of with **ifconfig**, so that the configuration is documented in one file. For **gated**, the metric set here overrides the metric set by **ifconfig**.

preference *pref*

Sets the preference for this interface. The value *pref* is a number between 0 and 255. **gated** prefers routes through interfaces with low preference numbers. The default preference for all network

passive　　　This keyword prevents **gated** from removing the interface from the routing table, even if **gated** believes the interface is down. By default an interface is removed when **gated** discovers that it is down. **gated** assumes that an interface is down when it stops receiving routing information through that interface. If you have only one network interface, or if you do not reliably receive routing information through that interface, use **passive** to keep the interface up. But if you are running a gateway that advertises that it can route data through this interface, allow the interface to default to an active interface so that you don't advertise the route when it is down.

martians {*martian_list*} **;**

This command defines a list of destination addresses, called the *martian_list*, for which routing information will not be accepted. Sometimes a misconfigured system sends out obviously invalid destination addresses. These invalid addresses, called *martians*, are rejected by the routing software. This command allows you to add to the list of martian addresses.

The entries in the *martian_list* are routing destinations written as IP addresses or as IP addresses with an associated *destination mask*. This structure, an IP address with an associated mask, is used repeatedly in the **gated** command language. When it is used, the destination mask is separated from the IP address by the keyword **mask** and is entered in dotted decimal form. If no mask is specified, the destination address is interpreted literally, only an address that exactly matches the destination is considered a match. If a mask is used, only the bits set to one in the mask are significant when comparing an address to the destination.

Here is a sample of each definition statement:

```
options gendefault ;
autonomoussystem 249 ;
interface 128.66.12.2 passive ;
martians {
     0.0.0.26
} ;
```

The statements in the sample perform the following functions:

- The **options** statement tells the system to generate a default route when it peers with an EGP or BGP neighbor.

- The **autonomoussystem** statement tells **gated** to use AS number 249 for its EGP or BGP packets.

- The **interface** statement tells **gated** not to remove the interface 128.66.12.2 from the routing table, even if **gated** thinks the interface is down.

- The **martians** statement prevents routes to 0.0.0.26 from being included in the table. This assumes that this invalid address is periodically appearing in the routing table.

Naturally these examples are contrived to make use of all the definition statements. It is unlikely that your system will use all of these statements in its configuration.

Protocol Statements

The second group of statements that may be included in the *gated.conf* file are the protocol statements. These protocol-specific statements occur after the definition statements and before the static or control statements. Protocol statements enable or disable protocols and set protocol options. There are protocol statements for SNMP, RIP, Hello, ICMP Redirect, EGP, and BGP. The structure of these statements falls into two categories—one structure for interior protocols and one for exterior protocols. SNMP is the only exception to this. The format of the snmp statement is:

snmp yes | no | on | off ;

> This command controls whether **gated** registers information with the SNMP daemon. SNMP is not a routing protocol and is not started by this command. You must run SNMP software independently. This statement only controls whether **gated** keeps the management software apprised of its status. Reporting is enabled by specifying **yes** or **on** (it doesn't matter which you use) and it is disabled with **no** or **off**.

NOTE

For the sake of brevity, this text explains only the first occurrence of any *gated.conf* parameter if it is used the same in subsequent commands. Only differences between commands are explained. For example, **yes | no | on | off** is not explained again, because it is always used in the same way to enable or disable a protocol.

The format of the protocol statements for all interior protocols is very similar. RIP is the primary example of an interior protocol, so let's start with the rip protocol statement.

The rip Statement

rip yes | no | on | off | quiet | pointopoint | supplier [{
    preference *preference*;
    defaultmetric *metric*;
    interface *interface_list* [**noripin**] [**noripout**];
    ...
    trustedgateways *gateway_list*;
    sourcegateways *gateway_list*;
}];

The rip statement enables or disables RIP. By default RIP is enabled. When enabled on a host, RIP listens quietly to routing updates; when enabled on a gateway, RIP supplies routing updates. You can change the default by using the keywords **quiet** or **supplier**. Regardless of whether the system is a host or a gateway, **quiet** forces RIP to be quiet, and **supplier** forces RIP to supply routing updates.

The argument **pointopoint** is only used in conjunction with the sourcegateways statement. If you specify **pointopoint**, RIP packets are only sent to the gateways listed in the sourcegateways statement. Normally RIP packets are broadcasted to every device on the network.

Several optional statements are associated with the rip statement. These are:

preference *preference*;
    Sets the **gated** preference for routes learned from RIP. The default preference for these routes is 100.

defaultmetric *metric*;
    Defines the metric used when advertising routes via RIP that were learned from other protocols. The default *metric* value is 16, which to RIP indicates an unusable route. This means that by default, routes learned from other protocols are not advertised as valid routes by RIP. This is the same for all protocols statements; the default metric is always the highest possible metric for the protocol. Set a lower value for *metric*, only if you want all routes learned from other protocols advertised at that metric. There are other ways to control the metric for individual routes.

interface *interface_list* [**noripin**] [**noripout**] ;

> Prevents RIP packets from being sent or received on certain network interfaces. The interfaces affected are defined in the *interface_list*. The list can contain interface names, IP addresses, or the keyword **all**. If **noripin** is specified, RIP packets received on the interfaces are ignored. If **noripout** is specified, RIP packets are not sent out from these interfaces. By default, RIP listens for packets on, and sends packets out, every available interface.

trustedgateways *gateway_list* ;

> Defines the list of gateways from which RIP accepts updates. The *gateway_list* is simply a list of host names or IP addresses. By default, all gateways on the shared network are trusted to supply routing information. But if the trustedgateways statement is used, only updates from the gateways in the list are accepted.

sourcegateways *gateway_list* ;

> Defines a list of gateways to which RIP sends packets. By default RIP packets are broadcast to every system on the shared network, but if this statement is used in conjunction with the **pointopoint** argument, RIP packets are sent only to the listed gateways.

The hello Statement

hello yes | **no** | **on** | **off** | **quiet** | **pointopoint** | **supplier** [{
> **preference** *preference* ;
> **defaultmetric** *metric* ;
> **interface** *interface_list* [**nohelloin**] [**nohelloout**] ;
>
> . . .
>
> **trustedgateways** *gateway_list* ;
> **sourcegateways** *gateway_list* ;

}] ;

This statement enables or disables Hello. By default, Hello is disabled. The default metric is 30000 (30 seconds is the highest possible Hello metric) and the default preference is 90. Unless the preference values are altered, routes learned from Hello are preferred over those learned from RIP.

The hello statement has basically the same options as the RIP statement. The only command differences are the keywords **nohelloin** and **nohelloout**, but they perform the same function for Hello as **noripin** and **noripout** do for RIP.

The redirect Statement

redirect yes | **no** | **on** | **off** [{
    preference *preference* ;
    interface *interface_list* [**noicmpin**] ;
    trustedgateways *gateway_list* ;
}] ;

This statement controls whether ICMP redirects are allowed to modify the kernel routing table. It does not prevent a system from sending redirects, only from listening to them. If **no** or **off** is specified, **gated** attempts to remove the effects of ICMP redirects from the kernel routing table whenever the redirects are detected. Remember that ICMP is part of IP; therefore, the redirects are not actually processed by **gated**. If you disable redirects, **gated** must actively remove the redirected routes from the routing table, which causes extra work. By default, ICMP redirects are enabled on hosts and disabled on gateways that run as RIP or Hello suppliers.

The default preference of a route learned from a redirect is 20. The interface statement disables redirects on an interface-by-interface basis. Redirects received via an interface listed in the *interface_list* are ignored. The trustedgateways statement enables redirects on a gateway-by-gateway basis. Only redirects received from a gateway listed in the *gateway_list* are accepted.

The structure of the protocol statements for the exterior protocols, EGP and BGP, varies slightly from those used for the interior protocols. EGP is the most commonly used exterior gateway protocol, so we'll start with its protocol statement.

The egp Statement

egp yes | **no** | **on** | **off** [{
    preference *preference* ;
    defaultmetric *metric* ;
    packetsize *maxpacketsize* ;
    group [**asin** *as_number*]
        [**asout** *as_number*]
        [**maxup** *number*]
        [**preference** *preference*] {
    neighbor *host*
        [**metricout** *metric*]
        [**nogendefault**]

```
            [acceptdefault]
            [propagatedefault]
            [gateway gateway]
            [interface interface]
            [sourcenet network]
            [minhello interval]
            [minpoll interval]
               ;

   . . .
   };
   . . .
}];
```

This statement enables or disables EGP. By default, EGP is disabled. The default metric for announcing routes via EGP is 255, and the default preference for routes learned from EGP is 200.

The **packetsize** argument defines the size of the largest EGP packet that will be sent or accepted. *maxpacketsize* is the size in bytes. Large packets consume more buffer space, but must be used for some networks. For example, Milnet core gateways send very large update packets. For systems attached to Milnet, set **packetsize** to at least 12288.

The egp statement has two clauses (subordinate parts)—the group clause and the neighbor clause. Use the group clause to define parameters for a group of EGP neighbors. Values set in a group clause apply to all neighbor clauses that follow it. There can be multiple group clauses, but each clause only affects the neighbor clauses that immediately follow it. The following parameters are set by the group clause:

asin *as_number*

> Only EGP packets with this autonomous system number are accepted from the listed neighbors. If you do not specify **asin**, the autonomous system number is not checked and all packets are accepted.

asout *as_number*

> Packets sent to the listed neighbors use this autonomous system number. If you do not specify **asout**, the number defined in the autonomoussystem statement is used.

maxup *number*

> Specifies the number of neighbors **gated** should acquire from this group. The default is to acquire all neighbors in the group.

preference *preference*

> Specifies the preference used for routes learned from these neighbors. This can differ from the default EGP preference set in the egp statement, so that **gated** can prefer one group of EGP neighbors over another—even though they all communicate with the system via EGP.

The neighbor clause defines one EGP neighbor. The only part of the clause that is required is the *host* argument which is the host name or IP address of the neighbor. All other parameters are optional. Any of these optional parameters can also be specified in the group clause if you want to apply the parameter to all neighbors. The optional neighbor clause parameters are:

metricout *metric*

> Used for all routes sent to this neighbor. This value overrides the **defaultmetric** value set in the egp statement, but only for this specific neighbor.

nogendefault

> Prevents **gated** from generating a default route when EGP peers with this neighbor, even if **gendefault** is set in the **options** directive statement.

acceptdefault

> Tells **gated** to accept the default route if it is received in an EGP update. Normally if a default route is contained in an EGP update, it is ignored. This parameter was created to allow systems attached to Milnet to accept a default route from the core gateways, because some core gateways announce a default route in lieu of sending out very large EGP update packets.

propagatedefault

> Tells **gated** to include the default route in EGP updates it sends. This allows the system to advertise the default route via EGP. Normally, default routes are not included in EGP updates. Only use this parameter if your system performs some special function. For example, if it acts as if it were a core gateway, or if it uses EGP to send routes to other computers within the same autonomous system.

minhello *interval*

Sets the interval between the transmission of EGP Hello packets.* The default Hello interval is 30 seconds. If the neighbor is very busy, it may not respond to the Hello. If it fails to respond to three Hello packets, the system abandons the attempt to acquire the neighbor. Setting a larger interval, say 3 minutes, gives the neighbor a better chance to respond. The interval can be defined as seconds, minutes:seconds, or hours:minutes:seconds. For example, a 3-minute interval could be specified as 180 (seconds), 3:00 (minutes), or 0:3:00 (no hours and 3 minutes).

minpoll *interval*

Sets the time interval between sending polls to the neighbor. The default is 120 seconds. If three polls are sent without a response, the neighbor is declared "down" and all routes learned from that neighbor are removed from the routing table. This can cause the routing table to be very unstable if a neighbor becomes congested and can't respond to rapid polls. A longer polling interval provides a more stable routing table. Again the interval is defined as seconds, minutes:seconds, or hours:minutes:seconds. A 10 minute polling interval entered in seconds is **minpoll 600**.

interface *interface*

Defines the network interface used to reach this neighbor. Normally the neighbor shares a network with the local system. **gated** uses the shared network, as determined by the neighbor's IP address, to send packets to the neighbor. If the local system and the EGP neighbor don't share a network, use this parameter and the two following parameters (**gateway** and **sourcenet**) to set up a path to the neighbor. These three parameters are normally used only in test configurations. Do not use this parameter if you share a network with the EGP neighbor.

gateway *gateway*

Identifies the next-hop gateway used for routes received from this neighbor. Use this with the **interface** parameter when the neighbor does not share a network with your system.

---

*Don't confuse this with the Hello protocol. Refer to the discussion of Hello and I-H-U packets in Chapter 7.

Because this neighbor does not share a network with you, the gateways specified in this neighbor's EGP updates will not be directly accessible from your system. For example, if the EGP neighbor is on Milnet, all of the gateways specified in the routing updates received from the neighbor will have Milnet (26.0.0.0) addresses. If your system is not on Milnet, placing these Milnet addresses directly into your routing table would be useless because TCP/IP routes must be next-hop routes. The *gateway* value lets you specify a valid next-hop gateway to be used for these routes. This is usually the same gateway that is used to reach the EGP neighbor. Do not use this parameter if you share a network with the EGP neighbor.

sourcenet *network*

This changes the network queried in EGP poll packets. By default this is the shared network. However, if the neighbor does not share a network with your system, the neighbor's network address should be specified here. For example, if the EGP neighbor is on Milnet (26.0.0.0) and your system is not, specify **sourcenet 26.0.0.0**. Do not use this parameter if you share a network with the EGP neighbor.

The bgp Statement

```
bgp yes I no I on I off [ {
      preference preference;
      defaultmetric metric;
      peer host
      [linktype [up I down I horizontal I internal]]
         [metricout metric]
         [asin as_number]
         [asout as_number]
         [nogendefault]
         [gateway gateway]
         [interface interface]
      ;
} ] ;
```

This statement enables or disables BGP. By default, BGP is disabled. The default preference is 150, and the default metric value is 65535. Unlike the RIP metric, the BGP metric does not play a primary role in determining the best route. The BGP metric is simply an arbitrary 16-bit value that can be used as one criterion for choosing a route. However, a BGP metric of all ones (65535) is used to indicate an unreachable destination.

The BGP protocol statement is almost identical to the EGP protocol statement. There are only two differences:

peer *host*

This statement identifies a BGP neighbor, called a "peer." The BGP protocol statement has no group clause. All parameters relating to a peer are specified in the peer statement. These parameters are a subset of the parameters used in the EGP protocol statement and their functions are the same. The only addition is the **linktype** parameter.

linktype [up | down | horizontal | internal]

This clause defines the type of link specified by the protocol when the connection between the local system and this peer is opened. If the peer has the same autonomous system number as the local system, the **linktype** defaults to **internal**. Otherwise it defaults to **horizontal**. These defaults are correct. Do not change them. The concept of up, down, and horizontal link types defined in RFC 1105 was removed from the BGP standard by RFC 1163. It is best to just ignore this parameter.

Static Statements

Static statements define the static routes used by **gated**. A single static statement can specify several routes. The static statements occur after protocol statements and before control statements in the *gated.conf* file. To **gated**, static routes are any routes defined with static statements. However, unlike the routes in a static routing table, these routes can be overridden by routes with better preference values.

The structure of a static statement is:

static {
    destination **gateway** *gateway* [**preference** *preference*] **;**
    destination **interface** *interface* [**preference** *preference*] **;**
} **;**

The static statement with the keyword **gateway** is the one you'll use. A static route is defined as a destination address reached though a gateway. This form of the static statement contains information similar to that provided by **route** commands and */etc/gateways* entries when they define static routes.

Only use the keyword **interface** if you have a single physical network with more than one network address—a rare occurrence. **ifconfig** normally creates only one destination for each interface. This special form of the static statement adds additional destinations to the interface.

The default preference of a static route is 50. **gated** favors static routes more than those learned through EGP (200), BGP (150), RIP (100), or Hello (90); but less than routes learned via ICMP Redirect (20). By default, only routes learned by ICMP redirects cause **gated** to override static routes. If you want other types of routes to override static routes, use the preference argument on the static statement to increase the preference number. Remember that high preference values mean less preferred routes.

The example below shows a static default route (0.0.0.0) through the gateway 128.66.12.1. The preference is set to 125 so that routes learned from RIP are preferred over this static route.

```
static  {
     0.0.0.0 gateway 128.66.12.1 preference 125 ;
   } ;
```

Control Statements

The final statements that can be included in the *gated.conf* file are the two control statements. One specifies which routes are accepted and what sources those routes are accepted from. The other statement defines which routes are advertised based on the source of the routes and the protocol used to advertise them. The two control statements are the *accept statement* and the *propagate statement*.

The accept Statement

The accept statement tells **gated** to accept, as valid, routes received from a specific protocol. There are two formats of the accept statement. The formats vary based on whether the routes are being accepted from an interior or an exterior protocol.

accept proto bgp | **egp as** *as_number*
      [**preference** *preference*] [{
      acceptance_list
}] ;

This accept statement for exterior protocols tells **gated** to accept routing information via BGP or EGP (depending on which is specified) from a specific autonomous system. The protocol that is the source of the routing information is defined by the keyword **proto**, followed by a keyword name for the protocol. For example, if the source of routes is BGP, use the keywords **proto bgp**. As we'll see later, this exact form is also used to specify an interior protocol on the other form of the accept statement.

The autonomous system that is the source of the routes is identified by the autonomous system number provided after the keyword **as**. Note this is *not* the number of your autonomous system; this is the number of the remote autonomous system from which you receive routes. Set the preference for routes learned from the remote AS using the keyword **preference** followed by the numeric preference value. If your system exchanges routing information with more than one other autonomous system, you can have multiple accept statements.

accept proto rip | hello | icmp [
    [**interface** *interface_list* | **gateway** *gateway_list*]
    [**preference** *preference*] {
    acceptance_list
}] ;

This form of the accept statement is for interior protocols. It differs slightly from the statements for BGP and EGP. Again the protocol that is the source of acceptable routes is identified, but with this command the source can be further limited. The optional **interface** and **gateway** arguments limit the effects of the *acceptance_list* to a certain interface or a specific gateway. Define the preference of routes learned from this source with the **preference** argument. The preference set in the accept statement overrides the preference of the protocol defined in the protocol statement. The accept statement defines the preference of the source of the routes which can be a protocol, an autonomous system, an interface, or a gateway.

Regardless of the source, the specific routes that are accepted is controlled by the *acceptance_list*. If no *acceptance_list* is defined, all routes received from the specified source are accepted. If any *acceptance_list* is defined, only those routes specifically contained in the list are accepted. The *acceptance_list* contains two types of entries. These are:

listen *destination* [**preference** *pref*] ;

        Defines an individual route that will be accepted. The route is defined by its *destination*, which is either an IP address, an address with a destination mask, the keyword **default**, or the keyword **all**. If a destination mask is specified, it defines which bits are significant when comparing an address to the destination address.* If the keyword **default** is used, a default route learned from this source is acceptable. If the keyword **all** is used, all routes are acceptable. The optional preference value applies to the individual routes accepted by this listen statement.

nolisten *destination* ;

Directs **gated** to ignore the specified route. The route is defined by its destination exactly as it was in the listen statement, and the same values are valid for destination.

As an example, assume we only want to accept routes from RIP that are for certain subnets and for no others. The following accept statement does this. The **accept proto rip** statement accepts all routes received from RIP, but the **listen** statements modify this so that only those explicitly identified routes are acceptable:

```
accept proto rip {
        listen 128.66.1.0 ;
        listen 128.66.2.0 ;
        listen 128.66.3.0 ;
        listen 128.66.4.0 ;
        listen 128.66.5.0 ;
} ;
```

The propagate Statement

The opposite of receiving routes from other systems is sending routes to them. The accept statement controls which routes received from other systems are used by **gated**, and the propagate statement controls which routes are advertised by **gated** to other systems. Like the accept statement, the syntax of the propagate statement varies slightly for interior and exterior protocols.

propagate proto bgp | egp as *autonomous system*
        [**metric** *metric*] {
        propagation_list
} ;

---

*Refer back to the discussion of the **martians** statement for a description of the destination mask.

propagate proto rip | hello
        [**interface** *interface_list* | **gateway** *gateway_list*]
        [**metric** *metric*] {
        propagation_list
} ;

This statement tells **gated** to advertise routes through the protocol specified after the keyword **proto**. The syntax of the propagate statement is almost identical to the syntax of the accept statement, and the values used for many of the parameters are identical. There are, however, a few differences:

- First, routes are not advertised using ICMP so the propagate statement does not include an **icmp** argument.

- Second, preference is only used by **gated** for evaluating inbound routing information; metric is used to advertise routes. Therefore, the propagate statement has a metric argument but no preference argument. If you use a metric value, it must be valid for the particular protocol used to advertise the routes. If a metric is not specified here, the default metric value from the protocol statement is used.

- Third, the structure of the *propagation_list* is different from the structure of the acceptance list.

The two forms of the *propagation_list* are shown below:

proto bgp | egp as *autonomous system*
        [**metric** *metric*] [{
        announce_list
}] ;

proto rip | hello | direct | static | default
        [**interface** *interface_list* | **gateway** *gateway_list*]
        [**metric** *metric*] [{
        announce_list
}] ;

The *propagation_list* defines which routes are advertised, and the source from which these routes were learned. Here the keyword **proto** precedes the name of the protocol from which the routes were *received*, unlike the keyword **proto** on the first line of the propagate statement that defines the protocol through which routes are *sent*.

In addition to the protocol names we have already discussed (bgp, egp, rip, and hello), there are three new values—**direct**, **static**, and **default**. **direct** means a route through a directly attached network interface. The destination of a direct route is a network to which the system directly connects. The value **static** means the route is defined by a static statement elsewhere in *gated.conf*. The value **default** means the route created by **gated** in response to the **gendefault** option. The generated default is not announced unless **gated** is directed to propagate the default route using this statement.

The **interface** and **gateway** options are used only with **rip** and **hello**. Respectively these options define the specific interface or gateway to be used as the source of the routes. This is identical to their functions in the accept statement.

The final component of the *propagation_list* is the *announce_list*. The *announce_list* is very similar to the *acceptance_list* used by the accept statement. If an *announce_list* is provided, only the routes on the list are advertised. If an *announce_list* is not provided, all routes learned from the source defined in the *propagation_list* are advertised. There are two *announce_list* statements. These are:

announce *destination* [**metric** *metric*]

> Defines a route that will be announced. The route is defined by its destination which can be either an address, an address with a destination mask, or the keyword **all**. If specified, the metric is applied to this route when it is advertised.

noannounce *destination*

> Specifies a route that will not be announced. Remember that if an *announce_list* is used, only the routes specified in the list are announced. To prevent the announcement of a few routes, but to allow the announcement of everything else, end your list of **noannounce** statements with an **announce all** statement.

The propagate statement can be confusing, because the same keywords and value are used twice in the command—first, to indicate the path through which the routes are propagated, and next to indicate the path through which the routes were learned. An example may help.

This propagate statement advertises routes via the RIP protocol through interface 128.66.12.3. All routes learned via RIP on the 128.66.1.5 interface are advertised, except for certain subnet routes (128.66.8.0, 128.66.13.0, and 128.66.15.0).

```
propagate proto rip interface 128.66.12.3
{
        proto rip interface 128.66.1.5
        {
                noannounce 128.66.8.0 ;
                noannounce 128.66.13.0 ;
                noannounce 128.66.15.0 ;
                announce all ;
        } ;
} ;
```

Preference Precedence

Before concluding this discussion of the **gated** configuration statements, a review of preference is in order. Each route has only one preference value associated with it, even though preference can be set in many places in the configuration file. A simple way of thinking about this is that the last preference value set for a route is the value used. (This is not a rule. This is just a way of thinking about preference that can make it more understandable.) The following sample statements from a *gated.conf* file illustrate this:

```
interface 128.66.12.2 preference 10 ;
rip yes preference 90 ;
egp yes ;
accept proto rip gateway 128.66.12.1 preference 75 ;
```

These lines set preference as follows:

- Direct routes through interface 128.66.12.2 have a preference of 10.
- RIP routes have a preference of 90.
- EGP routes, by default, have a preference of 200.
- Routes learned via RIP from gateway 128.66.12.1 have a preference of 75.

What preference value would be used for a route learned from gateway 128.66.12.1 via the RIP protocol through interface 128.66.12.2? It would be 75. The last preference applicable to routes learned via RIP from gateway 128.66.12.1 is defined in the accept statement. The preference applicable to other RIP routes is defined in the rip statement. The preference set on the interface statement only applies to routes through that interface to its directly connected network.

Table C-2 summarizes the preference values set in various configuration commands. The table lists the statements (some of these are clauses within statements) that set preference, and shows the types of routes to which each statement applies. The default preference for each statement is listed, and the table notes if the preference set in one statement overrides the preference set in another statement. The narrower the scope of a statement, the higher precedence its preference value is given, but the smaller the set of routes it affects. For example, the **listen** statement in the *acceptance_list* can only define the preference value for a single route, but no other statement can override that preference for that specific route.

Table C.2: Summary of gated Preference

Statement	Defines Preference of	Default Value
interface	direct routes	0
redirect	routes learned from redirects	20
hello	routes learned from Hello	90
rip	routes learned from RIP	100
bgp	routes learned from BGP	150
egp	routes learned from EGP	200
egp group	routes from a group of neighbors; overrides egp preference	no default
static	static routes	50
accept as	routes from a specific AS; overrides protocol preference	no default
accept interface	routes learned via an interface; overrides protocol preference	no default
accept gateway	routes learned from a gateway; overrides protocol preference	no default
listen	individual routes; overrides all other preference values	no default

This lengthy discussion illustrates the richness of the **gated** command language, its support for multiple protocols, and the fact that it often provides a few ways to do the same thing. **gated** provides a powerful set of configuration commands that the system administrator can use to control the routing environment.

D

named Reference

This appendix provides detailed information about **named** syntax, and the commands and files used to configure it. This is primarily a reference to use in conjunction with the information in Chapter 8. This information is useful to any domain administrator.

The named Command

The server side of DNS is run by the name server daemon, **named**. The syntax of the **named** command is:*

named [**–d** *level*] [**–p** *port*] [[**–b**] *bootfile*]

The three options used on the **named** command line are:

–d *level*   This option logs debugging information in the file
/usr/tmp/named.run. The argument *level* is a number from 1 to 9. A higher *level* number increases the detail of the information logged, but even when *level* is set to 1, the *named.run* file grows very rapidly. Whenever you use debugging, keep an eye on the size of the *named.run* file, and use SIGUSR2 to close and remove the file if it gets too large. Signal handling is covered in the next section.

It is not necessary to turn on debugging with the **–d** option to receive error messages from **named**. **named**

---

*Sun systems use in.named instead of named.

                displays error messages on the console and stores them in */usr/adm/messages*, even if debugging is not specified. The **–d** option provides *additional* debugging information.

–p *port*   This option defines the UDP/TCP port used by **named**. If this option is not specified, the standard port (53) is used. Since port 53 is a well-known port, changing the port number makes the name server inaccessible to standard software packages.

–b *bootfile*   This option specifies the file **named** uses as its configuration file. By default the configuration file is */etc/named.boot*, but the **–b** option allows the administrator to choose another configuration file. Note that the **–b** is optional. As long as the filename used for *bootfile* doesn't start with a dash, the **–b** flag is not required. Any filename written on the **named** command line is assumed to be the boot file.

Signal Processing

named handles the following signals:

SIGHUP   The SIGHUP signal causes **named** to re-read the *named.boot* file and reload the name server database. **named** then continues to run with the new configuration. This signal is particularly useful for forcing secondary servers to reload a database from the primary server. Normally the databases are downloaded from the primary server on a periodic basis. Using SIGHUP causes the reload to occur immediately.

SIGINT   The SIGINT signal causes **named** to dump its cache to */usr/tmp/named_dump.db*. The dump file contains all of the domain information that the local name server knows. The file begins with the root servers, and marks off every domain under the root that the local server knows anything about. If you examine this file, you'll see that it shows a complete picture of the information the server has learned.

SIGUSR1   The SIGUSR1 signal turns on debugging, and each subsequent SIGUSR1 signal increases the level of debugging. Debugging information is written to */usr/tmp/named.run* just as it is when the **–d** option is used on the **named** command line. Debugging does not have to be enabled with the **–d** option for the SIGUSR1 signal to work. SIGUSR1 allows debugging to be turned on when a problem is suspected, without stopping **named** and restarting it with the **–d** option.

SIGUSR2   The SIGUSR2 signal turns off debugging and closes */usr/tmp/named.run*. After issuing SIGUSR2, you can examine *named.run* or remove it if it is getting too large.

named.boot Configuration Commands

The */etc/named.boot* file defines the name server configuration and tells **named** where to obtain the name server database information. *named.boot* contains the following types of records:

directory *directory-path*
> Defines a default directory used for all subsequent file references anywhere in the **named** configuration. If **named** is forced to dump memory, the memory dump is stored in this directory.

primary *domain-name file-name*
> Declares the local name server as the primary master server for the domain specified by *domain-name*. As a primary server, the system loads the name server data base from the local disk file specified by name in the *file-name* field.

secondary *domain-name server-address-list file-name*
> Makes the local server a secondary master server for the domain identified by *domain-name*. The *server-address-list* contains the IP address of at least one other master server for this domain. Multiple addresses can be provided in the list, but at least the primary server's address should be provided. The local server will try each server in the list until it successfully loads the name server database. The local server transfers the entire domain database and stores all of the data it receives in a local file identified by *file-name*. After completing the transfer, the local server answers all queries for information about the domain with complete authority.

cache . *file-name*
> The cache command points to the file used to initialize the name server cache. This command starts with the keyword **cache**, followed by the name of the root domain (.), and ends with the name of the file that initializes the cache. This file can

have any name you wish, but it is usually called */etc/named.ca.* At a minimum, the */etc/named.ca* file contains the names and addresses of the root servers.

The cache command is included in almost every *named.boot* file. **named** will not develop a local cache of name server answers, and will function less efficiently, if the cache statement is not included in the configuration.

forwarders *server-address server-address* ...

The forwarders command provides **named** with a list of servers to try if it can't resolve a query from its own cache. In the syntax shown above, *server-address* is the IP address of a server on your network that can perform a recursive name server query for the local host. (A recursive query* means that the remote server pursues the answer to the query, even if it does not have the answer itself, and returns the answer to the originator.) The servers listed on the forwarders command line (the servers are also called "forwarders") are tried in order, until one responds to the query. The listed servers develop an extensive cache that benefits every host that uses them. Because of this, their use is often recommended. If you plan to use forwarders, your network administrator should define the list of forwarders for your network. The forwarders only develop a rich cache if they are used by several hosts.

slave   The slave command forces the local server to use only the servers listed on the forwarders command line. The slave command can only be used if a forwarders command is also present in the *named.boot* file. A server that has a slave command in its *named.boot* file is called a *slave server.* A slave server does not attempt to contact the authoritative servers for a domain, even if the forwarding servers do not respond to its query. Regardless of the circumstances, a slave server only queries the forwarders. The slave command is used when limited network access makes the the forwarders the only servers that can be reached by the local host. The slave command is not used on systems that have full Internet access because it limits the flexibility of those systems.

---

*Chapter 3 discusses recursive and non-recursive name server queries.

There are two *named.boot* commands that are no longer widely supported. You'll occasionally encounter descriptions of them in material written about name service, and for that reason they're discussed here. But don't use them in your configurations. They are:

domain *name*

> This command functions in exactly the same way as the domain command used in the *resolv.conf* file. This command is obsolete and will not be available in future releases of BIND. You don't need this command because the default domain name is easily defined by the **hostname** command or in *resolv.conf.*

sortlist *network network* . . .

> This is an obsolete command that causes **named** to prefer addresses from the listed networks over addresses from any other networks. Do not include this command in your *named.boot* file because it will not be supported in future releases of BIND.

Zone File Records

Two types of entries are used to construct a zone file: *control entries* that simplify constructing the file, and *standard resource records* that define the domain data contained in the zone file. While there are several types of standard resource records, there are only two control statements. These are:

$INCLUDE *filename*

> Identifies a file that contains data to be included in the zone file. The data in the included file must be valid control entries or standard resource records. $INCLUDE allows a large zone file to be divided into smaller, more manageable units.

> The *filename* specified on the command line is relative to the directory named on the directory statement in the *named.boot* file. For example: if the *named.boot* file for *almond* contains a **directory /etc** statement, and a zone file on *almond* contains an **$INCLUDE sales.hosts** statement, then the file */etc/sales.hosts* would be included in that zone file. If you don't want the filename to be relative to that directory, specify a fully qualified name, such as */usr/dns/sales.hosts*.

$ORIGIN *domainname*

> Changes the default domain name used by subsequent records in the zone file. Use this command to put more than one domain in a zone file. For example, a **$ORIGIN sales** statement

in the *nuts.com* zone file sets the domain name to *sales.nuts.com.* All subsequent resource records would be relative to this new domain.

The **named** software uses $ORIGIN statements to organize its own information. Dumping the **named** database, with the SIG-INT signal, produces a single file containing all the information that the server knows. This file, *named_dump.db*, contains many $ORIGIN entries used to place all of the domains that **named** knows about into a single file.

These two control entries are helpful for organizing and controlling the data in a zone file, but all of the actual database information comes from standard resource records. All of the files pointed to by *named.boot* contribute to the DNS database, so all of these files are constructed from standard resource records.

Standard Resource Records

The format of standard resource records, sometimes called RRs, is defined in RFC 1033, the *Domain Administrators Operations Guide.* The format is:

[*name*] [*ttl*] *class type data*

The individual fields in the standard resource record are:

name   This is the name of the object affected by this resource record. The named object can be as specific as an individual host, or as general as an entire domain. The string entered for *name* is relative to the current domain unless a fully qualified domain name is used.* Certain *name* values have special meaning. These are:

        A blank name field denotes the current named object. The current name stays in force until a new name value is encountered in the name field. This permits multiple RRs to be applied to a single object without having to repeat the object's name for each record.

  ..   Two dots in the name field refer to the root domain. However, a single dot (the actual name of the root)

---

*The FQDN must be specified all the way to the root; i.e., it must end with a dot.

also refers to the root domain, and is more commonly used.

@   A single at-sign (@) in the name field refers to the
current origin. The origin is a domain name derived
by the system from the current domain name or
explicitly set by the system administrator using the
$ORIGIN command.

*   An asterisk in the name field is a wildcard character.
It stands for a name composed of any string. It can
be combined with a domain name, or used alone.
Used alone, an asterisk in the named field means
that the resource record applies to objects with
names composed of any string of characters plus
the name of the current domain. Used with a
domain name, the asterisk is relative to that domain.
For example, *.*bitnet.* in the name field means any
string plus the string *.bitnet.*.

ttl   Time-to-live defines the length of time in seconds that the information in this resource record should be kept in the cache. *ttl* is
specified as a numeric value up to eight characters in length. If
no value is set for *ttl*, it defaults to the value defined for the
entire zone file in the *minimum* field of the SOA record.

class   This field defines the address class of the resource record. The
Internet address class is IN. All resource records used by Internet DNS have IN in this field, but it is possible for a zone file to
hold non-Internet information. For example, information used
by the Hessiod server, a name server developed at MIT, is identified by HS in the class field, and chaosnet information is identified by a CH in the class field. All resource records used in this
book have an address class of IN.

type   This field indicates the type of data this record provides. For
example, the A type RR provides the address of the host identified in the name field. All of the standard resource record types
are discussed in this appendix.

data   This field contains the information specific to the resource
record. The format and content of the data field varies according to the resource record type. The data field is the meat of the
RR. For example, in an A record, the data field contains the IP
address.

In addition to the special characters that have meaning in the name field, zone file records use these other special characters:

;   The semicolon is the comment character. Use the semicolon to indicate that the remaining data on the line is a comment.

( )   Parentheses are the continuation characters. Use parentheses to continue data beyond a single line. After an opening parenthesis, all data on subsequent lines is considered part of the current line until a closing parenthesis.

\x   The backslash is an escape character. A non-numeric character following a backslash (\) is taken literally and any special meaning that the character may ordinarily have is ignored. For example, \; means a semicolon—not a comment.

\ddd   The backslash can also be followed by three decimal numbers. When the escape character is used in this manner the decimal numbers are interpreted as an absolute byte value. For example, \255 means the byte value 11111111.

The same general resource record format is used for each of the resource records in a zone file. Each resource record is described below.

Start of Authority Record

The Start of Authority (SOA) record marks the beginning of a zone, and is usually the first record in a zone file. All of the records that follow are part of the zone declared by the SOA. Each zone has only one SOA record; the next SOA record encountered marks the beginning of another zone. Because a zone file is normally associated with a single zone, it normally contains only one SOA record.

The format of the SOA record is:

[*zone*] [*ttl*] **IN SOA** *origin contact* **(**
    serial
     refresh
     retry
     expire
     minimum
)

The components of the SOA record are:

zone   This is the name of the zone. Usually the SOA name field contains an at-sign (@). When used in an SOA record, the at-sign refers back to the domain name declared in the *named.boot* primary statement that points to this zone file.

ttl   Time-to-live is left blank on the SOA record.

IN   The address class is IN for all Internet RRs.

SOA   SOA is the resource record type. All the information that follows this is part of the data field and is specific to the SOA record.

origin   This is the host name of the primary master server for this domain. It is normally written as a fully qualified domain name. For example, *almond* is the master server for *nuts.com*, so this field contains *almond.nuts.com.* in the SOA record for *nuts.com.*

contact   The e-mail address of the person responsible for this domain is entered in this field. The address is modified slightly. The at-sign (@) that usually appears in an Internet e-mail address is replaced by a dot. Therefore, if *david@almond.nuts.com* is the mailing address of the administrator of the *nuts.com* domain, the *nuts.com* SOA record contains *david.almond.nuts.com.* in the contact field.

serial   This is the version number of the zone file. It is an eight-digit numeric field usually entered as a simple number, e.g., 117. However, the composition of the number is up to the administrator. Some choose a format that shows the date the zone was updated, e.g., 92031100. Others enter the serial number as two dot-separated numbers, e.g., 1.17.* Regardless of the format, the important thing is that the serial number must increase every time the data in the zone file is modified.

The serial field is extremely important. It is used by the secondary master servers to determine if the zone file has been updated. To make this determination, a secondary server requests the SOA record from the primary server and compares the serial number of the data in its cache to the serial number received from the primary server. If the serial number has increased, the secondary server requests a full zone transfer. Otherwise it assumes that it has the most current zone data. You must change the serial number each time you update the

---

****named** converts this form to a straight numeric form. 1.17 becomes 100017; 100.17 becomes 10000017. These results may not be what you expect.

zone data. If you don't, the new data will not be disseminated to the secondary servers.

refresh   This specifies the length of time that the secondary server should wait before checking with the primary server to see if the zone has been updated. Every *refresh* seconds the secondary server checks the SOA serial number to see if the zone file needs to be reloaded. Secondary servers check the serial numbers of their zones whenever they restart or receive a SIGHUP signal. But it is important to keep the secondary server's database current with the primary server, so **named** does not rely on these unpredictable events. The *refresh* interval provides a predictable cycle for reloading the zone that is controlled by the domain administrator.

The value used in *refresh* is a number, up to eight digits long, that is the maximum number of seconds that the primary and secondary servers' databases can be out of synch. A low *refresh* value keeps the data on the servers closely synchronized, but a very low *refresh* value is not usually required. A value set lower than needed places an unnecessary burden on the network and the secondary servers. The value used in *refresh* should reflect the reality of how often your domain database is updated. Most sites' domain databases are very stable. Systems are added periodically, but not generally on an hourly basis. When you are adding a new system, you can assign the host name and address of that system before the system is operational. You can then install this information in the name server database before it is actually needed, ensuring that it is disseminated to the secondary servers long before it has to be used. If extensive changes are planned, the *refresh* time can be temporarily reduced while the changes are underway. Therefore, you can normally set *refresh* time high, reducing load on the network and servers. Once (86400 seconds) or twice (43200 seconds) a day for *refresh* is adequate for most sites.

The process of retrieving the SOA record, evaluating the serial number and, if necessary, downloading the zone file is called a *zone refresh*. Thus the name *refresh* is used for this value.

retry   This defines how long secondary servers should wait before trying again if the primary server fails to respond to a request for a zone refresh. *Retry* is specified in seconds and can be up to eight digits long.

You should not set the *retry* value too low. If a primary server fails to respond, the server or the network could be down. Quickly retrying a down system gains nothing and costs network resources. A secondary server that backs up a large number of zones can have problems when *retry* values are short. If the secondary server cannot reach the primary servers for several of its zones, it can become stuck in a retry loop.* Avoid problems; use an hour (3600) or a half hour (1800) for the *retry* value.

expire   This defines how long the zone's data should be retained by the secondary servers without receiving a zone refresh. The value is specified in seconds and is up to eight digits long. If after *expire* seconds the secondary server has been unable to refresh this zone, it should discard all of the data.

expire is normally a very large value. 3600000 seconds (about 42 days) is commonly used. This says that if there has been no answer from the primary server to refresh requests repeated every *retry* seconds for the last 42 days, discard the data. Forty-two days is a good value.

minimum This is the value used as the default *ttl* in all resource records where an explicit *ttl* value is not provided. This is a number, up to eight digits long, that specifies how many seconds resource records from this zone should be held in a remote host's cache.

Make this a very large value. Most of the records in a zone remain unchanged for long periods of time. Hosts may be added to a zone, but host names (if they are well chosen) and addresses are very rarely changed. Forcing remote servers to query again for data that has not changed, just because it had a short *ttl*, is a waste of resources. If you plan to change a record, put a short *ttl* on that record; don't set the entire zone to a short *ttl* by setting a low *minimum*. Use a short *minimum* only if the entire database is being replaced. Use at least a week (604800), and a month (2419200) is even better. The *expire* argument has already told the secondary servers to keep the data for 42 days before deleting it. Why not tell the remote hosts to keep it a similar length of time?

---

*The server may alternate between periods when it fails to respond and when it resolves queries, or it may display the error "too many open files."

A sample SOA record for the *nuts.com* domain is:

```
@    IN  SOA  almond.nuts.com. david.almond.nuts.com. (
             92031101                ; serial
             43200                   ; refresh twice a day
             3600                    ; retry every hour
             3600000                 ; expire after 1000 hours
             2419200                 ; default ttl is one month
             )
```

Notice the serial number in this SOA. The serial number is in the format *yymmddvv*—where *yy* is the year, *mm* is the month, *dd* is the day, and *vv* is the version written that day. This type of serial number allows the administrator to track what day the zone was updated. Adding the version number allows for multiple updates in a single day. This zone file was created March 11, 1992, and it is the first update that day.

This SOA record also says that *almond* is the primary server for this zone and that the person responsible for this zone can be reached at the e-mail address *david@almond.nuts.com*. The SOA tells the secondary servers to check the zone for changes twice a day and to retry every hour if they don't get an answer. If they retry a thousand times and never get an answer, they should discard the data for this zone. Finally, if an RR in this zone does not have an explicit *ttl*, it will default to one month.

Name Server Record

Name server (NS) resource records identify the authoritative servers for a zone. These records are the pointers that link the domain hierarchy together. NS records in the top-level domains point to the servers for the second level domains, which in turn contain NS records that point to the servers for their subdomains. Name server records pointing to the servers for subordinate domains are required for these domains to be accessible. Without NS records, the servers for a domain would be unknown.

The format of the NS RR is:

[*domain*] [*ttl*] **IN NS** *server*

domain   The name of the domain for which the host specified in the *server* field is an authoritative name server.

ttl   Time-to-live is usually blank.

IN   The address class is IN.

NS   The Name Server resource record type is NS.

server   The host name of a computer that provides authoritative name service for this domain.

Usually domains have at least one server that is located outside of the local domain. The server name cannot be specified relative to the local domain; it must be specified as a fully qualified domain name. To be consistent, many administrators use fully qualified names for all servers, even though it is not necessary for servers within the local domain.

Address Record

The majority of the resource records in a *named.hosts* zone file* are address records. Address records are used to convert host names to IP addresses, which is the most common use of the DNS database.

The address RR contains the following:

[*host*] [*ttl*] **IN A** *address*

host	The name of the host whose address is provided in the data field of this record. Most often the host name is written relative to the current domain.
ttl	Time-to-live is usually blank.
IN	The address class is IN.
A	The Address resource record type is A.
address	The IP address of the host is written here in dotted decimal form, e.g., 128.66.12.2.

A *glue record* is a special type of address record. Most address records refer to hosts within the zone, but sometimes an address record needs to refer to a host in another zone. This is done to provide the address of a name server for a subordinate domain. Recall that the NS record for a subdomain server identifies the server by name. An address is needed to communicate with that server, so an A record must also be provided. The address record, combined with the name server record, links the domains together—thus the term glue record.

Mail Exchanger Record

The mail exchanger (MX) record redirects mail to a mail server. It can redirect mail for an individual computer or an entire domain. MX records are extremely useful for domains that contain some systems that don't run mail software. Mail addressed to those systems can be redirected to

---

*Chapter 8 describes the various **named** configuration files.

computers that do run mail software. MX records are also used to simplify mail addressing by redirecting mail to servers that understand the simplified addresses.

The format of the MX RR is:

[*name*] [*ttl*] **IN MX** *preference host*

name	The name of a host or domain to which the mail is addressed. Think of this as the value that occurs after the @ in a mailing address. Mail addressed to this name is sent to the mail server specified by the MX record's host field.
ttl	Time-to-live is usually blank.
IN	The address class is IN.
MX	The Mail Exchanger resource record type is MX.
preference	A host or domain may have more than one MX record associated with it. The *preference* field specifies the order in which the mail servers are tried. Servers with low *preference* numbers are tried first, so the most preferred server has a *preference* of 0. Preference values are usually assigned in increments of 5 or 10, so that new servers can be inserted between existing servers without editing the old MX records.
host	The name of the mail server to which mail is delivered when it is addressed to the host or domain identified in the name field.

Here is how MX records work. If a remote system understands how to use MX records and has mail to send to a host, it requests the host's MX records. DNS returns all of the MX records for the specified host. The remote server chooses the MX with the lowest preference value and attempts to deliver the mail to that server. If it cannot connect to that server, it will try each of the remaining servers in preference order until it can deliver the mail. If no MX records are returned by DNS, the remote server delivers the mail directly to the host to which the mail is addressed. MX records only define how to redirect mail. The remote system and the mail server perform all of the processing that actually delivers the mail.

Because the remote system will first try to use an MX record, many domain administrators include MX records for every host in the zone. Many of these MX records point right back to the host to which the mail is addressed, e.g., an MX for *almond* with a host field of *almond.nuts.com*.

These records are used to reduce the processing load of the remote computer. A nice gesture!

An important use for MX records is to allow mail to non-Internet sites to be delivered using Internet-style addressing. MX records do this by redirecting the mail to computers that know how to deliver the mail to non-Internet networks. For example, sites using **uucp** can register an Internet domain name with UUNET. UUNET uses MX records to redirect Internet mail addressed to these non-connected sites to *uunet.uu.net*, which delivers the mail to its final destination via **uucp**.

Here are some MX examples. All of these examples are for the imaginary domain *nuts.com*. In the first example, mail addressed to *hazel.nuts.com* is redirected to *almond.nuts.com* with this MX record:

```
hazel       IN    MX    10 almond
```

The second example is an MX record used to simplify mail addressing. People can send mail to any user in this domain without knowing the specific computer that the user reads his mail on. Mail addressed to *user@nuts.com* is redirected by this MX record to *almond*, which is a mail server that knows how to deliver mail to every individual user in the domain.

```
nuts.com.  IN    MX    10 almond.nuts.com.
```

The last example is an MX record that redirects mail addressed to any *host* within the domain to a central mail server. Mail addressed to any host, *hazel.nuts.com, peanut.nuts.com,* or *anything.nuts.com,* is redirected to *almond.* This is the most common use of the wildcard character (*).

```
*.nuts.com.  IN    MX    10 almond.nuts.com.
```

A couple of things to note about the examples. The *preference* is 10 so that a mail server with a lower preference number can be added to the zone without changing the existing MX record. Also notice that the host names in the first example are specified relative to the *nuts.com* domain, but the other names are not relative because they end in a dot. All of these names *could* have been entered as relative names, because they all are hosts in the *nuts.com* domain. Fully qualified names were only used to vary the examples.

Canonical Name Record

The Canonical Name (CNAME) resource record defines an alias for the official name of a host. The CNAME record provides a facility similar to nicknames in the host table. The facility provides alternate host names for the convenience of users, and generic host names used by applications (such as *loghost* used by **syslogd**).

The CNAME record is frequently used to ease the transition from an old host name to a new host name. While it is best to avoid host name changes by carefully choosing host names in the first place, not all changes can be avoided. When you do make a name change, it can take a long time before it becomes completely effective, particularly if the host name is embedded in a mailing list run at a remote site. To reduce problems for the remote site, use a CNAME record until they can make the change.

The format of the CNAME record is:

nickname [*ttl*] **IN CNAME** *host*

nickname	This host name is an alias for the official host name defined in the *host* field. The *nickname* can be any valid host name.
ttl	Time-to-live is usually blank.
IN	The address class is IN.
CNAME	The Canonical Name resource record type is CNAME.
host	The canonical name of the host is provided here. This host name must be the official host name; it cannot be an alias.

One important thing to remember about the CNAME record is that all other resource records must be associated with the official host name, and not with the nickname. This means that the CNAME record should not be placed between a host and the list of RRs associated with that host. The example below shows a correctly placed CNAME record:

```
peanut    IN    A        128.66.12.2
          IN    MX       5 peanut.nuts.com.
          IN    HINFO    SUN-3/60 "SUN OS 4.0"
          IN    WKS      129.6.16.2 TCP ftp telnet smtp domain
          IN    WKS      128.66.12.2 UDP domain
goober    IN    CNAME    peanut.nuts.com.
```

In this example the host name *peanut* stays in force for the MX, HINFO, and WKS records because they all have blank name fields. The CNAME record changes the name field value to *goober*, which is a nickname for *peanut*. Any RRs with blank name fields following this CNAME record would associate themselves with the nickname *goober*, which is illegal. An improper CNAME placement is shown below:

```
peanut    IN    A       128.66.12.2
goober    IN    CNAME   peanut.nuts.com.
          IN    MX      5 peanut.nuts.com.
          IN    HINFO   SUN-3/60 "SUN OS 4.0"
          IN    WKS     128.66.12.2 TCP ftp telnet smtp domain
          IN    WKS     128.66.12.2 UDP domain
```

This improperly placed CNAME record causes **named** to display the error message "goober.nuts.com has CNAME and other data (illegal)." Check */usr/adm/messages* for **named** error messages to ensure that you have not misplaced any CNAME records.

Domain Name Pointer Record

The Domain Name Pointer (PTR) resource records are used to convert numeric IP addresses to host names. This is the opposite of what is done by the address record that converts host names to addresses. PTR records are used to construct the *in-addr.arpa* reverse domain files.

Many administrators ignore the reverse domains, because things appear to run fine without them. Don't ignore them. Keep these zones up to date. Several programs use the reverse domains to map IP addresses to host names when preparing status displays. A good example is the **netstat** command. Some service providers, the anonymous **ftp** service on *uunet.uu.net* is the best example, use the reverse domains to track who is using their service. If they cannot map your IP address back to a host name, they reject your connection.

The format of the PTR record is:

name [*ttl*] **IN PTR** *host*

name   The *name* specified here is actually a number. The number is defined relative to the current *in-addr.arpa* domain. Names in an *in-addr.arpa* domain are IP addresses specified in reverse order. If the current domain is *66.128.in-addr.arpa*, then the name field for *peanut* (128.66.12.2) is 2.12. These digits (2.12) are added to the current domain (*66.128.in-addr.arpa*) to make the name *2.12.66.128.in-addr.arpa*. Chapter 4 discusses the unique structure of *in-addr.arpa* domain names.

ttl   Time-to-live is usually blank.

IN   The address class is IN.

PTR   The Domain Name Pointer resource record type is PTR.

host   This is the fully qualified domain name of the computer whose address is specified in the name field. The host must be specified as a fully qualified name because the name cannot be relative to the current *in-addr.arpa* domain.

There are many examples of PTR records in the sample *named.rev* file shown in Chapter 8.

Host Information Record

The Host Information (HINFO) resource record provides a short description of the hardware and operating system used by a specific host. The hardware and software are described using standard terminology defined in the *Assigned Numbers* RFC in the sections on *Machine Names* (hardware) and *System Names* (software). There are a large number of hardware and software designators listed in the RFC. Most name use the same general format. Names with embedded blanks must be enclosed in quotes, so some names have a dash (-) where you might expect a blank. A machine name is usually the manufacturer's name in uppercase letters separated from the model number by a dash; e.g., IBM-PC/AT or SUN-3/60. The system name is usually the manufacturer's operating system name written in uppercase letters; e.g., DOS or "SUN OS 4.0." Naturally the rapid changes in the computer market constantly make the data in the *Assigned Numbers* RFC out of date. Because of this, many administrators make up their own values for machine names and system names.

The format of the HINFO record is:

[*host*] [*ttl*] **IN HINFO** *hardware software*

host   The host name of the computer whose hardware and software is described in the data section of this resource record.

ttl   Time-to-live is usually blank.

IN   The address class is IN.

HINFO   HINFO is the resource record type. All of the information that follows is part of the HINFO data field.

hardware   This field identifies the hardware used by this host. It contains the machine name defined in the *Assigned Numbers* RFC. This field must be enclosed in quotes if it contains any blanks. A single blank space separates the hardware field from the software field that follows it.

software   This field identifies the operating system software this host runs. It contains the system name defined for this operating system in the *Assigned Numbers* RFC. Use quotes if the system name contains any blanks.

No widely used application makes use of the HINFO record; it just provides information. Some security-conscious sites discourage its use. They fear that this additional information helps intruders narrow their attacks to the specific hardware and operating system that they wish to crack.

Well Known Services Record

The Well Known Services (WKS) resource record names the network services supported by the specified host. The official protocol names and services names used on the WKS record are defined in the *Assigned Numbers* RFC. The simplest way to tell which well-known services are run on your system is to **cat** the */etc/services* file. If a service is not in that file, it should not be advertised on the WKS record. Each host can have no more than two WKS records; one record for TCP and one for UDP. Because several services are usually listed on the WKS record, each record may extend through multiple lines.

The format of the WKS record is:

[*host*] [*ttl*] **IN WKS** *address protocol services*

host   The host name of the computer that provides the advertised services.

ttl   Time-to-live is usually blank.

IN   The address class is IN.

WKS   The resource record type is WKS. All of the information that follows is variable information for the WKS record.

address   The IP address of the host written in dotted decimal format, e.g., 128.66.12.2.

protocol   The transport level protocol through which the service communicates—either TCP or UDP.

services   The list of services provided by this host. As few or as many services as you choose may be advertised, but the names used to advertise the services must be the names found in the */etc/services* file. Items in the list of services are separated by spaces. Parentheses are used to continue the list beyond a single line.

There are no widely used applications that make use of this record. It is only used to provide general information about the system. Again security-conscious sites may not wish to advertise all of their services. Some protocols, such as **tftp** and **finger**, are prime targets for intruders.

Experimental Resource Record

There are a few experimental resource records defined in the BIND documentation that are not defined in RFC 1033. These RRs have been in experimental status for several years and have never come into wide use. If included in your zone files, they will probably not be accessed by any remote sites. They are mentioned here for documentation purposes only.

All of the experimental records relate to mail delivery. Unlike the MX record, which centralizes special mail processing by redirecting mail to central servers, the experimental resource records attempt to distribute special mail processing by providing mail delivery instructions directly to the remote system. These RRs rely on the remote system to process the information provided by the records and deliver the mail according to the instructions they provide. Mail systems that can do this are not widely available.

There are four experimental records: the Mailbox (MB) record, the Mail Rename (MR) record, the Mailbox Information (MINFO) record, and the Mail Group (MG) record. Each experimental record is described below.

user [*ttl*] **IN MB** *host*

> The MB record provides the information needed to deliver mail addressed to *user@domain*. Each user in the domain has an MB record that points to the user's mail delivery host. When the remote system receives the MB record, it redirects mail addressed to *user@domain* to *user@host*. In the MX scheme, mail addressed to *user@domain* is redirected to the mail server for *domain*, and that server makes the delivery to the user. In this scheme, the remote system delivers the mail directly to the user based on the information from the MB record.

alias [*ttl*] **IN MR** *user*

> The MR record is used to deliver mail addressed to an alias user name to the actual user name. A corresponding MB record must accompany the MR record. The *user* field in the MR must match the *user* field in the MB record.
>
> Here is how it works. The remote system has mail addressed to *alias@domain*. It receives the MR and MB records and redirects the mail to the *user* from the MR record and the *host* from the MB record, so *alias@domain* becomes *user@host*.

name [*ttl*] **IN MINFO** *requests maintainer*

> The MINFO record defines the control information of a mailing list. The name of the mailing list is defined in the *name* field. Requests for additions and deletions from the mailing list are sent to the mailbox specified in the *requests* field, and problems are reported directly to the mailing address specified in the *maintainer* field. The MINFO record is associated with a list of MG resource records that define all of the individuals on the mailing list.

[*name*] [*ttl*] **IN MG** *member*

> The MG record defines the members of a mailing list. The name field contains the name of a mailing list, but it is usually blank because the MG records are associated with an MINFO record that defines the mailing list name. The *member* field is the full mailing address of a member of this mailing list. The mailing address is written with a dot in place of the at-sign. So if the mailing address *david@almond.nuts.com* is written in the member field of an MG record, it is` written as *david.almond.nuts.com*.
>
> The MINFO and MG records are used in the following way. A system has mail addressed to *name@domain* where *name* is the name of a mailing list defined by an MINFO record. The system receives the MINFO record and a group of MG records. It then sends a copy of the mail to the mailing address on each of the MG records.

All of these experimental resource records rely on capabilities that don't exist on many systems. If you decide to use these records, plan to use them only on your own network. Don't expect remote sites to be able to make use of them.

E

Sample sendmail.cf

This appendix contains the *sendmail.cf* file described in Chapter 10. This file was created from the *tcpproto.cf* file that comes with the **sendmail** 5.65 software release. The detailed modifications of the file are explained in Chapter 10, and the file listed in this appendix is heavily commented to make those modifications more understandable. The comments from the original *tcpproto.cf* file are boxed in pound signs (#). The comments we have added are boxed in plus signs (+).

This configuration was written explicitly for this book. It was modified for my desktop system following the modification scenario described in Chapter 10. I have used this configuration file on my desktop system a few times, and it works. But it should only be used as an educational tool. Use the **sendmail** configuration provided by your computer vendor to create your operational **sendmail** environment.

This configuration file makes the following assumptions based on the actual configuration of my system:

• This is the configuration of a standalone Sun workstation attached to a local Ethernet. The mailer paths and the paths for various files in the *Options* section might not be correct for other systems.

• The local Ethernet provides this host with direct access to the Internet.

• This host does not connect directly to a UUCP network.

• The host is named *cwh.cam.nist.gov*, which is a host in the *cam.nist.gov* domain.

The sendmail Configuration File

```
###########################################################
###########################################################
#####
#####            SENDMAIL CONFIGURATION FILE
#####
###########################################################
###########################################################
#++++++++++++++++++++++++++++++++++++++++++++++++++++++
#Like most sendmail configuration files, the first few sections of the
#file contain the data that is most likely to require custom
#configuration.  In this file, the sections are titled "Local
#information," "General Macros," "Classes," and "Version Number."
#++++++++++++++++++++++++++++++++++++++++++++++++++++++


##################
#  Local information  #
##################
#++++++++++++++++++++++++++++++++++++++++++++++++++++++
#The "w" macro defines the system's host name.  This value is defined
#internally by sendmail and does not usually require modification.  If
#your host is known by more than one host name, the multiple host names
#can be defined here by creating a class "w" that contains all of the
#names for your host.
#++++++++++++++++++++++++++++++++++++++++++++++++++++++
# Local host's internet aliases
#CwYOUR HOST'S NAME AND ALIASES


####################
#  General Macros  #
####################
#++++++++++++++++++++++++++++++++++++++++++++++++++++++
#   The "D" macro contains the name of the local domain.
#++++++++++++++++++++++++++++++++++++++++++++++++++++++
# local domain name
DDcam.nist.gov


#++++++++++++++++++++++++++++++++++++++++++++++++++++++
#If an MX record exists for the domain that this host is in, the domain
#name is defined in the "A" macro.  If no MX record exists, the host
#name ($w) is used.  "A" is used for rewriting the sender "From" address
#on outbound mail to hide the true host name, and to address outbound
#mail as if it was from the MX server.  This will only work if the
#MX mail server knows how to deliver mail to the users of this host.
#
#In this sample network, mail addressed to craig@nist.gov is properly
#delivered to craig@cwh.cam.nist.gov, because a server at the nist.gov
#level makes the proper deliver.  Therefore, "A" is defined as nist.gov,
#and the From address on mail sent out by this host is rewritten to
#user@nist.gov.
#
#This "A" macro was created as part of the debugging example in Chapter
```

#10, and is specific to this book. In other sendmail configurations,
#"A" will have another meaning.
#++
MX mail domain name
DAnist.gov

#++
#The "R" macro contains the name of the mail relay that can deliver UUCP
#mail for this host. This should be the name of closest host to your
#site that will make the delivery for you. If you have such a host on
#your local network, use that host.
#++
UUCP relay host
DRuunet.uu.net

#++
#As described in Chapter 10, all references to CSNET have been commented
#out. It would be cleaner to remove the lines completely, but because
#they were discussed in Chapter 10 they are left here for reference.
#++
csnet relay host
#DCYOUR_CSNET_RELAY_GOES_HERE

#++
#The "B" macro contains the name of a host that can relay Bitnet mail.
#Use a host on your local network, if you have one that is connected to
#Bitnet. Otherwise use one of the well-known Bitnet relays. There are
#several: pucc.princeton.edu, mitvma.mit.edu, umrvmb.umr.edu, vml.nodak.edu,
#cunyvm.cuny.edu, ricevml.rice.edu, uicvm.uic.edu, uga.cc.uga.edu,
#cornellc.cit.cornell.edu, vtvml.cc.vt.edu, and brownvm.brown.edu.
#++
bitnet relay host
DBcunyvm.cuny.edu

#++
#The "j" macro contains the full host name. On my system, the internal
#value set for "w" is the full host name that includes the domain.
#Therefore, the value of "w" can be used to set "j." If your system does
#not internally set "w" to the full host name, use Dj$w.$D to set the
#value of "j."
#
#To find out if your sendmail.cf sets the correct value for "j," start
#sendmail and:
telnet localhost 25
#This telnet command will connect to your sendmail. sendmail will
#display a single line of output. The value of "j" is the second field
#displayed on this line. After you check the value, type "quit" to
#disconnect from sendmail.
#++
my official hostname
Dj$w

```
##############
#   Classes   #
##############
#+++++++++++++++++++++++++++++++++++++++++++++++++++++++++++
#Class "I" contains special internal domain names.  These names are used
#for rewriting the mail that must be passed to the mail relays.  See the
#"Modifying Classes" section in Chapter 10.
#+++++++++++++++++++++++++++++++++++++++++++++++++++++++++++
# Internal ("fake") domains that we use in rewriting
CIUUCP BITNET


####################
#   Version Number   #
####################
#+++++++++++++++++++++++++++++++++++++++++++++++++++++++++++
#Macro Z contains the configuration file's version number.  It is
#modified every time the file is updated.  Keep a record of your
#modifications.
#+++++++++++++++++++++++++++++++++++++++++++++++++++++++++++
# 2.0  modified by Craig, per Chapter 10
#         - modified local information and general macros
#         - changed path for aliases and sendmail.st
#         - removed all references to CSNET and to .arpa
# 2.1  added macro A for MX mail domain
#         - modified S14 and S24 to delete class N and use macro A
DZ2.1


####################
#   Special Macros   #
####################
#+++++++++++++++++++++++++++++++++++++++++++++++++++++++++++
#In the following sections, "Special Macros," "Options," "Message
#Precedences," "Trusted Users," "Format of Headers," and "Rewriting
#Rules," changes are not usually required.
#+++++++++++++++++++++++++++++++++++++++++++++++++++++++++++
# my name
DnMAILER-DAEMON
# UNIX header format
DlFrom $g  $d
# delimiter (operator) characters
Do.:%@!^=/[]
# format of a total name
Dq$g$?x ($x)$.
# SMTP login message
De$j Sendmail $v/$Z ready at $b


##############
#   Options   #
##############
#+++++++++++++++++++++++++++++++++++++++++++++++++++++++++++
#In Chapter 10, we changed the value of option "A" to "/etc/aliases" and
#the value of option "t" to "EST,EDT" (Eastern Standard and Eastern
#Daylight Time).  We also deleted option "W."  These changes were made
#primarily as examples and are not usually required.
```

```
#++++++++++++++++++++++++++++++++++++++++++++++++++++
# location of alias file
OA/etc/aliases
# wait up to ten minutes for alias file rebuild
Oa10
# substitution for space (blank) characters
OB.
# (don't) connect to "expensive" mailers
#Oc
# default delivery mode (deliver in background)
Odbackground
# temporary file mode
OF0600
# default GID
Og1
# location of help file
OH/usr/lib/sendmail.hf
# log level
OL9
# default network name
ONARPA
# default messages to old style
Oo
# queue directory
OQ/usr/spool/mqueue
# read timeout -- violates protocols
Or2h
# status file
OS/usr/lib/sendmail.st
# queue up everything before starting transmission
Os
# default timeout interval
OT3d
# time zone names (V6 only)
OtEST,EDT
# default UID
Ou1
# load average at which we just queue messages
Ox8
# load average at which we refuse connections
OX12


#########################
#  Message Precedences  #
#########################

Pfirst-class=0
Pspecial-delivery=100
Pbulk=-60
Pjunk=-100
```

```
####################
#    Trusted Users    #
####################


Troot
Tdaemon
Tuucp


#######################
#    Format of Headers    #
#######################


H?P?Return-Path: <$g>
HReceived: $?sfrom $s $.by $j ($v/$Z)
        id $i; $b
H?D?Resent-Date: $a
H?D?Date: $a
H?F?Resent-From: $q
H?F?From: $q
H?x?Full-Name: $x
HSubject:
# HPosted-Date: $a
# H?l?Received-Date: $b
H?M?Resent-Message-Id: <$t.$i@$j>
H?M?Message-Id: <$t.$i@$j>



#########################
###    Rewriting Rules    ###
#########################


##############################
#  Sender Field Pre-rewriting  #
##############################
S1
#R$*<$*>$*          $1$2$3                    defocus


################################
#  Recipient Field Pre-rewriting  #
################################
S2
#R$*<$*>$*          $1$2$3                    defocus


##############################
#  Final Output Post-rewriting  #
##############################
S4


R@                    $@                        handle <> error addr


# resolve numeric addresses to name if possible
R$*<@[$+]>$*          $:$1<@$[[$2]$]>$3    lookup numeric internet addr


# externalize local domain info
```

```
R$*<$+>$*              $1$2$3                   defocus
R@$+:@$+:$+            @$1,@$2:$3               <route-addr> canonical


# UUCP must always be presented in old form
R$+@$-.UUCP            $2!$1                     u@h.UUCP => h!u


# delete duplicate local names
R$+%$=w@$=w            $1@$w                     u%host@host => u@host
R$+%$=w@$=w.$D         $1@$w                     u%host@host => u@host


###########################
#  Name Canonicalization  #
###########################
S3

# handle "from:<>" special case
R$*<>$*                $@@                       turn into magic token


# basic textual canonicalization -- note RFC733 heuristic here
R$*<$*<$*<$+>$*>$*>$*   $4                       3-level <> nesting
R$*<$*<$+>$*>$*         $3                       2-level <> nesting
R$*<$+>$*               $2                       basic RFC821/822 parsing


# make sure <@a,@b,@c:user@d> syntax is easy to parse -- undone later
R@$+,$+                @$1:$2                    change all "," to ":"


# localize and dispose of route-based addresses
R@$+:$+                $@$>6<@$1>:$2             handle <route-addr>


# more miscellaneous cleanup
R$+                    $:$>8$1                   host dependent cleanup
R$+:$*;@$+             $@$1:$2;@$3               list syntax
R$+:$*;                $@$1:$2;                  list syntax
R$+@$+                 $:$1<@$2>                 focus on domain
R$+<$+@$+>             $1$2<@$3>                 move gaze right
R$+<@$+>               $@$>6$1<@$2>              already canonical


# convert old-style addresses to a domain-based address
R$+^$+                 $1!$2                     convert ^ to !
R$-!$+                 $@$>6$2<@$1.UUCP>         resolve uucp names
R$+.$-!$+              $@$>6$3<@$1.$2>           domain uucps
R$+!$+                 $@$>6$2<@$1.UUCP>         uucp subdomains
R$+%$+                 $:$>9$1%$2                user%host
R$+<@$+>               $@$>6$1<@$2>              already canonical
R$-.$+                 $@$>6$2<@$1>              host.user


################################
#   special local conversions  #
################################

S6
R$*<@$=w>$*            $:$1<@$w>$3               get into u@$w form
R$*<@$=w.$D>$*         $:$1<@$w>$3
R$*<@$=U.UUCP>$*       $:$1<@$w>$3
```

```
##################################
#    Change rightmost % to @.     #
##################################

S9
R$*%$*                  $1@$2                First make them all @'s.
R$*@$*@$*                $1%$2@$3             Undo all but the last.
R$*@$*                  $@$1<@$2>            Put back the brackets.


##################
###   Mailers   ###
##################
#++++++++++++++++++++++++++++++++++++++++++++++++++++++
#The mailers do not usually require modification.  However in Chapter
#10, we did make some changes to the S and R rulesets of one of the
#mailers.  These changes will be noted later in this file.
#++++++++++++++++++++++++++++++++++++++++++++++++++++++


#########################################################
#########################################################
#####
#####          Local and Program Mailer specification
#####
#########################################################
########,#################################################

Mlocal, P=/bin/mail, F=rlsDFMmn, S=10, R=20, A=mail -d $u
Mprog,  P=/bin/sh,   F=lsDFMe,   S=10, R=20, A=sh -c $u

S10
R@                      $n                   errors to mailer-daemon


#########################################################
#########################################################
#####
#####          Local Domain SMTP Mailer specification
#####
#####   Messages processed by this specification are assumed to remain
#####   the local domain.
#####
#########################################################
#########################################################

Mtcpld, P=[IPC], F=mDFMueXLC, S=17, R=27, A=IPC $h, E=\r\n

S17

# cleanup forwarding a bit
R$*<$*>$*               $1$2$3               defocus
R$*                     $:$>3$1              canonicalize
R$*%$*<@$w>             $:$>9$1%$2           user%localhost@localdomain
```

```
# pass <route-addr>'s through
R<@$+>$*                    $@<@$[$1$]>$2           resolve <route-addr>


# map colons to dots everywhere
R$*:$*                      $1.$2                   map colons to dots


# output local host as user@host.domain
R$-                         $@$1<@$w>               user w/o host
R$+<@$w>                    $@$1<@$w>               this host
R$+<@$=w>                   $@$1<@$w>               or an alias
R$+<@$->                    $:$1<@$[$2$]>           ask nameserver
R$+<@$w>                    $@$1<@$w>               this host
R$+<@$->                    $@$1<@$2.$D>            if nameserver fails


# if not local, and not a "fake" domain, ask the nameserver
R$+<@$+.$~I>                $@$1<@$[$2.$3$]>        user@host.domain
R$+<@[$+]>                  $@$1<@[$2]>             already ok
# output fake domains as user%fake@relay


R$+<@$+.BITNET>             $@$1%$2.BITNET<@$B>     user@host.bitnet
#R$+<@$+.CSNET>             $@$1%$2.CSNET<@$C>      user@host.CSNET
R$+<@$+.UUCP>               $@$2!$1<@$w>            user@host.UUCP



S27


# cleanup
R$*<$*>$*                   $1$2$3                  defocus
R$*                         $:$>3$1                 now canonical form
R$*%$*<@$w>                 $:$>9$1%$2              user%localhost@localdomain


# pass <route-addr>'s through
R<@$+>$*                    $@<@$[$1$]>$2           resolve <route-addr>


# map colons to dots everywhere
R$*:$*                      $1.$2                   map colons to dots


# output local host as user@host.domain
R$-                         $@$1<@$w>               user w/o host
R$+<@$w>                    $@$1<@$w>               this host
R$+<@$=w>                   $@$1<@$w>               or an alias
R$+<@$->                    $:$1<@$[$2$]>           ask nameserver
R$+<@$w>                    $@$1<@$w>               this host
R$+<@$->                    $@$1<@$2.$D>            if nameserver fails


# if not local, and not a "fake" domain, ask the nameserver
R$+<@$+.$~I>                $@$1<@$[$2.$3$]>        user@host.domain
R$+<@[$+]>                  $@$1<@[$2]>             already ok


# output fake domains as user%fake@relay


R$+<@$+.BITNET>             $@$1%$2.BITNET<@$B>     user@host.BITNET
#R$+<@$+.CSNET>             $@$1%$2.CSNET<@$C>      user@host.CSNET
R$+<@$+.UUCP>               $@$2!$1                 user@host.UUCP
```

```
###########################################################
###########################################################
#####
#####            Internet SMTP Mailer specification
#####
#####    Messages processed by this specification are assumed to leave
#####    the local domain -- hence, they must be canonical according to
#####    RFC822 etc.
#####
###########################################################
###########################################################


Mtcp,    P=[IPC], F=mDFMueXLC, S=14, R=24, A=IPC $h, E=\r\n


S14


# pass <route-addr>'s through
R<@$+>$*                    $@<@$[$1$]>$2          resolve <route-addr>


# map colons to dots everywhere
R$*:$*                      $1.$2                  map colons to dots


# output local host in user@host.domain syntax
#++++++++++++++++++++++++++++++++++++++++++++++++++++++++++
#This ruleset referenced class "N", which is not defined in this
#configuration file.  The rule referencing "N" was commented out.  This
#ruleset also had a rule that would rewrite the sender address using the
#"% kludge" (u%h@gateway).  That rule was commented out and replaced with
#a rule that rewrites the sender address into user@domain using the MX
#domain name we stored in macro "A."
#++++++++++++++++++++++++++++++++++++++++++++++++++++++++++
R$-                         $1<@$w>                user w/o host
R$+<@$=w>                   $:$1<@$w>              this host
R$+<@$->                    $:$1<@$[$2$]>          canonicalize into dom
R$+<@$->                    $:$1<@$2.$D>           if nameserver fails
#R$+<@$=N.$D>                $@$1<@$2.$D>           nic-reg hosts are ok
#R$+<@$*.$D>                 $@$1%$2.$D<@$A>        else -> u%h@gateway
R$+<@$*.$D>                 $@$1<@$A>              else -> user@domain


# if not local, and not a "fake" domain, ask the nameserver
R$+<@$+.$~I>                $@$1<@$[$2.$3$]>       user@host.domain
R$+<@[$+]>                  $@$1<@[$2]>            already ok


# output internal ("fake") domains as "user%host@relay"

R$+<@$+.BITNET>             $@$1%$2.BITNET<@$B>    user@host.BITNET
#R$+<@$+.CSNET>             $@$1%$2.CSNET<@$C>     user@host.CSNET
R$+<@$+.UUCP>               $@$2!$1<@$w>           user@host.UUCP


S24


# put in <> kludge
R$*<$*>$*                   $1$2$3                 defocus
```

```
R$*                     $:$>3$1                 now canonical form


# pass <route-addr>'s through
R<@$+>$*                $@<@$[$1$]>$2           resolve <route-addr>


# map colons to dots everywhere.....
R$*:$*                  $1.$2                   map colons to dots


# output local host in user@host.domain syntax
#++++++++++++++++++++++++++++++++++++++++++++++++++++++++
#The same modifications for the class "N" and macro "A" as noted in
#ruleset 14 were made here.  It is common for the same rule to occur in
#multiple rulesets.
#++++++++++++++++++++++++++++++++++++++++++++++++++++++++
R$-                     $1<@$D>                 user w/o host
R$+<@$=w>               $:$1<@$w>               this host
R$+<@$->                $:$1<@$[$2$]>           canonicalize into dom
R$+<@$->                $:$1<@$2.$D>            if nameserver fails
#R$+<@$=N.$D>           $@$1<@$2.$D>            nic-reg hosts are ok
#R$+<@$*.$D>            $@$1%$2.$D<@$A>         else -> u%h@gateway
R$+<@$*.$D>             $@$1<@$A>               else -> u%h@gateway


# if not local, and not a "fake" domain, ask the nameserver
R$+<@$+.$~I>            $@$1<@$[$2.$3$]>        user@host.domain
R$+<@[$+]>              $@$1<@[$2]>             already ok


# Hide fake domains behind relays

R$+<@$+.BITNET>         $@$1%$2.BITNET<@$B>     user@host.BITNET
#R$+<@$+.CSNET>         $@$1%$2.CSNET<@$C>      user@host.CSNET
R$+<@$+.UUCP>           $@$2!$1                 user@host.UUCP



####################
###   Rule Zero   ###
####################


##########################################################
##########################################################
#####
#####           RULESET ZERO PREAMBLE
#####
#####   The beginning of ruleset zero is constant through all
#####   configurations.
#####
##########################################################
##########################################################


S0


# first make canonical
R$*<$*>$*               $1$2$3                  defocus
R$+                     $:$>3$1                 make canonical
```

```
     # handle special cases
     R$*<@[$+]>$*           $:$1<@$[[$2]$]>$3        numeric internet addr
     R$*<@[$+]>$*           $#tcp$@[$2]$:$1@[$2]$3   numeric internet spec
     R$+                    $:$>6$1
     R$-<@$w>               $#local$:$1
     R@                     $#error$:Invalid address    handle <> form


     # canonicalize using the nameserver if not internal domain
     R$*<@$*.$~I>$*         $:$1<@$[$2.$3$]>$4
     R$*<@$->$*             $:$1<@$[$2$]>$3
     R$*<@$->$*             $:$1<@$2.$D>$3           if nameserver fails


     # now delete the local info
     R<@$w>:$*              $@$>0$1                  @here:... -> ...
     R$*<@$w>               $@$>0$1                  ...@here -> ...


     #################################
     #  End of ruleset zero preamble  #
     #################################


     ##############################################
     ###   Machine dependent part of Rule Zero   ###
     ##############################################
     #++++++++++++++++++++++++++++++++++++++++++++++++++++++++
     #This section contains the part of ruleset 0 that reflects the mail
     #delivery capability of this host.  This section would be different for
     #a host that is only connected to a UUCP network or for one that is
     #connected to both UUCP and TCP/IP.
     #
     #As noted in Chapter 10, references to CSNET and the old ".arpa" domain
     #are commented out.
     #++++++++++++++++++++++++++++++++++++++++++++++++++++++++


     # resolve fake top level domains by forwarding to other hosts
     R$*<@$+.BITNET>$*      $#tcp$@$B$:$1<@$2.BITNET>$3    user@host.BITNET
     #R$*<@$+.CSNET>$*      $#tcp$@$C$:$1<@$2.CSNET>$3     user@host.CSNET


     # forward non-local UUCP traffic to our UUCP relay
     R$*<@$*.UUCP>$*        $#tcpld$@$R$:$1<@$2.UUCP>      uucp mail


     # hide behind our internet relay when talking to people in the arpa domain
     #R$*<@$*.arpa>$*       $#tcp$@$2.arpa$:$1<@$2.arpa>$3 user@host.arpa


     # but speak domains to them if they speak domains too
     R$*<@$*>$*             $#tcpld$@$2$:$1<@$2>$3         user@host.domain


     # remaining names must be local
     R$+                    $#local$:$1                   everything else
```

F

Selected TCP/IP Headers

In Chapter 11, *Troubleshooting TCP/IP*, several references are made to specific TCP/IP headers. Those headers are documented here. This is not an exhaustive list of headers; only the headers used in the troubleshooting examples in Chapter 11 are covered:

- the IP Datagram Header, as defined in RFC 791, *Internet Protocol;*
- the TCP Segment Header, as defined in RFC 793, *Transmission Control Protocol;*
- the ICMP Parameter Problem Message Header, as defined in RFC 792, *Internet Control Message Protocol.*

Each header is presented using an excerpt from the RFC that defines the header. These are not exact quotes; the excerpts have been slightly edited to better fit this text. However, we still want to emphasize the importance of using primary sources for troubleshooting protocol problems. These headers are provided here to help you follow the examples in Chapter 11. For real troubleshooting, use the real RFCs. You can obtain your own copies of the RFCs by following the instructions in Chapter 13.

IP Datagram Header

This description is taken from pages 11 to 15, of RFC 791, *Internet Protocol*, by Jon Postel, Information Sciences Institute, University of Southern California.

```
Internet Header Format

    0                   1                   2                   3
    0 1 2 3 4 5 6 7 8 9 0 1 2 3 4 5 6 7 8 9 0 1 2 3 4 5 6 7 8 9 0 1
   +-+-+-+-+-+-+-+-+-+-+-+-+-+-+-+-+-+-+-+-+-+-+-+-+-+-+-+-+-+-+-+-+
   |Version|  IHL  |Type of Service|          Total Length         |
   +-+-+-+-+-+-+-+-+-+-+-+-+-+-+-+-+-+-+-+-+-+-+-+-+-+-+-+-+-+-+-+-+
   |         Identification        |Flags|      Fragment Offset    |
   +-+-+-+-+-+-+-+-+-+-+-+-+-+-+-+-+-+-+-+-+-+-+-+-+-+-+-+-+-+-+-+-+
   |  Time to Live |    Protocol   |         Header Checksum        |
   +-+-+-+-+-+-+-+-+-+-+-+-+-+-+-+-+-+-+-+-+-+-+-+-+-+-+-+-+-+-+-+-+
   |                       Source Address                          |
   +-+-+-+-+-+-+-+-+-+-+-+-+-+-+-+-+-+-+-+-+-+-+-+-+-+-+-+-+-+-+-+-+
   |                    Destination Address                        |
   +-+-+-+-+-+-+-+-+-+-+-+-+-+-+-+-+-+-+-+-+-+-+-+-+-+-+-+-+-+-+-+-+
   |                    Options                    |    Padding     |
   +-+-+-+-+-+-+-+-+-+-+-+-+-+-+-+-+-+-+-+-+-+-+-+-+-+-+-+-+-+-+-+-+
```

Version: 4 bits

   The Version field indicates the format of the internet header.
   This document describes version 4.

IHL: 4 bits

   Internet Header Length is the length of the internet header in 32
   bit words. The minimum value for a correct header is 5.

Type of Service: 8 bits

   The Type of Service indication the quality of service desired.
   The meaning of the bits is explained below.

      Bits 0-2: Precedence.
      Bit   3:   0 = Normal Delay,   1 = Low Delay.
      Bits 4:   0 = Normal Throughput, 1 = High Throughput.
      Bits 5:   0 = Normal Reliability 1 = High Reliability.
      Bit 6-7: Reserved for Future Use.

```
        0     1     2     3     4     5     6     7
      +-----+-----+-----+-----+-----+-----+-----+-----+
      |                 |     |     |     |     |     |
      |   PRECEDENCE    |  D  |  T  |  R  |  0  |  0  |
      |                 |     |     |     |     |     |
      +-----+-----+-----+-----+-----+-----+-----+-----+
```

Precedence

      111 - Network Control
      110 - Internetwork Control
      101 - CRITIC/ECP
      100 - Flash Override
      011 - Flash
      010 - Immediate
      001 - Priority
      000 - Routine

Total Length: 16 bits

Total Length is the length of the datagram, measured in octets (bytes), including internet header and data.

Identification: 16 bits

An identifying value assigned by the sender to aid in assembling the fragments of a datagram.

Flags: 3 bits

Various Control Flags. The Flag bit are explained below:

Bit 0: reserved, must be zero
Bit 1: (DF) 0 = May Fragment, 1 = Don't Fragment.
Bit 2: (MF) 0 = Last Fragment, 1 = More Fragments.

```
  0   1   2
+---+---+---+
|   | D | M |
| 0 | F | F |
+---+---+---+
```

Fragment Offset: 13 bits

This field indicates where in the datagram this fragment belongs. The fragment offset is measured in units of 8 octets (64 bits). The first fragment has offset zero.

Time to Live: 8 bits

This field indicates the maximum time the datagram is allowed to remain in the internet system.

Protocol: 8 bits

This field indicates the Transport Layer protocol that the data portion of this datagram is passed to. The values for various protocols are specified in the "Assigned Numbers" RFC.

Header Checksum: 16 bits

A checksum on the header only. Since some header fields change
(e.g., time to live), this is recomputed and verified at each point
that the internet header is processed. The checksum algorithm is:

> The checksum field is the 16 bit one's complement of the one's
> complement sum of all 16 bit words in the header. For purposes of
> computing the checksum, the value of the checksum field is zero.

Source Address: 32 bits

> The source IP address. See Chapter 2 for a description of IP
> addresses.

Destination Address: 32 bits

> The destination IP address. See Chapter 2 for a description of IP
> addresses.

Options: variable

> The options may or may not appear in datagrams, but they must be
> implemented by all IP modules (host and gateways). No options were
> used in any of the datagrams examined in Chapter 11.

TCP Segment Header

This description is taken from pages 15 to 17, of RFC 793, *Transmission
Control Protocol,* by Jon Postel, Information Sciences Institute, University of
Southern California.

TCP Header Format

```
 0                   1                   2                   3
 0 1 2 3 4 5 6 7 8 9 0 1 2 3 4 5 6 7 8 9 0 1 2 3 4 5 6 7 8 9 0 1
+-+-+-+-+-+-+-+-+-+-+-+-+-+-+-+-+-+-+-+-+-+-+-+-+-+-+-+-+-+-+-+-+
|          Source Port          |       Destination Port        |
+-+-+-+-+-+-+-+-+-+-+-+-+-+-+-+-+-+-+-+-+-+-+-+-+-+-+-+-+-+-+-+-+
|                        Sequence Number                        |
+-+-+-+-+-+-+-+-+-+-+-+-+-+-+-+-+-+-+-+-+-+-+-+-+-+-+-+-+-+-+-+-+
|                    Acknowledgment Number                      |
+-+-+-+-+-+-+-+-+-+-+-+-+-+-+-+-+-+-+-+-+-+-+-+-+-+-+-+-+-+-+-+-+
| Data  |           |U|A|P|R|S|F|                               |
| Offset| Reserved  |R|C|S|S|Y|I|            Window             |
|       |           |G|K|H|T|N|N|                               |
+-+-+-+-+-+-+-+-+-+-+-+-+-+-+-+-+-+-+-+-+-+-+-+-+-+-+-+-+-+-+-+-+
|           Checksum            |         Urgent Pointer        |
+-+-+-+-+-+-+-+-+-+-+-+-+-+-+-+-+-+-+-+-+-+-+-+-+-+-+-+-+-+-+-+-+
|                    Options                    |    Padding    |
+-+-+-+-+-+-+-+-+-+-+-+-+-+-+-+-+-+-+-+-+-+-+-+-+-+-+-+-+-+-+-+-+
|                             data                              |
+-+-+-+-+-+-+-+-+-+-+-+-+-+-+-+-+-+-+-+-+-+-+-+-+-+-+-+-+-+-+-+-+
```

Source Port: 16 bits

    The source port number.

Destination Port: 16 bits

    The destination port number.

Sequence Number: 32 bits

    The sequence number of the first data octet (byte) in this segment
    (except when SYN is present). If SYN is present the sequence number
    is the initial sequence number (ISN) and the first data octet is
    ISN+1.

Acknowledgment Number: 32 bits

    If the ACK control bit is set, this field contains the value of the
    next sequence number the sender of the segment is expecting to
    receive. Once a connection is established this is always sent.

Data Offset: 4 bits

    The number of 32 bit words in the TCP Header. This indicates where
    the data begins. The TCP header (even one including options) is an
    integral number of 32 bits long.

Reserved: 6 bits

    Reserved for future use. Must be zero.

Control Bits: 6 single-bit values (from left to right):

    URG: Urgent Pointer field significant
    ACK: Acknowledgment field significant
    PSH: Push Function
    RST: Reset the connection
    SYN: Synchronize sequence numbers
    FIN: No more data from sender

Window: 16 bits

    The number of data octets (bytes) the sender of this segment is
    willing to accept.

Checksum: 16 bits

    The checksum field is the 16 bit one's complement of the one's
    complement sum of all 16 bit words in the header and text.

Urgent Pointer: 16 bits

    This field contains the current value of the urgent pointer as a
    positive offset from the sequence number in this segment. The

urgent pointer points to the sequence number of the octet following the urgent data. This field is only be interpreted in segments with the URG control bit set.

Options: variable

Options may occupy space at the end of the TCP header and are a multiple of 8 bits in length.

ICMP Parameter Problem Message Header

This description is taken from pages 8 and 9, of RFC 792, *Internet Control Message Protocol*, by Jon Postel, Information Sciences Institute, University of Southern California.

Parameter Problem Message

```
 0                   1                   2                   3
 0 1 2 3 4 5 6 7 8 9 0 1 2 3 4 5 6 7 8 9 0 1 2 3 4 5 6 7 8 9 0 1
+-+-+-+-+-+-+-+-+-+-+-+-+-+-+-+-+-+-+-+-+-+-+-+-+-+-+-+-+-+-+-+-+
|     Type      |     Code      |          Checksum             |
+-+-+-+-+-+-+-+-+-+-+-+-+-+-+-+-+-+-+-+-+-+-+-+-+-+-+-+-+-+-+-+-+
|    Pointer    |                   unused                      |
+-+-+-+-+-+-+-+-+-+-+-+-+-+-+-+-+-+-+-+-+-+-+-+-+-+-+-+-+-+-+-+-+
|      Internet Header + 64 bits of Original Data Datagram      |
+-+-+-+-+-+-+-+-+-+-+-+-+-+-+-+-+-+-+-+-+-+-+-+-+-+-+-+-+-+-+-+-+
```

Type

   12

Code

   0 = pointer indicates the error.

Checksum

   The checksum is the 16-bit ones's complement of the one's complement sum of the ICMP message starting with the ICMP Type. For computing the checksum , the checksum field should be zero.

Pointer

   If code = 0, identifies the octet where an error was detected.

Internet Header + 64 bits of Data Datagram

   The internet header plus the first 64 bits of the datagram that elicited this error response.

G

Reference for passwd+

This appendix provides a short reference to the command language used to construct password tests for **passwd+**. Even if you don't intend to write a custom **passwd+** configuration, you'll need a little understanding of the language just to read the sample configuration file, *pwsample*, that comes with the **passwd+** software.

The Configuration File

The **passwd+** configuration is stored in the */etc/password.test* file. The simplest way to configure **passwd+** is to copy the sample configuration file, *pwsample*, to */etc/password.test*. The most commonly required password tests are provided in the sample configuration file. It contains most of the same checks performed by **npasswd**, and many sites can use it with no additional configuration. *pwsample* contains the following:

```
# password tests
# format of the GECOS field
GECOS:          "%s %s" f s
GECOS:          "%[^,],%[^,],%s" n o t
FORCEGECOS:     "%s,%s,%s" n o t
# what to log
LOGLEVEL:       all,!debug      > /etc/passwd.log
#
# tests
#
# general tests
#
%#p<6                           password must be at least 6 chars long
```

```
%#b>0&%#v=0                        if alphabetic chars, must be mixed case
#
# people and office (etc.) stuff
# all these are in lowercase so we needn't worry about
# mixed cases
#
"%*p"="^%*u$"                     login name not allowed as password
"%*p"="^%-*u$"                    reversed login name not allowed as password
"%*p"="^%*f$"                     first name not allowed as password
"%*p"="^%-*f$"                    reversed first name not allowed as password
"%*p"="^%*s$"                     last name not allowed as password
"%*p"="^%-*s$"                    reversed last name not allowed as password
"%*p"="^%o$"                      office not allowed as password
"%*p"="^%-o$"                     reversed office not allowed as password
"%*p"="^%t$"                      phone number not allowed as password
"%*p"="^%-t$"                     reversed phone number not allowed as password
"%*p"="^%1*f%1*m%1*s$"            initials not allowed as password
#
# host name stuff
#
"%*p"="^%h$"                      host name not allowed as password
"%*p"="^%-h$"                     reversed host name not allowed as password
"%*p"="^%d$"                      domain name not allowed as password
"%*p"="^%-d$"                     reversed domain name not allowed as password
"%*p"="^%h.%d$"                   domained host name not allowed as password
#
# dictionary words -- look for strange capitalizations too
#
[/usr/dict/words] == "%p"         password matches dictionary entry
{tr A-Z a-z < /usr/dict/words} == "%*p" password is in dictionary
```

The lines that begin with # are comments. The comments imply that there
are several different sections to the configuration file, but there are really
only three: a section that defines the GECOS* data, a section that defines
logging, and a section that contains the password tests. The majority of the
file is the section that contains the various password tests. But before we
get to the password tests, let's look at the other two sections.

The GECOS Data

The GECOS† data from the */etc/passwd* file is used to set some values that
can then be used in the password test. The GECOS values are just a few of
the large number of predefined variables used by **passwd+**. All of the

---

*General Electric Comprehensive Operating System? No, this is the "user" data in the
/etc/passwd entry. Often called the *gcos-field*, this field contains the user's name and perhaps
telephone number.

†We use GECOS because **passwd+** does. You may be used to referring to this data as "gcos
data."

predefined variables are listed in Table G-1. Each variable is identified by a single character name. The predefined variables are identified by lower-case letters. User-defined variables must be identified by uppercase letters.

Table G.1: Predefined passwd+ Variables

Escape	Type	Meaning
a	number	count of alphanumeric characters
b	number	count of alphabetic characters
c	number	count of capital letters
d	string	domain name of the machine
f	string	first name of the user
i	string	initials of the user
l	number	count of lowercase letters
m	string	middle name of the user
n	string	full name of the user
o	string	the user's office
p	string	proposed password
q	string	current password (as typed)
s	string	surname of user
t	string	telephone number of user
u	string	login name of user
v	number	1 if mixed case, 0 otherwise
w	number	count of decimal digits

The sample configuration file uses the GECOS statements to set the values for the first name (f), surname (s), full name (n), office (o), and telephone number (t) of the user. The format of the GECOS field in your */etc/passwd* field is the format you should use in the GECOS statements in your */etc/pass-word.test* file. The sample file assumes that the format of GECOS data is:

firstname surname,office,telephone

The FORCEGECOS statement in the sample file forces this format to be used when **passwd+** writes GECOS data to the */etc/passwd* file.

Logging passwd+ Activity

The second section of the sample file defines the activities that **passwd+** will log. This is defined by the LOGLEVEL statement, which in the sample file is:

```
LOGLEVEL:      all,!debug      > /etc/passwd.log
```

The comma-separated list (all, !debug in this example) defines the type of information logged. The possible values used in this list are shown in Table G-2.

Table G.2: Logging Types for passwd+

Type	Meaning
all	turns on all logging types
clear	clears any types previously turned on
debug	logs extensive debugging information
item	logs the line number of the test that the password failed
result	logs the success or failure of each password change
syntax	logs syntax errors in the configuration file
system	logs system errors
use	logs usage of **passwd+**; who's changing what

An exclamation (!) mark in front of a logging type turns off that type of logging. For example, in the sample LOGLEVEL statement, all, !debug, turns on all types of logging except debug logging.

The last field in the LOGLEVEL statement tells **passwd+** how to dispose of the log output. In the sample, the log output is directed to the file */etc/passwd.log*. Table G-3 shows the various ways you can dispose of log output.

Table G.3: Redirecting Logging Output

Output Directive	Effect
I *command*	Output is input to *command*.
> *file*	Output is appended to *file*.
syslog	Output is written to syslog.
stderr	Output is written to standard error.

The first two sections of the */etc/password.test* file take only a few lines to define. The bulk of the file defines how to test new passwords.

Password Tests

The password tests check the proposed password (%p) to make sure that it is a "good" password. The checks are negative. If a password test evaluates to true, the password fails and is not added to */etc/passwd*. In other words, the proposed password is compared to numerous "bad" passwords. If it is not one of the "bad" passwords, it is assumed to be a "good" password.

The basic format of a password test is:

   value operator value   error message

The values are compared as specified by the operator, and if the comparison is true, the password fails and the error message is displayed.

Password tests can make comparisons between numbers, between strings, or between strings and patterns.* A comparison can be made between a string and a line from a file, or a string and a line of output from a program. If a file is specified in a comparison, the name of the file is enclosed in square brackets. If a program is specified, it is enclosed in curly braces. Comparisons to data from files and output from programs are commonly used for dictionary searches. For example:

```
[/usr/dict/words] == "%p"      password matches dictionary entry
```

This line from the *pwsample* file matches the proposed password (`"%p"`) against each individual line in the */usr/dict/words* file. By preventing users from selecting dictionary words for passwords, this type of test reduces the

---

*Strings are always enclosed in quotes. Patterns are combinations of **passwd+** string values and UNIX regular expressions.

danger of "dictionary guessing" being used to compromise the security of your system.

When a password is rejected by **passwd+**, the user is notified why the password is unacceptable. The message that notifies the user is taken directly from the test that the password failed. The last field in the password test is the error message. The error message must be separated from the comparison used in the password test by one or more tab characters. In the example above, the message "password matches dictionary entry" is displayed if the test is true.

The password tests are constructed using special **passwd+** escape sequences and operators. The details of the escape sequences and operators used in these tests are explained in the next section.

Escape Sequences

The value stored in a **passwd+** variable is retrieved using a special syntax called an *escape sequence*. Escape sequences are used in the password tests. The format of the escape sequence varies slightly depending on whether the variable is a number or a string.

The escape sequence for a number is:

> %[–]*escape*

All **passwd+** escapes sequences begin with a %, which indicates the start of an escape sequence. *escape* is the single-character name of this variable. For most numeric variables, the optional minus means that the value of the variable is subtracted from the length of the proposed password. For example, if the length of the proposed password is 10 and the value of %w is 2, then the escape sequence %-w is 8. The exception to this rule is *v*, which is a boolean. *v* can only be 0 or 1. If %v is 0, %-v is 1. If %v is 1, %-v is 0*.

The escape sequence for string values is slightly more complex:

> % [–] [*n1*][.*n2*] [^*|#*] *escape*

Again, % begins the escape sequence and *escape* is the single character name of the variable. But here the minus sign means that the characters of the string should be reversed. For example, if the value of %u is *craig*, the value of %-u is *giarc*.

---

*See Table G-1 for a full list of **passwd+** variables.

The arguments *n1* and *n2* are numbers that define the character positions of a substring within the string variable. Character positions are numbered starting from one. *n1* is the start of the substring, and *n2* is the end of the substring. Therefore, given that the value of %u is *craig*, %2.4u is *rai*. If *n1* is used without *n2*, it is interpreted as the number of contiguous characters starting from character 1, so %4u would be *crai*. To get just the fourth character of escape *u*, specify %4.4u, which would be *i* in our example.

The last group of optional arguments in the string escape sequence are called *format controls*. The four format controls define how the characters in the string are interpreted:

^   All alphabetic characters in the string are converted to uppercase.

*   All alphabetic characters in the string are converted to lowercase.

| The first character of the string is capitalized.

The length of the string is returned as opposed to the string itself. Assuming that %u returns *craig*, the sequence %#u would return 5.

These escape values can be compared and manipulated using most common operators. Strings can be compared against patterns using =~ to check for a match, and !~ to check for a pattern that does not match. Both strings and numbers can be compared for equality (==) or inequality (!=), while numbers can also be compared as less than (<), greater than (>), less than or equal (<=), and greater than or equal (>=). Numeric values can also be manipulated with the arithmetic operators: plus (+), minus (-), multiply (*), and divide (/), and with parentheses used for grouping. To use all of this would require some very fancy password processing!

Sample Tests

Two examples from the sample configuration file may help clarify the structure of **passwd+** tests. This first sample is a numeric comparison to check that the password is at least six characters long.

```
%#p<6                   password must be at least 6 chars long
```

The length (#) of the proposed password (p) is compared to 6. If the length is less than (<) 6, the password is rejected, and the user is notified with the message "password must be at least 6 chars long." If the test is false, the password is kept and passed on to the next test.

```
"%*p"=~"^%-*f$"          reversed first name not allowed as password
```

This second example compares a string to a pattern, as indicated by the =~ operator. It tests the proposed password to see if it is the user's first name, typed in reverse order. The string on the left hand side of this comparison is the escape sequence that returns the proposed password (p) forced to lowercase (*). The password is forced to lowercase to simplify the comparison.

In this example, the pattern on the right-hand side of the comparison contains both an escape sequence and some regular expression operators. A password test can contain anything that can appear in a regular expression, as well as a **passwd+** escape sequence. The ^ and the $ that occur before and after the escape sequence are regular expression operators that indicate the beginning and the end of the line. These operators force **passwd+** to compare the escape sequence %-*f to the entire line defined by %*p, and not just to part of it. The escape sequence %-*f returns the user's first name (f), forced to lowercase (*), and reversed (–). If this is the value used for the password, the password is rejected.

Final Words

The flexibility exists in the **passwd+** configuration language to create as complex a custom configuration as is needed. This rich and complex configuration language offers an endless variety of possible password tests. But before you decide to use **passwd+**, you should be aware that it is currently only available as an alpha release. If you choose to use this program, you must be willing to do some debugging.

passwd+ is available via anonymous **ftp** from *dartmouth.edu* in the compressed **tar** file *pub/security/passwd+.tar.Z.*

H

Software Sources

Throughout this book we have used free software that is available from the Internet via anonymous FTP. This appendix provides a consolidated list of that software. Table H-1 lists the programs in the order that they appear in the text. The table lists the FTP servers and directories from which the software can be obtained, and it lists the specific software files used to generate the examples in this book. The versions listed in the table, where that is applicable, are the ones used in this book. Some of these programs change frequently; check the server for the latest version of the program.

To retrieve any of these files:

1. **ftp** to the server listed in the table, and login to the anonymous FTP account.

2. **cd** to the directory listed in the table. If no directory is listed, you don't have to issue the **ftp** change directory command.

3. Enter the **binary** command to change to binary transfer mode. All of the files listed in the table, except *tcp_wrapper.shar*, must be transferred in binary mode.

4. **get** the filename listed in the table.

Table H.1: Free Software Used in This Book

Program	Server	Directory	File Name
SLIP	ai.toronto.edu	pub	slipware.tar.Z
PPP	archive.cis.ohio-state.edu	pub/ppp	ppp-sunos4.1.p16.tar.Z
gated	gated.cornell.edu	pub/gated	gated-2.0.1.14.tar.Z
sendmail	ftp.uu.net	mail/sendmail	sendmail.5.65.tar.Z
dig	venera.isi.edu	pub	dig.2.0.tar.Z
traceroute	ftp.ee.lbl.gov		traceroute.tar.Z
tcpdump	ftp.ee.lbl.gov		tcpdump.tar.Z
npasswd	ftp.cc.utexas.edu	pub/npasswd	npasswd.tar.Z
COPS	cert.sei.cmu.edu	pub/cops	cops.tar.Z
DES	kampi.hut.fi	alo	des-dist.tar.Z
wrapper	cert.sei.cmu.edu	pub/network_tools	tcp_wrapper.shar
archie	archie.sura.net	pub/archie/clients	c-archie-1.2.tar.Z
gopher	boombox.micro.umn.edu	pub/gopher/Unix	gopher0.9.tar.Z
WAIS	quake.think.com	pub/wais	wais-8-b4.1.tar.Z
passwd+	dartmouth.edu	pub/security	passwd+.tar.Z

The servers listed in this table are the servers we used to obtain the software used in this book. Most of the programs are available from several different servers; use **archie** to locate the nearest server that has the program you want.

Index

Z

Books That Help People Get More Out of Computers

Please send me the following:

❏ A free catalog of titles.

❏ A list of Bookstores in my area that carry your books (U.S. and Canada only).

❏ A list of book distributors outside the U.S. and Canada.

❏ Information about consulting services for documentation or programming.

❏ Information about bundling books with my product.

❏ On-line descriptions of your books.

Name _____

Address _____

_____

City _____

State, ZIP _____

Country _____

Phone _____

Email Address _____
(Internet or Uunet)

Books That Help People Get More Out of Computers

Please send me the following:

❏ A free catalog of titles.

❏ A list of Bookstores in my area that carry your books (U.S. and Canada only).

❏ A list of book distributors outside the U.S. and Canada.

❏ Information about consulting services for documentation or programming.

❏ Information about bundling books with my product.

❏ On-line descriptions of your books.

Name _____

Address _____

_____

City _____

State, ZIP _____

Country _____

Phone _____

Email Address _____
(Internet or Uunet)

NAME_____

COMPANY_____

ADDRESS_____

CITY _____ STATE _____ ZIP _____

BUSINESS REPLY MAIL

FIRST CLASS MAIL PERMIT NO. 80 SEBASTOPOL, CA

POSTAGE WILL BE PAID BY ADDRESSEE

O'REILLY & ASSOCIATES, INC.

103 Morris Street Suite A
Sebastopol CA 95472-9902

NAME_____

COMPANY_____

ADDRESS_____

CITY _____ STATE _____ ZIP _____

BUSINESS REPLY MAIL

FIRST CLASS MAIL PERMIT NO. 80 SEBASTOPOL, CA

POSTAGE WILL BE PAID BY ADDRESSEE

O'REILLY & ASSOCIATES, INC.

103 Morris Street Suite A
Sebastopol CA 95472-9902

About the Author

Daniel Gilly has been with O'Reilly & Associates since 1986. In addition to co-authoring *The X Window System in a Nutshell*, Daniel has had an editorial hand in several books in the X Window series, wrote the reference section of Volume Six, *Motif Programming Manual*, and revised the Nutshell Handbook, *Learning vi*, for its 5th edition.

For the past two years Daniel has been editor of the newsletter for MIT Crew. He has also written a musical comedy, a radio thriller, and a one-act play, all of which were performed at Boston area colleges. He graduated from MIT in 1985 with a B.S. in Mechanical Engineering. Having lived in the Boston area for ten years, Daniel moved to Silicon Valley in June 1992.

Colophon

Our look is the result of reader comments, our own experimentation, and distribution channels. Our distinctive covers complement our distinctive approach to technical topics, breathing personality and life into potentially dry subjects.

The illustrations featured on the cover of *UNIX in a Nutshell* for System 4 and Solaris 2.0 are football referees (or "refs", as they are frequently referred to). The referee poses, from left to right, are: 1st down, offsides, touchdown, pass interference, timeout.

Edie Freedman designed this cover from illustrations drawn by Arthur Saarinen. The referees were created in Adobe Illustrator. Supporting artwork was done in QuarkXPress.

The fonts used in the book are Garamond and Garamond book. Text was prepared using the troff text formatter and FrameMaker. Inside artwork was created in QuarkXPress.

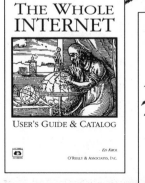
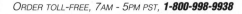

System Performance Tuning

By Mike Loukides

System Performance Tuning answers one of the most fundamental questions you can ask about your computer: "How can I get it to do more work without buying more hardware?" Anyone who has ever used a computer has wished that the system was faster, particularly at times when it was under heavy load.

If your system gets sluggish when you start a big job, if it feels as if you spend hours waiting for remote file access to complete, if your system stops dead when several users are active at the same time, you need to read this book. Some performance problems do require you to buy a bigger or faster computer, but many can be solved simply by making better use of the resources you already have.

336 pages, ISBN 0-937175-60-9

Essential System Administration

By Æleen Frisch

Like any other multi-user system, UNIX requires some care and feeding. *Essential System Administration* tells you how. This book strips away the myth and confusion surrounding this important topic and provides a compact, manageable introduction to the tasks faced by anyone responsible for a UNIX system.

If you use a stand-alone UNIX system, whether it's a PC or a workstation, you know how much you need this book: on these systems the fine line between a user and an administrator has vanished. Either you're both or you're in trouble. If you routinely provide administrative support for a larger shared system or a network of workstations, you will find this book indispensable. Even if you aren't directly responsible for system administration, you will find that understanding basic administrative functions greatly increases your ability to use UNIX effectively.

466 pages
ISBN 0-937175-80-3

COMPUTER
SECURITY
BASICS

Deborah Russell and G.T. Gangemi Sr.
O'Reilly & Associates, Inc.

Practical UNIX Security

By Simson Garfinkel & Gene Spafford

If you are a UNIX system administrator or user who needs to deal with security, you need this book.

Practical UNIX Security describes the issues, approaches, and methods for implementing security measures—spelling out what the varying approaches cost and require in the way of equipment. After presenting UNIX security basics and network security, this guide goes on to suggest how to keep intruders out, how to tell if they've gotten in, how to clean up after them, and even how to prosecute them. Filled with practical scripts, tricks and warnings, *Practical UNIX Security* tells you what you need to know to make your UNIX system as secure as it can be.

"Worried about who's in your Unix system? Losing sleep because someone might be messing with your computer? Having headaches from obscure computer manuals? Then *Practical Unix Security* is for you. This handy book tells you where the holes are and how to cork'em up.

"Moreover, you'll learn about how Unix security really works. Spafford and Garfinkel show you how to tighten up your Unix system without pain. No secrets here—just solid computing advice.

"Buy this book and save on aspirin."—Cliff Stoll
512 pages, ISBN 0-937175-72-2

Computer Security Basics

By Deborah Russell & G.T. Gangemi Sr.

There's a lot more consciousness of security today, but not a lot of understanding of what it means and how far it should go. This handbook describes complicated concepts like trusted systems, encryption and mandatory access control in simple terms.

For example, most U.S. government equipment acquisitions now require "Orange Book" (Trusted Computer System Evaluation Criteria) certification. A lot of people have a vague feeling that they ought to know about the Orange Book, but few make the effort to track it down and read it. *Computer Security Basics* contains a more readable introduction to the Orange Book—why it exists, what it contains, and what the different security levels are all about—than any other book or government publication.

464 pages, ISBN 0-937175-71-4

Managing UUCP and Usenet

10th Edition
By Tim O'Reilly & Grace Todino

For all its widespread use, UUCP is one of the most difficult UNIX utilities to master. Poor documentation, cryptic messages, and differences between various implementations make setting up UUCP links a nightmare for many a system administrator.

This handbook is meant for system administrators who want to install and manage the UUCP and Usenet software. It covers HoneyDanBer UUCP as well as standard Version 2 UUCP, with special notes on Xenix. As one reader noted over the Net, "Don't even TRY to install UUCP without it!"

368 pages, ISBN 0-937175-93-5

Using UUCP and Usenet

By Grace Todino & Dale Dougherty

Using UUCP shows how to communicate with both UNIX and non-UNIX systems using UUCP and *cu* or *tip*. It also shows how to read news and post your own articles and mail to other Usenet members. This handbook assumes that UUCP and Usenet links to other computer systems have already been established by your system administrator.

While clear enough for a novice, this book is packed with information that even experienced users will find indispensable. Take the mystery out of questions such as why files sent via UUCP don't always end up where you want them, how to find out the status of your file transfer requests, and how to execute programs remotely with *uux*.

210 pages, ISBN 0-937175-10-2

Understanding DCE

*By Ward Rosenberry, David Kenney,
and Gerry Fisher*

Understanding DCE is a technical and conceptual overview of OSF's Distributed Computing Environment for programmers and technical managers, marketing and sales people. Unlike many O'Reilly & Associates books, *Understanding DCE* has no hands-on programming elements. Instead, the book focuses on how DCE can be used to accomplish typical programming tasks and provides explanations to help the reader understand all the parts of DCE.

266 pages (estimated), ISBN 1-56592-005-8

Guide to Writing DCE Applications

By John Shirley

A hands-on programming guide to OSF's Distributed Computing Environment (DCE) for first-time DCE application programmers. This book is designed to help new DCE users make the transition from conventional, nondistributed applications programming to distributed DCE programming. Covers the IDL and ACF files, essential RPC calls, binding methods and the name service, server initialization, memory management, and selected advanced topics. Includes practical programming examples.

282 pages, ISBN 1-56592-004-X

Learning GNU Emacs

By Deb Cameron & Bill Rosenblatt

GNU Emacs is the most popular and widespread of the Emacs family of editors. It is also the most powerful and flexible. (Unlike all other text editors, GNU Emacs is a complete working environment—you can stay within Emacs all day without leaving.) This book tells you how to get started with the GNU Emacs editor. It will also "grow" with you: as you become more proficient, this book will help you learn how to use Emacs more effectively. It will take you from basic Emacs usage (simple text editing) to moderately complicated customization and programming.

The book is aimed at new Emacs users, whether or not they are programmers. Also useful for readers switching from other Emacs implementations to GNU Emacs.

442 pages, ISBN 0-937175-84-6

Learning the vi Editor

5th Edition
By Linda Lamb

For many users, working in the UNIX environment means using *vi*, a full-screen text editor available on most UNIX systems. Even those who know *vi* often make use of only a small number of its features. This is the complete guide to text editing with *vi*. Early chapters cover the basics; later chapters explain more advanced editing tools, such as *ex* commands and global search and replacement.

192 pages, ISBN 0-937175-67-6

Learning the UNIX Operating System

2nd Edition
By Grace Todino & John Strang

If you are new to UNIX, this concise introduction will tell you just what you need to get started, and no more. Why wade through a 600-page book when you can begin working productively in a matter of minutes?

Topics covered include:

- Logging in and logging out
- Managing UNIX files and directories
- Sending and receiving mail
- Redirecting input/output
- Pipes and filters
- Background processing
- Customizing your account

"If you have someone on your site who has never worked on a UNIX system and who needs a quick how-to, Nutshell has the right booklet. *Learning the UNIX Operating System* can get a newcomer rolling in a single session."—;login:

84 pages, ISBN 0-937175-16-1

MH & xmh:
E-mail for Users and Programmers

2nd Edition
By Jerry Peek

Customizing your e-mail environment can save you time and make communicating more enjoyable. *MH & xmh: E-mail for Users and Programmers* explains how to use, customize, and program with the MH electronic mail commands, available on virtually any UNIX system. The handbook also covers *xmh*, an X Window System client that runs MH programs.

The basics are easy. But MH lets you do much more than what most people expect an e-mail system to be able to do. This handbook is packed with explanations and useful examples of MH features, some of which the standard MH documentation only hints at.

728 pages, ISBN 1-56592-027-9

UNIX Text Processing

Learning
GNU Emacs

Debra Cameron and Bill Rosenblatt
O'Reilly & Associates, Inc.

Guide to OSF/1:
A Technical Synopsis

By O'Reilly & Associates Staff

OSF/1, Mach, POSIX, SVID, SVR4, X/Open, 4.4BSD, XPG, B-1 security, parallelization, threads, virtual file systems, shared libraries, streams, extensible loader, internationalization.... Need help sorting it all out? If so, then this technically competent introduction to the mysteries of the OSF/1 operating system is a book for you. In addition to its exposition of OSF/1, it offers a list of differences between OSF/1 and System V, Release 4 and a look ahead at what is coming in DCE.

This is not the usual O'Reilly how-to book. It will not lead you through detailed programming examples under OSF/1. Instead, it asks the prior question, What is the nature of the beast? It helps you figure out how to approach the programming task by giving you a comprehensive technical overview of the operating system's features and services, and by showing how they work together.

304 pages, ISBN 0-937175-78-1

POSIX Programmer's Guide

By Donald Lewine

Most UNIX systems today are POSIX-compliant because the Federal government requires it. Even OSF and UI agree on support for POSIX. However, given the manufacturer's documentation, it can be difficult to distinguish system-specific features from those features defined by POSIX.

The *POSIX Programmer's Guide*, intended as an explanation of the POSIX standard and as a reference for the POSIX.1 programming library, will help you write more portable programs. This guide is especially helpful if you are writing programs that must run on multiple UNIX platforms. This guide will also help you convert existing UNIX programs for POSIX-compliance.

640 pages
ISBN 0-937175-73-0

Managing NFS and NIS

By Hal Stern

A modern computer system that is not part of a network is an anomaly. But managing a network and getting it to perform well can be a problem. This book describes two tools that are absolutely essential to distributed computing environments: the Network Filesystem (NFS) and the Network Information System (formerly called the "yellow pages" or YP).

As popular as NFS is, it is a black box for most users and administrators. This book provides a comprehensive discussion of how to plan, set up, and debug an NFS network. It is the only book we're aware of that discusses NFS and network performance tuning. This book also covers the NFS automounter, network security issues, diskless workstations, and PC/NFS. It also tells you how to use NIS to manage your own database applications, ranging from a simple telephone list to controlling access to network services. If you are managing a network of UNIX systems, or are thinking of setting up a UNIX network, you can't afford to overlook this book.

436 pages, ISBN 0-937175-75-7

Power Programming with RPC

By John Bloomer

A distributed application is designed to access resources across a network. In a broad sense, these resources could be user input, a central database, configuration files, etc., that are distributed on various computers across the network rather than found on a single computer. RPC, or remote procedure calling, is the ability to distribute the execution of functions on remote computers outside of the application's current address space. This allows you to break large or complex programming problems into routines that can be executed independently of one another to take advantage of multiple computers. Thus, RPC makes it possible to attack a problem using a form of parallel or multiprocessing.

Written from a programmer's perspective, this book shows what you can do with RPC and presents a framework for learning it.

494 pages, ISBN 0-937175-77-3

UNIX Network Programming

Power
Programming
with

RPC

John Bloomer
O'Reilly & Associates, Inc.

Practical C Programming

By Steve Oualline

There are lots of introductory C books, but this is the first one that has the no-nonsense, practical approach that has made Nutshell Handbooks famous. C programming is more than just getting the syntax right. Style and debugging also play a tremendous part in creating well-running programs.

Practical C Programming teaches you how to create programs that are easy to read, maintain and debug. Practical rules are stressed. For example, there are 15 precedence rules in C (&& comes before || comes before ?:). The practical programmer simplifies these down to two: 1) Multiply and divide come before addition and subtraction and 2) Put parentheses around everything else. Electronic Archaeology, the art of going through someone else's code, is also described.

Topics covered include:

- Good programming style
- C syntax: what to use and what not to use
- The programming environment, including *make*
- The total programming process
- Floating point limitations
- Tricks and surprises

Covers Turbo C (DOS) as well as the UNIX C compiler.

420 pages, ISBN 0-937175-65-X

Using C on the UNIX System

By Dave Curry

Using C on the UNIX System provides a thorough introduction to the UNIX system call libraries. It is aimed at programmers who already know C but who want to take full advantage of the UNIX programming environment. If you want to learn how to work with the operating system and if you want to write programs that can interact with directories, terminals and networks at the lowest level, you will find this book essential. It is impossible to write UNIX utilities of any sophistication without understanding the material in this book.

250 pages, ISBN 0-937175-23-4

Managing Projects with make

2nd Edition
By Steve Talbott and Andrew Oram

Make is one of UNIX's greatest contributions to software development, and this book is the clearest description of *make* ever written. Even the smallest software project typically involves a number of files that depend upon each other in various ways. If you modify one or more source files, you must relink the program after recompiling some, but not necessarily all, of the sources.

Make greatly simplifies this process. By recording the relationships between sets of files, *make* can automatically perform all the necessary updating. The 2nd Edition of this book describes all the basic features of *make* and provides guidelines on meeting the needs of large, modern projects.

152 pages, ISBN 0-937175-90-0

Checking C Programs with lint

By Ian F. Darwin

The *lint* program checker has proven itself time and again to be one of the best tools for finding portability problems and certain types of coding errors in C programs. *lint* verifies a program or program segments against standard libraries, checks the code for common portability errors, and tests the programming against some tried and true guidelines. *lint*ing your code is a necessary (though not sufficient) step in writing clean, portable, effective programs. This book introduces you to *lint*, guides you through running it on your programs and helps you to interpret *lint*'s output.

"Short, useful, and to the point. I recommend it for self-study to all involved with C in a UNIX environment."—Computing Reviews

84 pages, ISBN 0-937175-30-7

DNS and BIND

By Cricket Liu and Paul Albitz

DNS and BIND is a complete guide to the Internet's Domain Name System (DNS) and the Berkeley Internet Name Domain (BIND) software, which is the UNIX implementation of DNS. DNS is the system that translates hostnames (like "rock.ora.com") into Internet addresses (like 192.54.67.23) Until BIND was developed, name translation was based on a "host table"; if you were on the Internet, you got a table that listed all the systems connected to the network, and their address. As the Internet grew from hundreds to thousands and hundreds of thousands of systems, host tables became unworkable. DNS is a distributed database that solves the same problem effectively, allowing the network to grow without constraints. Rather than having a central table that gets distributed to every system on the net, it allows local administrators to assign their own hostnames and addresses, and install these names in a local database.

418 pages, ISBN 1-56592-010-4

sed & awk

By Dale Dougherty

For people who create and modify text files, *sed* and *awk* are power tools for editing. Most of the things that you can do with these programs can be done interactively with a text editor. However, using *sed* and *awk* can save many hours of repetitive work in achieving the same result.

This book contains a comprehensive treatment of *sed* and *awk* syntax. Plus, it emphasizes the kinds of practical problems that *sed* and *awk* can help users to solve, with many useful example scripts and programs.

"*sed & awk* is a must for UNIX system programmers and administrators, and even general UNIX readers will benefit. I have over a hundred UNIX and C books in my personal library at home, but only a dozen are duplicated on the shelf where I work. This one just became number twelve."—Root Journal

414 pages, ISBN 0-937175-59-5

Programming Perl

By Larry Wall & Randal Schwartz

This is the authoritative guide to the hottest new UNIX utility in years, co-authored by the creator of that utility.

Perl is a language for easily manipulating text, files and processes. Perl provides a more concise and readable way to do many jobs that were formerly accomplished (with difficulty) by programming in the C language or one of the shells. Even though Perl is not yet a standard part of UNIX, it is likely to be available wherever you choose to work. And if it isn't, you can get it and install it easily and free of charge.

482 pages, ISBN 0-937175-64-1

UNIX for FORTRAN Programmers

By Mike Loukides

UNIX for FORTRAN Programmers provides the serious scientific programmer with an introduction to the UNIX operating system and its tools. The intent of the book is to minimize the UNIX entry barrier: to familiarize readers with the most important tools so they can be productive as quickly as possible. *UNIX for FORTRAN Programmers* shows readers how to do things that they're interested in: not just how to use a tool like *make* or *rcs*, but how it is used in program development and fits into the toolset as a whole.

"An excellent book describing the features of the UNIX FORTRAN compiler f77 and related software. This book is extremely well written."
—American Mathematical Monthly

264 pages, ISBN 0-937175-51-X

10.92